The Which? Guide
to the
West Country

The Which? Guide to the
West Country

Published by Consumers' Association
and Hodder & Stoughton

This book was researched and written by the *HOLIDAY WHICH?* team
CONTRIBUTORS *Val Campbell Tim Locke*
Polly Phillimore Kim Winter

Which? Books are commissioned and researched by
The Association for Consumer Research
and published by Consumers' Association,
2 Marylebone Road, London NW1 4DX, and
Hodder & Stoughton, 47 Bedford Square,
London WC1B 3DP

Typographic design by Tim Higgins
Cover artwork by Geoff Hunt
Maps by David Perrott Cartographics

First edition June 1991

British Library Cataloguing in Publication Data
The Which? guide to the West Country.
   1. England. Travel
   I. Consumers' Association
   914.2304859

   ISBN 0 340 51443 4

Typeset in Linotype Palatino by Wyvern Typesetting Limited Bristol

Printed and bound in Great Britain by Richard Clay Ltd, Bungay, Suffolk

Contents

Introduction

Peninsulas will always have a fascination for travellers. Britain's south-west corner is no exception, jutting out between the Bristol and English Channels – South Wales not so far to the north and Brittany considerably more distant to the south – reaching its maximum width of 72 miles from Countisbury to Prawle Point and tapering to nothing at Land's End. The journey through Somerset, Devon and Cornwall displays contrasts within a relatively small area that are often astonishing, almost making a nonsense of the idea of the West Country as a single region in anything except the purely geographical sense.

This book is intended as a guide, pointing the way to the best of the West Country's varied attractions. We have tried to be as comprehensive as possible, but have been selective where applicable: for instance, we have only described villages, landscape features and churches which stand out from the rest. We have mentioned the specific shortcomings of a place where your enjoyment might be spoiled were you to visit it unwarned. Probably the main problem with the West Country is its popularity, although admittedly the crowds provide the animation of traditional resorts like Torquay and Newquay. The Cornish coastal towns and villages, and certain honeypots elsewhere such as Widecombe-in-the-Moor, Clovelly and Dunster, can be spoilt by overcrowding in high season. Establishments calling themselves museums are everywhere – some professionally organised exhibitions of heritage, others amateur accumulations of bygones rescued from attics and junk-heaps, some good and some indifferent; you may come away feeling entertained, bored, informed or overdosed on nostalgia for its own sake.

If you can, avoid the most popular places in the school holidays; if you have to visit then and want to escape crowded beaches and traffic jams, some careful planning will reap dividends. Try visiting the most popular tourist spots first thing in the morning or last thing in the evening; Polperro and Land's End are two of several places that are easily reached on foot from elsewhere on the coast, and it's a supremely rewarding way to arrive for views and the excitement of anticipation. We found beaches by the road were packed out in July and August, although often a short walk along the coast path would reveal empty coves – some quite exquisite. Somerset and Devon, within easy reach of the M5, make good short-break territory from much of the rest of Britain. Somerset can be enjoyed all year round, only the Cheddar Gorge and a few places in Exmoor ever getting crowds large enough to intrude; Dartmoor has limited road access and occasionally the traffic squashes together but most of it is so lonely that you can always escape, especially on foot or horseback. Cornwall is just that bit further from the rest of the country and a long way to go for a weekend – unless you can afford to fly to Penzance; many places close down in the winter months, yet off-season it offers a mild climate and its charms can seem more authentic.

The West Country's coastline attracts devotees, drawn back year after year – not just for the famous bathing and surfing beaches of north Cornwall, or the yachting centres of the south coast, but also for the sheer diversity on this intricate seaboard. Feral goats graze on the slopes by the Valley of Rocks near Lynton. Contorted rock has been heaved into bizarre shapes by forces within the earth at Hartland Quay. Coast-path walkers brace themselves for the brunt of the wind on the highest cliffs in Cornwall near Crackington Haven. The shattered remains of Tintagel Castle cling to a rugged headland looking miles down

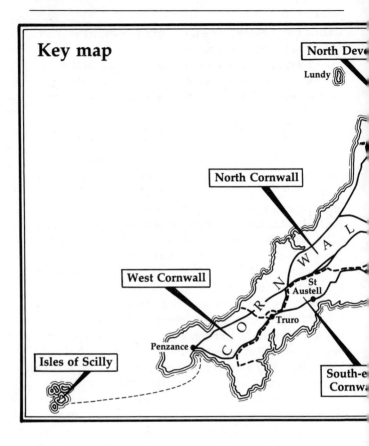

the coast, past Port Isaac where a cheerful clutter of cottages huddle around a harbour of lobster-pots and fishing boats. A dreamy haze of yellow sand-dunes and blue water provides the backdrop to Padstow, on the Camel Estuary. Gulls' cries echo around haunting remains of engine-houses from abandoned tin and copper mines, high up on the cliffs near St Agnes and Pendeen. Summer tourists pack St Ives and its narrow streets, while families indulge in beach games. Bird-watchers and tourists island-hop among the Scilly Isles, buying bunches of beautiful flowers to take home. Audiences at the Minack Open-Air Theatre come to see a show or a Shakespeare play in one of the

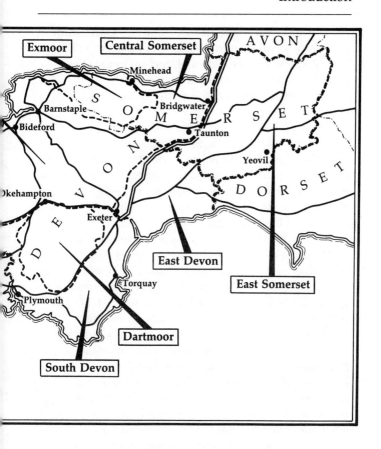

most remarkable settings on the Cornish coast. The
pastel-grey outline of St Michael's Mount shimmers
ethereally in Mounts Bay. On an August evening, a
pilot gig race at Cadgwith is followed by prize-giving,
the trophies displayed on paper-covered tea-chests,
and the music supplied by a brass band decked out in
purple blazers. Exotic gardens, flourishing in the mild
climate of the Helford river, slope down secretive
valleys to tidal creeks. Forests of yacht masts bob in the
great deep-water harbours at Falmouth and Fowey.
Plymouth sprawls, but claims one of the most dramatic
city sites in the country. Southernmost Devon looks
mellow, with two harbours providing much spectacle,

9

natural and man-made, at Salcombe and Dartmouth. Early nineteenth-century terraces at Sidmouth constitute the best seaside architecture in the West Country, with switchback sandstone cliffs immediately to the east: the genteel juxtaposed with the untameable.

Although some inland parts of the West Country are of little interest, much that is worth seeing lies away from the coast. Somerset has some of the most rewarding historical towns and villages, notably Wells, with its superb cathedral, Glastonbury and Dunster, as well as a multitude of fine churches with sandstone towers and medieval bench ends carved by local craftsmen; most of the county's best scenery is found in Exmoor National Park (which includes the coast and spills over into Devon), in the Quantock Hills and the limestone gorges of the Mendips. Dartmoor has the monopoly of landscape interest of non-coastal Devon with the highest and wildest ground in southern England, littered with granite tors and relics of early settlers; large expanses of the moor are sparsely populated today except by sheep and ponies. Both Exmoor and Dartmoor are places to be outdoors – organised sights are limited – though the climate is the region's least hospitable. Exeter has had to reconstruct itself after wartime bombing, but retains a great medieval cathedral. Inland Cornwall is a bit of everything – some unspoilt churches in the north part of the county in the neighbourhood of Launceston, Dartmoor-like wastes on Bodmin Moor, unbeautiful and unearthly landscapes created by the white spoil of the china-clay industry near St Austell; further west lies green farmland mingled with relics of mining near Redruth, and an important concentration of Bronze Age monuments superimposed on the pastures and moors of Penwith, Cornwall's westernmost extremity.

About this Guide

For the purposes of this guide we have defined the West Country as Cornwall, Isles of Scilly, Devon and Somerset. To break up the main body of the book into manageable sections the two national parks – Dartmoor and Exmoor – have chapters of their own, and each of the three counties is subdivided; maps with each chapter help you to plan your route and mark places to visit, and the text itself describes places of interest in each region.

At the end of each chapter we have introduced a two-tier highlight system. If you only have limited time in an area the ✷✷ sights are places we think you shouldn't miss; the ✷ places are the second division attractions that you should see if you have a little more time. The rest of the places mentioned are all worth visiting and we hope the book will be useful on every trip you take to the West Country.

After the highlights section in each chapter, we recommend a selection of hotels and bed and breakfast accommodation for the area, then list briefly a number of restaurants, pubs and cafés. The hotels are described in more detail in the *Which? Hotel Guide* and the restaurants are a selection taken from *The Good Food Guide*, *The Vegetarian Good Food Guide* and *Out to Eat*, all published by the Consumers' Association and Hodder & Stoughton.

Chapter Twelve, 'Walking in the West Country', describes some of the best walks in each area. These range from gentle strolls to some that involve serious climbing. Some walks are dealt with only briefly because the routes are well signed and easy to follow. There is advice on maps and books; it's wise to take an Ordnance Survey map with you if you're venturing off a well-trodden path, and a compass in case of sudden weather changes. At the end of each section we list other walks in the area, these are fully described in *The Holiday Which? Good Walks Guide* and *The Holiday Which? Town and Country Walks Guide*, both edited by Tim Locke and published by the Consumers' Association and Hodder & Stoughton.

About this Guide

Key to accommodation and restaurant prices

Hotels

£ Under £25   **£££** £35–£45   **£££££** Over £60
££ £25–£35   **££££** £45–£60

These prices are for bed and breakfast per person sharing a double room with bath. In some hotels bed and breakfast terms are not available; in these cases our price category is intended simply as a guide.

Restaurants

[ε] Under £10 for a 2-course meal with a drink.

East Somerset

*Ever-rewarding inland touring country for all seasons. The
wide watery saucer of the Somerset Levels, and the horseshoe
of higher ground from the Mendips to the Blackdown Hills,
reveal long dramatic perspectives as you travel; little roads
everywhere provide alternatives to the busy routes. East
Somerset is a pattern of rich farmlands varying abruptly with
the geology; villages of local stone are distinguished by
resplendent church towers; market towns are sleepy or hectic
according to a calendar independent of tourists. Even the
honeypots of Wells and Glastonbury keep – each in its own
way – an unspoilt individuality.*

The Mendip Hills

The Mendip Hills rise in a wedge along the county border
from foothills that merge with the Cotswolds to a 1,000-foot-
high point on the plateau above Wells and Cheddar. The
hills are formed largely of carboniferous limestone,
interspersed with old red sandstone and measures of
mineral-rich rock: lead in quantity, which was mined from
Roman times to the nineteenth century, and small amounts
of iron, copper and manganese, and calamine ore for zinc.
Further north there are coal measures. The quarrying of
Mendip stone also began with the Romans, and Doulting
stone from near Shepton Mallet was used for Wells
Cathedral.

   Under ground, the plateau is honeycombed with natural
holes, formed by water finding its level through the
carboniferous limestone, which very slowly dissolves,
leaving colourful cavities of harder rock. Bones have been
found in Mendip caves of both prehistoric animals – cave
bear, woolly rhinoceros – and their contemporary man; later,
Britons took refuge here in the post-Roman Dark Ages.
Above ground, high Mendip is studded with tumuli and flat

13

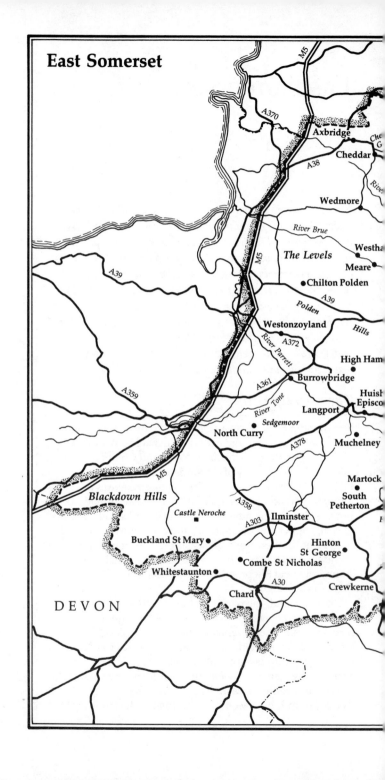

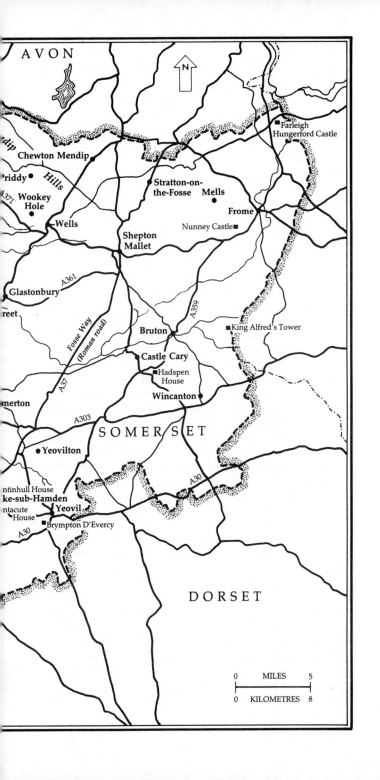

mysterious earth circles. The plateau is the only bleak place in this part of Somerset. Below the steep south-facing scarp, in immediate contrast, is one of the warmest and most sheltered areas. Market gardens famous for their strawberries offer produce on stalls along the road between Westbury and Draycott. From here, views out over the Levels are long but lumpy, not to be compared with the panorama from the top.

Just off the main road close to Wells, **Wookey Hole Caves** are worth a visit. The River Axe, green and deceptively still, flows through the sequence of caves; there are iron catwalks over cliffs, a sinister low swirling cavern, and a visceral vertical one, with bats. The guide recounts the ongoing exploits of cave divers, and the looting of stalactites by Alexander Pope for his Strawberry Hill Gothick grotto. The Witch of Wookey Hole, who was supposed to have lived in the caves, has a legend of her own, and the full story and relics are on display in Wells Museum (see p. 20). Tours emerging from underground pass through a genuine paper mill and a succession of attractions – fairground carousels, Tussaud waxworks, end-of-the-pier machines – with a little museum of geology and bones thrown in.

The road past Wookey Hole towards Priddy has the best viewpoint on this Mendip scarp, with a car park, and you can loop over the top and come down Cheddar Gorge. **Priddy** was a mining centre: it's more an area than a village, sparsely strung out from its green, where a sheep fair is held each August. The stack of ancient hurdles which sits on the green has been superseded by more modern arrangements, but remains as a token that the fair belongs here and not in Wells, whence it was transferred in 1348, a year of plague. There are pubs here, and several more isolated on the plateau roads; instead of miners they serve caving clubs now – the area is full of interesting holes to be investigated by experts.

The **Mendip plateau** is another world, with a perceptible drop in temperature. The few farms, huge fields and dry-stone walls resemble the Yorkshire Dales or Derbyshire; but this terrain includes a round green swell of earthworks and some steep woody clefts – one delightfully named Velvet Bottom. From around the Charterhouse crossroads there are outbreaks of 'gruffy' ground, the tussocks and grassy pits where lead was once dug out.

Between Axbridge and Cheddar, a mini-gorge towards

Shipham reaches the heights between stone quarries, but the more majestic one is **Cheddar Gorge**. It is generally agreed that this is best seen descending from the plateau and in winter, which has the double advantage of less obscuring foliage and fewer fellow-tourists. But even in summer, with a steady flow of coaches grinding round the bends and pausing in the lay-bys, the immense rosy-grey overhangs of sawn-off strata are awesome. At the bottom, Cheddar village is densely commercialised; the crowds attracted by cheese and caves support a long huddle of souvenir shops.

Of the **Cheddar Caves**, Gough's Cave is the best. Through passages the texture of angular Gruyère you reach stalactites and stalagmites, a domed cavern and a frozen cascade ('St Paul's' and 'Niagara'), vivid colours and *trompe l'oeil* reflections in still pools. The going is easy and the commentary a triggered recording, augmented by human guides at key points.

The Axe ought to be re-encountered at **Axbridge** but isn't. Just off the tourist route to Cheddar, this small ancient town has a lovely surprise of a square, odd-shaped and herringbone-paved, its houses coloured almond-green, plum-blue, pink and cream. One corner is overhung by the weathered sepia timbers of a fifteenth-century merchant's house named King John's Hunting-Lodge, a reference to the Mendip stag-hunts of Norman kings and Saxons before them. The house, timber-framed and studded in oak, has been restored and is now a small museum (open Apr to Sept, afternoons only). Itself revealing 500-year-old structural skills, it holds a collection of seventeenth-century silver and an iron bull-anchor, once used for bull-baiting. In another corner of the square, steps lead just as photogenically to an angle of the Perpendicular church, dating from medieval prosperity in wool. Its nave roof is elaborately plastered, its tower crossing fan-vaulted (but the beautiful eighteenth-century chandelier that hung here was stolen in 1988), and there are angels around the font and cavorting around the tomb of a soberly bonneted young matron. Axbridge's square also has two attractive restaurants with rooms and a traditional inn, and in the streets running off it are antique shops and an excellent antiquarian bookshop.

Wells

Wells, England's smallest cathedral city, has barely doubled
its thirteenth-century population of 4,000. It has light
industries, including dairy products and electronics, on its
western outskirts. But approaching from the east you see
only the intricate mass of the cathedral against green hills,
and you enter immediately the little streets that served the
medieval ecclesiastical precinct. Wells' Cathedral School,
now combining choristers and grammarians, occupies most
of the old houses in the area called the Liberty. Secluded
Vicars' Close takes the overspill and also still houses 'vicars-
choral' (altos, tenors and basses of the cathedral choir), and
the rest of these high-chimneyed, narrow fourteenth-century
houses are occupied by people working in the cathedral.
Vicars' Close is linked to the cathedral by the Chain Gate,
over which a covered way known as the Chain Bridge
enabled the vicars to cross from the Close into the cathedral
without dampening their robes in inclement weather. The
bridge pierces a long wall, which encloses cathedral, huge
Green and moated **Bishop's Palace** (open Easter Sat to end
Oct, Thurs, Sun and Bank Hol Mon, plus every afternoon in
Aug, 2 to 6). The Green is a peaceful spot, tucked behind the
market square and the cathedral. The moat and canal walk is
common ground, but as viewing the palace is restricted to
opening hours (see above) you may have to be content with
the turreted corners and drawbridge as you stroll around the
outside. The moat is home to a group of swans, which
appear at the sound of a bell. From Wells' Market Place you
pass through Penniless Porch, where beggars used to shelter
– so angled at a corner that you cannot anticipate the contrast
between civic bustle and the great calm space inside.

History in Wells is ecclesiastical. King Ine of Wessex first
built a church here, and for 200 years it was a peaceful Saxon
bishopric, until in 1088 a Norman bishop, John of Tours,
preferring Bath, pulled down the church and evicted its
canons. Robert of Lewes, bishop some 40 years later, did his
best to restore Wells' dignity and directed some work on the
church, but the new cathedral was not begun for nearly a
century. Other prelates coveted the greater riches of
Glastonbury – for a while in the twelfth century there was a
Bishop of Bath and Glastonbury, until the Pope decreed in
favour of Bath and Wells. The title Bishop of Bath and Wells

has been retained, in spite of the dissolution of Bath Abbey in 1539.

The building of **Wells Cathedral** began (the choir) in about 1180 and finished (the remodelled cloisters) in 1508. Over three centuries the work kept harmoniously to the careful plans of Bishop Reginald de Bohun, whose style was the earliest English Gothic; but there was a period between about 1290 and 1340 when Gothic inspiration advanced to brilliantly original treatment, and the dramatic solution of a major structural problem.

Three things are unforgettable at Wells. The recently restored west front, at its best in the late evening sunshine, is an amazing breadth of thirteenth-century sculpture covering screen, two flat-topped towers and buttress-shafts almost as detached as scaffolding. At the distance on the Green from which it is possible to take it all in, the door where people enter looks a mere mousehole. The external Doulting stone eroded badly, but inside the cathedral it looks brand new: and the second great impact is the white swirl of arches under the tower crossing, one boldly inverted on another, stone circles flanking their meeting-point. It looks extraordinarily modern, but it was done in 1315–22. Three such 'scissor' arches, inserted north, west and south, corrected the structural problem of a westward subsidence in the tower.

After the tower crossing you can take in the grace of all the cathedral's interior spaces, the rich details of carving, the stained glass and the famous clock. Thought to be the second-oldest clock in the world, its dial dates from the fourteenth century and as well as hours and minutes shows the position of the sun, dates of the lunar month and phases of the moon. Every quarter-hour the figure of John Blandiver kicks his heels and strikes the bell in front of him with a hammer, at which the horsemen rotate below as if in a mock tournament. (Salisbury Cathedral has a similar clock, claimed to be the oldest, made by the same craftsman, but with slightly less sophisticated mechanics.) On the north side, through a modest door, you come upon the third thing: the stairway to the Chapter House is a shock of pure pleasure, particularly if sunlight fills the vaulting and emphasises the off-centre wear of the steps. The flight both curves up to the right and continues ahead, divided yet whole. The round Chapter House itself, recently restored, where fan vaulting springs from a central pier, is most symmetrically exquisite; its approach is unsymmetrical magic.

Outside the precinct, Wells has a one-way street system around its shops, and car parks whose capacity is strained when Market Place fills up with stalls on Wednesdays and Saturdays. The small and interesting **museum** was relocated to 8 Cathedral Green in the early 1930s from a couple of rooms in the west cloister. Important features are the Iron Age finds from local cave excavations; other exhibits include the coarse comb, alabaster ball and bones of a tethered goat thought to have belonged to a medieval female inhabitant of the Wookey Caves, now known as the Witch of Wookey Hole.

St Cuthbert's, also worth looking in, is the largest parish church in Somerset (with a magnificent Perpendicular tower); its sixteenth-century ceiling, recoloured as new, has the verve of a gypsy caravan. Plenty of accommodation – hotels, inns and guesthouses – make the little city a convenient base.

East of the Mendips to Farleigh Hungerford

North-east of Wells, beyond intersecting Roman ridge roads, the scenery grows gentler, more complex and much more inhabited. Lanes squirm between sharp little hills and wooded valley bottoms to reach a score of villages, some of them utilitarian hamlets close to the stone quarries, others aristocratically charming. **Chewton Mendip** illustrates neither extreme but has an interesting church: Norman remnants survive in the mixed-up interior under a fine tower of Doulting stone. At **Stratton-on-the-Fosse** you can visit the great Gothic-Revival church of Benedictine **Downside Abbey**. It is the home of the Community of St Gregory the Great and the senior Benedictine monastery in Britain, with 50 members. Apart from numerous other parochial duties, the monks teach at the associated school, which currently has over 600 boys (mostly boarders). The abbey is of cathedral proportions, begun in 1872 and still unfinished – the west end stops at a rough temporary wall. Externally, it is massive, and weathered grey, but Giles Gilbert Scott's nave and slim transepts are all soaring white verticals, to steep rib vaulting in French thirteenth-century style. Ornament in the ambulatory chapels includes some very delicate modern carving, and in the south aisle is a lovely fifteenth-century

German wood sculpture of the Virgin and Child.

To the east, beyond the Fosse Way, the old Roman road that runs from near Sidmouth to the Humber, the last open stretches of hunting country end and the deep lanes grow labyrinthine. Prettiest of the villages is **Mells**, with its thatched and red-tiled cottages at the stream. Leading off to the churchyard yews is a straight street of terraced houses built in 1470, part of a plan to make a cruciform townlet of the village. Mells was an estate of Glastonbury Abbey until the dissolution of the monasteries, when it passed to the Horner family, who built an Elizabethan manor house here. Thereby originates one of our more political nursery rhymes: John Horner (Little Jack), as agent to the abbot, was reputedly carrying a placatory parcel of title deeds to Henry VIII, concealed under a pie crust, and the plum he pulled out was Mells. The last Horner heir was killed in the First World War, and in Mells' church the Horner chapel holds the unusual monument of a small equestrian statue – a change of medium for the painter Alfred Munnings. The church has stone angels in the nave, a complex two-storey porch and a tower elaborate even by Somerset standards.

Through the network of lanes south of Mells and a couple of miles from Frome, **Nunney Castle** is compact and outwardly complete within its tranquil moat. It was a family home in the fourteenth century, heavily crenellated by its soldier-lord, then gutted in the Civil War by Cromwell's men. An empty shell remains, four drum towers linked by walls as high, and standing within its roofless outline you look up four storeys imagining small-windowed rooms. Nunney brook (with white ducks) runs between the castle and an attractive village street of tiny market place and eighteenth-century weavers' houses; the high-set church has a painted St George and a chapelful of tombs, but deathwatch beetle has destroyed its wagon roof.

East of the Mendips, **Frome** (pronounced 'Froom') was a prosperous woollen-trade town which declined miserably in the nineteenth century and has been revived with modern industries in the twentieth. To its bustle of a shopping centre is added on Wednesdays and Saturdays a huge open market. The town's cheerful congestion is to be avoided on these two days if you're in a hurry – there is a bypass system. The main thoroughfare that swings uphill from the River Frome has many handsome buildings, but passing through it in heavy traffic gives you no hint of the pleasant street-browsing elsewhere. To the east are pedestrian bits: the post-medieval mix of little Cheap Street, with its central water-course, is all shops with swinging signs, while cobbled Gentle Street is domestic Stuart and Georgian and climbs up past the big parish church (very Victorianly restored). To the west up Catherine Hill lies a workmanlike warren of steeply curving terraces, enlivened by flights of steps with railings, an area of sombre colouring but interesting little specialist shops.

Down Frome's river in the extreme north-east corner of Somerset, you come abruptly on **Farleigh Hungerford Castle** as the A366 negotiates a ravine. Sir Thomas Hungerford turned a manor into a fortress in 1377, and his son's extensions enclosed the parish church, which became its chapel. Farleigh's towers are broken, but the castle still looks fierce. The Hungerfords were a doughty family. Thomas and his son were each Speaker of the House of Commons; a Robert spent seven years a prisoner in France, to end up attainted and executed in the Wars of the Roses; a Walter recovered Farleigh, but it passed to a daughter-in-law who was hanged at Tyburn for procuring and abetting a strangulation; another Walter, who walled up his wife for four years and tried to poison her, was executed for treason and unnatural vice. In the Civil War the castle was garrisoned by a Royalist Hungerford and taken by his Parliamentarian half-brother. A Restoration Edward, called 'the spendthrift', wasted the entire family fortune and sold the castle in 1686; by 1701 it was reported ruinous. In the church below the battlements the simple white nave (with a fresco of St George) has an added chapel crammed with Hungerford tombs like elaborate furniture packed in store, and below is a grisly little crypt revealing pillaged coffins.

Shepton Mallet to Wincanton

A fine roof is the pride of **Shepton Mallet**, in the church with a capped stump of a spire (through medieval economy or a change of fashion). The solid barrel vault, with angels at its beams, is one of the richest in England, never repeating a carved design in 350 panels and 300 bosses, as dense as foliage. Shepton Mallet declined with the demise of the wool industry, and while gloves and shoes, brewing and Babycham restored its prosperity, it is still very agricultural, the permanent site of the Bath and West Show. Its centre is a

pedestrian precinct, carefully modernised around the old
Market Cross with hexagonal pillared arcade and the
surviving 'shamble', a market stall. Visiting motorists,
seeking 'town centre' direction in Shepton's outer swirl,
should follow the 'car park' sign.

Bruton, in its valley, is a self-contained and harmonious
little town of mellow roofs and warm grey stone, with a
medieval aspect from the river. The dovecote on the green
skyline behind the big handsome church is a remnant of an
Augustinian abbey, whose buttressed wall follows the street
called Plox opposite King's School (founded in 1519). A pack-
horse bridge still spans the Brue, and eighteenth-century
cloth-merchants' houses line old crooked streets of one-way
traffic. Bruton seems untouched by modernity, let alone
tourism, but is not as sleepy as it looks: an art gallery and a
good restaurant – Clair de Lune (with rooms) – flourishes in
the High Street among the antique shops.

East of Bruton, on the Somerset border and visible for
miles, **King Alfred's Tower** stands reputedly on the spot
where he raised his standard against the Danes. It was put
up in 1772, providing some local employment as well as
commemorating his victory. **Castle Cary**, to the south-west,
has only the foundations of a hillside Norman castle; its
prettiest features are the pond and a little round Georgian jail
with a pepperpot top. Just to the south, **Hadspen House**
gardens, designed by Mrs Hobhouse, who is now at
Tintinhull (see p. 24), has many interesting and unusual
plants both to admire and to buy from the excellent nursery
(open all year, exc Jan, Tues to Sat, 10 to 5; plus Sun, Apr to
Oct, 2 to 5).

In **Wincanton**, bypassed by the A303, fine old inns recall
the years when 17 coaches a day stopped here; today, the
inns are just as busy when there's a race meeting. The A303
passes close to the steep wooded hill which is the site of
Cadbury Castle, four concentric grassy ramparts almost a
mile round. Evidence suggests that there were fortifications
here in the Stone and Iron Ages, reused by the Romans and
Saxons. Excavation in the 1960s revealed also some sixth-
century defences (including the foundations of a cruciform
church), which made this a candidate for King Arthur's
Camelot – controversy raged, visitors flocked.
All is quiet now, but the view is worth the effort up a steep
muddy path.

West of Cadbury the landscape is flat and the skies

distracting with aeroplanes from the Royal Naval Air Station at **Yeovilton**. The planes can be observed here at close quarters in the **Fleet Air Arm Museum** (open daily, 10 to 5.30 (4.30 Nov to Mar)), where the exhibits range from 1914 veterans to Concorde 002.

Yeovil to Ilminster

Industrial **Yeovil** is no holiday town – though unexpectedly convenient as a serious shopping centre – but just west of it begins a thicket of small-scale hills, pretty villages and houses to visit. The biscuit-gold Ham stone quarried at Ham Hill, close to the village of Stoke-sub-Hamdon, and used in south Somerset's finest buildings, is everywhere in evidence. **Brympton D'Evercy**, near Odcombe, is a particularly attractive lived-in manor house with large gardens and vineyard, grouped idyllically with church, stables and the priest's house, which contains a **museum** strong on cider-making (open Easter and May to Sept, daily exc Thurs and Fri, 2 to 6). The grander Elizabethan symmetry of **Montacute House** (open Mar to Oct, daily, 12 to 6; house closed Tues), now National Trust, stands in fine formal gardens below the pointed hill (*mons acutus*) where an eighteenth-century folly marks the site of a Norman castle. The rows of clipped Irish yews and raised walks above borders of shrub roses give vantage-points from where you can fully appreciate the architecture of both house and garden. Montacute's plasterwork, panelling, tapestries and furniture are all splendidly ostentatious, and at the top, in the Long Gallery, paintings from the National Portrait Gallery show faces from the history books – the handsome statesmen preferred by Queen Elizabeth, the dark-eyed favourites of James I. Although the official opening times do not reflect it, the motto attached to the front door suggests the geniality of earlier times: 'Through this wide opening Gate none come too early none return too late'.

Ham Hill itself has a hill fort, much disrupted by Roman quarrying, lushly overgrown around a switchback of grassy paths. **Stoke-sub-Hamden**, just below, has rare Norman carving in its church. At Tintinhull you can visit the garden of **Tintinhull House** (open Apr to Sept, Mon, Weds, Thurs and Sat, 2 to 6), not large but delightfully planned and planted in the 1930s as a series of different 'rooms'. The house is mainly sixteenth century with an early eighteenth-century west front, but is not open to the public.

Across the A303 to the north, **Martock** is a linear village of Ham stone cottages and more important houses near the church, including the late thirteenth-century Treasurer's House – a rector of Martock was treasurer at Wells. The church interior, spacious and light, is a glory of Somerset-style decoration, its beamed and many-panelled roof embellished with angels, much larger than those at other churches and all different.

The church at **South Petherton** is less of a marvel, but this large attractive village has other pleasures including the Global Village company, which imports a wide range of decorative goods and furniture from over 30 countries to sell in two shops here and several other West Country branches.

Hinton St George is a gem among Ham stone villages (though its great house is not open) – a near-perfect street of Tudor, Jacobean and Georgian pedigree and a pinnacled fifteenth-century church.

Of the three towns in this corner of Somerset, **Ilminster** most repays a visit. It is expanding with industrial outskirts, and its High Street is the A303, but downhill to the south is a mellow market place kept tranquil by a one-way system in the narrow Georgian streets and the provision of a huge car park. An open-sided market hall fills one end of the square, and the little shops of Silver Street beyond face the magnificent church whose central tower and crossing is modelled on that of Wells Cathedral.

Crewkerne to the Somerset Blackdowns

The A30 wriggles through the market centre of **Crewkerne** between old-established industries – tough textiles were made here for the navy, and webbing is still a speciality. The chief reason to pause is the church, set quietly above the town centre: it is cruciform, like Ilminster's, and very light, with lavish windows behind a west front of cathedral pretensions.

Between Crewkerne and Chard, under the ridge of Windwhistle Hill, the wildlife park of **Cricket St Thomas** (open daily 10 to 6 (5 Nov to Mar)) occupies an estate described in the Domesday Book. Exotic animals and birds seem entirely content here, in rolling wooded parkland and pretty riverscapes around elegant Cricket House. The house was rebuilt by Sir John Soane after a fire in the eighteenth century; it is not open to the public, but is recognisable as the manor in the television series 'To the Manor Born'.

At **Chard** the A30 traffic forges straight up the mile-long slope of the main street, seeing the best of the town, an attractive succession of Georgian and Victorian buildings with some Elizabethan frontage (surviving a major sixteenth-century fire) opposite the projecting pillars and gable of the Guildhall.

Beyond Chard to the west, Somerset's border meanders north-west through the **Blackdown Hills**. In total, these form a complex maple-leaf shape extending spurs far down into Devon. The Countryside Commission, preparing to make this an official Area of Outstanding Natural Beauty, calls it 'archetypal English landscape'. Somerset's part of the Blackdowns has the high ridge of Staple Hill running west, with a steep scarp facing north above Taunton and Wellington.

Behind the hill, complicated folded foothills border the Levels. This is terrain where you get lost in deep-hedged lanes full of flowers in spring, up hill and down dale in a farming patchwork of tiny fields, random riverlets and undiscovered pretty villages – **Combe St Nicholas** around a green; **Whitestaunton** scarcely bigger than church and manor house; **Buckland St Mary** a hillside scatter of coloured cottages. Even high up on the stretches of open heath, vistas from the Blackdowns are usually tantalising glimpses through woodland below. A two-mile nature trail through forest which was once royal hunting territory leads to **Castle Neroche**, one of the few big viewpoints: it's an ancient earthwork at the eastern end of the high ridge, used by the Normans before they moved to Montacute. At the western end, on the highest point of the Blackdown Hills, the **Wellington Monument** obelisk is both landmark and more accessible vantage-point, illuminated at night. It commemorates the Duke of Wellington, victor of Waterloo, who took his title from the town.

The Somerset Levels

From the Blackdowns to the Mendip ridge, the low flat Somerset plain resembles East Anglia more than anywhere in the West Country, and is in fact unique in Britain. Strictly speaking, the **Levels** are on the belt of coastal clay that is the western boundary of the flatlands; inland flood plains are called the Moors. Higher ground separates the rivers – the central ridge of the Poldens is the most perceptible – and there are more dramatic single outcrops of hard rock, from Brent Knoll (440 feet) to little Burrow Mump (just under 80 feet). The obvious charm of this area is the long romantic view, particularly a misty, mystic perspective of Glastonbury Tor, but the reality of life and work in the wetlands is constant vigilance and unromantic drainage technology. Exploring the area off the roads is not encouraged and it is just as well that a moving car is – short of the M5 in rain – an excellent means of appreciating the landscape. Even on the network of ditch-lined local routes you can rarely stop the car without causing obstruction. But parking areas are provided at places with a viewpoint or a possible stroll.

In earliest recorded history here, man occupied islands and ridges in a flooded marsh from which the waters receded in summer, leaving the pastures the Saxons called *somer saete* ('summer pasture'), thus naming the county. It was an area inaccessible, uncomfortable and unpopular. King Arthur's healing paradise of Avalon is romantic legend; the story of King Alfred holed up on **Athelney** at the low ebb of his resistance against the Danes has guerrilla realism, whether or not he burned the good wife's cakes. Athelney was 'surrounded on all sides by very great swampy and impassable marshes so that no one can approach it by any means except in punts' (so described by a medieval observer); the monastery Alfred later founded there proved unattractive to Saxon monks, and had to be staffed with foreigners.

The rivers flowing sluggishly across the plain were – and are – liable to flood from both directions: by excess of water from the horseshoe surround of hills, or the rivers meeting a tidal surge of sea. Behind the Levels' clay bank, spring tides in the Bristol Channel rise ten feet higher than the inland moors. The Romans first cut drainage channels, but no more impression was made by man until the twelfth and thirteenth centuries, when much of the land was owned by the Abbot of Glastonbury or the Bishop of Bath and Wells. Then sea walls and river banks were built up, and farming land reclaimed – the abbot left himself a fishpond at Meare Pool – and in 1485 the first tidal sluice doors were set across the mouth of the River Brue at Highbridge. After the dissolution of the monasteries not much more was achieved before the eighteenth century; in 1607, sea-water flooded inland as far as Glastonbury.

A new pattern was imposed on the landscape from 1770, when rights of grazing and peat-cutting on common land gave way to enclosure into small plots. Ditches, called rhynes, edged rectangular fields; new channels were dug, straightening and strengthening the rivers' flow. King's Sedgemoor Drain, one of the major channels, got its sea-lock in 1794, and the River Axe in 1806. The Brue's medieval sea-doors were replaced in the nineteenth century, and during the Second World War a large waterway, the Huntspill river, was dug and given a barrier. Only the estuary of the Parrett is too wide to block. The stopping of tide-water for a few hours causes fresh-water flooding if the rivers are high – as regularly happens on a small scale, and sometimes very badly, as in December 1979. Two years later an exceptional sea surge drove up the Parrett, demolished coast defences towards Burnham and drowned over 5,000 acres of farmland in salt water. But pumping-stations, modern field drainage systems and constant care of the rhynes normally control the whole great fluctuating sponge, allowing productive farming.

Shallow flooding is not all bad news: winter 'spillwater' from the agriculture of the surrounding hills both enriches the soil and makes the Levels one of Britain's most important wetland habitats for wildlife. Wading birds breed in large populations – lapwing, curlew, redshank and snipe; in winter Bewick's swans are among the regular migrants. Otters survive here, and there are 22 species of butterfly, and 80 of water beetle.

In wet meadows and along the rhynes, some marsh plant families have survived, the species preserved in the peat. West Sedgemoor and several other areas are Sites of Special Scientific Interest, designated not without opposition from farmers, as it means scrutiny of many farming operations that might damage natural flora and fauna. There are National Nature Reserves (requiring permits to visit) at Bridgwater Bay and Shapwick Heath, and an RSPB reserve on West Sedgemoor with free access to a moors path and a hide from which to observe a large heronry.

Heading north-east from the Blackdowns, you see first the most beautiful southern part of the Levels. **Sedgemoor** is mostly pasture-land for cows, intensely green in summer, its flat dividing grid of rhynes made visible by the pollarded willows along the flowery edges. Once down in this grid, it is a slight hump as the dead-straight little road crosses water that gives you a slim, gleaming perspective each way between avenues of shaggy stumps. Basket-making has been a local industry since the thirteenth century: commercial withy willows, looking like reeds, are grown in beds. Artists' charcoal and furniture are made too, but demand for willow peaked during the Victorian taste for wickerwork and has declined drastically in the age of plastic. Now it is presented as an interesting craft industry with basket shops and a visitor centre along the Withy Way between **Burrowbridge** and **North Curry**. An extension of this is the Curry Moor Trail, through withy beds and meadows and along the River Tone, a good way of seeing the landscape at close quarters from a car park base.

Burrowbridge is a key crossroads in exploring Sedgemoor, under the miniature tor of **Burrow Mump** that rises unexpectedly in the flat prospect like an infant brother of Glastonbury Tor equally tempting to climb and much less of an effort. There are vague connections with King Alfred's monastery of the fen fastnesses, but the little tower at the top is eighteenth century. At Burrowbridge the Tone joins the River Parrett, flowing north between increasingly substantial banks which are often the highest and driest site for a line of houses. Following rivers is the worst way to look at the scenery: the rivers are invisible unless you storm the bank, and the adjacent roadway is liable to be closed for maintenance.

Working pumping-stations do not usually welcome visitors, but at **Westonzoyland** you can see the restored (and superseded) beam engine built in 1830 to pump water from rhyne to Parrett. Westonzoyland's church – worth visiting for its splendid example of an angel-supported Somerset roof – entered history in July 1685 at the Battle of Sedgemoor, which ended the rebellion of the Duke of Monmouth, illegitimate son of Charles II, against the unpopular James II. Monmouth lost his gamble, and merciless retribution at Judge Jeffreys' Bloody Assizes awaited all who had survived supporting him (see p. 30). The parish register records: 'There was killed of the rebels upon the spott about 300. . . About 500 prisoners brought into our church, of which there was 79 wounded, and 5 of them died of their wounds in our church.'

Turning upstream at Burrowbridge, the tidal limit of the Parrett is reached at grey-stone **Langport**. Through traffic in its narrow main street is encouraged to miss its attractive hilltop bit, where there is a fine view south from the churchyard (and the church has rare medieval glass in its east window). Langport's 'hanging chapel', built for fifteenth-century town guilds, projects on a substantial arched gateway over the main road, which goes on to **Huish Episcopi** half a mile east. Known as Huish until the twelfth century, the village then came under the control of the Bishop of Bath and thenceforward was called Huish Episcopi. The road skirts Huish's celebrated church tower, rising perfectly proportioned in marvellous pinnacles and traceries of golden Ham stone, set off by the local blue lias (a

The Pitchfork Rebellion and the Bloody Assizes

After the Civil War, Charles II lived in an uneasy peace. His staunchly Catholic brother James, Duke of York was the rightful successor to the throne but his illegitimate son, James, Duke of Monmouth had the support of the Protestants.

In 1680 Monmouth went on a tour to the West Country and then to Sussex and the Midlands a couple of years later. These 'Progresses', as they became known, showed the strength of his support both with the ordinary people and the Whig landowners. He had a following of several thousand as he travelled from Longleat through Ilchester, staying at such places as Brympton d'Evercy (see p. 24), Ilminster, Chard and Forde Abbey on his way to Exeter. Promises of military support encouraged extremists to contemplate the assassination of the king and the Duke of York; their schemings were unsuccessful but resulted in Monmouth's exile to Holland in 1684.

He was still there when his father died a year later and the Duke of York became James II. He decided to return and try to challenge his uncle's autocratic power. On 11 June 1685 with inadequate money, three ships and only 80 men, Monmouth landed at Lyme Regis. For the three weeks that followed, Monmouth's rebel army, never more than 8,000 strong, often less, marched through West Dorset, East Devon and Somerset. Pursued by the king's army sent from London to crush them, they were constantly on the move. The king's forces together with the local militia made quite daunting opposition for Monmouth's untrained soldiers, considered a mere band of ill-armed

type of limestone rock). There's a useful car park to admire it from.

Muchelney (the name means 'large island'), two miles south of Huish, has neat houses with a mullioned-window style appropriate to (and probably looted from) its former abbey. A small Benedictine monastery was founded very early here on 'the large island' – sometimes cut off by winter floods. Refounded after the Danes destroyed it, the monastery thereafter made the best of its seclusion. By the fourteenth century it was being rebuked for unseemly luxury; from its dissolution in 1538 enough remains of the

---

farmers and cloth-workers. Their over-confidence was nearly their undoing when, on 5 July, the rebel army took them by surprise, attacking at night when they were sleeping. There was a point during the ensuing battle of Sedgemoor when the king's army came close to defeat but finally, on 6 July, the rebels were overwhelmed; they fled, pursued and ruthlessly butchered in the fields and moors close by. The casualties were recorded as 700 dead and 300 wounded of Monmouth's army; the king's army claiming only 27 dead and 200 wounded.

Monmouth escaped but he was too serious a threat to the throne to be left alive. He was caught, found guilty of treason and executed on Tower Hill on 15 July. Any of his followers who survived the battle were rounded up and made examples of, the king hoping to deter any future rebellions. The Autumn Assizes, later known as the Bloody Assizes, were conducted by Lord Chief Justice Jeffreys and four colleagues, first in Winchester, then Dorchester, Exeter, Taunton, Bristol and Wells. Speedy beheading followed sentencing except for anyone who had dared plead not guilty or had come over from Holland with Monmouth – these unfortunates were hanged. Over 300 rebels were despatched by Judge Jeffreys and his panel.

This wasn't the end of it: after hanging or beheading, the corpses were dismembered, quarters of the bodies salted, boiled and tarred, then distributed for long-term public exhibition. Towns and villages in Dorset, Somerset and Devon were forced to display these gruesome reminders until William of Orange came to the throne in 1688 and allowed their burial.

Over 1,000 rebels who survived trial with their lives were transported to the West Indies where they faced ten years of slavery. Very few returned home.

---

abbot's grand lodging to indicate his lifestyle. Next to the abbey site, the parish church has a delightfully incompetent roof-painting of outrageous angels in bosom-revealing Elizabethan dresses. The thatched Priest's House is an intact fourteenth-century survival (open by appointment with its tenant).

Further east, **Somerton**, on a ridge of farmland, was an important centre to the Saxons (who always preferred high ground) and was the county town in the thirteenth century. It is today a sedately pleasing market town, all light grey stone, the well-spaced meeting place of many (but not major) roads. At its centre, the low octagonal market cross is seventeenth century and the church tower thirteenth, but they are a harmonious pair; inside the church sobriety was abandoned in the fourteenth century with an extravagantly modelled roof. Broad Street, around the corner, is a surprisingly elegant boulevard of eighteenth-century town houses and a grand coaching-inn, now the Red Lion Hotel. In the other direction are antiques, local shops where you could put together a picnic of high quality, more old inns and a bookshop that not unreasonably proclaims itself the best in Somerset. Three miles south off the Ilchester road, the lovely little manor house of **Lytes Cary** is open in summer in the afternoons on Wednesday (Somerton's early-closing day) and Saturday.

West of Somerton – due north of Langport – the ridge has a maze of steep lanes in which you come upon **High Ham**, very small, which has a church by a pretty green and a thatched windmill. From here the northward road takes you out across King's Sedgemoor much more peacefully than the A361: there is not a building in sight for miles, and if you're lucky not a vehicle – just willows, cows and the immense green flatness. Then, at the Poldens ridge, the A39 runs eastwards to **Street**, where the big attraction is the **Shoe Museum** (open Easter to Oct, Mon to Sat, 10 to 4.45 (4.30 Sat)). It is run by the Clark family, who set up their shoe business here in 1825, and the factory continues to provide employment for a large proportion of Street's population. To the west on the A39 the Roman route runs through workaday villages on the slopes; its views are intermittent, and never both sides at once. One of the best glimpses southwards is from Cock Hill near **Chilton Polden**. Crenellated Chilton Priory, the eye-catching roadside building almost opposite, is neither medieval nor a priory but a church-style nineteenth-century house. If you turn east at the ridge, there is a minor road (signposted Ivythorne) which leads to Walton Hill, with the double prospect of Sedgemoor and Glastonbury.

After the Poldens, to the north, you come to the peat zone. The peat accumulated between about 4500 BC and AD 400. Prehistoric inhabitants' timber trackways have been discovered, radio-carbon dated to 2900 BC. The oldest settlement was at **Meare**, where an Iron Age lakeside village was built on piles and stilts. Centuries of peat-digging by hand only made small inroads on the accumulated layers, up to 20 feet deep, stretching on each side of the River Brue. Now it is dug by machine at the rate of half a million tons a year, supplying Britain's garden centres and grow-bags. Areas being worked are black with exposed wet peat, which is cut and dried with factory precision, then stands about in great chocolate-brown heaps, sprouting weeds until scooped by yellow diggers. Worked-out areas look scruffy and derelict. It is uncertain what will happen when the peat has been exhausted. One possibility is the creation of the 'Avalon Lakes' as an area combining water storage, flood control, recreation and nature conservation. The Peat Moors visitor centre is near **Westhay**, where there is also the only roadside parking place for miles, and a pretty stretch of the Brue with swans.

Pasture-land and pollarded willows begin again on each side of the Isle of Wedmore, biggest in the Levels, where King Alfred brought the Danish leaders, defeated and forcibly baptised, to conclude the peace treaty of 878. **Wedmore**, the isle's substantial central village, is well supplied with urbane little shops and a couple of pubs among pretty Georgian houses. Above the pulpit in its big, prominent church there is a richly coloured fifteenth-century wall-painting of St Christopher carrying Christ; the painting is visibly superimposed on at least one earlier version.

Glastonbury

Over to the east of the plain, **Glastonbury** exerts a compelling attraction, apparently as it has since man first contemplated the supernatural. Legends surround the town's origins as a Christian sanctuary: Joseph of Arimathea came here and buried the Holy Grail near the source of Chalice Well; on Wearyall Hill his staff took root as the everlasting Glastonbury Thorn. There are Irish connections with St Patrick and Welsh ones with St David. Glastonbury is the burial place of three Saxon kings, and possibly of that greatest British hero, King Arthur, reputedly brought mortally wounded after his last battle to the Isle of Avalon. This legend gained much force in 1191, when, the story goes, grave-digging monks discovered the bones not only of Arthur but of his Queen Guinevere, still distinguishable by some golden locks of hair – which at a touch turned to dust. A leaden cross in the grave was inscribed *Hic Jacet Sepultus Inclytus Rex Arturius in Insula Avallonia* – 'here lies buried the renowned King Arthur in the Isle of Avalon'. In 1278 the bodies were enshrined with great ceremony in the abbey choir. The discovery had been a timely one for Glastonbury, stimulating support during the slow rebuilding of the abbey after fire had destroyed the Norman foundations. What finally rose in its place was the greatest Benedictine establishment in England, with a cathedral of a church. Vast landholdings contributed to the abbey's wealth, which increased throughout the Middle Ages until the dissolution of the monasteries: in 1539 the abbey was devastated, and its last abbot hanged and quartered on the Tor.

On its site, in the care of the Church of England, a few majestic remnants stand in greensward and avenues of trees, with a layout traced on the ground. The shell of the Lady Chapel is there, and of the nave two tall piers and some of the south wall survive; they are tantalising fragments, tracing in details of arch and ornament the transition in style from Norman to Gothic. On its own across the grass, the Abbot's Kitchen survives intact to its octagonal roof and lantern with smoke-holes, the only evidence of a great complex of secular monastic buildings where now there is undulating grass. Other buildings survive outside the precinct: the great fourteenth-century barn of the abbey farm is now the centre of the excellent **Somerset Rural Life Museum** (open all year, Mon to Fri, 10 to 5, Sat and Sun, 2 to 4 (6, Mar to Oct)) on the outskirts of Glastonbury towards the Tor, and at Meare, down the Brue, is the neat barn-like Abbot's Fish House. In Glastonbury High Street the Tribunal, the abbey's court-house, has a small, many-windowed, fifteenth-century frontage; and the sumptuous stonework of the Pilgrims' Inn (now the George Hotel) suggests luxury rather than piety.

The abbey site makes an L-shape of Glastonbury's town

centre: the abbey's entrance gatehouse is in the short arm
from the Market Cross, and none of the abbey is visible from
the long arm of the High Street, dominated instead by the
fine tall tower of the parish church. Here the sheepskin and
anorak shops are outnumbered by those serving
Glastonbury's counter-culture of mythology, magic and
magnetic vibrations, which attracts its own crowds of
pilgrims all summer. Boutiques and arcades of vivid clothes,
bookshops full of New Age and alternative literature, posters
advertising mystical tours, meditation and 'healing
workshops' provide a jumble of exotic interest. The Tor,
chief focus of all this, usually has to be approached, as well
as climbed, on foot – its paths start from Wellhouse Lane,
half a mile from the top of the High Street, and parking is
limited to a few street spaces near the garden of the Chalice
Well spring. It's a stiff climb up smooth, steep contours to
the remnant of the fourteenth-century chapel on the top.
You plod up at a suitably holy pace, avoiding cow-pats and
hoping the view will be worth it – which it is, on a good day,
extending from the Bristol Channel to Salisbury's cathedral
spire. But whatever the distant visibility, the immediate
satisfaction is to stand at last, islanded in space, on this
shapely summit which has drawn the eye so often from the
Somerset roads below.

Highlights

** *Axbridge, Blackdown Hills, Cheddar Gorge,
Glastonbury, Mendips, Montacute,
Sedgemoor, Wells.*

* *Brympton D'Evercy, Cheddar Caves,
Hinton St George, Ilminster, The Levels,
Lytes Carey, Somerton, Tintinhull,
Wookey Hole.*

Where to stay

For a key to prices, see p. 12

Barwick
Little Barwick House

Barwick, Yeovil, Somerset
BA22 9TD. Tel Yeovil
(0935) 23902

An attractive white-painted
Georgian house on the edge of
the village with a pretty garden.
Very unlike a hotel in its
informality – although there's
no fault in the service or food –
the main emphasis is on the
restaurant, which is open to
non-residents. Veronica Colley
cooks everything to order so
reservations are staggered. The
ground-floor sitting-room is
cosy with well-used
comfortable chairs and rugs on
the parquet floors. The dining-
room has a huge window
overlooking the garden, and
very high ceilings, but is
softened by rugs and pink-
clothed tables. Bedrooms are all
different: quite simply
furnished with antiques and
bric-a-brac.
£££ *Open all year exc Xmas and
New Year. Closed some Sundays
and Mondays*

Glastonbury
Number 3

3 Magdalene Street,
Glastonbury, Somerset
BA6 9EW. Tel Glastonbury
(0458) 32129

Just beside the abbey, this listed
Georgian house calls itself a
restaurant with rooms rather
than a hotel. There are three
comfortable, spacious double
bedrooms with lots of original
pieces and their own

bathrooms. The dining-room
might be a bit over the top for
some tastes, being richly
decorated and quite formal, but
the food is good. An upstairs
sitting-room is lighter with
comfortable chairs and a cosy
atmosphere.
£££ *Closed first 3 weeks Jan*

Hatch Beauchamp
Farthings

Hatch Beauchamp, Somerset
TA3 6SG. Tel Hatch Beauchamp
(0823) 480664

Only about five miles from
Taunton and the M5, this partly
Georgian house is conveniently
situated, with a small pretty
garden where guests are
encouraged to sit in summer. It
is a small (six bedrooms) hotel,
rather old-fashioned in style
and immaculately neat and
clean. The Coopers, whose
home it is, welcome their guests
and take great care of them.
Bedrooms and public rooms are
comfortable if a bit uninspiring.
££££ *Closed early Jan*

Oakhill
Oakhill House

Bath Road, Oakhill, Somerset
BA3 5AQ. Tel Oakhill
(0749) 840180

Set in four acres of gardens just
outside Shepton Mallet, this is
an unusual hotel. You are
aware of the clucking of various
fowl (the Durnells raise their
own) around the Georgian
house, some of which may
appear on your plate later.
Inside, collections of china-

faced dolls and old typewriters are used as decorative features in some of the public areas. It is comfortable enough for the reasonable prices. Some of the bedrooms are huge, but single rooms can be cramped; all have their own bathrooms.

££–£££ Open all year. Restaurant closed Sun and Mon evening

Seavington St Mary
The Pheasant

Seavington St Mary, Nr Ilminster, Somerset TA19 0QH. Tel South Petherton (0460) 40502. Fax (0460) 42388
The first impression of a neat well-tended place – shrubs and lawns are immaculate, with No Dogs signs very clear – is carried throughout this hotel. The partly thatched buildings have been converted from a seventeenth-century farm, and the cosy bar and dining-room have beams and inglenook fires. Everything is neatly co-ordinated. The bedrooms each have their own distinctive style but all are comfortable and with modern equipment.

£££ Closed 26 Dec to 10 Jan, restaurant closed Sat lunch and Sun evening

Shepton Mallet
Bowlish House Restaurant

Wells Road, Shepton Mallet, Somerset BA4 5JD. Tel Shepton Mallet (0749) 342022
On the outskirts of the town, Bowlish House is recognisable by its fine Palladian façade with central pillars and steps up to the entrance. The main rooms are grandly proportioned but not intimidating, particularly the bar with painted panels, high-backed chairs and old

photographs. Bedrooms vary, large high-ceilinged rooms on the first floor, more quirky shapes higher up, but all are individually furnished with antiques and knick-knacks and have their own bathrooms.

£ Open all year, exc 24 to 27 Dec

Somerton
The Lynch

4 Behind Berry, Somerton, Somerset TA11 7PD. Tel Somerton (0458) 72316
On the edge of this attractive town, the hotel has a decent-sized garden, very well kept. The eighteenth-century stone house has been simply but well decorated in keeping with its style – elegant without being overdone. Light is quite a feature, streaming in through windows and the glass roof extension in the centre, making interesting patterns. The 10 bedrooms are a good size with neat, attractive furnishings and lots of comforting extras.

£££ Open all year

Ston Easton
Ston Easton Park

Bath, Somerset BA3 4DF. Tel Chewton Mendip (076 121) 631. Fax (076 121) 377
If you want to treat yourself to a night of luxury in a fine Georgian house in lovely landscaped grounds this is the place for you. It is expensive but it will be difficult to find fault. The rooms are large and grand with every detail of decoration and furnishing attended to. The main drawing-room is almost too much with its Corinthian columns and carved eagle of Jupiter but it is all faithful to the period of the house. The library

is easier to relax in – panels and mahogany bookshelves with some comfortable sofas and chairs – and guests can take tea by the fire. The bedrooms are beautifully done, some huge, all with antiques and fine pictures and lots of luxurious extras. Food and service is of the same high standard.

£££££ *Open all year*

Where to eat

For a key to prices see p. 12

Ashcott
Ashcott Inn
50 Bath Road, Ashcott. Tel Ashcott (0458) 210282
Friendly, welcoming pub with fish dishes as a speciality.
[£] *Open all week, Mon to Sat 11–2.30, 5.30–11, Sun 12–3, 7–10.30. Closed Christmas Day*

Barwick
Little Barwick House
Barwick, Yeovil. Tel Yeovil (0935) 23902
Dinner only. Set menu with daily additions. Good roasts with plenty of vegetables.
Open Mon to Sat, 7–9

Bruton
Claire de Lune
2–4 High Street, Bruton BA10 0EQ. Tel Bruton (0749) 813395
Dinner only. Small restaurant in an old storehouse with a set menu of elaborate dishes.
Open Mon to Sat, 7–10 (10.30 Sat)

Castle Cary
Old Bakehouse
High Street, Castle Cary. Tel Castle Cary (0963) 50067
A homely atmosphere in this vegetarian shop and café. Lots of wholesome dishes with mainly organic ingredients
[£] *Open Tues to Sat 9.30–5.*

Cranmore
Strode Arms
Cranmore. Tel Cranmore (074 988) 450
Fifteenth-century pub with beamy interior and reliable pub food.
[£] *Open all week noon to 2; Mon to Sat 7–9.30 (10 Fri and Sat). Closed Christmas Day*

Glastonbury
Number 3
Magdalene Street, Glastonbury. Tel Glastonbury (0458) 32129
Dinner only. Tasty, unpretentious cooking in a very strongly decorated dining-room.
Open Tues to Sat 7–9.15. Closed Jan

Mells
Bell Inn
Lower Mendip nr Bath. Tel Mells (0373) 812316
Seventeenth-century beamy village pub with tasty home-made cooking such as rabbit casserole or steak & kidney.
[£] *Open all week, noon to 2, 7–10.30. Closed Boxing Day*

Montacute

Milk House

The Borough. Tel Martock
(0935) 823823
Fifteenth-century house
furnished with antiques;
wholefood cooking combined
with classic French.
*Open Wed to Sat 7–9, Sun noon
to 2*

North Perrott

Manor Arms

North Perrott, Crewkerne. Tel
Crewkerne (0460) 72901
Lively pub serving simple
dishes. Jolly atmosphere.
*[£] Open Tues to Sun noon to 2,
Tues to Sat 7–9.45.*

Shepton Mallet

Bowlish House

Wells Road. Tel Shepton Mallet
(0749) 342022
Good atmosphere. A
reasonable choice of dishes well
cooked.
*Open all week 7–9.30. Lunches by
arrangement*

Ston Easton

Ston Easton Park

Ston Easton. Tel Chewton
Mendip (076 121) 631
A grand country house hotel
with formal dining-room. Set
menu at dinner gives six choices
at each course.
*Open all week 12.30–2, 7.30–9.30
(10 Fri and Sat)*

Wells

The Cloister Restaurant

West Cloister, Wells Cathedral,
Wells. Tel Wells (0749) 76543
Simple cloister café/restaurant
in the Cathedral. Fairly basic
but very wholesome.
*[£] Open Mon to Sat 10–5 Sun 2–
5, (Nov to Feb 4.30). Closed 2
weeks Christmas, Good Friday*

Fountain Inn

1 St Thomas Street, Wells. Tel
Wells (0749) 72317
Fifteenth-century pub with a
good range of out of the
ordinary pub food.
*[£] Open all week, Mon to Sat
11.30–2, 6–10, Sun noon to 2,
7–9.30. Closed Christmas Day and
Boxing Day*

Central Somerset

This triangle of country, bounded by the Bristol Channel to the north, the M5 to the south and east and Exmoor National Park to the west, does not attract visitors in anything like the numbers that gravitate towards better-known areas west and east. Yet although the coast has little of interest, apart from birdlife on a spectacular scale, rural England at its deepest is found inland on and around the Quantock Hills and the broad vale to its west, through which snake the steam and diesel trains of Britain's longest private railway line. Sandstone church towers beckon anyone with a love of unspoilt country churches – here they are in number and quality, carved bench ends, brass candelabras, oak wagon roofs, medieval screens and all. Once away from the busy towns close to the M5, there is a series of towns and villages with docile small-scale charm, such as Milverton, Stogumber, Stogursey and Nether Stowey. Country houses stand beside or close by many of its villages, but Gaulden Manor is the only one regularly open to public view.

Bridgwater to Brean Down

Bridgwater, bypassed by cross-country traffic on the M5, has the gruff red-brick suburbs and factory zones of an industrial town but one or two good things in the centre. Bisecting the town, the River Parrett provides the key to the town's early prosperity as a port with access to the Severn Estuary; the town's prosperity declined with the death of the local cloth industry. Vestiges of early industrial buildings line either side of this tidal waterway, crossed by a late-Victorian bridge with ornate lamps that sets a decidedly jolly mood. Because of fighting in the Civil War, when the town was under siege – held by Royalists, although the townsfolk were pro-Cromwell – nothing of the medieval town survives, save one or two half-timbered buildings and St Mary's Church, and the brick industrial town has only piecemeal eighteenth-century survivals. Admiral Robert Blake (1598–1657) dominates Fore Street in statue form, standing high above the shoppers. Blake's uneventful first 40 years in country life were followed by a parliamentary career. He soared to fame as a commander in a period of British naval supremacy, during which time the British defeated the Dutch, rid the English Channel of pirates, took Jamaica from Spain and dominated some of the Mediterranean.

Behind Blake's statue is the imposing but substantially restored St Mary's, in which Blake was baptised. Noted for its tall and graceful tower, the church possesses in its dark interior a Jacobean screen and a notable seventeenth-century altar-painting *The Descent from the Cross* by a Bolognese artist.

Also close by the statue is the absorbing **Admiral Blake Museum** (open daily exc Christmas Day and Boxing Day, Mon to Sat, 11 to 5; Sun, 2 to 5), which contains Blake mementoes – including his travelling compass and sea chest – a model in the Shipping Room of the now-closed Bridgwater Docks at the turn of the century, and a miscellany of local history, with sepia photographs of works outings, antique cameras, a history of brick-making in Bridgwater, and a multitude of tin soldiers within a glass case portraying the Battle of Sedgemoor (see p. 30).

Castle Street, probably the best complete street of its date in the West Country, is strongly unified early Georgian (begun in 1723), its brickwork carefully preserved. The Bridgwater Arts Centre at numbers 11–13 is a venue for music, drama, dance and amateur operatics, and has temporary art exhibitions; it closes in August. Castle Street leads into King Square, which dates from the late eighteenth century but which was never completed. Its plum-brown brick houses, shaded by a horse chestnut tree at the centre, are now solicitors' offices and surgeries. The whole square stands on the site of Bridgwater Castle, which was destroyed in the Civil War.

Further north and above the mouth of the River Parrett, **Burnham-on-Sea**, a small seaside resort, is a much quieter cousin of Weston-super-Mare. Sand-castles, donkeys and a short pier supply the foreground for a prospect over the Bristol Channel to the South Wales coast, with Brean Down protruding to the north and the Quantocks visible in the west. Just off the beach itself, one of the town's two

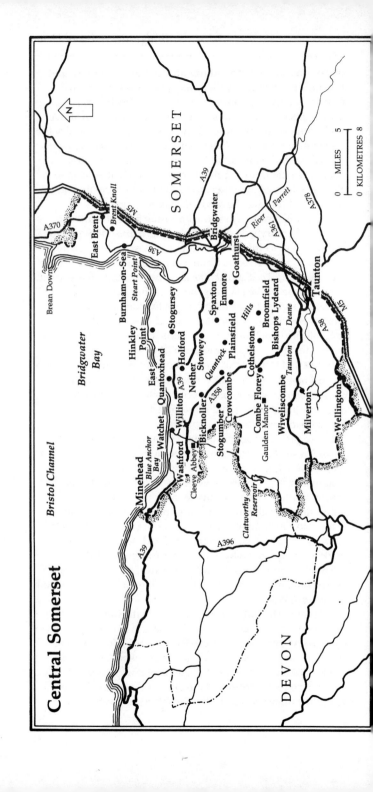

lighthouses is built on stilts over the water; the other, taller and more conventional, lies inland. The pair together act as a navigational aid for shipping. The parish church, its tower tilting on sandy foundations, is a relic of the original village, which has otherwise virtually disappeared, and contains a real surprise: the much-restored interior is the unlikely setting for a set of carved figures by the great seventeenth-century sculptor and wood-carver Grinling Gibbons, assisted by Arnold Quellin. There are nine cherubs, six behind the altar and three incorporated into a nineteenth-century memorial by one of the windows, and two graceful angels in front of the font in the baptistery. The figures were originally in the chapel at Whitehall Palace, which was destroyed by fire in 1698. They passed on to Westminster Abbey and thence in 1820 to Bishop King of Rochester, vicar of Burnham (and dean of St Paul's).

Inland from Burnham-on-Sea, **Brent Knoll**, a hill of knob-like appearance, is of modest height but towers above a flat coastal plain that was once sea-bed. A signposted path leads up to the site of the hill fort, located from a local path map displayed at the churchyard entrance in **East Brent**; the church tower soars over the fields. The church interior (which may be locked) contains a delicate plaster ceiling of 1637 in the nave and some good bench ends. On the Burnham side of the hill, **Brent Knoll** church has unique carved bench ends depicting a satirical tale of a fox in bishop's attire being defrocked, pilloried and hanged. Thus, uninhibited side-swipes are made at clerical greed – topical at the time as the abbot of Glastonbury was trying to divert the parish tithes for his own uses.

North of Burnham-on-Sea, the long, straight coast road leads past sand-dunes and the holiday camps and caravans around Brean until it ends at **Brean Down**. From the car park, a steep flight of concrete steps climbs up 320 feet and on to the down, the most significant piece of Bristol Channel coastal scenery east of Exmoor. Projecting nearly a mile out to sea, the rabbit-nibbled turf makes for an exhilarating walk, unrivalled in the vicinity for views, which include the Mendips, Brent Knoll, the Quantocks, Hinkley Point power-station, North Hill (above Minehead), Dunkery Beacon on Exmoor, Steep Holm and Flat Holm (in the Channel), Swansea, Cardiff and the Brecon Beacons. Weston-super-Mare lies almost immediately on the other side. Geologically, this carboniferous limestone hill belongs to the Mendip chain, although it is completely detached from the rest and was an island in prehistoric times when sea-level reached its maximum height. Tilting of rock strata, brought about by movements within the Earth, is evident in the cliffs themselves, which drop precipitously on the southern side. The maritime climate and geology are the cocktail for a rare plant life (making Brean Down a Site of Special Scientific Interest) that includes the rare white rock-rose, here in profusion in its most northerly site, dwarf sedge, goldilocks and Somerset hair grass (not found in England outside the Mendips). Common blue and marbled white butterflies flit among the wild flowers, while at the far end of the down binocular-clad birdwatchers monitor the progress of kestrels, cormorants, waders and rock-pipits.

If it seems a serene place now, its history is very different. In the last century the Brean Down Harbour Company was formed, with the object of building a railway line along the length of the down to connect the main railway network with a new harbour here. The harbour scheme got as far as the foundation stone ceremony, with cannon fired and town band hired, but proved ill-fated, as the foundation stone was washed out on the tide the following morning. The scheme was abandoned soon after.

At the end of the down stand the grey derelict ruins of Brean Down Fort, part of Lord Palmerston's chain of four Bristol Channel fort defences, erected to protect the docks of Bristol, Avonmouth, Cardiff and Newport. Built to accommodate 50 men, the fort was closed after an explosion deliberately and mysteriously caused by a gunner in 1900, but it had a renaissance in the Second World War, when it was rearmed. Close by, a length of rail survives from one of several experiments developed here by the Miscellaneous Weapons Development of the Admiralty.

The Quantock Hills

A range of hills with its toe nearly in the sea and rising to 1,261 feet at Wills Neck, stretching 12 miles from West Quantoxhead in the north-west to the brink of Taunton in the south and to North Petherton in the east, the Quantocks have an inscrutable charm of their own. Villages are folded into the landscape, lanes are maze-like and high-hedged, little-frequented and not always signposted; roadside views are blocked by dense vegetation, except for dips in the lane revealing glimpses of the hills themselves above silent glades and shady combes. The top can be reached by car either on the Crowcombe to Nether Stowey road or up the no-through road from Plainsfield. Once you are up there, you can walk along a breezy moorland track, a prehistoric highway dotted with cairns and burial mounds from the Bronze Age, look out for wild ponies and red deer, and enjoy grand views over the Bristol Channel to the Glamorgan coast, Exmoor and the Blackdown Hills. The Quantocks have more than just a passing resemblance to Exmoor itself, though they are a shade tamer, their finite extent is more obvious and their lower reaches more populated. Unlike Exmoor, the Quantocks have never been a royal hunting-forest, although the staghounds and hunts will be out in spring and late summer. The villages below the slopes, standing amid fertile red-earth farmland, tell of wool-trade prosperity: opulent country houses and churches with noble towers, hallmarks of the Quantock landscape.

The multitude of quiet lanes that comprise the eastern approaches to the area from Bridgwater have inviting views. Before you reach the hills proper, a number of villages deserve a look. **Goathurst** comprises a village street of pastel-shaded and sandstone cottages; Halswell House (1689) to the south, now converted into flats, stands in what remains of its park, with an ornamental rotunda and temples. **Broomfield** lies up a slope and far from the madding traffic. Nearby **Fyne Court** now houses the headquarters of the Somerset Trust for Nature Conservation, which owns over 40 nature reserves in the county. Here is an interpretation centre, with information about the county's natural history. The trees are magnificent, and there are woodland trails through the grounds, particularly good for children. The old manor, which was largely destroyed by fire in 1894, could easily have been destroyed before that when its most celebrated resident, Andrew Crosse (1784–1855), was working out his early experiments with electricity. Known locally as 'the thunder-and-lightning man', and regarded with awe as something of a magician, he attempted to obtain electrical current from the air by means of masts connected to a brass conductor installed in the organ loft of the house; family silver was melted down for the pure silver required for this. A mast is still attached to an oak tree, and copper wire is still unearthed periodically in the grounds. Down the lane, Broomfield church possesses another superb collection of bench ends, mostly sixteenth century, beneath a wagon roof adorned by 47 shield-bearing angels.

Further south, close to Cheddon Fitzpaine, is **Hestercombe Garden**. Hestercombe House has been the headquarters of the Somerset Fire Brigade since the early 1950s and is not open to the public. The garden (open all year, Mon to Fri, 9 to 5, plus Sat and Sun, 2 to 5, May to Sept). Originally designed by Sir Edwin Lutyens in collaboration with Gertrude Jekyll, had deteriorated during the Second World War and restoration started only in 1973. Faithful to the design, the remarkable terraces and vistas have been restored, and some of the old-fashioned varieties of plants donated by gardeners from all over England. The result is worth a visit.

To the north, **Enmore** has red-stone farms and cottages amid red-earth fields. Eighteenth-century Enmore Castle, near the church, was visited in 1807 by Coleridge, here to meet John Perceval, Earl of Egmont, who was an ardent admirer of Coleridge's work. Lichen mottles the sandstone walls of the church at nearby **Spaxton**, whose sixteenth-century bench ends include the renowned but misnamed Fuller's Panel, depicting a clothworker with the tools of his trade and a roll of cloth. Farmers' boys recorded their presence here in 1728 by carving their names and farms on the pews. At **Plainsfield**, hand-woven and home-spun woollen goods are on offer at Quantock Weavers (which also runs weaving and spinning courses).

Nether Stowey, further north and just off the A39, is the largest Quantocks village, which attracts literary pilgrims seeking out Coleridge's cottage (open Apr to Sept, Tues to Thur and Sun, 2 to 5). Thomas Poole, a village tanner and self-taught bibliophile who lived and worked in Castle Street on a site behind Poole House, arranged the tenancy for his poet friend. Coleridge stayed with his family for three years in 'dear Stowey', from December 1796. It was a period of creativity for him. During a walk to Dulverton with Wordsworth, who was staying at Holford (see p. 47), the two poets had a conversation that produced the ideas for 'The Ancient Mariner', and while on a visit to a farmhouse near Culbone (see p. 67) near the coast he wrote his unfinished masterpiece 'Kubla Khan'. He also composed Part One of 'Christabel' here. The days in the romantic scenery of the area brought Coleridge and Wordsworth closer together and fired their imaginations to make a profound impact: 1798 saw the publication of the *Lyrical Ballads*, one of the great cornerstones of English literary romanticism.

The cottage was much altered in the nineteenth century, but the National Trust has set up two of the four surviving low-beamed rooms as a museum to the poet and his circle, with manuscripts and memorabilia, and the rooms furnished as they might have been.

Ranged around a Y-shape of streets, the village itself is densely packed together, with red-tiled cottages fronting directly on to the street, and invites a short exploration. A stream, which Coleridge dubbed 'the gutter of Stowey', runs down the street; if you fall in it, a saying goes, you will stay in the village for ever. Thomas Poole's tannery has gone, but his life is summarised on a plaque beside the entrance to the church; the plaque states: 'his originality and grasp of mind counterbalanced the deficiencies of early education'. Beyond the tea-shop, the Quantocks visitor centre, next to the library, provides limited tourist information.

To the north-west, and also just off the A39, **Holford** is scattered close to the heads of Hodder's Combe and Holford Combe, both delicious valleys of mature oaks and beeches with alluring paths that run alongside clear streams and on up to the hilltops; by the north side of Hodder's Combe stands a curious restored dog-pound with a heraldic motif. William and Dorothy Wordsworth stayed at Alfoxton Park, now a hotel, at the edge of the village, in 1797, providing companionship for Coleridge: Wordsworth penned 'Lines Written in Early Spring' here, while Dorothy recorded in her journal the ferns, periwinkles and trees. A Home Office official also paid a visit, checking out the radical Wordsworths and Coleridge at a time, following the French Revolution, when there was a considerable feeling of unease about any possibility of revolutionary upsurges on this side of the Channel. The poets' nocturnal walks with camp-stools and notebooks, their northern accents and Dorothy's brown complexion had aroused local suspicion, and Coleridge's servants had overheard talk of Spinoza as 'spy noser'. Eventually, the official dismissed the Wordsworths and Coleridge as harmless cranks.

Villages on the west side of the hills lie just off the main road, the A358. **Bicknoller** church, its churchyard a splash of purple hydrangeas, has carved Tudor bench ends with leaf and floral designs, and twentieth-century ones depicting the church and village stocks; the fan-vaulted screen was carved by craftsmen from the Dunster area. Outside the porch, on the left as you enter, a now-illegible verse (reproduced in the form of a rubbing displayed in the tower) reads:

O, who would trust this world
or prize what's in it
That gives and takes and chops
and changes every minit.

Coleridge used to walk over the Quantocks to the pub (still extant) in Bicknoller. Halsway Manor (signposted from the main road), not generally open to the public but visible from the road, has a Tudor appearance, though has been much altered subsequently. It is now a residential folk centre, also used for conferences and seminars.

At **Crowcombe**, notices on the fifteenth-century Church House – the village hall – advertise occasional teas, a summer art exhibition and the Bicknoller Flower Show; adjacent, behind high walls, is the former village pound, where stray animals used to be kept. Opposite, a driveway fringed by mountain ashes forms a vista for Crowcombe Court, an imposing early-Georgian house of brick and Ham Hill stone, now a retirement home. The churchyard echoes to the distant whistle of a steam train on the West Somerset Railway (see p. 52). Inside the church is a very fine array of pre-Reformation bench ends, many with a fertility theme (vines and the ancient spirit known as the Green Man in particular), mixing Christian and pagan. On the roadside close by, a stepped medieval stone cross stands by itself at the site of the defunct village market, its steps worn by vendors and their wares.

Taunton to Stogumber

A major commercial centre for the West Country, and the county town of Somerset, **Taunton** draws visitors to its Brewhouse Theatre, farmers to its important twice-weekly cattle market and cricket fans to Somerset's main county ground. But it is predominantly a busy and important shopping town, much of it rather unremarkable to the eye. The best it has to offer visually is concentrated within yards of the old Market House, a red-brick eighteenth-century building now stranded amid traffic. Immediately behind it, Tudor House (now called Monmouth Bar) is the only half-timbered house in the town. Hammett Street, Taunton's finest, consists of plain, plum-coloured brick eighteenth-century terraces with white porticoed porches. This short street perfectly frames the vista of St Mary Magdalene's tower, all 163 feet of it, a faithful 1862 rebuilding, in Ham Hill stone and Quantock old red sandstone, of the graceful fifteenth-century original, which was deemed unsafe. Go inside the largest parish church in Somerset, two aisles and a nave making the plan almost square, for a neck-craning view of an elaborate Tudor roof with gilded angels, and modern shield motifs depicting art, music, outer space and electricity.

Entered through a thirteenth-century gateway from the main road, Taunton Castle now houses the **Somerset County Museum** (open all year, Mon to Sat, 10 to 5; closed Bank Hols exc May and August), a professionally displayed and spaciously presented exhibition. A particularly strong archaeology section features a mosaic of Dido and Aeneas from the site of a Roman villa at Low Ham (near Langport), a dug-out canoe *c*.350 BC discovered by the River Brue, a cist (burial chamber) with occupant from Culbone, and part of a walkway made of matted hazel and willow found submerged in marshy land near Glastonbury and dating from *c*.2900 BC. Dolls, military costumes, ceramics (including Han dynasty vases) and seventeenth-century silverware are also represented.

The castle itself was where in 1497 Perkin Warbeck was proclaimed king after his expedition against Henry VII, and the venue for the Bloody Assizes of 1685 after the Battle of Sedgemoor (see p. 30), when in the Great Hall Judge Jeffreys condemned 508 followers of the Duke of Monmouth, some to be hanged, drawn and quartered in Taunton. The Norman castle was besieged in the Civil War and much of it lay in ruins until restoration in the eighteenth century; the eastern gatehouse now forms part of the Castle Hotel (see p. 60). Nearby, the Norman Garden, excavated and restored in the 1930s, offers surprising peace and seclusion.

Curious visitors may like to seek out three minor features of the town: Bath Place, a narrow and easily missed alley off the High Street, has seventeenth- and eighteenth-century shop-fronts now refurbished and occupied by small boutiques selling picture frames and jewellery – it leads out at the far end to bland civic buildings lightened by Georgian terraces in The Crescent to the left; Vivary Park, entered by white iron gates at the far end of the High Street, has a mildly preposterous Edwardian fountain, multi-coloured with sculpted daffodils, cherubs riding fish, lions spouting water, and storks – the effect not that far removed from garden gnomery; and adjoining the post office in North Street, the British Telecom Museum displays vintage historical telephone and telegraph equipment.

Taunton Deane, a vale of russet-soil farmland, prized for its fertility since Roman times and perhaps before, extends northwards and westwards from Taunton, the low land bounded by the Brendon and Quantock Hills, with the Blackdown Hills close by to the south. This is famous cider-apple country; on the A38 between Taunton and Wellington, **Sheppy's Cider** has a functioning cider press adjoining orchards, where you can see the cider-making process and buy the result; antique agricultural tools and devices are on show in one of the outbuildings. Of the two towns in the vale apart from Taunton, **Wellington** is the larger, a textile centre on the A38 west of Taunton. This has both industrial and market-town character, with a fifteenth-century church possessing an imposing sandstone tower (there's little else in the town worth going out of your way for).

Cider

Wold Zam could never goe vur long
Wi'out his jar or virkin;
A used the zider zame's twur ile
To keep his jints vrim quirken.

The West Country's favourite tipple meant more than a pint in the pub: for generations it was the stuff of life. In Somerset every man, woman and child drank it. In the Levels particularly, it was a more wholesome drink than the water, and enlivened a diet of bland bread and porridge, salty meat and fish. Farm workers were poorly paid, and it was standard practice to make up wages with the 'cider truck', an allowance that might be a couple of pints a day in winter but increased to a gallon or more at harvest-time. The going rate to attract extra labour was two quarts a day for a man and one quart for a boy, but in practice consumption was prodigious – to swing a scythe from dawn until dusk, a labourer got 'cidered up' on half a gallon before breakfast and sweated out replenishments all day.

Most farmers managed the once-in-a-lifetime outlay on a cider press, and the farm's supply was produced convivially after the day's work was done, a sweet-smelling task in a lamplit barn. The

Further north, **Wiveliscombe**, a former cloth-weaving town, is quietly uneventful apart from a curious tile-hung Victorian library in medieval style and, south-east of the church, a surviving gate from the manor house used by the bishops of Bath and Wells when on pastoral duty in this area. The town stands at the western fringe of Taunton Deane, with pleasant hilly country to the north-west merging imperceptibly into the Brendon Hills. Attractively set **Clatworthy Reservoir** has some visitor amenities, including a picnic site on its eastern side, a nature trail and a footpath around its partly wooded four-mile perimeter.

Milverton, to the south-east, has irregular terraces of colour-rendered cottages, and the wisteria-hung Georgian houses of local sandstone in North Street telling of days of prosperity when the weaving trade flourished. Sited on a rise, the church looks over a yew to the distant Blackdown Hills, with the Wellington Monument (see p. 26) just visible on top. Inside the church, a set of bench ends, very fine even

---

apple crop was first crushed to small juicy pieces in a mill that resembled a mangle, and the resulting 'pomace' was stacked on the press in carefully constructed 'cheeses', between layers of clean straw or cloth. The top was screwed down on a four-foot stack of 'cheeses', to be pressed gradually over a week.

From a trough at the bottom, the juice was transferred to wooden casks with the bunghole open and left to ferment. It first went through a violent frothy stage, with daily topping up of juice to prevent air entering, and then, once the froth subsided, was firmly 'bunged down' and left for at least a month and sometimes six. A variety of additives improved the liquor: blackberries, elderberries and currants were popular for flavour, and there are stories of horseshoes thrown in for iron content and a leg of beef or mutton for 'body' – all absorbed by the power of the fermenting apple juice. But these refinements were for the high-quality cider on which the farmer's social reputation rested; his labourers drank weaker stuff, even a second pressing, diluted with hop-water to stop it turning to vinegar.

The flavour depended chiefly on the blend of cider apples. The main types are the bitter-sweets and the bitter-sharps, both high in astringent tannin, closely related to crab-apples and useless for

by Somerset standards, was mostly carved by local craftsmen about 1540–60 and includes portraits of royals, symbols of the martyrdom of the apostles and, in the south aisle, a depiction of the spies of Eschol returning to Moses with a bunch of grapes.

Bishop's Lydeard church, also known for its sixteenth-century bench ends – a windmill with its miller, a Quantocks stag and a ship feature in the carvings – has a vast and noble tower dominating a flat landscape. On the western edge of this large, suburban-flavoured village lie the terminus, goods shed and renovation depot for the **West Somerset Railway**, a privately run line on which steam and diesel trains haul brown-and-cream ex-British Rail carriages (1950s-style, with compartments and string luggage racks) to Minehead. The route follows the broad, green valley between the Quantocks

---

cooking or eating. Somerset has traditionally excelled in the grafting skills needed for robust stock and distinctive varieties – Stoke Red and Kensington Black, Sweet Coppin and Tremlett's Bitter, Tom Putt and Yarlington Mill.

Farming methods changed, and cider ceased to be an essential. Orchards where cattle grazed under the trees were grubbed to make room for more profitable crops. While the Victorians had a liking for ciders and perries (cider made with pears), these drinks had a poor reputation by the twentieth century.

The traditional English cider was rescued by the companies that began production on a larger scale and popularised it all over the country. 'Foreigners' may prefer it sweet and sparkling, but the big manufacturers – the Taunton Cider Company, and Showerings of Shepton Mallet – also make it strong, still and dry. Traditional farmhouse methods have always been used at Perry's Cider Mills (telephone Ilminster (0460) 52681) near Ilminster and Sheppey's Cider Farm near Taunton (telephone Bradford-on-Tone (0823) 461233), both of which are open to visitors on most days. At Pass Vale Farm near Martock (telephone South Petherton (0460) 40782), home of the Somerset Cider Brandy Company, you can buy the celebrated Burrow Hill cider bottled or draught from the barrel. You can usually put in an order for Somerset Cider Brandy, too, but you may have to wait a year or more for your bottle. This distinctive cousin of French Calvados, made here in England's only licensed distillery, takes at least four years to mature.

---

and Brendons, runs through Williton, the halfway point, where steam trains stop for replenishment at the water tower, and reaches the coast at Watchet; it then snakes inland to Washford before rejoining the sea at Blue Anchor for the final few miles across sea-level expanses of farmland. When British Rail closed the railway in 1971, Somerset County Council bought the line and leased it to the newly formed West Somerset Railway Company. Today, the 20-mile line is the longest privately owned railway in Britain; the complete journey takes something over an hour, but seven intervening stations can be used for a shorter trip. A railway museum and shop operate at Washford, where you can also stop off for Cleeve Abbey (see p. 57). A chartered bus service connects Bishop's Lydeard with the British Rail station at Taunton.

Cothelstone, a couple of miles north of Bishop's Lydeard, has a manor house (not open) built in Stuart times, easy to view from the road, occupying a lovely site in landscaped parkland on the brink of Quantocks woodlands. In 1685 its owner, Lord Stawell, refused to entertain Judge Jeffreys following the barbarity of the Bloody Assizes; Jeffreys avenged him by hanging two of the Monmouth rebels outside the manor.

Further west, on the far side of the speedier A358, unclassified lanes wind through undulating pastoral landscapes and unassuming scattered hamlets, with **Gaulden Manor**, east of Tolland, providing an objective. Dating from the twelfth century, this was once a possession of Taunton Priory, its pond, which still survives, providing the monks with fish. After the Reformation, ownership of the manor passed to the Turberville and Wolcott families. The former was the family of Hardy's *Tess of the d'Urbervilles*; the family's Dorset home, Woolbridge House, in Wool, appears in the novel as Wellbridge House. Thirty-minute guided tours by the present owners of the manor (open Easter Sun and Mon, May to early Sept, Sun, Thurs and summer Bank Hols, 2 to 5.30) take in three main rooms, fleshed out with descriptions of the antiques they have collected, which include sixteenth- to nineteenth-century furniture and porcelain. The highlight is the Great Hall, with an elaborate plastered ceiling added in the sixteenth century by James Turberville, Bishop of Exeter, Turberville coats of arms above the fireplace, roundels depicting King David with his harp and the Angel of Death blowing a trumpet, and

53

a frieze showing religious tableaux. The other rooms seen are a kitchen, reputedly haunted, a small room off the Hall serving as a chapel, and a bedroom with another Turberville coat of arms. After the tour you can sit in an informal tea-shop, which has its own tea-garden.

A few miles to the east, the village of **Combe Florey** has a brief moment of grandeur, with an arched sandstone gate-house of 1593 presenting a glimpse into a park, but the old manor, for which this was the gate-house, was rebuilt further up the slope some 80 years later. From 1829 to 1845 the house was home of rector Sydney Smith, who expressed himself 'extremely pleased' with his parish, 'a very pretty place in very beautiful country'. He found his house 'like the parsonages described in novels', but stated that his neighbours looked 'very much like other people's neighbours; their remarks are generally meteorological'. Smith's wit will probably be remembered for ever: he enjoyed gentle pokes at his own profession ('Don't you know, as the French say, there are three sexes: men, women and clergymen'), and invented that famous definition of Heaven as 'eating *pâté de foie gras* to the sound of trumpets'. Novelist Evelyn Waugh lived at the house for the last years of his life, from 1956 to 1966, completing *Unconditional Surrender*, the final part of the *Sword of Honour* trilogy here. Waugh is buried beside his wife Laura at the top of the churchyard, in a private plot just inside the adjacent park (reached by taking a kissing-gate in the top right-hand corner of the churchyard and turning left). The church itself has medieval bench ends, a wagon roof and some fine tombs, including a cross-legged knight.

Just south of a pottery at Vellow lies **Stogumber**, on a hillside, with marigolds and wallflowers in compact cottage gardens, and thatch or tiles above colour washes of pink, buff, dark orange or cream. There is scarcely a jarring note, from the antique shop at the bottom end, past an antique road sign faintly pointing to Bicknoller and the station (a mile out of the village, on the West Somerset Railway) and past seventeenth-century ex-almshouses to the dominating gargoyle-embellished church tower at the top. The church has a spacious interior with typical west Somerset features, including a wagon roof, Bridgwater-made brass candelabra and carved bench ends. In one aisle a bier stands ready for use: '2/6d a day, 3/6d if cleaned', reads its sign.

Bridgwater Bay to Blue Anchor Bay

The River Parrett feeds into Bridgwater Bay, a southern expanse of the Bristol Channel, just west of Burnham-on-Sea. The bay's coast is an area of tidal mud-flats partly fringed by marshes – a windswept and silent place of appeal to birdwatchers – and overlooked by Steart Point, on the west of the Parrett. Wildfowl and waders are seen in profusion, and the bay is an important moulting ground for shelduck, seen all year round feeding on the mud or in flight across the Bristol Channel. Spring brings about two hundred curlews and five times that number of whimbrels. Thousands of ducks appear in winter, to spectacular effect. You can find the uncommon yellow-horned poppy growing on the shingle.

Most of this little-visited coast between Steart Point and the seaward end of the Quantocks is accessible only on foot in a few places. The flat scenic uniformity is rudely interrupted by the block-like bulk of **Hinkley Point**, Britain's largest nuclear power-station. Guided tours around the reactors take place most mornings and afternoons (these must be booked – telephone Combwich (0278) 652461; you can go along without booking for tours at 2.15 throughout July and Aug).

Lying inland, and a world away from Hinkley Point, **Stogursey** deserves a look for two things. One is the church, which is easy to pass by: but its uninspiring white-rendered exterior belies an interesting interior. It was once a Benedictine priory church, founded by William of Falaise *c*.1100. Inside the entrance, some home-made Friendly Society banners feature a human-looking moustachioed lion with a unicorn and slogans such as 'Go and Do Thou Likewise' and 'Lord Speed the Plough'. 'Before-and-after' pictures by the door show how Victorian restoration made this part of the church somewhat bland. Further into the church comes the big surprise, dark and powerful Norman portions revealing themselves: rounded arches and vaulting and wide steps leading to a plain altar. This is the best-preserved Norman church in the county, embellished by Tudor bench ends and a Bridgwater brass chandelier of the eighteenth century. A notice will help locate a fossilised ichthyosaurus in the flagstoned floor, well preserved and amazingly incongruous.

Stogursey's other attraction is its castle, well hidden at the southern side of the village, but found by walking along Castle Street for a hundred yards and branching right on to a signposted path along a raised walkway. The moat, curtain wall and pretty thatched gate-house (private) soon come into view; the keep was destroyed in the Wars of the Roses. This was the stronghold of the Courcy family, the old village name Stoke Courcy at some time being corrupted into the present one.

West of the power-station, the coast is unspoilt and little visited except by occasional walkers and fossil collectors looking for ammonites. From the car park at Listock there is easy access to the Coast Path and a shingle beach. Further west, **East Quantoxhead**, hidden on a no-through road and somewhat timeless in character, is a perfect composition of duck-pond, thatched cottages and Jacobean grey-stone Court House. The latter, owned by the Luttrell family of Dunster Castle, adjoins the church, which has gigantic ammonite fossils embedded into its walls.

Holiday camps around St Audrie's Bay sprawl most of the way along the coast to **Watchet**, a working port – far from conventionally pretty but with an authentic enough character around its harbour. The cargo-ship *Celtic Navigator* is often in dock, offloading timber for the town's paper mill, whose chimney is visible by St Decuman's, the parish church high up in town and lying well inland. Families promenade out to the diminutive lighthouse at the end of the West Pier. Cobbles and period-style lamp-posts tell of an attempt in the 1980s at giving the sea-front a facelift.

In the last century, Watchet was an important outlet for iron ore excavated from the Brendon Hill mines. Photographs of Watchet as it was can be seen in a small museum (open Easter to Sept, daily, 10.30 to 12.30, 2.30 to 4.30, plus 7 to 9 in July and Aug), which also contains replica Anglo-Saxon coinage from the Watchet mint and memorabilia connected with the harbour.

The lonely position of St Decuman's represents a determined attempt to escape the ravages of the sea. It stands close to a holy well (reached via a track west of the churchyard) and has well-preserved roofs and a finely carved screen. Coleridge very likely had this church and harbour in mind when he described the departure of the Ancient Mariner:

The ship was cheered, the harbour cleared,
Merrily did we drop
Below the Kirk, below the hill,
Below the lighthouse top.

Signposted off the busy crossing of main roads that rather spoils Williton is **Orchard Mill museum** (open all year, Tues to Sun, 10 to 6; closed Tues in winter). The watermill machinery and wheel are intact, but not operating, and the mill rooms are full of endearing and slightly dusty clutter – old vacuum cleaners, thatchers' tools, cheese presses, sheep brands and enough pitchforks to mount a rebellion. Built in 1616 for the Wyndham estate, the mill retains the original iron bars on its windows, protection from tenant farmers who were much exploited by the manorial system obliging them to bring all their grain here.

On the main road at **Washford**, the railway station houses a neatly arranged museum for the West Somerset Railway (see p. 52), with old station signs and photographs – of fairly minor interest for those who are not train-buffs, but a reason for getting out here if you are travelling along the line. South of the main road and just out of the village lies the remarkable **Cleeve Abbey**. These ruins of a Cistercian abbey are of great interest for the extent to which the monks' living-quarters have survived, normally the portion of an abbey to have most disappeared. Enough is here to evoke the Cistercian lifestyle, aided by succinct descriptive captions erected here and there by English Heritage.

The complex is entered at the gate-house, whose preserved effigies of Christ, Mary and child seem to have been placed too high for Henry VIII's men to wreak damage on them. Considerable alterations took place when the building was used as a farm, and parts have recently been restored, but there are some outstanding features in addition to the intactness of the general layout. Most impressive of all is the magnificent arch-braced collar timber roof of the refectory, with crowned angels on the trusses and the whole illuminated by traceried windows. The most conspicuous feature of the earlier (thirteenth-century) refectory is a fine tiled floor decorated with heraldic motifs, now open to the elements. Wall-paintings survive in the dorter (dormitory) and refectory ranges. On the upper floor of the east range, the dorter provides an excellent idea of the monks' living conditions – built in the thirteenth century as one room to house up to 36 monks, and later partitioned into

cubicles. Downstairs lie the vaulted library and
chapter-house.

Minehead

Easily the biggest and liveliest seaside resort in Somerset,
Minehead divides neatly into two very distinct halves. South
and east of the main street (Park Street/The Parade/The
Avenue) lies a residential suburb thick with guesthouses and
holiday lets, set in straight, spacious roads. This area is
fronted by a long promenade, with the terminus of the West
Somerset Railway (see p. 52) at one end, passing a string of
amusement parlours to reach Somerwest World, a large
Butlin's camp (open to day visitors) which has a wide range
of family attractions – and a strong smell of chips. On
the promenade, families sniff a healthy-seeming sea breeze;
a booking pavilion advertises deep-sea fishing-trips and
coach-tours of Quantocks villages. The sandy beach is large
enough at high tide and vast at low. The Avenue, still
very much tree-lined, is the busiest part of town in the
evening, with bars and steak-and-chips cafés doing a brisk
trade.

To the north there is an abrupt transition to Edwardian
villas with verandahs and sloping gardens of neat lawns
shaded by palms and cypresses, centred on Blenheim
Gardens and its bandstand. Beyond rises the formidable
mass of North Hill, wooded on this side, the beginning of the
Exmoor coast. The sea-front here is less fussy, more of a well-
preserved fishing-village. From the harbour, by a battery of
cannons, the *Balmoral* cruises up the Bristol Channel to
Clevedon and Steep Holm. The *Waverley* also operates from
here, sailing along the Exmoor coast and around Lundy
Island.

At the sea-front stands the signpost ('Poole 500 miles')
marking the start of the South-West Peninsula Path. The
coast path rises straight away. To reach St Michael's Church,
leave the path at the first fork and go along Church Path and
then up St Michael's Hill. This short walk is well worth the
effort, not just for the view over Grabbist Hill and (with
tower) Conygar Hill near Dunster, but for the building itself.
Below the clock, a carving represents God holding a crucifix,
while on the right (east) side St Michael weighs souls and
Mary tips the balance against the weight of a devil. Inside is
an intricately carved screen, a medieval illuminated missal

encased in the west wall, an early-seventeenth-century pulpit, and the green-coated, red-capped sculpted figure of 'Jack Hammer', who used to strike the clock bell but has been moved to his present position by the door.

Church Steps, directly below the church, is a picturesque corner of Minehead, with two-up, two-down thatched colour-washed cottages beside a stepped path. Further uphill, leafy outskirts give way to a maze of woodland paths up North Hill and into Exmoor National Park.

Highlights

** *Brean Down, Cleeve Abbey, Quantock Hills and villages.*

* *Bridgwater, Crowcombe, Gaulden Manor, Milverton, Minehead, Nether Stowey, Stogumber, Stogursey, Taunton, West Somerset Railway.*

Where to stay

For a key to prices, see p. 12

Kilve
Meadow House
Sea Lane, Kilve, Somerset TA5 1EG Tel Holford (027 874) 546
As the name suggests, a rural hotel surrounded by fields. The main rooms are in the converted rectory and other bedrooms in the separate fifteenth-century thatched cottage across the courtyard. There are plenty of places to relax: a reading room and separate sitting-room with comfy sofas, and a games room complete with billiard table. Bedrooms are decorated in bright, fresh colours and prints, and even have real coffee and biscuits for guests to help themselves to. A set dinner is served at 8 pm.
£££ *Open all year, exc Christmas week*

Langley Marsh
Langley House
Langley Marsh, Wiveliscombe, Somerset TA4 2UF Tel Wiveliscombe (0984) 23318 Fax (0984) 24573
A very civilised small hotel off the main road in immaculately kept gardens. The house is part-sixteenth- part-eighteenth-century and is filled with fine pieces of furniture. The sitting-room is elegant but not uncosy, with rugs on the parquet floor and comfortable well-upholstered sofas. Personal

service is provided by Peter and Anne Wilson. He is the chef and produces delicious set dinners. Anne makes sure guests have everything they need, and the atmosphere is friendly and relaxed. Bedrooms are well-designed and comfortably equipped. Not cheap.

£££   *Closed Feb*

Taunton

The Castle

Castle Green, Taunton.
Tel Taunton (0823) 272671
The wisteria covered building dominates Castle Green. It has been a hotel for over 300 years, but its origins go back to the eighth century. Modern Taunton is creeping up on the Castle but you can still find peace in the restored Norman Garden. The public rooms are neat and fairly formal; the dining-room particularly so and dinner is a celebrated and expensive occasion. The bedrooms are immaculately co-ordinated, varying in style, size and price but are all comfortable and well-equipped. It's a smart hotel mainly used by business people in the week and locals out for a special treat.

££££   *Open all year*

Vellow

Curdon Mill

Vellow, Williton, Somerset TA4 4LS Tel Stogumber (0984) 56522
A friendly base for exploring the area, this pink-stone mill beside a farm and surrounded by neat unfussy gardens was opened by the Criddles as a hotel about five years ago and has many unusual features. The dining-room on the second floor is large and airy, spreading across the width of the mill, with dark wooden tables and a dresser; the old wheel shaft, still attached to the roof, is a decorative feature. When booking, visitors are sent an extended menu. You can send back your choice or take pot luck from the set menu on arrival. The sitting-room, also upstairs, is pretty and comfortable, as are the bedrooms, which are all individually furnished. Opportunities for croquet players, fishing and hunting.

££   *Open all year*

West Bagborough

Higher House

West Bagborough, Nr Taunton, Somerset TA4 3EF Tel Taunton (0823) 432996
This attractive welcoming place is well hidden away in the Quantock Hills. Mullion windows overlook the hills and after the stillness of the night you are likely to be woken by the crowing of the next door farm's cockerel – it is a truly rural experience. The sitting-rooms are homely and cosy, with a snooker table at the end of one of them. Guests all eat dinner together promptly at 8; the anti-social can eat out at the local pub and still have the benefit of their comfortable, pretty bedrooms.

£   *Open all year, exc Christmas*

Where to eat

For a key to prices, see p. 12

Brent Knoll
Goat House Cafe

Bristol Road, Brent Knoll. Tel
Brent Knoll (0278) 760995
As the name suggests this shop
sells goat products. The café's
menu places less of an
emphasis on this and you can
get sandwiches, baked
potatoes, pizzas etc.
Unlicensed.
*Open all week, Mon, Wed, Thurs,
Fri, Sat 9–5.30. Tues 12–5.30,
Sun 10–5.30*

Bridgwater
Nutmeg House Restaurant

Angel Crescent 8–10 Clare
Street, Bridgwater TA6 3EN. Tel
Bridgwater (0278) 457823
A daily roast, open sandwiches
or a baked potato are some of
the choices at lunch. Evening
meals are more expensive.
*Open Mon to Wed 9.30–5, Thurs
to Sat 9.30–5, 7–late. Closed Sun
and Christmas Day*

Langley Marsh
Langley House Hotel

Langley Marsh. Tel
Wiveliscombe (0984) 23318
Very attractive house set
dinners served in a formal but
cosy dining-room.
*Open all week orders 8–9, (8.30 Fri
and Sat)*

Monksilver
Notley Arms

Monksilver. Tel Stogumber
(0984) 56217
Beamy village pub serving a
selection of freshly cooked
dishes including pasta and
stir-frys.
*[£]   Open all week Mon to Sat 12–
2, 7–9.30; Sun 12–1.45, 7 to 9.
Closed Christmas Day and first 2
weeks Feb*

Taunton
The Castle

Castle Green, Taunton. Tel
Taunton (0823) 272671
Delicious food in formal
surroundings (see p. 60).
Open all week 12.30–2, 7.30–9

Pizza Piazza

39 East Street, Taunton. Tel
Taunton (0823) 322087
Lots of Pizzas.
[£]   Open all week 11 am–11.30 pm

Williton
White House Hotel

Williton. Tel Williton
(0984) 32306/32777
A nice treat for dinner. Starters
and puddings their speciality.
*Open all week orders 7.30–8.30;
closed Nov to mid May*

Exmoor

One of Britain's smallest National Parks, preserved for its coastal and hill scenery and for its importance to the naturalist. Exmoor reveals itself at its best on and near the coast around Lynton, Lynmouth, Selworthy and the Hunter's Inn, and inland in the vicinity of Dunkery Beacon and the valleys of the Barle and the Exe. The area can be superficially covered in a long weekend or explored thoroughly by car and on foot in a couple of weeks. While there is little that is genuinely rugged away from the coast, the rolling moors and sparsely populated farming country and a handful of villages yield a largely unexploited charm in their remote character. Dunster, an oasis of historic interest and a visual delight, should not be missed.

Minehead to Lynmouth

North Hill presents a formidable natural barrier just west of Minehead, 800-foot slopes shelving steadily to the sea, planted with mixed trees and rhododendrons by the Luttrell family of Dunster. An unfenced no-through road starting beyond Minehead parish church provides easy access, leading past panoramic viewpoints at Bratton Ball and Selworthy Beacon before giving out beyond a car park. From near here, a path leads down a narrow combe to **Selworthy** itself, also reached by taking the road from the A39 into the tiny village. Selworthy has little to it, but it's one of the most pleasingly perfect of the West Country's many small-scale essays in whitewashed thatch amid a glorious setting (and jams of tourists if you are unlucky). Above, the white church gleams and looks out towards Dunkery Beacon. The church's south aisle, with a wagon roof ornamented by wall-plates with angels bearing shields and by bosses with Passion symbols and the face of Christ, is Somerset's finest, and the

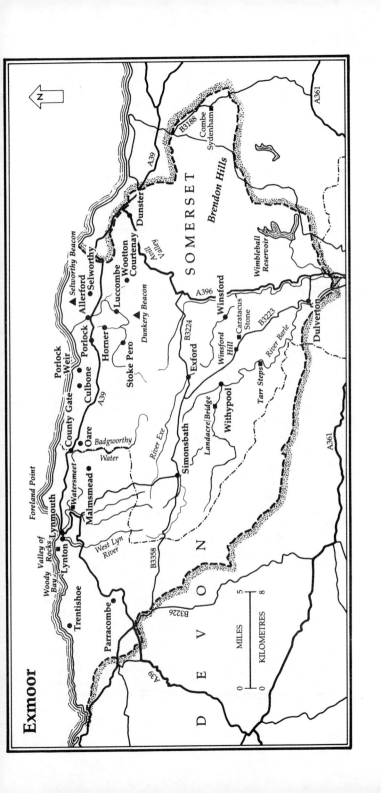

church in its entirety is on an impressively grand scale. Also in the village stands a tithe barn with fourteenth-century moulding depicting a sheep, pig and corn sheaf.

Allerford, the next village to the west, has a pretty two-arched pack-horse bridge which provides a classic postcard shot, nestling below hanging oak woods below Selworthy Beacon. Its thatched primary school, operational from 1821 until 1981, has become the **West Somerset Museum of Rural Life** (open Easter to mid-Oct, Mon to Sat, 10.30 to 12.30, 2 to 4.30), which has an interesting schoolroom kept as it would

Exmoor National Park

Within its 265 square miles, Exmoor National Park displays exquisite diversity – a fascinating and totally unspoilt coast with a distinctive grandeur of its own, deeply incised river valleys, rolling and at times spectacularly empty hills, and some fine viewpoints. Among all this, elusive red deer roam the deciduous woodlands, Exmoor ponies frequent the moors, Exmoor Horn sheep and Devon Red cattle graze enclosed pastures, and circling buzzards mew in silent skies. Apart from the drama of the sandstone cliffs and the cragginess of the Valley of Rocks, Exmoor is curvaceous and subdued in appearance, a plateau land interrupted by tiny combes and gentle undulations. Geologically, it came about when the present-day sandstones, grits and slates were sand on the sea-floor, which became lifted up by forces from within the Earth, leaving a steep slope on the northern side and dipping gradually to the south. Thereafter, quick-flowing streams and rivers, several of which rise from the 1,600-foot-high plateau called the Chains, sculpted much of the rest.

Maps sprawl the legend 'Exmoor Forest' over the middle of the area, referring no longer to trees – the largest survival of ancient woodland, which once covered much of the area, is further east around Horner Water – but to a royal hunting-forest (never much hunted by kings, however) where you can find the much-prized and still extant Exmoor deer herds. The entire area was leased from the Crown from 1508. Wardens had maintained forest law from Norman times and continued to do so until 1814. The wardens ensured the preservation of the deer and controlled stock-grazing. Apart from a 100-acre enclave of farmland created by James Boevey

have looked in the early years of the century (children are encouraged to try out the clothes, classroom slates and games), complete with £sd sums on the blackboard and a poster showing correct postures for boys. As its name suggests, there's the ubiquitous collection of crafts, tools and domestic paraphernalia here too, but this one is larger than average, featuring a dairy, a laundry, a typical Exmoor hearth and numerous local photographs.

Porlock, further west on the A39, harbours one or two attractive paths, such as The Drang, which wind between

---

at Simonsbath in the seventeenth century, the forest was moorland. Settlements established by the Saxons kept to the valleys – a pattern that survives today.

That primeval character turned out to be a fragile one, as deep ploughing was used as the solution to turning the waterlogged, peaty land into productive farmland. Most of the royal forest was acquired in the early nineteenth century by John Knight, who built a huge estate wall and introduced profitable farming and new breeds; he had sold out by the end of the century to Earl Fortescue, and the estate later became fragmented. Probably the most drastic changes to the landscape occurred in the 30 years after the Second World War, with nearly 20 square miles of Exmoor being converted into farmland or new forest; the Chains only just escaped a blanket covering of Forestry Commission plantations. The designation of Exmoor as a National Park in 1954 did not initially safeguard the moor itself; only when the greening of farmers' attitudes began in the 1970s, and subsidies for ploughing moorland ended, did voluntary management agreements really take off, and what moorland remains now looks safe.

Exmoor's compact size and abrupt changes of mood make it rewarding to explore. The coast and accompanying hills deserve the most attention. Prime inland attractions are Dunkery Beacon and Dunster, but a drive, walk or horseback ride across the central expanses should not be missed either. Although Exmoor has a wet climate – even in summer it can be a bleak place when rain swirls and the cloud-level is low – sudden dry, sunny spells produce memorable results: purple moors and green patchworks of fertile lands are illuminated, and clear-weather views extend over the Bristol Channel to Glamorgan and even the Brecon Beacons.

cottage gardens. By leaving the main road you can appreciate something of its scenic position at the foot of Porlock Hill and on the edge of the fertile, low-lying vale that stretches to Porlock Bay and was once sea-bed. Porlock's centre has something of an urban air, with a range of shops selling saddlery, country wear and walking boots, but the traffic can be overpowering. If you need to stop off to shop, you may like to pay a visit to the small museum you can park beside the nearby tourist information centre; or to look for historic graffiti on the canopied tomb in the parish church.

From the village there is a three-way choice of roads westwards. Steepest is the A39, which takes almost perpendicular hairpins up the once-notorious Porlock Hill, climbing 1350 feet in under three miles, not a great trial for today's cars (although caravans are advised to take the toll road), but formerly a signal for charabanc passengers to get out and walk and for Austin Sevens to overheat before reaching the top. The views from here are memorable, with Dunkery Beacon to the south and Porlock Bay and Selworthy Beacon to the north and east. For traffic to avoid the worst of the much-feared slope, a toll road was built, zigzagging gradually from the Ship Inn in Porlock up through woods and into the open; this has now become a popular scenic ride. Another route, the Worthy Combe Toll Road, climbs from **Porlock Weir**, a quiet resort village with a well-

The Exmoor Coast

The thin coastal strip, with its immediate hinterland, from Minehead to Combe Martin has the monopoly of Exmoor's most distinctive scenery, with moorland hills coming right down to the cliffs, while close by are some delectable inland combes with shady rivers. Seaward bluffs are bold and assertive, windswept and excitingly rugged, sea-level only reached at a few shingly or rocky bays and coves; the absence of bathing beaches has precluded resort development, the cliffs being more the preserve of sea-birds and walkers; if you want sand and good swimming, head for Minehead (see p. 58). From the road you get some fine glimpses of the best of the coast, notably on Porlock Hill, at County Gate, in the Valley of Rocks and by Holdstone Down.

positioned hotel (see p. 81) overlooking sailing dinghies on a raised pebbly shore, but formerly a busy little port with herrings, salt, limestone, yarn and hide all passing through.

The toll road leads up to a gate-house, where you are requested to pull a slightly improbable hand-bell contraption to summon the attention of the gate-keeper. Beyond, there is parking space, from where it is worthwhile taking a signposted path for a mile to **Culbone** church, which is inaccessible by public road. The path leads through woodlands created by Lord Lovelace, who had been inspired on visits to Italy to romanticise his estate, peppering it with grottoes, turreted follies and a section of foot-tunnel, as well as planting rhododendrons, oaks and pines. The church is the smallest complete parish church in England, 34 feet by 12. The site dates probably from Saxon times, but the building is basically Norman in structure. Visionary artist Samuel Palmer painted the scene of the church in its deep valley, and Coleridge wrote 'Kubla Khan' in a remote farmhouse nearby, only to have his inspirational opium dream broken off by the (alleged) arrival of that famous nobody 'the person from Porlock', leaving the masterpiece unfinished.

The countryside associated with *Lorna Doone* (see p. 68) extends over much of Exmoor, but the centre of the Doones' activities seems to have been in the Oare and Badgworthy Valleys. A minor road drops from the A39 and crosses Oare Water at tellingly named Robber's Bridge to reach **Oare** church, remarkable for the number of visitors who come here to see the site of an entirely fictitious event: here, in Blackmore's novel, Lorna Doone was shot by Carver Doone on her wedding day. The adjacent manor house was Farmer Snow's fictional home, and John Ridd lived in an imaginary farm in the valley. Blackmore, whose grandfather was rector of Oare (1809–42), has a monument in the church.

At **Malmsmead** a pack-horse bridge spans Badgworthy (pronounced 'Badgery') Water and the Somerset–Devon border, the county boundary also going through **County Gate**. Picnickers and walkers congregate at both places, lured by picnic sites, inviting paths and lovely views of gentle river valleys rubbing shoulders with blustery moorland. Ordnance Survey maps and signposts refer to Badgworthy Water as Doone Country or Doone Valley, and the popular level walk from Malmsmead southwards along the river passes another memorial to

Blackmore on its route to the increasingly lonely Exmoor heartlands.

The two waters, Badgworthy and Oare, merge to become the East Lyn River, which, north-west of the hamlets of Brendon and Rockford, gouges out one of Exmoor's most enthralling scenes as East Lyn merges with West Lyn at **Watersmeet**: waterfalls and superb oak woods on plunging slopes, with wagtails and bobbing dippers above the water. Standing by the meeting of the two rivers, an 1830s fishing-lodge is now run by the National Trust as a café serving lunches and cakes, with tables and chairs set up on the lawn under a huge Monterey pine. The plant Irish spurge

Lorna Doone

The most successful novel of Richard Doddridge Blackmore (1825–1900), Lorna Doone *is a minor classic of romance and high adventure (and some would say melodrama). The novel is set in remote Exmoor and based on a real family of bandits, the Doones, who terrorised these parts in the late seventeenth century. The now-tranquil valley of Badgworthy Water (see above) is actually labelled as Doone Country on Ordnance Survey maps. It was in the valley that real and fictional Doones seem to have carried out their activities; in 1969 a memorial was erected here to commemorate the centenary of the novel's publication. Tom Faggus, the gentleman highwayman and Judge Jeffreys, the Bloody Assizes judge (see p. 30), appear in the novel and were real characters living at the time of the Monmouth Rebellion.*

Blackmore's story begins with the murder of a farmer, father of 12-year-old John Ridd, by the outlawed Doones. The story revolves around its hero John, his determination to avenge his father's murder and his love for Lorna, whom the Doones have kidnapped from a noble family. A dramatic scene near the end of the book is set at Oare church (see p. 67), which has consequently become a tourist attraction.

Blackmore was a shy man who had retired from his work as a barrister and teacher because of poor health. A legacy enabled him to devote himself to his Teddington garden and to writing. His early novels Clara Vaughan *and* Cradock Nowell *failed to make mass sales, and* Lorna Doone *languished for the first year and a half after publication before it caught the public imagination.*

(*Euphorbia hyberna*) makes one of only two mainland appearances in these woods. The best way of appreciating the natural wonder of the valleys is to follow the footpath along the river to Lynmouth, or even better to climb from Ye Olde Cottage Inne on the B3234 on the south-east side of Lynton and take the path zigzagging up through trees and along the top of the Lyn and Myrtleberry Cleaves: this gives a grandstand panorama of the whole river system, and the wafer-thin hill lining the north side of the valley, with Countisbury clifflands, the highest in England, beyond. The Exmoor coast reaches its northernmost tip at Foreland Point, whose lighthouse can be visited in daylight hours by those prepared for a 1½-mile walk from Countisbury.

Lynton and Lynmouth

These two small resorts make up the largest centre of population in Exmoor. Lynton stands on the hill, ignoring the sea, while Lynmouth is huddled at sea-level 400 feet below. Zigzagging paths and a cliff railway, the steepest in the world when constructed in 1890, connect the two. Their site is virtually without equal in the south-west, at the meeting of the Lyn gorge, the Valley of Rocks and the culmination of the great cliffs of Foreland Point to the east.

Beyond straggling outskirts, the centre of **Lynton** has a solid, Victorian appearance, a line of sedate guest-houses with rusticated eaves, a turn-of-the-century town hall in Arts and Crafts style and the three-storey Valley of Rocks Hotel with an arcaded lounge rising the height of the building. Comfortably sleepy in its secure streets, Lynton is like an elderly relative dozing through a tumultuous thunderstorm – an incongruous juxtaposition, with scenery of this majesty right on its doorstep, notably the Valley of Rocks and Lyn Cleave (see above), where deep wooded combes lie side by side with huge moorland cliffs. The town has one formal sight, **a museum** (open Easter to end Aug, Mon to Fri, 10 to 12.30, 2 to 5; Sun, 2 to 5) of pleasingly unrelated local artefacts housed in an old cottage, with a sign from the long-defunct Lynton and Lynmouth Station in its front garden. Sloping Queen Street is a survival of the pre-Victorian village centre.

Lynmouth is smaller but more bustling in daytime, with holiday-makers wandering along a row of craft-cum-gift shops, and cream teas being consumed behind diamond-leaded tea-room windows. Much of the village was swept away in a dreadful flash flood in 1952, when nine inches of rain fell within 24 hours and 90 million tons of water surged down the Lyn Valley. But apart from a small display in the Memorial Hall, there's little to show for the flood damage until you see pictures of the village as it was. What remains is mostly Victorian prettification (partly reconstructed), with one or two thatched buildings from its days as a fishing village, and a terrace of cottages built for workers at a hydro-electric station which supplied Lynton and Lynmouth before most towns in the country had electricity. There are plenty of opportunities to while away a summer afternoon on a range of undemanding activities – putting and tennis, a sea-water swimming pool, a model railway layout and a brass-rubbing centre. But it's more the setting than anything that draws visitors. Blacklands Beach, reached by crossing the footbridge in the village centre, is stony but finely sited,

Inland Exmoor

Today moorland is the exception and enclosed pasture the rule, but the landscape is still strikingly empty, sparsely superimposed by villages in deep vales and by vestiges of prehistoric habitation high up, with humps of Bronze Age barrows discernible. Driving over inland Exmoor involves close-up views of hedgerows until a cattle-grid brings you out on to open unfenced land of bare and expansive horizons, where ponies and sheep spill on to the road. Exmoor ponies are not wild in that they are all owned by someone, but they roam freely all year round. They are descended from a herd of just 20, the Anchor Herd from Ashway Farm, west of Dulverton. The National Park Authority occasionally tops up the stock when numbers dwindle.

The central moor has a covering of coarse purple moor grass and whortleberries (bilberries) for the most part, with blue heath speedwell, heath-spotted orchids and bog pimpernel also putting in an appearance. Traditional purple-flecked heathery uplands are found more around the edges, in the Dunkery area, along the coast, and on Holdstone and Winsford Hills. If you have an Ordnance Survey map of the area and wish to see the best of the moor from the car, make for the roads shown as unfenced (indicated with broken

looking to the highest cliffs in England around Countisbury. Close to the beach, near the river-mouth, a salmon trap made of wattle hurdles still functions. There is also a charming riverside path along the Lyn through National Trust woodlands to the café at Watersmeet (see p. 68). Glen Lyn Gorge was the site of the hydro-electric installation, washed away in the flood; for a fairly hefty admission fee it offers an exhibition room and a steep path up to a small waterfall.

Lynton to Combe Martin

The **Valley of Rocks**, just west of Lynton, made a strong impression on Shelley, Coleridge and Wordsworth. Its quintessentially romantic flavour is undeniable: a short dry valley (very likely the former bed of the River Lyn before it diverted course to break through to the sea at Lynmouth)

---

instead of continuous lines). The finest drives include those from Luccombe or Porlock, over the west shoulder of Dunkery Hill to Exford, from Exford south over Winsford Hill towards Dulverton, from Dulverton to Twitchen via Molland Common on the south side of the National Park, and (for a short distance) from Simonsbath north on the B3223 towards Lynmouth.

Over 700 red deer, Exmoor's natural and most magnificent deer species, inhabit the area, notably in the Horner, Hawkcombe, Worthy and Grabbist woods, and around Croydon Hill. Standing about 44 inches at the shoulder and some six feet from antler to antler, these shy creatures are the objective for the controversial Exmoor hunts. Stag-hunting takes place during much of the year – mid-April to the end of May and mid-August to mid-September for stags, and mid-September to mid-April for hinds – with the three staghound packs, the Quantock, the Tiverton and the Devon and Somerset. Roe deer, migrants from Dorset and Hampshire, can sometimes be glimpsed in the Haddoe Valley, in the woods around Selworthy and on the Brendon Hills. Fallow and sika deer are both species that have escaped from deer parks, the former from Dunster and Nettlecombe Court (now found near Monksilver and on Croydon Hill) and the sika from Pixton and Dulverton (inhabiting the Mole and Bray Valleys on Exmoor's southern fringes).

71

running for a mile and a half parallel to the sea and with bizarre rock outcrops gracing its brackeny margins. Fanciful names adhere to most of the forms, such as Ragged Jack, the Cheese Wring and Chimney Rock; horned, feral but docile goats – found nowhere else on Exmoor – graze the slopes. The scene looks at its best from Castle Rock, the most prominent feature, which has a hair-raising 400-foot drop on its seaward side and was the home of Aggie Norman, a madwoman whom Blackmore is thought to have made into Mother Meldrum in *Lorna Doone*. A folly prominent on the far side of Wringcliff Bay is Jennifred's Leap, named after Jennifred de Wichehalse, who was jilted in the 1680s by Lord Auberley and hurled herself from the cliff.

All is scenic enough from the road, but as soon as you leave your car you will wish that the over-prominent car park and roundabout could vanish into the ground. A much more exciting way in is to walk around the coast path by taking the road between the church and the Valley of Rocks Hotel in Lynton. After narrowing to a tarmac path, with pleasant views of the sea below and the grassy cliffs above, the walk gives a phenomenal view as the valley reveals itself.

To reach **Woody Bay**, north-east of Martinhoe, means walking down from the top, which requires no small effort to get back up again. But the bay is a fine one, backed by sandstone cliffs and a dribbling waterfall. Further west is the more accessible and more frequently visited **Heddon's Mouth**, reached by a level walk from the well-signposted Hunter's Inn along the densely wooded Heddon Valley. At the minute 'mouth', an old lime-kiln is all that remains of a small port from where lime fertiliser used to be shipped across the Bristol Channel.

Trentishoe tries to ignore the sea, sheltered by the slope and looking into the Heddon Valley and its tributary. A tiny church contains a rare musicians' gallery of the type so often ripped out in the last century when organs were installed, with a notch cut out to allow the free movement of the double bass player's bow. For the most complete picture of this western corner of Exmoor, continue west from Trentishoe until you reach the car park at the foot of Holdstone Hill, from where it is an easy stroll to the top.

Parracombe church, a few miles further inland, deserves a special detour as an outstanding example of a totally unrestored medieval church. In the nineteenth century when a new church was built in the village, it was proposed that the old one be demolished. But a campaign spearheaded by John Ruskin in 1879 resulted in the church's salvation. Its interior wonderfully evokes a country church of pre-Victorian England – box pews, worn with age and raised at the back in theatre fashion for the benefit of the church band (with coat pegs still in place), the humblest of screens, pulpit with a sounding-board suspended overhead, rough plaster walls and an uneven flagstoned floor, all under an ancient roof. Organ, stained glass and encaustic floor tiles are conspicuously absent. To reach it, turn off the A39 and follow the Old Church signs.

The Barle Valley

Simonsbath, Somerset's westernmost settlement, seems to be signposted from every other road junction in central Exmoor. It appears insignificant when you get there: a dip into the valley to a hotel, Simonsbath House (see p. 81), by the junction of the B3223 and the B3358. But historically Simonsbath marks the beginning of the taming of the great moor, for here in the seventeenth century James Boevey acquired what had been royal hunting-forest but had passed to the state after the Civil War; after the restoration of the monarchy, Boevey stayed on as a tenant farmer. Further farming activity took place when John Knight lived in Simonsbath House in the nineteenth century. Knight was a disciple of Coke of Holkham in Norfolk, a great 'improving landlord'. He carried out stock-rearing experiments, built a reservoir (Pinkworthy Pond, at the head of the Barle), improved local roads and built a 29-mile wall around his estate, of which traces can still be seen around Badgworthy and Brendon. His son Frederick introduced Cheviot sheep, ideal for the harsh climate, and was farming 9000 acres when he died in 1897.

A riverside path south-eastwards passes the site of **Wheal Eliza** (marked Flexbarrow on OS maps), where copper, iron and manganates mining were carried out for 300 years. Frederick Knight's efforts in the mid-nineteenth century were hampered by drought (foiling the operation of the waterwheel) and a shortage of funds, and his grandiose scheme to build a railway to the coast at Porlock Weir to supply the iron industry of South Wales came to nothing. Across the river, a carefully positioned Victorian photograph on an information board shows the scene of the working mine. A mile further on, **Cow Castle** is the grassy ramparts of an Iron Age fort on top of the hill.

Landacre Bridge, south-east of Simonsbath, gives a glimpse of typical upland Exmoor, a popular spot for sitting by the Barle in a remote bracken-clad combe and taking in the quiet scene. Further downriver, horses pause photogenically for a drink under the old stone bridge at **Withypool**, nestling in the valley at a point where roads dropping from the open moor converge.

Winsford Hill, between the Barle and the Exe, followed along its spine by the B3223, makes an enjoyable high-level drive on the open moor. At the mild summit, by the trig point on the north of the road, are the three **Wambarrows**, Bronze Age burial mounds, looking out over the central moor and northwards to Dunkery Beacon. Close by, just 100 yards from the road and south-east of the crossroads with the turns to Winsford and Knaplock/Tarr Steps, the **Caratacus Stone** leans drunkenly beneath a stone shelter protecting it from the elements and from curious ponies. Its Latin inscription, *Cara(t)aci nepus* ('descendant of Caratacus'), probably belies its origin, which is thought to be just after the Roman occupation. One theory is that it is a memorial to a nephew or kinsman of Caradoc, a tribal leader who led a revolt against the Romans. Later, the stone was used as a boundary marker of the hunting-forest.

The road signposted near the Caratacus Stone gives the easiest access to **Tarr Steps**. The 'steps' are in fact a complete clapper bridge across the Barle, the finest and largest bridge of its kind in the country, comprising 17 gritstone slabs. The river in spate has demolished it many times, the last time in 1952, but the structure's origins are at least medieval, perhaps much earlier, and at some point in its life it collected the reputation as a sunbathing place for the devil. If you have time, the walk upriver along one of Exmoor's loveliest river paths is rewarding, although you need to allow two hours each way to reach Withypool.

Dulverton lies adjacent to the Barle but takes little notice of it. Its compact and almost picturesque small streets concern themselves with country life and make only a few minor concessions to tourism. As well as an ironmonger's and a dealer in guns and fishing gear, there's a second-hand bookshop and an old-fashioned tea-room with a 'Tea with Hovis' sign. The streets bustle with walkers and sightseers squeezing past four-wheel drives; the town hall is the focus for much of the town's activities, the setting one week for a house-clearance auction, the following week for the amateur dramatic society's summer performance. The National Park's headquarters, housed in a former workhouse, are at the bottom of the town and incorporate a visitor centre.

The Exe Valley and Dunkery Beacon

North of Dulverton and away from the main roads, **Winsford** has well-groomed thatch, and visitors trying to locate the eight bridges: five are easily found in the centre over the narrow River Winn, one can be detected on a nearby cul-de-sac, and two more obscure ones are on the Exford road, spanning the Exe. The Royal Oak (see p. 83), all clotted-cream rendering and elaborate thatch, complete with a thatched squirrel above the entrance and a vintage AA sign, steals the show in the village centre. In its less sedate days it provided rich pickings for Tom Faggus, a 'gentleman highwayman'; Blackmore used him as a character in *Lorna Doone*, and drew upon local colour for the novel from conversations at the inn. The village's most famous son, Ernest Bevin – statesman, Foreign Secretary and trade unionist – was born in 1881 in a cottage opposite the post office: look for the plaque.

Further up the Exe, **Exford** looks cheerful: picnickers on a village green fringed by a miscellany of cottages and hotels. It has been an important crossing point over the Exe since the Bronze Age, but until the nineteenth century it was little more than a scattering of farmsteads and cottages. Then John Knight was instrumental in levying a road rate, and built a road connecting the village with the outside world. The village became a busy community, an important point on the cross-country route and on the Exe; blacksmiths and carpenters carried out trade, schools were set up and the settlement built up around its green. Three hotels stand by the green, and one of the four smithies still functions as a totally unsmartened-up and workaday affair, in a modest building over the bridge. The cacophony of barking you are likely to hear comes from the Devon and Somerset Staghounds, whose kennels are beside the hunt stables in the village centre: meets are held from August to April. At Exford Horse Show, held in August, the best pony breeds can be seen. The church stands well up the hill and away from the rest of the village, but is worth a look for its fine screen, moved from West Quantoxhead church. To the right of the porch, a wall tablet commemorates a woman who died aged 106 – perhaps an Exmoor record.

Dunkery Beacon (north-east of Exford), the outstanding and most visited natural attraction in inland Exmoor, is the 1,704-foot-high summit of Dunkery Hill, a sprawling and uncomplicated form some four miles long from east to west, and Exmoor's highest point. Its breathtaking view, one of southern England's grandest, extends over 16 counties and points well over 100 miles apart, ranging from Dartmoor in the south, Bodmin Moor in Cornwall to the west, the Brecon Beacons and Welsh Marches to the north and the Mendips in the east. A beacon placed by the summit cairn provided part of a nationwide chain of warning beacons lit in time of danger. The cairn can be reached easily by walking up a broad track from the car park three-quarters of a mile to the east, on the road from Wheddon Cross to Webber's Post.

More intricate and secretive are the woodlands around the snaking valley of **Horner Water** just to the north, containing ancient oak woods and a great variety of lichens; further planting was carried out by the Acland family, once major landowners in Exmoor. The woodlands harbour red deer and a diverse wildlife, and parts are accordingly designated as a Site of Special Scientific Interest. Inviting woodland paths through secluded glades lead off the road at **Horner**, where you can enjoy the tea-garden after a walk along the valley.

Luccombe, leafy and tucked away, has a thatched post office by the churchyard and only occasional sightseers. At **Wootton Courtenay**, nearby, backpackers down their rucksacks to pause for refreshment at the shop and to take in the village's lovely view southwards across the Avill Valley and the eastern tip of Dunkery Hill. High above, modest **Stoke Pero**, a church (substantially restored) without a village, lies just above the Horner woodlands and has the distinction of being Exmoor's highest church.

The Rivers Barle and the Exe both have their sources in the empty Chains of central Exmoor – the name given to a huge unpopulated expanse stretching about 12 miles from the National Park's western boundary and dotted with Bronze Age barrows. These rivers rapidly deepen to carve out steep-sided, meandering valleys, where clear, shallow waters slide over iron-tinted stones. The best of both valleys can be experienced only on foot – the road occasionally follows the rivers for a short stretch, such as the Exe east of Winsford and the Barle west of Dulverton. The two rivers merge south-east of the latter town.

Dunster and the Brendon Hills

Dunster, south-east of Minehead and one of the showpiece small towns of England, has something of a theatre-stage effect: a broad main street of colour-washed cottages in creams, peppermint green, Battenburg pink and yellow, and with an octagonal yarn market at its top end. Gracing it all, Dunster Castle towers from its hillock, as romantic as a Rhenish *Schloss* yet somehow quintessentially English in its statement of feudalism. At the opposite end of the street from the castle, the eighteenth-century Coneygar Tower stands high in the woodlands at the mouth of the Avill Valley; the tower was built to punctuate the view from town and castle. In season, Dunster's self-consciousness gives it something of the air of a museum, and there is perhaps one gift-shop too many, but its ordered perfection and sense of time-warp are instantly enchanting. If in summer it is always bustling, it positively throbs with life during the day of the Dunster show, held in August on the edge of town inside and around white marquees, with cattle and dog shows, horticultural competitions and cake stalls – an insight into local country life.

The **castle** (open Mar to Nov, daily exc Thurs and Fri, 11 to 5 (12 to 4 Oct and Nov)) occupies a site dating from Saxon times. The gate-house dates from the thirteenth century, and parts of the main structure from then to the fifteenth century, but the castle had two thorough rebuildings in the seventeenth and nineteenth centuries. Both were carried out by the Luttrell family, who acquired the estate in 1376 and remained owners until the National Trust took over the castle in 1976. The seventeenth-century work that survives includes a superb staircase, the carved embellished hand-rail with oak scrolls and elm flowers which Sir Nikolaus Pevsner rates on a par with the work of Grinling Gibbons; the Leather Gallery contains leather wall-hangings probably of French or Flemish origin depicting the story of Antony and Cleopatra, and a sumptuous plaster ceiling in the dining-room. But the extensive alterations made after 1867 by Anthony Salvin, the fashionable country-house architect of the day, pervade the house – so what one sees is a romanticised effect, an admirable example of the living quarters of a Victorian aristocrat. Dark oak panelling lines the downstairs rooms, proportions are generous but not overpowering, and there are wonderful views on all sides over town, grounds and deer park.

Dunster church, built as part of a Benedictine priory, has a carillon which plays a different hymn tune for each day of the week – a slightly lethargic rendering of 'O Worship the King' for Wednesdays. Its sophisticated and partly Victorianised interior is chiefly memorable for its fifteenth-century wagon roof and flat south aisle roof, a medieval screen that is said to be the widest in England and a monument to Elizabeth Luttrell. The north door leads into the former priory garden, still walled and now public.

Two prominent buildings in town also have religious connections: where the road kinks, fourteenth-century Nunnery House, picturesquely slate-hung, had nothing to do with nuns but was a priory guest-house (even today it offers B&B), and the Luttrell Arms was probably the town residence for the Abbott of Cleeve. The octagonal, open-sided yarn market is unmistakable. Here, transactions took place for the smooth kersey Somerset cloths, 'Dunsters', 'Tauntons' and 'Bridgwaters' among them. A cannon-ball hole inside the building can still be seen, dating from the siege of Dunster Castle, the last Somerset stronghold of the Royalists in the Civil War, holding out against Cromwell's men led by Robert Blake to whom they eventually ceded.

Approached along narrow Mill Lane, the mill-race running along one side, the seventeenth-century **water-mill** gives a rare glimpse of a working mill producing flour. The mill is unique in having twin 'overshot' wheels – fed with water at the top and creating power by moving under the weight of the water contained in buckets attached to the wheel. After a look round the machinery, granary and collection of country bygones, you can buy flour made on the premises; there is an attractive tea-room in a converted barn.

Close by the mill, on the very edge of town, is the Gallox Bridge, a tiny pack-horse bridge over a brook with thatched cottages grouped beside, and so called because gallows used to stand here. By keeping left on the other side you enter the deer-park; the deer are no longer restricted to this area – they roam the nearby woods that are crowned by the ramparts of Iron Age Bats Castle. From here there are excellent views of Dunster Castle.

South of Dunster lie the **Brendon Hills**, a complex area of hills and deep valleys, much of it intensively farmed and the rest mostly afforested by Forestry Commission plantations. What few villages exist are well down the slopes, and it is from here, particularly around Luxborough, that the Brendons look their best; nearby Croydon Hill is also densely forested, but as good a bet as any for a sighting of red deer. The road along the crest of the hills is disappointing scenically, but passes close to a disused mine building at Burrow Farm. This is just about all that remains of a once flourishing iron-ore industry. Haematite ore extracted here was shown at the Great Exhibition in 1851 and attracted the attention of a Welsh ironmaster, who organised a syndicate, brought in miners from various parts of the country and founded the Brendon Hills Iron Ore Company. From 1853 it produced three-quarters of a million tons for the iron-smelting industry at Ebbw Vale in Glamorgan, peaking in 1877; miners' cottages, stores and a chapel were built at Gupworthy, but the business was wiped out by the revival of Spanish competition and was abandoned from one day to the next in 1878, leaving Gupworthy a ghost town (and today an insignificant hamlet). There are still traces in the forest of the remarkable inclined plane which used to take railway wagons 1,200 feet up the one-in-four slope of the escarpment, part of a journey from the Brendon Hills to Watchet: empty wagons from Watchet were hauled up by the weight of the laden ones on their way down.

Tucked into the south-eastern corner of the National Park, barbecue aromas waft from picnic sites at **Wimbleball Reservoir**, which is attractively set and has a lakeside walk. Exmoor's eastern extremity, **Combe Sydenham** (open Mar to Oct, Sun to Fri, 10 to 5), a country park, consists of a manor house being restored from a very derelict state. The house possesses a charming tale: Elizabeth Sydenham, wooed by Sir Francis Drake, had nevertheless become engaged to another man, but at the church door an object, which came to be known as 'Drake's cannonball', miraculously dropped between bridegroom and bride, which Elizabeth took to be an omen, and so married Drake instead. The cannonball, which is probably a meteorite, is kept on display in the house. Fly-fishing for trout (beginners as well as the initiated are welcome), 'magic story trails' and forest walks are the main outdoor activities.

Highlights

** *Dunkery Beacon and Horner Water, Dunster, Parracombe Old Church, Valley of Rocks, Watersmeet and the Lyn Valleys.*

* *Allerford, Barle Valley (Dulverton, Tarr steps and Withypool), Exford, Heddon's Mouth and the Ladies' Mile, Holdstone Down, Lynmouth, Malmsmead and Badgworthy Water, Selworthy and Selworthy Beacon, Winsford, Woody Bay.*

Where to stay

For a key to prices, see p. 12

Combe Martin

Coulsworthy House

Combe Martin, Devon
EX34 0PD. Tel Combe Martin
(0271) 882463
You can see the sea in the distance from this splendidly situated hotel high up above the village on the western side of Exmoor. The mainly eighteenth-century house is run by the Anthonys with their daughter and son-in-law, and the emphasis is on informality; the place has a homely and lived-in atmosphere. You can relax in the comfortable sitting-room or bar and savour a delicious dinner cooked by Alison (the daughter) in the pretty dining-room. The bedrooms, most with bathrooms, are all different, sloping ceilings adding extra charm to the top-floor rooms. Great trouble is taken with everything and many of the guests are regulars.
££££ *Closed mid-Dec to mid-Feb; rest closed Sun evening*

Hawkridge

Tarr Steps Hotel

Hawkridge, Dulverton, Somerset TA22 9PY. Tel Winsford (064 385) 293
A very peaceful, secluded spot a few hundred yards from the Tarr Steps. The hotel is tucked up in the woods beside the narrow lane that ends at the ancient bridge. It is run as a relaxed country home with a mixture of chintz and plain wooden furniture. Very reasonably priced and sporting orientated, you can hunt, shoot and, most particularly, fish: wellington boots and fishing rods line the hallway. Bedrooms are all different, comfortable and spacious with old pine furniture and lacy bedspreads. No TVs here.
£££ *Closed Jan to Mid-Mar*

Lynmouth

Rising Sun

Mars Hill, Lynmouth, Devon.
Tel Lynton (0598) 53223
Raised slightly from the road,

this glorified pub/hotel is very much in the centre of things. The beamed fourteenth-century inn is very cosy in winter but can be a bit dark in summer. Latticed windows overlook the boats and harbour and for more privacy there's a garden for residents only. The bar area and oak-panelled dining-room give guests plenty of places to sit although they're also very popular with tourists. A narrow slanting staircase – be careful not to hit your head – leads to a few of the bedrooms but most are a few yards up the hill in adjoining cottages. They are well furnished and comfortable, some with sea views.

£££ *Open all year*

Parracombe
Heddon's Gate Hotel

Heddon's Mouth, Parracombe, Barnstaple, Devon EX31 4PZ. Tel Parracombe (059 83) 313

The white-painted house is in itself not particularly distinguished-looking but it has a great setting. Terraced gardens lead to the woods and from the house the views beyond to the sea and the valley are beautiful. Inside, the style is part Victorian, part twenties, with beaded lampshades, a covered screen and blue and white willow-patterned plates displayed on the wall. Guests are bidden to dinner by the gong and the set menu allows for a choice of main course. The bedrooms are all different and some in the main house have themes such as the Japanese and Chinese rooms and Grandmama's.

££££ *inc dinner Closed Jan to week before Easter; mid-week Nov to Dec*

Porlock Weir
Anchor Hotel and Ship Inn

Porlock Weir, Somerset TA24 8PB. Tel Porlock (0643) 862636 Fax (0643) 862843

In a lovely position overlooking the pebble beach and harbour at Porlock Weir, only one and a half miles from Porlock, but a much quieter spot. The Anchor Hotel forms the main part and is comfortably traditional in decor with good-sized public rooms and plain bedrooms and bathrooms; the Ship Inn is an older building and is more pubby, with lower beamed ceilings, smaller rooms and a bar that is a popular local haunt. Residents can use the bars and restaurants of either.

£££–££££ *Open all year*

Simonsbath
Simonsbath House

Simonsbath, Exmoor, Somerset TA24 7SH. Tel Exford (064 383) 259

At the crossroads of two small Somerset lanes in the heart of Exmoor, this is a lovely spot. Very little disturbs the peace here and the hotel provides old-fashioned comfort: soft old sofas and armchairs, open fires, rugs, magazines and newspapers lying around. The panelled library/bar has a huge old fireplace and a couple of comfortable armchairs. Bedrooms are all different in size, shape and furnishings; here too the comfort is from big old beds and antiques rather than designed co-ordination.

£££ *Closed Dec, Jan*

Wheddon Cross
Raleigh Manor

Wheddon Cross, Nr Dunster, Somerset TA24 7BB. Tel Timberscombe (0643) 841484
This nineteenth-century stone manor house in the middle of Exmoor was built as a hunting lodge and has wonderful views right down to the Bristol Channel. Inside there's a mixture of informal and formal decor with stripped wooden doors and banisters and lots of plants, dark red and pink walls in the dining-room and gold and cream in the sitting-room. Bedrooms are a reasonable size and furnished with an assortment of antiques; all have en suite bathrooms.
££ *Closed Nov to end Mar*

Winsford
Royal Oak Inn

Winsford, Minehead, Somerset TA24 7JE. Tel Winsford (0643 85) 455 Telex 46529 ROAK G
Right in the centre of the village the Royal Oak has been an inn for hundreds of years and has a timeless look; baskets hang from the thatched roof, with flowers trailing down over creamy walls. Inside, low ceilings, beams and stone fireplaces show its medieval origins. This is a great meeting place for locals as well as walkers stopping off for much needed refreshments. Three sitting-rooms housing an extensive collection of ceramic animals give residents plenty of space to sit quietly away from the often jolly throng in the bars. Traditional English food is served in the simple, beamed dining-room. Bedrooms are

quite fussy with cream and gold painted furniture; the more modern ones are across the courtyard.
£££ *Open all year*

Withypool
Royal Oak Inn

Withypool, Somerset TA24 7QP. Tel Exford (064 383) 506/7
Another very attractive inn in the heart of Exmoor. It's a cosy, friendly place with lots of hunting trophies including stag's antlers and foxes' heads arranged on the walls. Both bars have low ceilings and bench-seats but the residents' bar is carpeted and snugger. Guests can choose to eat in here or in the restaurant in the evening; decorated in blues and pale browns with chintzy ruffled curtains, the dining-room is smart and atmospheric and you have an option of three to five courses. The bedrooms, most with their own bathrooms, are all differently decorated and are comfortable.
££ *Open all year, exc 25, 26 Dec*

Woody Bay
Woody Bay Hotel

Woody Bay, Parracombe, North Devon EX31 4QX. Tel Parracombe (059 83) 264
Built in the 1890s as a hotel, it is sited on a steep wooded slope leading down to the rocky coastline, giving sea views to most of the rooms. It's a homely place, with no TVs or telephones in the rooms, and guests are encouraged to play games or read books in the sitting-room warmed by an open fire they can study maps and plan the next day's walk.

The decor generally is quite plain and simple: high-backed bench seating in the dining-room, copper-topped tables in the bar and simple, pretty bedrooms. Packed lunches and

bar snacks are available at lunchtime as well as a three-course daily menu in the evening.

££ *Closed early Jan to mid-Feb; limited opening Nov to mid-Mar*

Where to eat

For a key to prices see p. 12

Dunster

Tea Shoppe

3 High Street, Dunster. Tel Minehead (0643) 821304
Traditional home cooking in this early fifteenth-century cottage, cooked on the aga.
[£] *Open all week Mar to Oct and Christmas Hols 10–6 (weekends only 1 Nov to Christmas) Closed 2 Jan to mid-Mar*

Exford

The Crown

Exford. Tel Exford (064 383) 554
A seventeenth-century pub/hotel; cosy atmosphere and a lovely spot in the heart of Exmoor.
Open all week 12–2, bar/bistro 7–9.30, restaurant 7.30–9.30

Dulverton

Ashwick House

nr Dulverton. Tel Dulverton (0398) 23868
Large country house in very secluded position. You need to book a couple of days in advance because residents take priority.
Open Tue–Sat 7.15–8.30; and Sun 12.15–1.15, 7.15–8.30

Crispins

26 High Street, Dulverton. Tel Dulverton (0398) 23397
An attractive bistro in the centre of town. Enterprising menu includes good choice for vegetarians.
Open all week, Mon to Sat 12–2, 7–9.30; Sun 12 to 2 Closed Feb, Mon in winter

Lynmouth

The Rising Sun

The Harbour, Lynmouth. Tel Lynmouth (0598) 53223
Pretty pub/hotel on a slope beside the harbour right in the centre of things. You can eat in the bar or the panelled dining room (see p. 69).
Open all week 12–2, 7–8.30

Porlock Weir

The Anchor Hotel & The Ship Inn

Porlock Weir. Tel. (0643) 862753
You can eat in either place: the Ship Inn is smaller and pubbier but both have a good atmosphere (see p. 66).
Open all week. Bar snacks 12–2 (12.30–1.45 Sun) 7.30–9 Closed 3 weeks Jan

Simonsbath

Simonsbath House

Simonsbath, Exmoor National Park. Tel Exford (064 383) 259

Comfortable and secluded place for any meal of the day (see p. 73).
Closed Dec, Jan

Winsford

Royal Oak Inn

Winsford, Exmoor National Park, Winsford. Tel Winsford (064 385) 455
Traditional village inn; pretty exterior and lots of warm and cosy rooms inside (see p. 75)
Open all week 12–2, 7.30–9.30

Withypool

Royal Oak Inn

Withypool. Tel Exford (064 383) 506/507
Lovely pub/hotel with a couple of snug bars and an attractive, cosy dining-room
Open all week 12–2 (1.30 Sun), 7–9

North Devon

North Devon's nickname of the Golden Coast derives today largely from the superb stretches of sandy beaches at Woolacombe, Saunton and Westward Ho!, which draw swimmers and surfers in their hundreds. In the past, however, the epithet was more likely to refer to the rich pickings available to smugglers and wreckers who took full advantage of the treacherous rocky headlands and caves around Hartland Point, Lundy and Clovelly. Today Clovelly is one of the most popular tourist spots in north Devon, but Hartland Point, pounded relentlessly by the Atlantic, still retains its feeling of windswept isolation. Likewise, a trip to the tiny granite isle of Lundy is popular with birdwatchers and those who want to get away from it all. The rival estuary towns of Barnstaple and Bideford are not really tourist centres, but contain enough of interest for a casual visitor, while the family resorts of Ilfracombe, Woolacombe and Westward Ho! offer more traditional seaside facilities and entertainment. Inland, the rolling hills of central Devon are crossed by a web of steep sunken lanes lined with hedged banks, feathery ferns and magenta cranesbill, and country pubs and village life provide more interest than specific sights. Two exceptions are the towns of Great Torrington, with its glass factory and rose gardens, and Tiverton, with an excellent museum and attractive church.

Combe Martin to Barnstaple

Right on the edge of Exmoor National Park, **Combe Martin** is a large village that straggles for a mile and a half along the sheltered valley of the Umber, ending in a shingly beach between high cliffs. From the tiny harbour, ships used to ferry cargoes of strawberries – which crop earlier here than

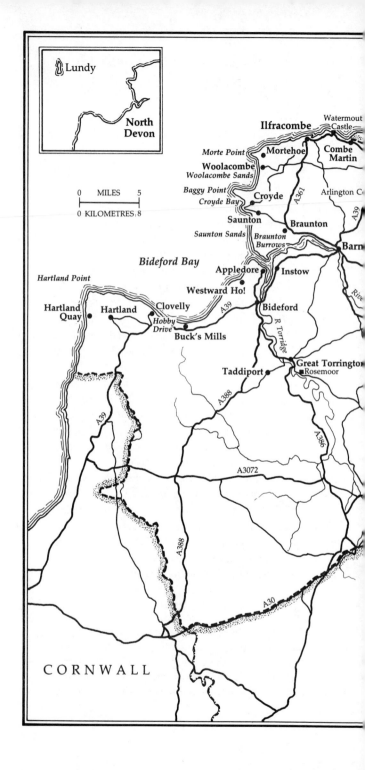

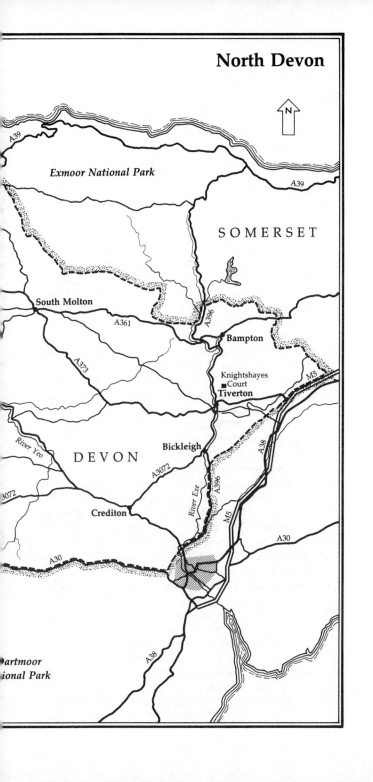

elsewhere because of its sheltered aspect – to other ports for export. Now there's just a small fishing industry here and the bay is more popular with tourists and windsurfers.

In medieval and Tudor times the village became wealthy from lead and silver mines in the area. Disused shafts are said to run beneath the main street, but the most obvious remains are the ruins of the chimney of Knap Down Mine, last worked in 1875, on a hill to the north of the village. In Combe Martin itself, the Pack of Cards Inn is the quirkiest feature. Built by eighteenth-century gambler George Ley to celebrate a lucky streak at cards, the crooked white building with its multiple chimney-stacks looks rather like a card house itself; each of the four floors has 13 doors, and the whole building has 52 windows. Inside are various nooks and crannies where local men hid from the press-gangs who used to put ashore here. There's another memorial to George Ley in the less worldly surroundings of the Gothic parish church of St Peter ad Vincula, with its pretty painted rood-screen.

Two other tourist attractions are the **Combe Martin Motor Cycle Collection** (open May to Sept, daily, 10 to 6) and the **Wildlife Leisure Park** (open Mar to end Oct, daily, 10 to 4.30) – monkeys, meercats and wallabies. Children will also love **Watermouth Castle** (opening times vary telephone: Ilfracombe (0271) 867474), on the A399 halfway between Combe Martin and Ilfracombe; a castellated mansion built in 1825, it is now a theme park, with a model railway, fairy-tale tableaux and a steam carousel.

To the west on the A399, **Ilfracombe**, the largest resort in north Devon, developed during Victorian times after the railway reached the coast in 1874. The Victorian pavilion nestles beneath Capstone Hill on the sea-front amid neat public gardens and pitch-and-putt greens, while stately bay-windowed B&Bs rise in terraces above the town. For a good view over the town climb up from the small harbour to the chapel of St Nicholas on Lantern Hill. Built in the fourteenth century as a seamen's chapel, complete with lantern, its red light still guides ships safely into the harbour. To the east, Hillsborough Hill offers great views, on clear days, of Combe Martin and Lundy Island. The remains of Ilfracombe's first prehistoric settlement, an Iron Age fort, are also here.

Ilfracombe's **museum** (open Easter to end Oct, daily, 10 to 5.30, also, June to end Sept, daily 7.30 to 10; Nov to Easter, Mon to Fri 10 to 12.30), housed in a former hotel laundry, is a testimony to the Victorian passion for collecting: neatly labelled drawers are crammed with birds' eggs, beetles, butterflies and moths, while stuffed birds and animal heads decorate the walls. Photographs of the damage caused by the two great fires of Ilfracombe, in July 1896 and September 1983, are on display, as well as a newspaper cutting reporting on the last passenger railway service from Ilfracombe to Barnstaple in 1970: 'The death occurred on Saturday of the Barnstaple to Ilfracombe railway line. It was 96 and had been ill for some time. Fifteen miles of it was closed.'

The Tunnels Beaches were also a Victorian creation. Welsh miners were paid 8d a day to pickaxe through the cliffs to the coves beyond. Separate bathing pools for ladies and gentlemen were made using the natural curve of the rocks, and a bugler was posted between the pools to sound the alarm should any lascivious male try to creep round to the ladies' pool. Old sepia photographs just inside the entrance to the beaches show sedate scenes of swimmers in stripy costumes emerging from a neat row of wooden changing cubicles. Winter storms have done their worst, and the gentlemen's pool no longer exists, but the ladies' pool is still visible for six hours out of every 12, as the tide rises and falls. The beach isn't wonderful, consisting of coarse grey sand, shale and rocks, but it's sheltered, with lots of rock-pools for the curious.

The coastline changes direction at **Morte Point**, a jagged headland of slate covered in scrubby gorse, now under the care of the National Trust. According to an old Devonshire proverb, 'Morte is the place which Heaven made last and the Devil will take first' – a reference to the numerous shipwrecks that have taken place in this area. In 1852 five ships came to grief here on the Morte Stone, the sunken reef at its tip; it wasn't until 1879 that a lighthouse was built on Bull Point to the north to warn vessels of the dangers along this stretch of coast.

At **Mortehoe**, further inland, the small fourteenth-century church of St Mary contains a curious mosaic, almost Byzantine in style, over the chancel arch, and some lovely Tudor carved bench ends depicting local worthies as well as more religious subjects like a chalice and 30 pieces of silver. The tomb of Sir William Tracy, rector of Mortehoe who died in 1322, is in the south transept. Many like to believe that the tomb in fact belongs to Sir William de Tracy, one of the murderers of Thomas à Becket in 1170, but as the chantry in which the tomb stands was not built until 1307, this is unlikely.

Protected by the sloping Woolacombe Downs, the three-mile stretch of **Woolacombe Sands** south of Morte Point is one of the best in north Devon. The rolling Atlantic breakers, sandy beach and rock-pools make it popular with surfers and families alike. There's no shortage of hotels, B&Bs and campsites in Woolacombe itself.

Baggy Point, separating Woolacombe Sands from the equally popular **Croyde Bay**, also belongs to the National Trust and offers two and a half miles of bracing walks. The sea has worn a huge cave, Baggy Hole, in the cliffs of sandstone and grit, which is accessible by boat at low tide. Inland, in the pretty village of **Croyde** itself, the small **Gem, Rock and Shell Museum** has an interesting collection of

Smugglers' Tales

Them that asks no questions isn't told a lie.
Watch the wall, my darling, while the gentlemen go by!

After customs duties were introduced in 1272 by Edward I to help pay for the wars against France, smuggling really took off, particularly in Devon and Cornwall. It reached its peak in the second half of the eighteenth century, when nearly four million gallons of gin and five to six million pounds of tea were being brought in illegally each year. The local Devon communities, with their knowledge of the coast and secret landing places, saw nothing wrong with 'fair trading', as they called it. Magistrates and even vicars were involved – churches made good hiding places for contraband.

At first smuggling was relatively easy, as enforcement officers were overworked and outnumbered. They were also poorly paid, which led many of them to accept bribes to overlook the furtive goings-on. The Reverend R. S. Hawker, a Cornish vicar, described how a bag of money would be left in a rocky hollow to be collected by an excise man, who would then be approached by one of the smugglers with the cheery phrase, 'Sir, your pocket is unbuttoned'. The corrupt excise man would reply, 'Ay! Ay! But never mind, my man, my money's safe enough', and the smugglers would be satisfied that their boats could safely go out that night.

polished stones and jewellery as well as shells from all over the world.

From Croyde the B3231 runs along the clifftops with views across the five-mile expanse of **Saunton Sands** and **Braunton Burrows**. Saunton Sands, the third of the beaches in north Devon that earned this area the nickname of the Golden Coast, is much loved by swimmers, surfers and windsurfers. Behind, the 1500 acres of sand dunes that make up Braunton Burrows National Nature Reserve also house a golf course and an army firing range, in use when red flags are flying. The peace of the area is often shattered by low-flying jets from the RAF station at Chivenor, which also acts as a base for helicopters sent on rescue missions along the coast.

Braunton itself, still classed as a village, is rapidly developing as a satellite town of Barnstaple, with new

---

The coast of north Devon is pockmarked with smugglers' caves and paths. Dingle Hole, a cave along Hobby Drive, is a natural rock fault that leads down to the shore. Around the smugglers' caves in the Valley of Rocks, a coastguard and the smuggler he was trying to arrest fell to their deaths from the cliffs as they struggled in combat. From caves in Lee Bay, contraband goods were carried along old paths to Somerset. And in Lynmouth the thatched cottages down by the harbour were once used for storage.

After the war against France ended in 1815 the increased availability of men and money improved the efficiency of the coastguards, and the smugglers had to devise more ingenious methods of getting their goods ashore. In 'crop-sowing', several tubs were tied to a length of rope, weighed down with heavy stones and anchors, and thrown overboard. Later, when the coast was clear, innocuous fishing boats would haul the tubs up and hide them under their nets before burying them in sand to be collected later. Sometimes the tubs would be submerged for so long that their contents would go off – they were then known as 'stinkibus'.

The incentive of large profits encouraged creative thinking. Boats were built with false bottoms, tobacco was plaited inside ropes, a turkey was stuffed with rare silk. But as law enforcement improved and customs duties were reduced, smuggling in Devon and Cornwall declined, and bravado tales of swashbuckling heroism became a thing of the past.

---

housing estates and industrial warehouses. Thirteenth-century St Brannock's Church is out of the town centre, in the narrow streets of the old village up on the hillside. St Brannock, a Celtic missionary and priest, is supposed to have arrived in north Devon from Wales in the sixth century by floating over the sea on a stone coffin. Legend has it that his original choice of site for the church was just behind where it stands today, but every time the building was started it fell down. Finally St Brannock was told in a vision to build the church where he found a white sow and her litter, and he obeyed. The story is depicted on one of the coloured bosses, showing the sow and her five piglets, on the plain cradle roof above the font. The carved ends of the chestnut pews, similar to those of St Mary's Church in Mortehoe, are also striking; one shows St Brannock with his cow, which he was supposed to have miraculously brought back to life after it had been chopped up and cooked.

From Braunton the A361 runs alongside the sluggish, silted up estuary of the River Taw to **Barnstaple**, which is the main town of north Devon and claims to be the oldest in England. Today Barnstaple is a pleasant market town with an unpretentious feel: there are few of the endless tea-shops and craft centres that characterise much of tourist-oriented Devon. At low tide the piers of the town's fifteenth-century bridge stand well clear of the water, encouraging local youths to climb down on to the concrete bases and fish with rod and line in the remaining foot or so of water. Two hundred yards downstream from the bridge, the Georgian colonnades of **Queen Anne's Walk**, topped with a farthingaled queen with gilded crown and mace, front what used to be the merchants' exchange when Barnstaple still reigned supreme as a trading port. Merchants agreed deals across the Tome Stone in the presence of a witness without signing contracts. The two stone quays that originally stood next to the exchange were demolished to build the first railway station in 1872, and a new quay was built just downstream at Castle Quay, where sea-going vessels still unload today.

On the other side of Castle Street, a grassy tree-covered mound is all that remains of Barnstaple's castle, which back in Domesday times stood at the meeting-point of the Taw and Yeo rivers. It's now an environmental study area. Below is the modern red-brick library and the cattle market, which is still held every Friday – providing a good excuse for Barnstaple's pubs to remain open all day.

From the cattle market the pedestrianised alley of Holland Walk leads to the High Street. At number 85, opposite the T-junction, a wall plaque commemorates the fact that John Gay, author of *The Beggar's Opera*, was born here in 1685. Further along, the Grecian pillars of the Georgian **Guildhall**, built in 1826, were designed by Thomas Lee, architect of Arlington Court (see p. 94). Behind it lies the town's famous **Pannier Market**, a great railway hangar of a place, with iron girders supporting the sloping glass roof. Before the market was built in 1855, traders simply sold their goods from baskets, or panniers, along the High Street. Today's goods are far more varied: fresh eggs and dairy produce, sheepskin moccasins, fluorescent socks, and fruit and vegetables alternate with summer craft and antique markets to catch the tourist trade. **Butchers Row**, running beside the Pannier Market, was built at the same time to house 33 butchers' shops. More variety is evident here too, with fishmongers and greengrocers and signs advertising 'Cream by post'.

Paternoster Row is a more peaceful thoroughfare connecting the High Street with Boutport Street. Buskers play beneath the trees between St Peter's Church on one side and St Anne's Chapel on the other. The grassy slopes rise above the paths because of the number of bodies that have been buried there over the years. **St Anne's Chapel**, now a museum, was once a grammar school, where John Gay was a pupil. Some say that the twisted broach spire of **St Peter's** is the result of being hit by lightning; others maintain that it's simply been warped over time. The building dates mostly from the fourteenth century but was heavily restored between 1866 and 1882 by Sir Gilbert Scott. One of the seventeenth-century memorials inside is to Richard Beaple, a mayor of the town and father-in-law of wealthy cloth merchant John Penrose, whose 20 granite **almshouses** can still be seen in Litchdon Street. Neatly arranged around a cobbled courtyard with a central water-pump that once served all the buildings in the compound, the almshouses still bear the scars of bullet holes dating from clashes during the Civil War. Barnstaple, which came out in favour of the Parliamentarians, was captured by the Royalists in 1643 but was retaken by the Parliamentarians under Fairfax three years later.

Further along Litchdon Street, the windows of the cream- and brown-tiled Brannams pottery are filled with the company's famous terracotta wares, though the factory itself has moved out of Barnstaple to the Roundswell Industrial

Estate just off the A39 (museum and guided factory tours; open Mon to Sat, 9 to 5, and in July and Aug, Sun, 10 to 4).

Back at the parish churchyard the narrow alley of Church Lane twists round to meet the High Street again. Here there are more almshouses, built by wealthy seventeenth-century merchants Gilbert Paige and Thomas Horwood. Next door is Alice Horwood's school, erected for '20 poor maids', now a café.

The **Museum of North Devon** (open all year, Tues to Sat, 10 to 4.30) beside the roundabout at the south end of town is worth visiting. It opened in 1990 and, as its name suggests, concentrates on everything Devonian: minerals, nineteenth- and early twentieth-century north Devon pottery, fossils, and a section on marine life are beautifully displayed, well lit and labelled. There's a Victorian section with a rather horrifying cabinet full of brilliantly coloured beetles and bugs (dead) collected by Victorians from tropical rain forests and made into brooches. More rooms are planned.

Further inland, where the A39 meets the River Yeo, stands **Arlington Court and Park** (house open Easter to end Sept, Sun to Fri, BH Sat, 11 to 6; Oct, Sun to Fri, 11 to 5; park open all year daily during daylight hours). The architect Thomas Lee showed his liking for the Greek revivalist style in a severely plain white building embellished only with a pillared portico. Before the National Trust inherited Arlington, it had been the home of the Chichester family since it was built in 1820. The house contents are largely the legacy of one woman – Rosalie Chichester, aunt of Sir Francis Chichester – who lived at Arlington for 84 years until she died in 1949. She was an obsessive collector who travelled all over the world. According to the National Trust, Rosalie Chichester had amassed '75 cabinets full of shells, 200 model ships, several hundred pieces of pewter, 50 punch ladles, 30 tea caddies, 2 cases of candle snuffers, 2 cases of Maori skirts and African clubs, 5 large cases of stuffed birds, hundreds of snuff boxes, a large stamp collection with some 52,000 specimens, 30 volumes of Christmas and greetings cards, 40 paperweights, 29 watches, numerous mineral specimens, medals, coins, books (including five sixteenth-century books unknown to bibliographers), brass and glass objects, a cupboard full of camera equipment and "a case of bombs and zepplin bits". Although many of these treasures have been sold and passed on, the house still contains much of Miss Chichester's pewter, shell and model ship collection. But she didn't stop at inanimate objects: she also created her own wildlife park after visiting national parks in Australia, and Jacob sheep and Shetland ponies still roam the grounds of Arlington. The National Trust has also housed its own carriage collection in the former stables.

Great Torrington to Hartland

Great Torrington, perched high above the Torridge valley, is perhaps best known to tourists for the **Dartington Crystal and Glass Centre** (open all year, Mon to Fri, 9 to 5, Sat, 9.30 to 4; tours all year, Mon to Fri, 9.30 to 3.30), with a series of exhibits tracing the history of English glassware, a video presentation and a fully working replica of an eighteenth-century glass cone. You can also go on a factory tour to see the various stages of glass blowing and finishing, and there's a shop where you can buy Dartington ware and seconds at reduced prices.

Great Torrington is old enough to have merited a mention in the Domesday Book, and its castle must be one of the first to have suffered from lack of planning permission: in 1228 the sheriff of Devon ordered that it be pulled down because it had been erected without King's licence. Today's bowling green, where ladies in cream sweaters and white hats confer about the score, is said to be on the site of the original castle keep. The remains of the walls, however, are nineteenth century, built by Lord Rolle. A prominent local family, the Rolles did a great deal for Torrington, funding a charity school, building a canal to link the town with Bideford, and leasing property to allow the Torridge Vale Buttery factory, forerunner of today's Dairy Crest plant, to be set up.

From the castle walls the roofless Pannier Market leads to the market square, with its Gothic fountain, erected by Mark Rolle in 1870, a fifteenth-century coaching inn and the pillared town hall, which houses the tourist office and a small local museum, with old uniforms, anvils and tools, and coins. There's also a display on the former leper colony at Taddiport, just across the river, with photographs of lepers working in the fields.

The most famous incident in Great Torrington's history was also a turning point in the Civil War. A Royalist stronghold, Great Torrington was captured in a surprise attack by General Fairfax in 1646. The Parliamentarians imprisoned the 200 captured Royalists in the church, little knowing that this had been the Royalists' arsenal, with 80 barrels of gunpowder stored there. Somehow the ammunition went up, killing the prisoners and destroying most of the building. The church, largely rebuilt in 1651, contains a copy of the famous Black Madonna of Czestochowa, the installation of which caused some controversy locally, and monuments to relatives of Sir Joshua Reynolds. The artist and Dr Johnson both stayed in nearby Palmer House, built in 1752 by John Palmer after he had married Mary Reynolds, Sir Joshua's sister.

Just south-east of the town the Royal Horticultural Society's gardens at **Rosemoor** (open Easter to end Sept, daily, 10 to 6, Mar and Oct, daily, 10 to 5; Nov to Dec, daily, 10 to 4) have beautiful roses, herbaceous borders and divided areas like the Kitchen Garden and Stone Garden.

The A386 follows the Torridge north to Charles Kingsley's 'little white town' of **Bideford**. This owes its existence to the **Long Bridge**, 667 feet long with 24 arches of varying widths. Before the bridge was built travellers used to cross the ford by boat: Bideford's name has its origin in 'By-the-Ford'. Then in the fourteenth century legend has it that the parish priest, Sir Richard Gurney, had a dream telling him exactly where a bridge should be constructed. The bridge, built of wood, had arches of different widths according to the lengths of timber available; when it was rebuilt at the beginning of the sixteenth century many of the old timbers were simply encased in stone – and the irregular arches were preserved.

Responsibility for the bridge used to lie with the Bridge Trust, made up of 18 prominent Bideford men known as Feofees. They used their income from properties owned in and around Bideford to pay for the upkeep and maintenance of the bridge. But in 1968 the two arches nearest to the town started to crack, and the bridge had to be closed for several months to carry out extensive repairs. Since then the bridge, now a listed Ancient Monument, has come under the care of the Department of Transport. You can see a model of the bridge during various stages of its development in the public library. A new bypass bridge carrying the A39 was opened further downriver in 1987.

From the bridge a busy tree-lined road runs beside the quay, which is crowded with parked cars. Locals believe that England's first cargo of tobacco was unloaded here by Sir Walter Raleigh. But it was another swashbuckling Elizabethan, Sir Richard Grenville, whose founding of colonies in Virginia and Carolina started off 200 profitable years trading with the New World, before the wool trade with Spain, Holland and France developed. The Grenville family have long been connected with the town: they made it into a borough at the beginning of the thirteenth century, and an effigy of Sir Thomas Grenville, who died in 1513, as well as an epitaph to Sir Richard, can still be seen in St Mary's Church. In the nineteenth century, however, European wars and increasing piracy led to the decline of Bideford's port and shipbuilding industry.

From the quay the town rises steeply in a series of parallel streets – Bridge Street, High Street, Mill Street, Gunstone Street – lined with mainly Victorian architecture. The exception is Bridgeland Street, where some wealthy seventeenth-century merchants' houses survive. The Red House, now an antique shop, was built with red tiles rather than brick to avoid paying brick tax. The Freemasons' Hall opposite used to be the home of one Thomas Stuckley, who believed that cleanliness might spread infection: when he died in 1730 his house was absolutely filthy, with money piled up in corners covered in dust and cobwebs.

Bideford's Pannier Market, held on Tuesdays, sits at the top of Bridge Street, in the upper half of the town, amid a gaggle of shops selling antiques and bric-a-brac. One of the most interesting is Scudder's Emporium – a real warren of rooms crammed with old furniture, prints, books, stuffed animals, and so on. For more conventional shopping needs, the shops on the modernised High Street and pedestrianised Mill Street should fit the bill.

On the other side of the River Torridge, **East-the-Water** once housed most of Bideford's prosperous shipyards, but today is mostly noted for the seventeenth-century Royal Hotel, where Charles Kingsley stayed when he was writing *Westward Ho!* A white marble statue of the author stands at the end of the quay back across the water. Behind him is Victoria Park, with a set of Spanish guns captured from the Armada fleet, and the Burton Art Gallery, which displays work by local artists.

Moving north the A386 continues to follow the Torridge estuary to **Appledore**. Unlike many places in the area, Appledore's shipyards have moved with the times and still turn out ships of considerable size. But with the modern shipyards tucked away almost out of sight further up the estuary, it's easy to gain the impression that Appledore is little more than an attractive fishing village. Pastel-washed cottages along the river back on to tiny cobbled courtyards filled with flowers, overlooking the boats and beaches of Instow. These cottages used to be the homes of local boat-builders and fishermen, but many are now holiday homes. Further up the hill the modern bungalow development is less picturesque, but it's worth climbing up and taking the footpath across Staddon Hill past the white cottage called 'The Lookout' for a fine view of Bideford Bay, Lundy and Westward Ho! Except at high tide, you'll also be able to see the waves breaking over the infamous Bideford Bar, a shifting sandbank across the entrance to the Torridge estuary that has caused many shipwrecks in the past. Today all large ships have to be guided in and out of the estuary by Trinity House pilots.

To overcome the problem, the locals constructed a type of boat peculiar to the area, called a polacca. This could be sailed backwards to negotiate the Bar. The **North Devon Maritime Museum** (open Easter to end April and Oct, daily, 2 to 5.30; May to end Sept, daily, 11 to 1, 2 to 5.30) in Odun House has models of polaccas, as well as displays of wartime activities – for example, testing mud shoes and mud sledges round the sewage outfall pipe at Bideford East-the-Water. One of the more imaginative – and more hopeless – projects was the development of the Great Panjandrum: basically a giant catherine wheel packed with high explosives and propelled by a large number of rockets. The idea was that it would rush up the Normandy beaches and break through Hitler's Atlantic Wall, thus allowing the Allies to pour through the gap. After several trials on the beach at Westward Ho! the army boffins, who included one Lt Commander Norway – otherwise known as the author Neville Shute – decided that they were ready to demonstrate the weapon to the army's top brass in January 1944. Unfortunately the demonstration went horribly wrong: 'The wheel hit bumps in the sand and veered off course, one of the steering cables snapped, rockets detached and flew wildly among spectators, and in the end the Great Panjandrum fell on its side in a heap of smoke and flame.' Needless to say, the Allies had to rely on more conventional methods for their D-day landings.

Today the beaches of **Westward Ho!** are more popular with surfers, who love the Atlantic rollers that break on to the two-mile stretch of golden sand, backed by a huge pebble

ridge. The town itself was developed in the nineteenth
century to commemorate Charles Kingsley's book, but the
pier and some of the original houses were washed away in a
storm. Rudyard Kipling was also educated here, at the
United Services College, and set the exploits of *Stalky & Co* in
this area. Today the town's literary connections are few –
Kipling's Kitchen Café serves chicken and chips, and hot
donuts – but it's a popular resort, with a bingo hall, skating
rinks and Victorian terraces of souvenir shops.

Back on the main A39 coast road, **Buck's Mills** is a smaller,
less commercialised version of its western neighbour
Clovelly, with a steep road lined with pretty cottages and
ending in a gravelly beach. In earlier times the village was
supposed to have been inhabited entirely by people named
Braund, descendants of dark-haired, brown-eyed Iberian
immigrants who came to Britain about 3000 years ago. Now
the locals are rather more mixed, but many Braund
descendants still visit the West Country every year in search
of their roots.

If you're heading west for north Devon's most famous
fishing village, **Clovelly**, the nicest approach is along the
Hobby Drive. This one-way three-mile unmetalled track (fee
payable) winds through ancient woodland with occasional
glimpses of the coastline below. The drive was started in
1811 by Sir James Hamlyn Williams and his wife Diana,
partly as a hobby (hence the name) and partly to provide
employment for the locals during the Napoleonic Wars. It
took about 30 years to complete. In 1899, a stretch of several
hundred yards that ran along the edge of a precipitous slope
collapsed on to the beach below, and a new section had to be
built further up.

On reaching Clovelly you'll be directed to the large car
park above the village. Here you have to pay an admission
charge to enter the visitors' centre and walk down into the
village – one way of controlling the many thousands of
visitors who swarm here every year. The steep cobbled main
street of Up-a-long/Down-a-long, built on the dry bed of a
stream, is true to the picture postcard views: slate-roofed,
whitewashed cottages spill down the hill to the tiny harbour
with its terraced sea wall. Flowers tumble out of hanging
baskets and window-boxes, and the milkman makes his
deliveries by sledge instead of float. It's undoubtedly too
twee for some, but undeniably popular all the same. The
street is stepped to make the climbing easier, but Land Rover
trips ease the long haul for the elderly or disabled.

Clovelly's parish church, standing slightly above the rest of the village, contains several memorials to members of the two families most closely associated with Clovelly – the Carys and the Hamlyns. The Carys, originally from Cockington in south Devon, acquired Clovelly by marriage in about 1370. Clovelly's quay was built by George Cary (1543–1601) for the sum of £2000, and it was his son William who was featured in *Westward Ho!* by Charles Kingsley. Legend also has it that a member of the Cary family removed all the lead from the church roof to make bullets for the Royalists. When the last generation of Carys died childless in 1738, Clovelly was sold to the Hamlyn family. It was Christine Hamlyn, who died in 1936 aged 80, who devised the policies to keep Clovelly unspoiled by tourism. Many of the cottages bear her initials and a date, showing when they were refurbished. By all accounts an autocratic and imperious woman, she also forbade anyone to put up hoardings, build new bungalows or hotels, or set up ice-cream or souvenir stalls.

From Clovelly, drivers must return almost to the A39 before they can turn west along the A3248 to **Hartland**, set amid windswept moorland and bowed, stooping trees. The magnificent parish **church of St Nectan**, named after a fifth-century Welsh hermit, is actually a couple of miles further on, at Stoke. The story goes that the church was founded by Countess Gytha, mother of King Harold, as thanks to God for saving her husband from being drowned in a storm. The church tower, second highest in Devon, acts as a landmark for sailors along this treacherous coast. Countess Gytha herself is depicted in one of the windows in the south aisle, while the windows in the north aisle show the three kings traditionally linked with Hartland: King William with the Domesday Book and part of the Bayeux tapestry; King Alfred and his burnt cakes; and King Arthur with the Holy Grail and Excalibur. The chancel has a fine painted oak reredos carved with figures of saints, and the bosses on the wagon roof of the north aisle show symbols depicting a Christian's progress through life. The Pope's Chamber, a small room above the north porch where the sexton used to sleep, contains Jacobean pulpit panels carved with 'God save Kinge James fines', bought in 1609 for £1 13s 4d. The inscription wasn't added until 1625, the year King James died; it's thought that the last word 'fines' refers to his death.

Close by the church is **Hartland Abbey**, occasionally open to the public. The castellated twelfth-century building was the last to survive Henry VIII's dissolution of the monasteries, finally being given to William Abbott, sergeant of the king's wine cellar, in 1539. It's now home of Baronet Hugh Stucely, and contains photographic exhibitions, pictures, furniture and porcelain.

From Stoke the road winds down the precipitous cliffs backing the wild coast surrounding **Hartland Quay**. A quay was built here by William Abbott and was Hartland's gateway to the outside world for three centuries, as boats loaded with coal, lime and wood fought their way through the surf to unload. The lead for the church roof arrived by this route. The incessant storms that rage along this coast finally swept the quay away in the last century, and were also responsible for the many shipwrecks in the area. The **museum** (open Easter, end May to end Sept, daily, 11 to 5), next to the Hartland Quay Hotel, has detailed records of many of the wrecks.

From the museum the single street runs down to the extraordinary beach, where the layers of sandstone, shale and slate have been forced up against each other in enormous zigzags, some with tunnels beneath eroded by the sea. Sea anemones and barnacles inhabit the pools that form in the clefts between the kelp-scattered ridges of rock; further out, fishermen with rod and line brave the wind in yellow oilskins.

Two miles further north the coast makes a sharp right-angled turn at **Hartland Point**. The white, rounded form of the lighthouse resembles a Greek church when seen against the blue skies of a summer day, but the pounding waves dashing on the rocks below are a reminder of its true purpose. Before the lighthouse could be built a road had to be cut in the cliff, as the site was inaccessible by land; the initial surveys were done offshore in a small boat. During construction in 1873 the *British Trident*, a Canadian timber ship, was wrecked and ended up just below the partially completed lighthouse. The remains of the last victim, the Panamanian *Johanna*, which came aground less than 400 yards from the lighthouse on 31 December 1982, still lie rusting on the rocks below.

South Molton to Crediton

The market town of **South Molton**, the focus of a large agricultural area, was historically important, lying on the Taunton-Barnstaple coaching route and profiting from the wool and cloth trade. Today it's rather less busy, mainly thanks to the completion of the north Devon link road, which bypasses the town. Centred on the rather elongated town square of Broad Street, South Molton is a pretty mixture of Georgian and Victorian buildings, with a lively cattle market on Thursdays.

The main places of interest are all on Broad Street. In the centre is the Medical Hall, now a chemist's shop, with an unusual wrought-iron balcony supported by four Ionic columns. The eighteenth-century town hall, its pillared portico overlapping the pavement, contains the **museum** (open late Feb to end Nov, Tues, Thurs and Fri, 10.30 to 12.30, 2 to 4; Wed and Sat, 10.30 to 12.30), with displays including old fire engines and weights and measures. On the opposite side of the road is the church of St Mary Magdalene, which contains a series of stained glass windows commemorating local Victorian and Edwardian worthies.

A more unusual attraction is the **Quince Honey Farm** (on North Road, open Easter to end Sept, daily, 9 to 6; Oct, daily, 9 to 5), a plain, two-storey building with displays showing how honey is made, collected and put into jars. You can see real beehives, in locations as diverse as postboxes and tree-trunks, and buy honey and beeswax in the shop.

From South Molton the A361 east is the fastest route to Tiverton but if you have more time the longer scenic route is the B3227 through rolling agricultural scenery via **Bampton**. A quiet market town on the edge of Exmoor, Bampton has peaceful streets lined with plain Georgian cottages. Nothing but a mound remains of King Stephen's castle, but the churchyard boasts two yew trees said to be over 500 years old.

Heading on the A396 towards Tiverton, it's worth taking a detour to **Knightshayes Court** (garden open April to Oct, daily, 11 to 6 (5 Oct), house open Sat to Thurs, and Good Fri, 1.30 to 6 (5 Oct); closed Fri). Although the property is probably better known for its very attractive gardens, the extraordinary Victorian country house itself is certainly worth a visit. It was originally designed by the Gothic

Revivalist architect William Burges for the Heathcoat-Amory family, who were local lace-manufacturing magnates. Burges was better known for designing churches than houses, and his enthusiasm for the medieval seemed limitless: 'I was brought up in the thirteenth-century belief and in that belief I intend to die.' Once the house was structurally complete the cost and flashiness of his plans for the interior design – colourful friezes and borders, extravagant chimneypieces, ceilings covered in tiny circular mirrors and stucco, and stained glass – horrified the conventional John Heathcoat-Amory so much that another, 'safer' decorator, John Crace, was hired to finish the job. Even the toned down result was too much for some: succeeding generations of Heathcoat-Amorys have dismantled some of the more colourful and distinguishing features of the house. The National Trust has worked hard to restore several of the lost eccentricities, but copies of Burges's fantastic medievalist designs, on display opposite the ticket desk, show that there is still a long way to go.

It was Heathcoat-Amory's grandfather, John Heathcoat, who established the family fortune, walking 200 miles to **Tiverton** from Loughborough in 1816 after his lace factory had been attacked by a mob of drunken Luddites. The factory he built on the banks of the Exe still continues to provide local employment – lace for the wedding outfits of both Princess Anne and the Princess of Wales was produced here. The excellent **museum** (open Feb to Dec, Mon to Sat, 10.30 to 4.30) has several of Heathcoat's original machines on display, including the oldest in existence, invented in 1808 and built in 1853. Other displays include the Railway Gallery, with the 'Tivvy Bumper' (Great Western Railway locomotive 1442), a recreated village smithy and various medical contraptions, including a Victorian cure for constipation, provided by companies such as Moore's Patent Medical Machines: '. . .improved pump for drawing the breasts of nurses, inhalers in metal for applying the vapour of vinegar, etc to inflamed throats and of glass for inhaling iodine, chlorine, etc trusses, bandages, etc of every description. . . wire leech appliers, medical spoons, etc.'

It was as well that Heathcoat came along when he did, for by the beginning of the nineteenth century Tiverton was in danger of following the declining fortunes of the woollen industry, on which it depended so heavily. In 1730 the town was said to have 56 fulling mills, manufacturing Tiverton 'kersies' – coarse woollen worsted in red, blue and green. Peter Blundell, a local merchant who made his fortune from kersies, left a generous bequest when he died in 1601 to found a free grammar school. Blundell's School, known as the Eton of the west, was originally built in 1604, with some of the roof timbers said to come from wrecked ships of the Armada. Famous pupils include R. D. Blackmore, whose *Lorna Doone* opens in the forecourt of the school, and the Reverend John 'Jack' Russell, the well-known hunting parson. Samuel Wesley, John Wesley's brother, was the school's headmaster for a while. In 1882 the school moved to bigger premises a mile along the road; Old Blundell's (not open to the public) is now owned by the National Trust.

Another beneficent cloth merchant was John Greenway, whose property in the town in 1524 was valued at £150, making him the richest man in Tiverton. His almshouse in Gold Street provided rooms for five old men and a chapel where they could pray for the souls of their benefactors – Greenway and his wife Joan. For good measure, inscriptions on the walls outside exhort passers-by to 'Have grace ye men and ever pray, For the souls of John and Jone Greenway'. But Greenway's biggest scheme for self-aggrandisement was to build a chantry chapel on to St Peter's Church. Although there are some scenes from the life of Christ, the most prominent carvings are more for Greenway's own glorification, depicting his ships, his merchant's mark and him and his wife kneeling on either side of the Virgin Mary.

Next door to the church is **Tiverton Castle** (open Easter to end Sept, Sun to Thurs, 2.30 to 5.30), built as a royal fortress in 1106. A Royalist stronghold during the Civil War, the castle was besieged by the Parliamentarians under Sir Thomas Fairfax in 1645. After three days a lucky shot from a Parliamentarian cannon broke one of the drawbridge chains, and the castle was taken. A copy of Fairfax's report is on display in the castle. There's also a large number of clocks, collected by one of the previous owners, Ivar Campbell, and sets of armour dented where they have been 'proofed' (tested to see whether they will hold).

From Tiverton the A396 winds south beside the Exe to **Bickleigh**, a classic Devon village of thatched cottages and country gardens lining the river, with a pretty five-arched bridge, said to be haunted by a headless knight. **Bickleigh Castle** (open Easter, early April to end May, Wed,Sun and BH, end May to early Oct, Sun to Fri, 2 to 5), a strange mix of

Norman chapel, fourteenth-century gate-house, and cob and thatch farmhouse, was, like Tiverton, a Royalist stronghold during the Civil War. Fairfax wreaked damage here too, destroying the north and west wings and damaging the gate-house. The owner, Sir Henry Carew, restored the gate-house and added the thatched farmhouse. After his death in 1681 the property fell into neglect, and its restoration, begun at the beginning of this century, has been continued by the present owners, Norma and Noel Boxall. The tiny chapel has folding Cromwellian chairs; much of the furniture in the rest of the castle is Tudor. The original moat has been converted into a beautiful water-garden.

Crediton, on the main Exeter-Barnstaple road, is most noted for the fact that Winfrith, later to become St Boniface, was born there in 680. Unfortunately, a series of fires in the eighteenth century destroyed much of the historic medieval town, but the huge red sandstone Holy Cross Church, originating in the eleventh century, still stands at the end of the High Street.

Lundy

Lundy HIGH, IT *will be dry,*
Lundy LOW, IT *will be snow,*
Lundy PLAIN, IT *will be rain,*
Lundy in HAZE, FINE *for days.*

Apart from its role as a weather-vane for north Devon, the island of Lundy is a great spot for those wanting to get away from it all. Lying about 12 miles north of Hartland Point, this granite outcrop, little more than three miles long by half a mile across, is a popular destination for birdwatchers, who board the *MS Oldenburg* loaded down with telescopes and field-glasses. Lundy is the first land sighted by migrant birds after several thousand miles, and more than 400 different species have been spotted there. The nesting colonies have, however, declined over the years, but kittiwakes, guillemots, razorbills and, most famous of all, puffins, still return to the cliff ledges each year. It's from the puffin that Lundy gets its name: *lunde* means puffin in Norse, and the suffix *ey* means island.

As for human inhabitants, Lundy seems to have been quite a haven for pirates, smugglers and law-breakers. The tone was set by some of the earliest owners, the Marisco family, who came over with the Normans. William de Marisco defied Henry II's orders to hand Lundy over to the Knights Templar in 1160, and was fined for his trouble. His nephew, also called William, used the island as a base for his piratical activities, and was later hanged, drawn and quartered for his part in a plot to murder the king.

The Mariscos having been dealt with, Lundy passed through the hands of several royal governors and other families, including the Salisburys and the Duke of Clarence. In Elizabethan times the Grenville family took possession of the island, with Sir Walter Raleigh named as one of the trustees. Despite the swashbuckling reputations of Raleigh and Sir Richard Grenville, the island was used as a base by several pirate outfits, and in 1595 Queen Elizabeth admonished Sir Barnard Grenville for neglecting his inheritance and threatened to take over the island herself. But no sooner had one group of pirates been chased off than others muscled in, from as far afield as Turkey and Spain; according to the account of one aggrieved local, 'They burned our farms, took away our young sheep and our daughters and left us only old ewes and old women.'

Then came the Civil War. Sir Bevil Grenville, who had inherited Lundy, was a staunch Royalist, and on his death King Charles handed the island over to Thomas Bushell, a mining prospector who supported the Royalist cause with coins and precious metals from his mint in Aberystwyth. When the Royalists were defeated, Bushell remained on Lundy, surrendering only when he was guaranteed a free pardon and the continued rights to his mines and other estates on the mainland.

The island once again fell prey to marauding freebooters. During the reign of William and Mary a party of French privateers, pretending to be Dutch, landed and asked if they could bury their captain in the island's cemetery. The coffin, however, turned out to contain not a body but a cache of arms, with which the privateers held the natives prisoners, robbed them of their valuables, and destroyed their guns and fortifications before taking to the seas again.

Lundy seemed to bring out the worst, even in apparently respectable citizens. At the beginning of the eighteenth century the island was leased to Bideford merchant Thomas Benson, who was elected MP for Barnstaple in 1747. As well as smuggling, Benson diverted convicts bound for penal colonies in Virginia and Maryland to Lundy, where he used them as slave labour in his quarries. His antics finally came to light when he set fire to one of his own ships in order to claim on the insurance, but he managed to escape to Portugal, where he died in 1772.

Lundy's most settled period began in 1834, when William Hudson Heaven bought the island for 9000 guineas. Under the ownership of the Heaven family, which lasted until 1918, Lundy became known as 'the Kingdom of Heaven'. A road linking the landing beach to the lighthouse was built, and many agricultural improvements were made. Heaven's son, the Reverend Hudson Grossett Heaven, was responsible for building St Helena's Chapel, ambitiously capable of seating 165 people (the current permanent population is fewer than 20).

The final eccentric attracted by Lundy's granite charms was Martin Harman who, during his ownership from 1925 to 1954, came to regard the island as his independent kingdom, issuing his own coins and stamps. The stamps – featuring puffins – are still in use today, but Harman lost his court case defending his right to issue his own coinage, despite arguing that Lundy was outside the jurisdiction of the realm and that he therefore could not be tried in the county court. After his death his son took over Lundy until 1968, when the National Trust, with the help of a British millionaire living in the Bahamas, bought the island. The Landmark Trust, which leases Lundy from the National Trust, has converted some of the old buildings into holiday accommodation, and all requests for accommodation should be made in advance (telephone Littlewick Green (0628) 825925, Mon to Fri, 9 to 5.30).

If you're not planning to stay on the island, you can still visit Lundy on a day-trip: *ms Oldenburg* leaves from Bideford throughout the year and during the summer from Ilfracombe as well. The approach to the island is very scenic in late spring, when the rhododendron thickets on the eastern coast are a mass of pink. Landing Beach at the southern end is too shallow for the boat to sail right up to the shore, so a smaller craft makes a series of trips to ferry passengers to the landing jetty. From here a steep path climbs up to the remains of the castle, the church and the village. The cosy Marisco Tavern serves pub food and Lundy beer, brewed on the island, while the adjoining general store sells souvenir puffin mugs, tea towels and other items, as well as basic provisions like rice and sugar. The High Street – little more than a track –

continues past the Linhay Discovery Centre, with books and displays on the history, geography and wildlife of the island.

The village soon runs out, and the emptiness of Lundy begins. The main track carries on, over the three walls dividing the island into quarters, to the North Light, no longer staffed but controlled from the South Light near the Landing Beach. It's a bleak, windy walk through bracken, heather and springy grass tussocks. The trail along the eastern coast is greener and more sheltered, through earthy rhododendron groves and passing occasional goats and rabbits. Most birdwatchers, however, head for Jenny's Cove, about halfway along the western coast. Here they huddle behind rocks or bushes, seeking what protection they can from the powerful Atlantic winds, telescopes trained on distant wheeling specks.

Highlights

** *Clovelly, Hartland Point and Hartland Quay, Knightshayes Court, Tiverton – church and museum.*

* *Appledore, Arlington Court, Great Torrington, Lundy.*

Where to stay

For a key to prices, see p. 12

Barnstaple

Lynwood House

Bishop's Tawton Road, Barnstaple, Devon EX32 9DZ. Tel Barnstaple (0271) 43695 Fax (0271) 79340
On the outskirts of Barnstaple this well-kept Victorian house is an excellent touring base and is also used by business people. You can enjoy good food and have everything you need in the bedrooms, including trouser press, TV with teletext, direct dial telephone and two armchairs to make up for the lack of a sitting-room. The bar, with bench seating and walls decorated with black and white photographs, is both smart and cosy. The dining-room is immaculate, with highly polished tables laid with fine glass and silver, and the extensive menu has a strong emphasis on fish dishes; there's a separate vegetarian menu.
£££ *Open all year*

Bishop's Tawton
Downrew House

Bishop's Tawton, Barnstaple, Devon EX32 0DY. Tel Barnstaple (0271) 42497/46673 Fax (0271) 23947

Surrounded by its own golf course about a mile from the village, this part-seventeenth-century part-Queen Anne house offers lots of other sporting as well as business facilities. The public rooms are spacious and comfortable, with a grand piano in the library and a particularly light, pretty dining-room. You can choose from a range of bedrooms, varying in furnishings and prices, both in the main house and the annexe. New owners in 1990 plan more changes.
££££ *Open all year*

Halmpstone Manor

Bishop's Tawton, Barnstaple, Devon EX32 0EA. Tel Swimbridge (0271) 830321 Fax (0271) 830826
A lovely and very rural setting, down a narrow lane past a farm: the view from the house is over acres of Devon countryside. The owners are friendly and welcoming, Charles Stanbury acting as host and barman, while Jane, his wife, commands operations in the kitchen. The sitting-room with real fire is light and airy in contrast to the small panelled dining-room. Bedrooms are a treat: extremely comfortable, even luxurious, and bathroom extras include fluffy bathrobes and paracetamol.
££££ *Open all year exc Christmas Day*

Croyde

The Whiteleaf at Croyde

Croyde, Nr Braunton, Devon EX33 1PN. Tel Croyde (0271) 890266
On the outskirts of Croyde, this efficiently run guest-house is a very good-value base. A small

garden and parking area set the undistinguished 1930s house back from the road. Flo and David Wallington are a well-practised team; he cooks, she does the rest. You order from a good choice of dishes and wines by 6.30 and eat at about 8. It's a small, fairly intimate place where you help yourself to a drink, and all guests eat at the same time – although at separate tables. Both bedrooms and public rooms are immaculately clean and neat.
£–££ *Closed part of Dec and Jan; 2 weeks in April/May and in July/Aug*

East Buckland

Lower Pitt Restaurant

East Buckland, Barnstaple, Devon EX32 0TD. Tel Filleigh (059 86) 243
It calls itself a restaurant with rooms and there are only three simple bedrooms: light with pretty fabrics and their own bathrooms. It becomes very busy at weekends, and the Lyons were building a conservatory extension in 1990 which should ease the crush at the bar. In spite of its popularity it is a peaceful spot near the church in the village and makes an excellent base for touring the area.
££ *Open all year*

Huntsham

Huntsham Court

Huntsham, Nr Bampton, Devon EX16 7NA. Tel Clayhanger (039 86) 365/366 Fax (039 86) 456
A very original hotel run more as a private home with visitors. There's no formality; guests help themselves to drinks and

all eat at the huge 24-seater table in the panelled dining-room. There's plenty to do whatever the weather: croquet, tennis, billiards, chess and, above all, music. Bedrooms are named after composers, you will never be short of a piano to play and there's a huge collection of records. Public rooms are large and comfortable with open fires, parquet floors and plenty of places to retire with a book. Bedrooms, all with their own bathrooms, are similarly comfortable.

££££ *Open all year*

Knowstone

Masons Arms

Knowstone, South Molton, Devon. Tel Anstey Mills (039 84) 231/582

Opposite the church this thirteenth-century thatched pub is a very jolly place. Heavy black beams are hung with a collection of ancient bottles and beside the fireplace is an old bread oven. The owners are very hospitable, as are the locals, and even the dog, Charlie, seems pleased to see visitors. There's plenty of choice with both bar food and more substantial dishes, and the inviting atmosphere makes it worth stopping for a night or two. Bedrooms are varied, with uneven floors and simple cottagey furnishings.

£ *Open all year*

Lewdown

Lewtrenchard Manor

Lewdown, Nr Okehampton, Devon EX20 4PN. Tel Lewdown (056 683) 256/222 Fax (056 683) 332

The Elizabethan creeper-clad manor is a Grade II-listed building and is surrounded by large gardens. The proportions are huge and the new owners are tackling the vast job of refurbishing both the reception rooms and bedrooms. The dark panelling, embossed ceilings and oil portraits can be oppressive in the daytime but in the evening the mullioned windows and huge fires give a splendid atmosphere. Every room has fine features: carvings, painted panels, interesting pictures. Bedrooms are grand and comfortable with modern bathrooms.

££££ *Closed last 3 weeks Jan*

South Molton

Whitechapel Manor

South Molton, Devon EX36 3EG. Tel South Molton (076 95) 3377 Fax (076 95) 3797

It is a difficult place to find so make sure of clear directions from the owners. This extremely attractive Grade I-listed Elizabethan manor house is set slightly into the hill. Pretty tiered gardens stretch down to the parking area hidden below so nothing impairs the view. The house has been painstakingly restored over the last three years: the Jacobean carved oak screen separating the hall from the spacious, comfortable sitting-room is just one example. Bedrooms are attractively furnished, all different, and well equipped. Public rooms are elegant without being formal and John and Patricia Shapland are very welcoming hosts. Food is good and expensive.

££££ *Open all year*

Spreyton
Downhayes

Spreyton, Crediton, Devon
EX17 5AR. Tel Bow (0363) 82378
Guests need to be sociable to
enjoy a stay at Prue Hines's
attractive farm guest-house.
The three rooms, one sharing a
bathroom with the Hines, are
light and pretty with co-
ordinated fabrics and pine
furnishings. There's a
comfortable lounge with TV and
open fire for guests, who all eat
together in the small dark-red
dining-room. It's unlicensed
but guests are encouraged to
bring their own wine.
£ *Open all year, exc 20 to 29 Dec*

Woolacombe
Little Beach

The Esplanade, Woolacombe,
Devon EX34 7DJ. Tel Barnstaple
(0271) 870398
Overlooking Woolacombe
Sands this is one of the row of
hotels on the Esplanade. A
small hotel, it is full of lovely
pieces collected by Brian and
Nola Welling, who used to be
antique dealers. Dinner is
served in the long thin dining-
room, again surrounded by
attractive things including
polished cabinets of china.
Modern bedrooms are
unelaborate with cheerful
chintz, dralon headboards and
white chipboard furniture.
£ *Closed Nov, Dec, Jan, Feb*

Where to eat

For a key to prices see p. 12

Barnstaple
Heavens Above

4 Bear Street, Barnstaple. Tel
Barnstaple (0271) 77960
Vegetarian café with pine
furniture and paintings for sale.
Different hot dish every day at
lunchtime.
[£] *Open Mon to Sat 10–5 Closed
Sun, Christmas and Boxing Day,
Good Fri, Easter Mon*

Lynwood House

Bishop's Tawton Road,
Barnstaple. Tel Barnstaple
(0271) 43695
Attractive restaurant with
rooms (see p. 108). You might
have homemade sausages, fish
soup or an omelette. Good for
lunch or dinner.

[£] *Open all week 12–2 (exc Sun),
7–10*

Bideford
Sloops

Bridge Street, Bideford. Tel
Bideford (0237) 471796
Some unusual grills such as
bananas wrapped in bacon and
some more traditional fare in
this friendly café/bar/
restaurant.
[£] *Open Tues to Sat 10.30–2,
6.30–9 Closed Sun and Mon*

Banks Coffee Shop

16 High Street, Bideford. Tel
Bideford (0237) 476813
An ex-bank, now a simple café/
snack place for pies, quiches
and a daily changing hot dish.

[£] Open Mon to Sat 9–5 (2.30 Wed in winter); extended hours in summer

Bolham

Knightshayes

Knightshayes Court, Bolham.
Tel Tiverton (0884) 259416
A National Trust property with
a very good café/restaurant.
Homebaking and real ice cream.
[£] Open all week April to Oct, 11–5.30 Oct, Nov, Dec Wed to Sun, 11–5.30. Closed Jan and Feb

East Buckland

Lower Pitt

East Buckland, Barnstaple. Tel
Filleigh (059 86) 243
Former farmhouse restaurant
with rooms, adventurous home
cooking.
Open Tues (Mon in summer) to Sat, 7–9

Eggesford

Gardens Restaurant

Eggesford Garden Centre,
Eggesford, nr Barnstaple. Tel
Chumleigh (0769) 80250
As the name suggests, an
informal restaurant at the
garden centre. Choose from
baked potatoes, pies or quiches
and serve yourself with salads.
[£] Open all week 10–6 (5 winter)

Ilfracombe

Whites

12 Beach Road, Hele Bay,
Ilfracombe. Tel (0271) 862821
Home cooking in a cosy
restaurant. Home-baked bread
and lots of sauces.
Open Tues to Sat, 7–9.30

Lewdown

Lewtrenchard Manor

Lewdown. Tel (056 683) 256

Elizabethan manor house
internally decorated in
Victorian/Jacobean style. It's an
original place with delicious
cooking. Snack lunches every
day.
Open all week 12– 2.30, 7.15–9.30

Lynton

Hewitt's

North Walk, Lynton. Tel
(0598) 52293
Overlooking the Bristol
Channel, this Victorian hotel
offers high quality cuisine and
is open to non-residents for
lunch and dinner by prior
arrangement.
Open all week 12–2, 7–9

South Molton

Stumbles

East Street, South Molton. Tel
South Molton (076 95) 3683
Wine-bar in the centre of town;
tasty, reliable cooking.
Open Mon to Sat 12.30–2.15, 7.30–9.30

South Molton

Whitechapel Manor

Tel. South Molton (076 95) 2554
and 3377
Ring up for directions to this
lovely house. A special place for
a gourmet lunch or dinner in
quite a formal dining-room.
Open all week 12–2, 7–8.45

Torrington

Rebecca's

8 Potacre Street, Torrington. Tel
Torrington (0805) 22113
Shop and restaurant with
simple, good cooking; daytime
food cheaper than the dinner
menu.
[£] Open Tues to Sat 12–2, Mon to Sat 7–10 Closed Sun

Weare Giffard

Cyder Presse

Weare Giffard, nr Bideford. Tel
Bideford (0237) 475640
A very busy and popular whitewashed country pub serving
good, filling dishes.
[£] *Open Tues to Sun 12.30–1.45,
7–9.45*

Exeter and East Devon

An area for gentle exploration rather than high activity or beach inertia. The switchback coastline makes fine walking but lacks sandy space until it flattens out at the Exe estuary, with its low-key family resorts and retirement havens. South of the bisecting A30 are pretty river-valley villages and high open heaths; north, fertile farmland and deep lanes, hill forts and hamlets. There are some fine churches, but historic sightseeing is concentrated in Exeter, easily reached and a complete change of key. The city has much dull post-Blitz building but a whole and glorious cathedral, remnants of many centuries and a global collection of boats.

Exeter

More than once in Devon you come across the allegation 'X was a market town when Exeter was furzy down', and indeed not much is known of Caer Isc, the Celtic 'stronghold on the river'. But the Romans installed the Second Augustan Legion in a fortress above this strategic crossing-point of the River Exe, and made their walled frontier town of Isca Dumnoniorum the headquarters and communications centre for the south-west: so it has been ever since. Saxon Exanceaster was defended by King Alfred but twice ravaged by the Danes, and in 1050 Edward the Confessor transferred the bishop's see from undefendable Crediton to make Exeter a cathedral city. After the Battle of Hastings, Bishop Leofric gave sanctuary to the mother of Harold but declared for William the Conqueror, who refrained from punishing the city and entered by the east gate as the queen escaped by the west. Norman Excestre gained Rougemont Castle on its red sandstone hill, and a new cathedral. Exeter's relationship with the English Crown remained a constant: the Semper Fidelis motto bestowed by Elizabeth I saw it through the Civil War with the adaptability of the Vicar of Bray, and it only

drew the line at James II, supporting the Duke of
Monmouth's rebellion before welcoming William of Orange.

While playing the key West Country role in England's
politics, wars and religious upheavals, this was a city of hard
work and corporate pride. As cloth market and mercantile
port it had three rich centuries – by the end of the
seventeenth, Celia Fiennes, that most hard-headed
sightseer, reported: 'It turns the most money in a week of
anything in England.' As industrial competition took over in
the eighteenth century Exeter became more genteel, settling
down from a hum of polite society to a civilised place of
retirement after the Napoleonic Wars; and it expanded
steadily but not dramatically through the railway age, adding
twentieth-century suburbs to Georgian and Victorian
quarters.

In 1942 bombs devastated half the city centre. In 1949 the
future Queen Elizabeth II crossed a totally flattened area to
stand on a modest construction called the Commemorative
Feature – aligned on to the north tower of the cathedral,
which was to be the vista at the end of the new street called
Princesshay – and formally opened the city's rebuilding
programme. This took 20 years and was inevitably
controversial. Modern Exeter starts halfway up the High
Street, and to the south the road system cuts off the city
centre from the river and old quay; a 1970s shopping
development has rearranged a network of old back streets.
But no tall buildings challenge the towers of the cathedral,
which dominate in every view; and its immediate
surroundings were opened up by the removal in 1971 of St
Mary Major, a nineteenth-century church occupying the site
of the cathedral's Saxon predecessor. Now, all its serene
complexities of pale stone can be properly seen across the
grassy expanse within the Close: the heart of Exeter, and
overwhelming reason for a visit.

The outer and inner bypass roads and central one-way
system, which attempt to keep Exeter's traffic flowing, may
seem designed to swirl the motorist straight out again, but
there are ten car parks within a convenient walk of the
cathedral and as many again around the rest of the city
centre. To explore all the interesting bits takes much more
than a day, if only because the Maritime Museum, not to be
missed, is some distance away – and can absorb hours. The
tourist information office is to the north, in the modern part
of town, opposite the bus station; Quay House

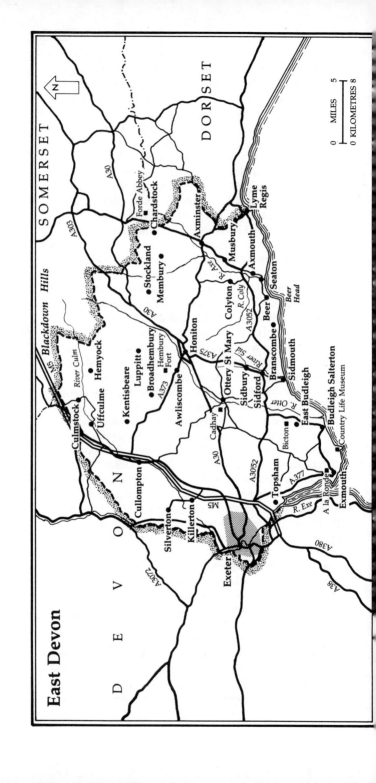

East Devon

Interpretation Centre by the river can also provide some maps and guides.

Exeter Cathedral's Norman towers, massive and straight as fortresses, acquired their pinnacles when the cathedral was transformed into buttressed Gothic, completed with Bishop Grandisson's fourteenth-century image screen of saints and cross-legged kings on the west front. Inside, ribbed pillars of Purbeck marble rise in the central avenue of Gothic vaulting, the longest unbroken span of it in the world. After the first impact of glorious light-filled spaces, the eye is drawn to the delicate screen between nave and choir: apparently there has always been an organ perched on its middle – perfectly placed for acoustics – but the seventeenth-century organ case has an owlish over-importance. Binoculars help in the nave with the coloured bosses and the musical angels of the minstrels' gallery; in the choir, the soaring Bishop's Throne is one superlative of fourteenth-century carving, and the set of 49 bizarre little misericords another; there is old glass, an astronomical clock and extremely handsome tombs.

The Close and Cathedral Yard make up the attractive triangle around the cathedral's green – chestnut trees and Bishop Hooker's statue above ground, and invisible below it the Roman bath-house archaeologists found when St Mary Major was demolished. At the corner a historic jostle of buildings includes the shop which was once Mol's Coffee House, Dutch-gabled in the nineteenth century but otherwise elaborately Tudor; the cramped little red church of St Martin's, its simple nave askew; and the Royal Clarence, the first English inn to describe itself 'hotel', French-style, in 1769. The rest of Cathedral Yard is a pleasant mix of stucco and Georgian, but east, at numbers 10 and 11 The Close, a medieval courtyard house of utter charm can be glimpsed past its archway and great studded door.

In the thirteenth century Exeter's future as a river port was compromised by a weir (or wear) constructed downstream on the Exe. Countess Wear takes its name from Isabella de Fortibus, Countess of Devon, who built it: her grievances against the citizens of Exeter included non-payment of her bailiff's tithes of fish. Soon, ships could come no further upstream than Topsham, which flourished. After nearly 300 years of litigation Exeter got a canal, and the quayside renewed its activity. Now, in the canal basin parallel to the river, and in warehouses and a former fish market, the

Maritime Museum (open daily exc Christmas Day and
Boxing Day, 10 to 5 (6 July and Aug)) collects boats from all
over the world. They are restored by the International Sailing
Craft Association (ISCA) in a huge galleried hall once an
electricity generator, then displayed with a hands-on policy
and a sense of fun. Elegant, exotic, frivolous and ridiculous
craft can be wobbled and sat in; you can compare groups
(ferry, fishing, racing boats), board the colourful medley
moored in the basin, boat yourself about. You can also eat
here in the licensed restaurant, a lofty warehouse room with
mainstream cooking and salads, gingham and candles, and
ships in bottles. On this side of the river there is ample
parking space.

On foot, Exeter's old Quay is reached from the museum or
vice versa by a manual chain ferry that dates from 1750 or by
a new suspension bridge. The latter has much to do with the
urban renewal programme of houses and flats which has
radically altered the view from the quay and the atmosphere
– it can help to reflect that buildings rather than grass and
trees were the old riverside scene. The Quay, since its
appearance (as Liverpool) in television's 'Onedin Line', has
been revitalised with cafés and nightclubs. Beyond the
Prospect pub, the tall warehouses built into the red cliff are
being revamped; antiques and craftwork fill smaller houses.
The Interpretation Centre stresses maritime Exeter, with a
film show in its loft, and the handsomest building is the 1678
Customs House. Boat-trips operate in summer, and you can
walk for miles along the river and canal.

In the centre of Exeter is the city's oldest crossroads, where
High Street and Fore Street, North Street and South Street
meet; the streets formerly ran from the four gates in the city
walls. North-east along High Street, pedestrianised except
for the city minibuses, the literally outstanding building is
the **Guildhall** (open all year, Mon to Sat, 10 to 5, subject to
civic requirements, telephone Exeter (0392) 77888 to check):
its proud Elizabethan frontage spans the pavement. Behind
this, the building itself dates from 1330. Its hall has a fine
timbered roof, and the portraits include Lely's of the princess
Henrietta, presented to the city by Charles I. Other vivid old
buildings – or their narrow frontages – are preserved in this
part of the street. Behind it is the Guildhall shopping centre
of mixed modern pastiche, where the tiny sandstone church
of St Pancras sits isolated in a precinct behind Marks and
Spencer. Queen Street was cut straight through the old

layout in Queen Victoria's time; it offers the **Royal Albert Memorial Museum** (open all year, Tues to Sat, 10 to 5.30), which has fine displays of West Country silver and clocks, and the excellent coffee-house next door. The post-war end of High Street is wide, and its brick buildings dull and horizontal, in contrast to the crowded verticality of the medieval streets, but shrubs and flowers help. Uphill to the north, a Norman gate-tower still stands at the entrance to the civic offices on the site of Rougemont Castle, and **Rougemont House Museum** (open all year, Mon to Sat, 10 to 5.30, plus Sun afternoons July and Aug) holds Devon history. The gardens beyond fill a great defensive ditch made for William the Conqueror, and climb to a stretch of the old walls. To the south, the line of the walls can be followed around the Georgian and floral sweep of Southernhay.

In South Street the fourteenth-century **White Hart Inn** survives, once the first hospitality for arrivals through the great south gate; and there's an oasis of a café (see p. 132), with a garden, behind the fascinating shop Global Village (a branch of a Somerset enterprise); in the old Meeting House hall. Out along North Street the Iron Bridge of 1830 oversails a valley: steps get you down to an under-view of its decorative design in Lower North Street.

Fore Street has some interesting eighteenth-century houses behind drab nineteenth-century shop-fronts, and **Tuckers Hall**, similarly inconspicuous, is a Reformation conversion of the guild chapel of the Tuckers (or Fullers), rich inside with panelling and the original magnificent wagon roof. West up The Mint you can visit the museum in the eleventh-century remnants of **St Nicholas Priory**; parallel to the east, cobbled Stepcote Hill is the picturesque way down to an area desolated both by the Blitz and by modern traffic requirements. Photographers angle out the surroundings as they frame the diverting clock of St Mary Steps church – it has three bright little jacks – and a narrow timbered house which was bodily moved about 70 yards in 1961 to accommodate the new road system. Stepcote Hill was the original route down to the river crossing: a few of the 18 arches of the thirteenth-century bridge can be seen in a grassy dip between the traffic. Underpasses from here assist progress on foot towards the area of the Quay.

Town trail walks literature is widely available, and the information office supplies details of Exeter's many guided tours.

Topsham to Exmouth

About three miles down the Exe by road or riverside footpath, **Topsham** overlooks a peaceful waterscape of moored dinghies and mudflats' birdlife, between the straight-ruled line of the M5 bridge and the marshy estuary inflow of the River Clyst. As a river port Topsham benefited at Exeter's expense from Countess Isabella's medieval weir; most of its buildings date from its three prosperous centuries. The best – often the only – chance of parking in this narrow little town is at the Exeter end. High Street and Fore Street are lined with friendly little shops and antique pubs beginning with the Salutation Inn; Ferry Road along the estuary reveals the warehouses and shipyards of Topsham's busy years as a merchant port. There is hardly an ugly building – the whole town is a conservation area – but the most pleasing part is the Strand, running from the Town Quay to end at a peaceful walk along the sea wall. Here is a row of stuccoed seventeenth-century merchants' houses, built of Dutch bricks brought home as ballast, variously Dutch-gabled and bow-windowed, with many decorative doorways and glimpses of courtyard gardens. At number 25 the little local museum is open three afternoons a week. Time a visit to include a traditional pub lunch – in Topsham you're spoilt for choice among handsome sixteenth-century inns. The Bridge overlooking the river, and the Globe in Fore Street, are both recommended (see p. 134).

Further downriver from Topsham and on the coast is **Exmouth**, east Devon's big family-holiday resort. The town's mass of twentieth-century suburban development has swallowed up local villages among its access roads. Exmouth's great asset is its two-mile-stretch of long sandy beach, unique on a shingly coastline. This is backed up by plenty of attractions and amusements to supplement a bucket-and-spade holiday and keep children entertained on a wet day. From the western point you can take boat-trips up the Exe, and in summer a passenger-ferry goes over the river to Starcross. There is still a working dock area on the river side of Exmouth, rebuilt in the late nineteenth century when the town also got its long sea wall and Marine Drive. East along the sea-front the beach ends at a line of bathing huts under a rocky headland, and the oldest hotels climb in the sea-facing terraces begun in the late eighteenth century.

Exmouth, earliest watering-place in Devon, was rather fashionable then; it was eclipsed by Torquay, which the railway reached first. Exmouth's style became based on family holiday-makers from Exeter and the surrounding countryside, and stayed unchanged as its trade multiplied. Now, respectable small hotels offering weekly terms make up the streets around the town's shopping centre, undistinguished architecturally but pleasant enough with its trees and gardens.

In the northern outskirts, off the A376, the house **A La Ronde** (open 8 April to end Oct, daily exc Fri & Sat, 11 to 6, 11 to 5 during Oct only) is an extraordinary period-piece built for two Devon ladies in 1798 after a Grand Tour abroad; it stayed in the family until early 1991 when it was sold to the National Trust. Sixteen-sided, it sprouts dormer windows in all directions on its grassy eminence; from its 60-foot blind inner octagon a tour reveals eccentric rooms, Gothic passages and a gallery, all densely embellished with the skills and collections of the Misses Parminter – shells and feathers, silhouettes and needlework, sand and seaweed art. At Sandy Bay, three miles east, the big **World of Country Life Museum** (open Easter to Oct, daily, 10 to 5) expands into steam engines, vintage cars and acres of parkland with deer, Highland cattle and llamas – only some of the assorted animals.

Budleigh Salterton to the River Sid

Budleigh Salterton, east of Exmouth, is small-scale and low-key, a quiet resort of the nineteenth century and retirement favourite of the twentieth. It has a traffic-tight main street well stocked with tea-shops, and up a side street the Salterton Arms (see p. 132) for a good pub lunch. Across the roadside stream, a thatched but dignified museum deals with the lower Otter Valley: salt was panned in the river estuary just east. Budleigh's long beach is steep banks of big round pebbles, with fishing boats winched high and heaps of net and lobster-pots. On the Marine Parade a blue plaque marks the house of Sir John Millais, who painted 'The Boyhood of Raleigh' by the sea wall.

On the high ground between the Otter and the Exe, lanes and B-roads reach a fine viewpoint at Woodbury Common. Up the Otter, the church at **East Budleigh** has over 60 carved bench ends of unusually varied motifs, including faces, ships and the Raleigh coat of arms – the future Sir Walter was born a mile west at Hayes Barton, a sixteenth-century manor house, modernised in the late nineteenth century. A bridge crosses to the working water-mill at Otterton; and at **Bicton Park** (open Mar to Oct, daily, 10 to 6) besides a layout of playgrounds and themed attractions, there are acres of parkland and fine Italian gardens which make an elegant contrast with the villages' flower-decked cob and thatch. The Woodland Train, which sounds like a good way of getting around the park, is disappointing. It chugs laboriously along an uninspired track through the arboretum – you could walk it faster.

Sidmouth, like Exmouth, has undistinguished inland suburbs, but once through them you find an old-fashioned resort of considerable charm. Sidmouth is set between sheer red cliffs rising to 500 feet: to the west they break into spectacular erosions at Ladram Bay, to the east their outline is backed by the distant white mass of Beer Head. The 'tide-washed golden sand' of the official guidebook is only evident at very low tide; much of the beach is pebbles, into which at

Cob and thatch

More than any other county, Devon has kept the informal charm of this building combination: steep thatch pulled down over deep-set cottage windows, walls gently irregular, every angle rounded. Cottages all over Devon were built of cob, and in the east until about 1850 so were most farmhouses and parsonages – Walter Raleigh's birthplace, Hayes Barton, is a well-known Tudor example. Thatch needs renewing after about 50 years, but cob walls have survived for centuries – particularly in Devon, perhaps because of the firm local tradition that 'all cob wants is a good hat and a good pair of shoes'.

The 'shoes' were the foundation plinth of stone or rubble masonry, about a foot high and three feet thick. On to this the builders forked the cob, a mixture of local mud and chopped straw, brought to the right degree of semi-wetness by a laborious treading process often performed by cattle. The straw was a binding agent, and, unlike wattle-and-daub construction, needed no supportive shuttering while it was drying, but building was slow: after each foot or so of height the cob wall had to dry out, topped with more straw, before another layer was added. As it dried, the cob was pared and

the fishing-boat end the amiable River Sid disappears after a
pretty east-town passage with a ford and plenty of ducks.
Gentry and aristocracy in search of relaxation at home while
deprived by the Napoleonic Wars of travel abroad first
stayed, then built houses, at 'select Sidmouth'; low-grade
amusements are still at a minimum, though there are plenty
of souvenirs. If the atmosphere was sedate, the architecture
was lively: from Regency Gothic to sympathetic Victorian,
the Esplanade hotels and many houses around the town
have curvaceous gables, sharp leaded windows, fanlights
and porticoes, canopied balconies, plasterwork and thatch.
John Betjeman called the more fantastic combinations 'the
apotheosis of the cottage *orné*'. The eastern side of town has
plenty of small hotels and guest-houses in pretty gardens,
and also holiday flats – Sidmouth's appreciative clientele is
getting younger.

Behind the Esplanade narrow shopping streets form a
triangle before expanding up the High Street, and tall trees in
St Nicholas' churchyard make a tranquil enclave of Church
Street and the town's museum, which has quantities of

---

*smoothed and angled. All depended on the builder's eye: sometimes
on a sloping site a whole building slants a little, and often cottage
walls lean slightly inwards, less thick at the top. The colour of the
local material – red from Devon sandstone, grey and buff from the
clays and shales – can be seen in barns and garden walls, but
habitable buildings were plastered over and protected with limewash in cream or white or brighter tints. This was essential
waterproofing, for if exposed to rain cob would revert to mud. A coat
of tar on the plinth did the same job, and also discouraged burrowing
vermin.*

*The 'good hat' of thatch needed only a light framework nailed to
the building's rafters, and was relatively light – cob could not
support a heavier roof. Traditional 'Devon reed' is actually straw,
usually wheat, in clean unbroken lengths of about three feet – the
modern version is specially grown, and at threshing is protected
from damage by being passed through a machine called a comber,
hence 'combed wheat reed'. It is laid like true Norfolk water reed, the
butts of the stalks forming the exposed surface of the roof; rather
than flowing down over it, rain drips from stalk to stalk until it falls
clear from the overhanging eaves. Water penetration eventually
makes thatch rot, but not all of it is necessarily stripped off during*

Regency prints, Victoriana and old photographs, and offers architectural guided walks around the town. Other attractions include vintage model trains in Field's department store, a repertory theatre, Sunday concerts by the Sidmouth Silver Band, and the 18-hole golf course.

East of the Sid it's several miles before you can reach the sea again by car, but from Salcombe Hill you can walk half a mile of nature trail to the top of the cliffs for a vertical view of Sidmouth. (Approach the edge with caution; the Upper Greensand underlying this stretch of coast is crumbly stuff.)

The Sid is only six miles long and its valley is a distinctive, straightforward drive. The Blue Ball pub at **Sidford** is a good place at which to stop for lunch (see p. 133), but **Sidbury** is the more attractive village, with a couple of cream-tea cafés among its cob and thatch. Under the Norman and medieval church, restorers in 1898 discovered a Saxon crypt. From Sidbury the A375 slants up the steep valley side with brief dramatic green views to Gittisham Hill.

---

repair: under much modern thatch in Devon is a quantity of medieval original, smoke-blackened from a central hearth.

A roof is thatched from the eaves up, stitched or hooked to its bottom framework and its anchoring rods of hazel or willow. The reed is 'dressed' into position with a specially surfaced square board called a leggett. At the top, the roof is finished off with a ridge roll, traditionally fixed with flexible hazel – this is the most vulnerable area, latterly often protected from birds and windy weather with wire netting. Decorative flourishes and 'straw dollies' (often birds or animals) are the whims of modern owners rather than traditional practice.

Thatching thrives in Devon, a skill in continuous use over the centuries, still mastered by apprenticeship and long training, much as it was in the Middle Ages. Time-consuming cob construction inevitably died out when brick became widely available – though Down St Mary got a new cob bus shelter in 1978. Cob and thatch cottages are often individually listed buildings, or protected as contributing to the general character of a Conservation Area. Long and low, settled into comfortable lines under their fresh limewash, they are quintessential Devon.

Branscombe to Axmouth

South of the A3052, two or three narrow roads make their
way steeply towards the sea at **Branscombe**. Too small and
hard to get at to have attracted early development, this
community of sheltered scattered cottages has been secured
since the 1960s by the National Trust, which has provided a
big car park at Branscombe Mouth. The only buildings by the
sea are the old coastguard cottages up a steep track (now a
small hotel; see p. 131) and the Sea Shanty café. Branscombe
is no longer undiscovered, but it is restrained – as is the
homeward procession of walkers' and picnickers' cars
through the little lanes at the end of the day. The village
begins half a mile back with a couple of good pubs (see
p. 132) and an old smithy; flower-smothered thatched
cottages string out along the gentlest of the converging
valleys to the west. The simple, graceful little Norman
church is full of good things, from its oak-beamed roof and
Elizabethan gallery to its eighteenth-century three-decker
pulpit; there are fragments of medieval wall-paintings, and a
graphic monument to a lady of the manor whose 'several
children' by two husbands add up to 20.

The steepest valley road, to the east, is the short cut to
Beer. The name (like bere and beare) implies woods, but the
white cliffs that squeeze Beer are smoothly grass-topped.
Beer Head is the last outcrop of southern England's chalk,
and pale Beer Stone has been prized since Roman times as
building material, soft and very easy to carve ornamentally
when first quarried, hardening on exposure to air. A mile
inland, the complex caverns of the quarry have guided tours.
Beer is a cheerful little resort, pretty and immensely popular,
full of cafés and souvenir shops but still firmly a fishing
village with strong stubby boats beached in the pebbly cove
and trips from the jetty. A vigorous spring accompanies the
long village street – during the drought of 1989 it was the
object of envious discontent as a stand-pipes situation
threatened in Devon – and what little space there is at the sea
is full of accommodating steps and seats, agreeable paths
and viewpoints. A large proportion of the visitors come from
adjacent **Seaton**, and east of the valley you're soon in the
bungalow hinterland of its wide safe bay.

There was once a considerable port here, at the mouth of
the River Axe and the start of the Romans' Fosse Way; but by

medieval times a landslip from Seaton's eastern cliff had begun incurable blockage of the harbour by a bank of shingle. Further east toward the Dorset border and Lyme Regis, three-quarters of a mile of Dowland Cliff split off and sank into the sea overnight, on Christmas Eve 1839; this stretch of dense growth and difficult walking is now known as The Landslip. From a subdued fishing village, Seaton was slowly encouraged into a resort in the mid-nineteenth century. It now has promenade amusements and a sprawl of chalets, and, with none of the dignity of Sidmouth, goes all-out for the family holiday in spite of a lack of sand. The star attraction is its tramway, taking the route, once a railway, up the west bank of the Axe, a river wide and marshy in the stretch behind its narrowed sea exit. From the Axmouth road on the opposite bank there is the bizarre prospect beyond the reeds and birdlife of a narrow-gauge double-decker tram in swaying progress.

The Seaton Tramway terminates at Colyford. West of the Axe and up its own River Coly from Colyford is **Colyton**, a most confident little place, settled by the Saxons in a particularly pretty area of combes and rolling hills, rich in the Middle Ages among manors and prosperous farms. Below its oblong square, complete with town hall, is the extremely handsome church, topped with an octagonal lantern. It's rather distinguished inside, with enjoyable monuments: the small white effigy of Margaret Beaufort, married to one of the Courtenay Earls of Devonshire who owned Colyton (until Henry VIII executed the earl of 1538); and lying back to back, each on an elbow, the coloured figures of John and Elizabeth Pole, prominent in a chapelful of local Poles.

A village now, **Axmouth** was also a big Roman port, and later a market town. It was much burned in the Civil War, suffered with Seaton from the ending of river business, and dwindled finally with the coming of the railway in 1868. It now has a neat sloping street, pretty cottages and some finer houses of the sixteenth and seventeenth centuries; Christ and St Peter painted in the fifteenth, on two Norman pillars of its church; and a thatched inn. Beyond the Axe is some high border country – not the much-adjusted modern border between counties but hill-fort territory of the Iron Age. A chain of forts follows the Axe Valley, two of them in Devon, at Hawkesdown Hill north of Axmouth and at Musbury Castle. **Musbury**'s church, below the hill, has a splendid three-couple monument to the Drake family, not including Sir Francis, whose origins were elsewhere and obscure.

Ottery St Mary to the Dorset border

Westwards from the high ridge crossroads called Putts
Corner, the B3174 drops down to **Ottery St Mary**, a
serviceable little web of a town with much modest Georgian
building, pretty but not picturesque except around its high-
set parish church, one of the finest in England. Bishop
Grandisson, who completed Exeter Cathedral in the
fourteenth century, rebuilt St Mary's too, as a collegiate
church for a community of priests, with a chancel as long as
the nave and a Lady Chapel beyond. Clerestory light reveals
all the fine carved detail, starting with the impact of the
Grandisson tombs, canopied effigies in pale stone between
pillars of the nave. The Dorset (south) aisle, added in the
sixteenth century, is superbly fan-vaulted, and has quirky
little capital-carvings including two owls and an elephant.
Victorian restoration left a north wall covered in a tile mosaic
as ugly as period linoleum, but also set vivid colour in the
east window to splash on the stonework of the Lady Chapel.
The lectern's eagle is a gilded bird with an air of benign
enquiry, presented by Bishop Grandisson; the bishop
appears on a roof boss, and his shield is everywhere.

Samuel Taylor Coleridge has a memorial tablet (profile and
albatross); the poet's father was vicar here, and headmaster
of the grammar school. The river of his birthplace and
boyhood inspired a late bad sonnet: 'Dear native brook! wild
streamlet of the West!' The Otter flows peaceably through
water-meadows down past Tipton St John, which has a
Victorian church, and Newton Poppleford, medieval market
town now main-road village with many thatched white
cottages. Just upstream of Ottery St Mary is **Cadhay**, a Tudor
manor house with a lovely Elizabethan courtyard (open July
and Aug, Tues, Weds and Thurs, plus late May and Aug
Bank Hols, 2 to 5.30). The Great Hall, in the north wing, has
a fine timbered roof thought to be from an earlier house
dated around *c*.1420.

From the south, the view of **Honiton** is one long enticing
swoop straight up to a church. It's a Georgian town on a
Roman road, bypassed and no longer an A30 bottleneck,
pleasant to explore. There are antiques and old books among
its shops, cafés (see p. 133) and coaching-inns, a pottery, and
a market on Tuesdays and Saturdays in summer. Next to the
incongruous but handsome neo-Norman church, built in

1837, is one of the few buildings to survive town fires of the early eighteenth century: Allhallows Chapel (fifteenth century) is now Honiton's crammed and fascinating museum. Its local exhibits include the bones of exotic prehistoric animals discovered in the bypass excavations, and its pride is Honiton lace. Protestant refugees from Brussels and Antwerp to Elizabethan England brought finesse to the cottage industry of east Devon – no more confined to Honiton than Brussels sprouts to Brussels, but sold here, on the coaching-route. It was most in demand in the nineteenth century, and Queen Victoria's £1000 wedding dress was made in Beer and Branscombe. There are demonstrations of its eye-straining labour with patterns and bobbins and pins, and beautiful intricate samples. The Honiton Lace Shop has some too, and sells modern lace.

Down a side alley – the town is not entirely linear, and new shopping arcades are repeating old patterns – the tiny tourist office is particularly well stocked with information on the whole of east Devon and Exeter.

Beyond Honiton is upland country, bisected by the A30 and the upper valley of the River Otter. Hamlets are tiny, the villages far apart, 'sights' few and visitors rare. It's an area to explore in leisurely detail, with a picnic – you may be miles from a pub. To the east, **Stockland** has one (see p. 133), an ancient Church Ale House serving the fifteenth- to seventeenth-century farmsteads scattered around the parish; it also has a tall, graceful church. On the ridge topped with a television transmitter to the south-east, Stockland Great Camp was a formidable hill fort. Only half of it remains, but the rampart rises 40 feet. **Membury** also has a fort, enclosing three acres and with a complex entry route; the fort was probably part of the frontier defences between the Dumnonii of Devon and the Durotriges of Dorset. **Chardstock** found itself in Devon after the border adjustment of 1896; its church was overwhelmingly rebuilt in the 1860s, but its George Inn is thatched and medieval and has an enormous fireplace. A couple of miles further east (in Dorset) is **Forde Abbey**, a twelfth-century Cistercian monastery altered during the sixteenth and seventeenth centuries to a grand country house. Covering over 30 acres, the celebrated gardens of tranquil beauty have their origins in the eighteenth century (garden and plant centre open all year, daily, 10 to 4.30; abbey open Easter to end Oct, Sun, Weds and Bank Hols, 1 to 4.30).

South of Chardstock is **Axminster**, of carpet fame (the business, begun in 1755, has now been revived and welcomes visitors at the new factory near the station). The town has a pleasant layout of curving main street and two squares, and is of very ancient origin but is now mostly respectable nineteenth century. St Mary's parish church on its central green has a fine Tudor porch and gargoyles, and interesting things within, from a beautiful twelfth-century effigy to a modern carpet.

Blackdown Hills

North-west of the A30 and the pastoral upper Otter Valley, the **Blackdown Hills** resume a steeply varied terrain full of viewpoints above the deep lanes. Little Dumpdon Hill near **Luppitt** is a good one, rising to 850 feet and a crowning earthwork. Luppitt, very small, is set among farms mentioned in the Domesday Book. The cruciform church is famous for its Norman font, sculpted with barbaric relish – there is a centaur fighting dragons, and men driving a nail into a human head. Further east, **Hemyock** proves rather dull in spite of the castle enticingly marked on the tourist map, which is the scant remains of a fortified house by the church. **Culmstock** has dwindled since the heyday of the woollen industry along the River Culm – it has an old water-powered mill, converted now to dwellings. Culmstock church keeps a treasure in a glass case, a richly wrought fifteenth-century cope of gold velvet. At **Uffculme**, which was an important woollen centre, Coldharbour Mill has been revived as a working wool museum, and the church is spanned by the longest rood screen in Devon.

At the western edge of the Blackdown Hills on a last high spur – north of **Awliscombe**, whose church also has a remarkable rood screen of Beer stone – **Hembury Fort** is the most important of all the area's forts. It was occupied in neolithic times and reinhabited in the Iron Age, when its ramparts and ditch were built; the Romans made use of it too. There is still much to excavate, and it is unsignposted and difficult to get at on its excellent defensive site; if you are driving from Awliscombe, the A373 traffic labouring up the hill can make turning or stopping impossible. But if you spot the turn, and find the path, a vast view and an immense sense of achievement reward you. Among local villages that take their names from the fort, **Broadhembury** is deservedly much visited: disarmingly pretty and immaculately preserved. Trim thatched cottages and the inn flank a meeting of roads (wide enough for calling coaches), and an avenue of chestnuts leads to the late fourteenth-century church, in which some attractive detail survived the Victorian sprucing up.

Kentisbeare has a church distinguished by its chequer-patterned tower, alternating pale Beer stone with the local sandstone – for this is the edge of 'red Devon' and the Exeter basin. Here too the rood screen spans the church. There are some interesting tombs, and on a capital a carved woolpack and a Tudor ship. The appealing cob-and-thatch building by the churchyard is the medieval priest hall.

Cullompton, across the M5, is a busy little market town – so busy that for parking purposes it is worth knowing that early-closing day is Thursday. Some Tudor houses survived a nineteenth-century fire, in small 'courts' off the long main street, and the town has a grand church rebuilt in its heyday as a woollen centre, in a spirit of competition with Tiverton: the 100-foot tower, rose-red picked out and pinnacled in white, is both trademark and landmark. Inside, the wagon roof is richly carved and coloured above Beer stone arcades and space for 1000 people; coloured screen and Jacobean gallery span its width, and there is some fascinating carving – faces on capitals, and a gruesome oak Golgotha in the fan-vaulted Lane aisle named after its cloth merchant donor.

Towards Exeter, **Silverton** is one of the oldest villages in Devon, Saxon-planned and spacious. The handsome church is fifteenth and sixteenth century, but the older thatched cottages down Fore Street have a shaggy antiquity quite unlike Broadhembury's showpiece row. Back towards the motorway, **Killerton** (open end Mar to end Sept, every day exc Tues, 11 to 6 (5 in Oct)) is east Devon's only National Trust stately home rebuilt as two-storey Georgian for the seventh Ackland baronet in 1778. Very plain from the front, the back of the house shows the many nineteenth-century additions made necessary by the increasing size of the tenth baronet's family. Some of the rooms have rather disconcerting dummy people displaying a costume collection. Close to the house the gardens are Edwardian, and the park rolls into the distance from a steep wooded spur with its own earthwork and a panoramic view.

Highlights

** *A La Ronde, Cadhay, Exeter, Forde Abbey, Topsham.*

* *Axmouth, Beer, Branscombe, Broadhembury, Colyton, Honiton, Sidmouth.*

Where to stay

For a key to prices, see p. 12

Branscombe

The Look Out

Branscombe, nr Seaton, Devon
EX12 3DP Tel Branscombe
(029 780) 262
As its name suggests, The Look
Out is on top of a cliff with
wonderful views over Lyme
Bay and west towards Star
Point. All the good-sized
comfortable bedrooms have sea
views and armchairs in which
to appreciate them; the rooms
are attractively and simply
decorated with modern
bathrooms. Downstairs is
almost open-plan, a low
beamed room with a wooden
panelled grid dividing the
dining area from the sitting-
room. A log fire, lots of
interesting pieces, rugs on
polished flagstones, and good
service – the hotel has a subtle
sophistication but is cosy and
welcoming. A great base.
£££ *Closed mid-Dec to mid-Jan;
rest closed Mon*

Exeter

The Forte

Southernhay East, Exeter,
Devon EX1 1QF Tel Exeter
(0392) 412812 Telex 42717
THFEX G Fax (0392) 413549

Right in the centre of Exeter
close to the cathedral this is a
recently opened Trusthouse
Forte hotel. The Regency style
runs throughout, both in the
architecture and the good-
quality reproduction furniture.
Fabrics, curtains and carpets all
co-ordinate in the public rooms
and the good-sized bedrooms.
In addition to all the usual
facilities it has a health club with
swimming pool, sauna and
solarium. No single rooms were
built so it is very expensive for
the single traveller or business
person. Good leisure-break
prices.
£££££ *Open all year*

Whimple

Woodhayes

Whimple, Nr Exeter, Devon
EX5 2TD Tel Whimple
(0404) 822237
This large white house on the
edge of the village provides
well-thought-out comfort and
service. Large plump armchairs
and sofas in pale colours in both
sitting-rooms, coal-effect fires
and light Muzak create quite a
soporific atmosphere, and the
fairly formal dining-room is an
elegant setting for the seven-

131

course dinner. The bedrooms by contrast are more old-fashioned, furnished with a mixture of pieces, bobble-

fringed curtains and fern wallpaper, and are very homely and comfortable.
£££ *Open all year*

Where to eat

For a key to prices see p. 12

Branscombe
Fountain Head
Branscombe. Tel Branscombe (029 780) 359
Picturesque fourteenth-century inn with plenty of places to sit inside and out. Cosy and relaxed atmosphere. Homemade pies and lots more.
Open all week Mon to Sat 11–2.30, 6.30–11 (2 and 10.30 in winter), Sun 12–2, 7–10.30

Masons Arms
Branscombe. Tel Branscombe (029 780) 235
Fourteenth-century inn, cosy with beams and flagstones; good, traditional English cooking.
[ɛ] *Open all week 12–2, 7–9*

Broad Clyst
Killerton
Killerton House, Broad Clyst, Exeter. Tel Exeter (0392) 881345
Delicious homemade dishes in the attractive café. Fortify yourself with a glass of estate wine.
[ɛ] *Open Mar to end Sept Wed to Mon 11–6 (5 in Oct) Closed one week Easter*

Budleigh Salterton
Salterton Arms
Chapel Street, Budleigh Salterton. Tel Budleigh Salterton (03954) 5048

Good food and a friendly welcome in this neat, comfortable pub. Seafood a speciality.
[ɛ] *Open all week 11–2.30, 5.30–11*

East Budleigh
Grasshoppers
16 High Street, East Budleigh. Tel Budleigh Salterton (039 54) 2774
A small gift shop and cáfe-tea room serving homemade scones, soups, baked potatoes and other snacks and savouries.
[ɛ] *Open Tues to Sat 10–5.30, Sun 2.30–5.30 Closed Christmas Day and Boxing Day, 1st week May and 2 weeks Nov*

Exeter
Café at the Meeting House
38 South Street, Exeter. Tel Exeter (0392) 410885
In the gallery of a converted chapel, lunchtime food is purely vegetarian, fish dishes are added in the evening and salads are always available.
[ɛ] *Open Tues to Sat 11–5, 7.30–9.30, Mon 11–5 Closed bank holidays*

Cooling's
Gandy Street, Exeter. Tel Exeter (0392) 34183/4
Interesting vegetarian selection and good puddings. Open long hours.
[ɛ] *Open all week 12–9.30*

Gallery Café

Exeter and Devon Arts Centre,
Bradninch Place, Gandy Street,
Exeter. Tel Exeter (0392) 219741
Original vegetarian dishes and
lots of salads in the Arts Centre.
[£] *Open Mon to Sat 12–2.30*
Closed bank hols, 2 weeks at
Christmas

Herbies

North Street, Exeter. Tel Exeter
(0392) 58473
Simple decor with pine tables
and chairs serves vegetarian
and vegan food.
[£] *Open Tues to Fri, 11–2.30, 6–*
9.30 Sat 11–4 Mon 11–2.30

Pizza Piazza

44–45 Queen Street, Exeter. Tel
Exeter (0392) 77269
Popular pizza place.
[£] *Open all week 11 am–11.30 pm*

Tudor House

Tudor Street, Exeter. Tel Exeter
(0392) 73764
Oak ceilings and mullioned
windows are only some of the
features of this beautifully
restored building. Imaginative
fish, meat and game dishes.
Open Tues to Sat, 12.15–1.45,
7.15–9.45

Honiton

Honeybees

110 High Street, Honiton. Tel
Honiton (0404) 43392
Quite a cluttered, informal
wholefood café. Mainly coffees,
teas and cakes but it also offers
simple, mainly vegetarian,
lunches.
[£] *Open Mon to Sat 9–5*

Lympstone

River House

The Strand, Lympstone. Tel
Exmouth (0395) 265147
A lovely, peaceful setting by the
River Exe. Good sized portions,
maybe a bit too rich for some.
Plenty of choice.
Open Tue to Sun 12–1.30, 7–9.30
(10.30 Sat)

Newton Poppleford

Jolly's

The Bank, Newton Poppleford.
Tel Colaton Raleigh (0395) 68100
A very comfortable and
attractive setting with sitting-
room and dining-room. Purely
vegetarian with very filling
main courses.
Open Tues to Sat 12–2, 7–9 Mon
7–9

Sidford

Blue Ball

Sidford. Tel Sidmouth
(0395) 514062
Thatched fourteenth-century
inn. A friendly place run by the
same family for over 70 years.
Wide selection of food
including steaks, omelettes and
traditional roasts.
Open all week, Mon to Sat 10.30–
2.30, 5.30–11 Sun 12–3, 7–10.30

Stockland

Kings Arms

Stockland. Tel Stockland
(040 488) 361
A strong emphasis is put on
food here. Lots of choice and
plenty of space in this friendly
pub. You can also sit in the
garden or on the front terrace in
summer.
Open all week, Mon to Sat 12–3,
6.30–11 Sun 7–10.30

Topsham

The Bridge

Elmgrove Road, Topsham. Tel
Topsham (0392) 873862
A charming, old-fashioned
sixteenth-century pub. Popular

with locals. Food is mainly pasties and sandwiches.
Open all week 12–2, 6–10.30 (11 Fri and Sat)

The Globe

Fore Street, Topsham. Tel Topsham (0392) 873471
Attractive and comfortable sixteenth-century coaching inn. Good home cooking.
Open all week 11 am–11 pm

Toppers

41 Fore Street, Topsham. Tel Exeter (0392) 874707
Only one meat dish on offer here; mainly vegetarian with a few fish dishes.
Open Tue to Sun 6.30–10.30 (9.30 Sun), Sat and Sun 12.30–2.30

South Devon

The large sweep of Devon's southern coastline, from Exeter to Plymouth, is the most heavily touristed part of Devon. Most popular are the English Riviera resorts of Torquay, Paignton and Brixham, where the mild climate and traditional seaside atmosphere draw young families and retired couples alike. But Devon's best beaches are further south – Blackpool Sands, Bantham, Bigbury on Sea. Here, too, are bracing cliff walks. Enthusiasts can walk the whole of the South Devon Coast Path, but for the less energetic the stretch between Bolt Head and Bolt Tail provides an impressive introduction. In wet weather the historic streets and museums of Totnes and Dartmouth, in their picture-postcard settings on the Dart, should satisfy, while a trip on one of the steam-powered railways usually appeals to all ages. Salcombe, popular with sailing enthusiasts, and Kingsbridge are small but have an afternoon's worth of charm, while Plymouth provides an excellent chance to learn about some of the great events in English maritime history and do some shopping.

Starcross to Newton Abbot

Heading south from Exeter and Topsham the A379 veers back towards the Exe estuary at **Starcross**. Here, one of the old pumping-houses of Brunel's atmospheric railway has been opened as a small museum (open Easter to end Oct, Mon to Sat, 10–6, Sun 2.15–6; Nov to Easter Sat 10–6, Sun 2.15–6), with an audio-visual show and working display models. Before Brunel's time, locomotives couldn't go uphill very easily unless they were pulled by horses. The railway used the idea of a vacuum to help power the trains. Brunel didn't actually invent the system, but as director of the South Western Railways Board he commissioned the railway to run

South Devon

Dartm
National

Tamar Valley

A384

Tavistock

Morwellham Quay

River Tavy

Yelverton

River Plym

■Buckland Abbey

River Tamar

A386

CORNWALL

A38

Plymouth

A38

A379

**Newton
Ferrers**
**Noss
Mayo**

Bigb

Bigbury-on-Sea

Burgh Island

Bant

Thurles

H
B
T

| 0 | MILES | 5 |

| 0 | KILOMETRES | 8 |

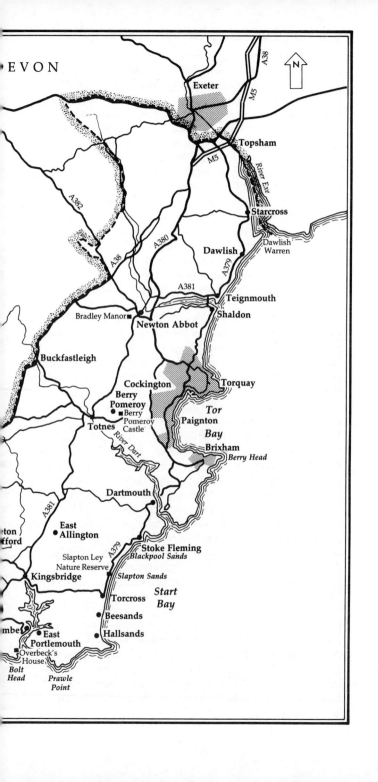

between Exeter and Newton Abbot in 1847. Anxious to persuade a parsimonious board that the idea was worth pursuing, he underestimated the budget required, and then tried to save money by using smaller pipes and leaving off the protective weatherproof plates. Unfortunately, the smaller pipes didn't work – resulting in 25 miles of customised pipeline having to be scrapped – and the lack of weatherproofing meant that the leather seals cracked, letting in air and ruining the vacuum system. Further trouble was caused when the whale and seal oil applied to the leather to keep it soft attracted rats, some of which were sucked into the vacuum and landed up in the engine room! Despite the problems, when the system worked it was very effective, with trains reaching speeds of up to 70 miles per hour. In the end, however, the setbacks and cost were seen as being greater than the advantages, and the railway was closed down.

It's difficult to believe as you approach, but **Dawlish Warren**, right at the mouth of the Exe, is a 505-acre nature reserve. Stretching beyond the mass of caravan parks, holiday centres and amusement complexes at the mainland end is a double sand spit one and a half miles long. Although the area was declared a bird sanctuary in 1934, this didn't stop RAF bombers using the beach for target practice during the Second World War. Today, as well as about 180 species of birds, the dunes support 450 types of flowering plants. The local council organises guided nature walks featuring various aspects of the wildlife.

Dawlish itself is centred on a long grassy park through which the Dawlish Water flows in a series of sedate, stepped falls to the sea. Mallards and moorhens bob and dabble, while black swans glide more gracefully past the bowling green. You reach the sandy beach by passing beneath the red, green and gold arches of the Victorian railway bridge. Notable past visitors drawn by the town's attractions have included Jane Austen, John Keats and Charles Dickens, who made it the birthplace of Nicholas Nickleby.

Keats also visited **Teignmouth** on his travels, a fact commemorated by a plaque at 20 Northumberland Place in the western part of town. Keats was not the only Victorian to find the air congenial; the Den, an area of sandy waste-ground given to the town by the Earl of Devon in 1869, was soon laid out with lawns and gardens, and became the fashionable place to be seen promenading. Backed with turreted Victorian guesthouses, B&Bs and coffee houses, the Den overlooks Teignmouth's long beach of coarse red sand and the modern pier, which looks rather like a clump of mobile homes on stilts. The original Victorian pier, shortened in the 1960s when part of it was discovered to be unsafe, was once used to segregate male and female bathers.

The busy port area is tucked away west of the bar that lies across the mouth of the estuary, and is easy to miss. Thanks to a thriving trade in ball clay, used by potters, Teignmouth is not wholly dependent on fishing and tourism, though the days when Dartmoor granite was shipped from here to build the British Museum or London Bridge have long gone, and the last shipyard closed in 1968.

A wooden bridge linking Teignmouth with **Shaldon**, just across the water, was first built in 1827, but in 1838 it was found to be full of shipworm and had to be closed for three years. Today's road bridge is more sturdy, but a passenger-ferry from the Harbour Beach at Teignmouth still operates (in season only), landing visitors on Shaldon's red pebble-strewn sand. **St Peter's Church**, right next to the Shaldon end of the bridge, has a splendid barrel roof in granite, supported by flying buttresses. The architect Edmund Sedding originally intended the church to have a tower, but the weight would have been too great for the foundations. The interior has a lovely chancel screen of Gothic tracery and carved figures of the Virgin Mary and four saints. The pulpit, in black, pink and grey marble, is surrounded by ornately carved Beer stone columns, while a white marble John the Baptist holding a clam-shell forms an unusual font.

From the church a walk along the river takes you past pretty cottages and private conservatories decked with hanging baskets, and into a labyrinth of Georgian houses centred on a triangular bowling green. In the past local fishermen used the green as a drying ground for their nets, while the grand houses were the homes of wealthy traders and ships' captains. Today, on every Wednesday during the summer, the green becomes the venue for '1785 day', when the villagers dress up in Georgian costumes and set up craft markets.

From the village you can walk or drive up to **the Ness**, a red sandstone headland with a long smugglers' tunnel leading to an attractive sheltered beach at the bottom. At the top is Ness Farmhouse, a peaked cottage with dishevelled thatch where Nell Gwynne is supposed to have stayed for a few days. Shaldon Wildlife Trust (open Easter to end Sept, daily, 9 to 6; end Sept to Easter, daily 10 to 4), a breeding centre for rare and endangered species, is also here.

At the head of the Teign estuary, **Newton Abbot**'s position made it a natural junction for both railway and road systems. As a town serving the needs of local people rather than as a tourist attraction in its own right, Newton Abbot is well known for its markets: general market on Wednesdays and Saturdays with cattle also on Wednesdays, and antiques all day Tuesdays in East Street. The fourteenth-century tower of St Leonard's Church (the rest was pulled down last century) now stands on a traffic island.

Just outside the town, **Bradley Manor** (open April to end Sept, Wed 2–5; a couple of Thursdays in April and Sept), owned by the National Trust, is a fifteenth-century manor house with white gables and oriel windows. The great hall contains a Renaissance screen and the walls are emblazoned with Queen Elizabeth I's coat of arms.

Torquay to Totnes

Torquay, at the northern end of the wide sweep of Torbay, is the main resort of the English Riviera. Stacks of hotels and guest-houses streaming over the rocky contours testify to the popularity of Torquay's mix of classy shopping centres, family fun and balmy atmosphere – yes, those palm trees along the front are real. The beaches of coarse red sand are not as good as those at Paignton, but the pretty harbour buzzes with yachts and motorboats, offering cruises and fishing-trips. In Victorian times, the town 'built to accommodate invalids' offered special temperature-controlled baths (hot, tepid, vapour, shower and cold) at the end of the pier for those not healthy enough to enter the sea itself. Its gentility exasperated Rudyard Kipling, who described it as 'a place as I do desire to upset it by dancing through it with nothing on but my spectacles. Villas, clipped hedges and shaven lawns, fat old ladies with respirators and obese landaus . . .'.

Earlier inhabitants were probably less genteel. **Kents Cavern**, one of the oldest human dwelling places discovered in Britain, was excavated by the chaplain of Torre Abbey, Father John MacEnery, after being shown the caves by his friend Thomas Northmore in 1825. During his four years of digging and exploration he discovered hundreds of bones of animals long extinct in England, including mammoths, bison and rhinoceros, as well as flint tools made by prehistoric man. After his death his results and findings were lost for several years, and it wasn't until 30 years later that his achievements were recognised and he was proclaimed a pioneer in the scientific excavation of caves. His work was continued in 1865 by William Pengelly, a founder member of the Torquay Natural History Society, who discovered a fragment of human jaw complete with teeth embedded in a stalagmite. Today Kents Cavern can be visited on a 45-minute guided tour (open April to Oct, daily, 10 to 6 (9 in July & August exc 6 Sat)). The skulls of the bear and other animals are quite interesting (though the best findings are in Torquay museum), but the stalactite and stalagmite formations are less impressive.

Torquay's other well-known sight is the square, ivy-covered **Torre Abbey**, set back from the beach behind a putting green. It was founded in 1196 by a group of Premonstratensian monks from Welbeck Abbey, following the order of canons established at Prémontré in France in 1120, and attracted trade and commerce as well as caring for the sick and the poor. After Henry viii's dissolution of the monasteries, the abbey was left to decay until in 1598 the Ridgway family converted some of the remaining buildings into a private family home. In 1662 the property was bought by the Cary family, who became associated with the place for the next 250 years, and remodelled it in Georgian style. Torre Abbey (open end Mar to Nov, daily, 10–6) is now used by the local council to display its art collection, which includes a lovely bust of Othello by Calvi and *The Children's Holiday* by William Holman Hunt. The magnificent tithe barn in the grounds is rumoured to be haunted by the ghost of the 'Spanish Lady', a young Spanish lieutenant's fiancée who disguised herself as a sailor so that she could travel with her love on the ill-fated Armada expedition. They were both captured and held prisoner in the barn, where she fell ill and died, but he recovered and returned to Spain. Her ghost, it is said, can be heard crying and sobbing for her lost love.

Cockington village, on a hill above Torquay, is a clutch of immaculate thatched cottage 'shoppes', with horse and carriage rides along leafy lanes adding to the carefully cultivated old world atmosphere. Even the most modern addition to the village – the Drum Inn designed by Sir Edwin Lutyens – was built to blend in with surroundings. The plain white Cockington Court, set amid rolling grounds, was the ancestral home of the Carys before they moved to Torre Abbey; it now houses a tea-room. The small church has an unusual Renaissance pulpit carved with cherubs bearing elephants' ears and rams' horns.

South along the coast, **Paignton** tends to live in the shadow cast by Torquay's exuberance. Paignton's beaches are better – wide, with finer red sand and not so much of the gritty shingle that makes its appearance around Torquay – but the town itself offers less in the way of entertainment and nightlife. Those opting for a civil marriage, however, might prefer Paignton, for the council offices are housed in **Oldway Mansions**, former home of the Singer family. (You can look around the ground floor and glimpse into the upstairs ball room and registry if no ceremonies are taking place.) Isaac Singer's original mansion of 1874 was a yellow-brick villa, but his son altered it in a style more associated with Versailles than with seaside Devon, giving it a sweeping Italianate marble staircase, ceiling frescoes and a gallery of mirrors. The Paignton Room on the ground floor has old sewing machines, watercolours of Paignton and other memorabilia.

At the other extreme, Kirkham House is a plain, sparsely furnished example of a late medieval stone house, restored in 1960. Nearby, St John's Church has an elaborate chantry, carved with figures of Nicholas Kirkham and his family as well as the Twelve Apostles and other saints. In the churchyard the pink sandstone Coverdale Tower is all that remains of the old palace of the bishops of Exeter.

One of south Devon's two steam railway lines, the **Paignton and Dartmouth Steam Railway** (open Mar, Easter, Nov, Sun; April, May & Oct, Tues, Thurs & BHs; June to Sept, every day 10.15 to 5; Dec, Santa specials) – the other is the South Devon Steam Railway (see p. 144) – runs between Paignton and Kingswear. The seven-mile trip along the coast, with views of Goodrington Sands, wading herons and Dartmouth Naval College, gives you a taste of what travel was like in the days of the Great Western Railway. The coaches are painted in the old GWR colours of cream and brown, but can be quite a squash, with jostling parties of excited schoolchildren. It's better to pay a small amount extra and sit up front in the Devon Belle observation coach, behind the engine. From the leather seats you can watch the clouds of steam billowing from the engine funnel and hear the hooter blowing.

Heading east from Paignton along the A385 towards Totnes, it's worth taking a slight detour to see the romantic remains of **Berry Pomeroy Castle** (open Easter to end Sept, daily, 10–6), sited slightly outside the village of Berry Pomeroy itself, above the Gatcombe valley. There's little unusual about the approach to the angled towers of the gate-house, but the medieval walls hide the remains of a Renaissance mansion and loggia, added by Edward Seymour, uncle of Edward vi, when he bought the castle from the Pomeroys in 1547. His execution in 1552 meant that his designs remained unfinished, and in 1690 the castle was abandoned altogether.

The ruined castle at **Totnes** (open end Mar to end Sept, daily, 10–6; Oct to end Mar, Tues to Sun, 10–4; closed 1 Jan and 24 to 26 Dec) is rather older – a classic Norman motte and bailey straight out of a primary-school textbook. Intending to intimidate the townspeople, the Normans could have saved themselves the trouble, as Totnes – unlike Exeter – surrendered without a blow. Strategically, however, building the castle was undoubtedly a good move, commanding as it does a good view of the town, the surrounding hills and the River Dart. From the castle medieval Fore Street slopes steeply down to the river. The weather-boarded Butterwalk, a gallery supported by pillars with shops beneath, got its name from the days of open-air markets when butter had to be kept in the shade to stop it from melting. Further down, the castellated white and blue arch of East Gate, which marked one of the three medieval entrances to the town, was destroyed by a fire in September 1990 and is now under restoration. You can still, however, climb up to the ramparts to visit the sixteenth-century Guildhall (open April to end Sept, Mon to Fri, 10 to 1, 2 to 5), where the panelled council chamber is still in use.

Further down Fore Street the **Brutus Stone** commemorates a local legend that Totnes was the first place where Brutus the Trojan set foot when he colonised Britain: 'Here I stand and here I rest and this good town shall be called Totnes.' The **Elizabethan Town House Museum** (open Easter to end Sept, Tues to Sat, 10 to 5.30, Sun 2 to 5, October to Easter Tues to Sat 10 to 4.30) retains its original frontage (many of the other Tudor buildings on Fore Street were refaced with weatherproofing during the nineteenth century, disguising their earlier origins). It has an interesting collection of artefacts, including a set of false teeth carved out of ivory, and an exhibition on Charles Babbage, who invented a prototype computer and was a pupil at the local Edward VI grammar school.

At the bottom of the hill a stone needle monument commemorates William Wills, a local explorer who with Robert Burke was the first to cross Australia, but died of starvation on the return journey. The quayside around the bridge has been redeveloped in recent years, with old warehouses converted to shops, cafés and riverside apartments, but boats still ply the river with cargoes of timber. Across the bridge is the **Totnes Motor Museum** (open Easter to end Oct, daily, 10 to 5.30), two floors of displays of children's pedal-cars, racing cars, and an amphicar for crossing the river. Next door, from the steamer quay, you can take a cruise down the river to Dartmouth. Alternatively, the **South Devon Steam Railway** runs steam trains on a circular route from Buckfastleigh. You don't need to be a railway buff to enjoy the trip, which takes you on a journey of about seven miles along the scenic Dart Valley.

Just north of Totnes, the **Dartington Cider Press Centre** (open all year, Mon to Sat, 9.30 to 5.30; mid July to mid Sept, Sun, 9.30 to 5.30) sells various crafts, including pottery seconds by Janice Tchalenko, crystal and glass, knitwear and toys.

Brixham to Kingsbridge

The third of the resorts on the English Riviera, **Brixham** is better known for its fishing fleet than for beach holidays. Sheltered by Berry Head on the southern curve of Tor Bay, the small harbour contains a replica of Sir Francis Drake's *Golden Hind*, looking rather incongruous amid the bobbing fishing vessels and leisure cruisers. A rather ugly statue of Prince William of Orange overlooks this busy medley, marking the spot where he landed in 1688 to lay claim to the throne from James II. The harbour is lined with amusement arcades and shops selling the usual paraphernalia associated with seaside holidays – shellfish, ice-cream, fish and chips, shellcraft and bright pink rock – while the gloomy tanks of the aquarium contain a few miserable-looking fish. The British Fisheries Museum, charting the times when Brixham was the foremost fishing port in the West Country, has been closed until further notice.

East of Brixham, **Berry Head** has the remains of a coastal fort built during the Napoleonic Wars; the closest Napoleon ever got to England was when he was kept in the *Bellepheron* moored off Berry Head in 1814. The area is now a nature reserve, with breeding colonies of sea-birds returning every year to nest in the limestone cliffs.

South of Brixham the road forks; either route will get you to **Dartmouth**, by the higher or lower car ferry. Whichever you choose, the short trip across the Dart gives you a chance to admire the proud lines of Britannia Royal Naval College and the jumbled tiers of neat white houses rising above the river. The steep wooded valley with its deep-water harbour made Dartmouth a favourite port for both assembly and defence: the English contingent of Second and Third Crusades left from here, and 800 years later 480 vessels sailed for the Normandy beaches. Twin castles, on either side of the mouth of the estuary, watch over the anchorage; in the fifteenth century a chain could be drawn up between them as defence. **Dartmouth Castle** (open Easter to end Sept, daily, 10 to 6; Oct to Easter, Tues to Sun, 10 to 4; closed 1 Jan, 24 to 26 Dec) was one of the first castles to be designed for artillery, with proper gunports rather than just enlarged arrow slits, though the artillery itself was still fairly primitive: guns were strapped down on flat wooden beds rather than mounted on wheeled carriages. The fort was used as a Royalist garrison during the Civil War after Dartmouth, having declared for Parliament, was captured by Prince Maurice. Two earthwork forts built at this time above the castles on either side of the harbour show how military engineering had progressed, allowing wider fields of fire.

In Dartmouth itself, **Bayard's Cove** by the lower car ferry was another small fort built at the beginning of the sixteenth century with artillery in mind. The Pilgrim Fathers, in their ships *Mayflower* and *Speedwell*, called in here in 1620, but had to return to Plymouth when the *Speedwell* sprang a leak. In more recent times the cobbled courtyard was used as another location for the television series 'The Onedin Line'.

The steep-sided valley that made Dartmouth such an attractive defensive port was less of an advantage to the merchants during the town's seventeenth-century heyday. Eager to cash in on increasingly lucrative business with the New World, the merchants found that lack of flat land meant they were unable to expand as much as they wanted. Their solution was extensive land reclamation; much of the lower part of the town, including Foss Street and the market place, was once a muddy pool. The labyrinth of streets in this area now contains art galleries, craft shops, yacht chandlers and classy restaurants. The wonky, half-timbered Butterwalk overlooking the moored yachts of the Boat Float contains the Dartmouth Museum, with displays of model ships and other historic exhibits.

Further up the hill, where the river's edge used to be, the half-timbered pub, The Cherub, built in about 1380, is Dartmouth's oldest remaining building. Nearby St Saviour's Church, rebuilt during the seventeenth century, has some lovely ironwork doors with leopards' heads, and an eighteenth-century hand-pumped fire engine hidden behind a curtain. The unusual Jacobean pulpit is carved with roses, fleurs-de-lis and a portcullis.

From Dartmouth the A379 runs south to meet the coast at Stoke Fleming, with views of small, sandy, secluded coves. The closest of these is **Blackpool Sands**, a popular stretch of dark golden beach where windsurfing and canoeing are on offer. Despite the name, the endless stretch of **Slapton Sands** is a raised bank of mostly shingle, protecting the reedy marshes and 1000-year-old fresh-water lake behind, part of Slapton Ley Nature Reserve. A stone obelisk commemorates the fact that Slapton Sands was used for target practice by American troops in 1943 and 1944 when preparing for the D-Day landings. Because live ammunition and bombs were used, 3000 local people were given six weeks to evacuate their homes, many of which were destroyed. The training was not without loss for the troops either. An American convoy accidentally ran into a group of German E-boats out in Start Bay, and two American craft were torpedoed and sunk, with the loss of 749 men and their armoured vehicles. A Sherman tank in the car park commemorates the unhappy incident.

Beyond Torcross, at the southern end of Slapton Sands, you can join the South Devon Coast Path, but drivers wanting to explore the southern extremity of Devon are faced with a web of twisting, single-track roads. **Beesands** has a coarse shingle beach and a few fishing cottages. **Hallsands**, now consisting of a hotel and a couple of cottages, was once a thriving fishing community of 37 houses. It was destroyed by a series of severe winter storms in 1917; dredging operations in Start Bay 15 years earlier are believed to have caused the beach-level to drop by 13 feet, thus destroying the village's natural protection. From here, the bay curves east to end at the lonely white lighthouse on **Start Point**, where in Elizabethan times captured pirates were hung in chains as a warning to the crews of passing ships.

At **Prawle Point**, Devon's most southerly spot, a tiny white lookout clinging to the cliffs looks down on the series of small coves scooped out by the waves. Westwards, the frond-like inlets of the Kingsbridge estuary are really a series of flooded valleys. **East Portlemouth** may be a poor relation of Salcombe across the estuary, but its small sandy beach is better – and less crowded – than anything Salcombe has to offer. Although the distance between East Portlemouth and Kingsbridge at the head of the valley is only about three miles as the crow flies, the convoluted route that wends its way round the creeks of the estuary, crossing at least one ford, almost triples this.

Kingsbridge itself has a hilly main street with narrow cobbled medieval passages running off it, delighting in names like Squeezebelly Lane. The town is small enough for the Victorian town hall to double up as the cinema and theatre; next door is the Shambles, a row of covered shops and cafés similar to the Butterwalks of Dartmouth and Totnes. St Edmund's Church behind has an interesting tombstone of 'Robert commonly called Bone Phillip', who made a living by charging a penny to act as a scapegoat: 'Here lie I at the Chancel door, Here lie I because I'm poor, The further in the more you'll pay, Here lie I as warm as they.'

Kingsbridge's **Cookworthy Museum** open April to Oct, Mon to Sat, 10.30 to 5, housed in an old grammar school, is named after the local William Cookworthy who discovered a way of making English hard-paste porcelain, a secret that in the eighteenth century was still only known by the Chinese. He had teething problems: some of his glazes were thick and rather lumpy, or became stained or tinged during firing, and difficulties with the mixing of raw materials led to spiral wreathing or stretching in thrown items. The museum devotes one room to Cookworthy and has an interesting selection of agricultural implements, Victorian and Edwardian toys, and a reconstructed pharmacy.

Although the town mill no longer exists, you can still see one of the two leats that used to provide the water-power. The western stream runs beside the Western Backway path, bridged by slabs to allow people access to and from their

147

gardens. The eastern stream, which used to run beside the Eastern Backway, has been directed under ground because of problems with flooding.

Salcombe to Newton Ferrers

Popular with the yachting fraternity because of its sheltered site, **Salcombe** is also a favourite place for a family holiday. The waterside walkways and jetties are crowded with sailors and landlubbers alike, with lots of blue guernseys and yellow wellies in evidence. Children fish for crabs with weighted lines and nets; adult tastes can be satisfied by more sophisticated fishing tackle and boats for hire. The busyness of the narrow streets, crammed with antique shops, art galleries, yacht chandlers and houses the colour of sugared almonds, means that parking outside the town centre is a good idea, even if the walk down to the harbour is a bit steep.

For non-sailors, Salcombe has a couple of beaches at South Sands and North Sands, though neither is very large; East Portlemouth is better. It's also a good area for walks: the South Hams Group of the Ramblers Association publishes a booklet, *17 Country Walks Around Salcombe*, with maps of suggested routes.

The ruins of Fort Charles, on an outcrop near North Sands, represent the last Devonian outpost of Royalist resistance during the Civil War. For four months Sir Edmund Fortescue and his troops held out against the siege, so impressing the Parliamentarians that when he finally did surrender he was allowed to march back to his mansion at East Allington with full honours.

From Salcombe a very narrow winding road leads up to what must be one of the best sited museums and gardens in the country at **Overbeck's House** (Museum open Easter to end Oct, daily, 12 to 5; garden open all year, daily, 10 to 8, or sunset if earlier). Otto Overbeck, the research chemist who originally owned the house, believed that he had invented an electrical rejuvenator that could tone and cure 'all illnesses . . . with the exception of malformation and germ diseases'. One such machine is on display in the house, together with a varied collection of exhibits reflecting Overbeck's other interests, such as a German polyphon, or clockwork musical box, commemorative china and stuffed animals and birds. It's the terraced garden, however, that steals the show, with

exotic palms and banana trees testifying to the mildness of
the climate. From the picnic spot at the top of the garden
there are dramatic views over the estuary.

The five miles of cliffs from **Bolt Head** to **Bolt Tail** ('bolt' is
Anglo-Saxon for 'arrow') provide no shelter for ships in
distress, and many have come to grief here. Among them
was the *Herzogin Cecilie*, a Finnish clipper that hit the Ham
Stone near Soar Mill Cove in 1936. She did not, however,
sink immediately, and was towed round to Starehole Bay in
the hope that she could be saved. But further storm damage
put an end to that, and on a still day you can still see her
shadowy remains in the water below Sharp Tor.

Tucked in behind Bolt Tail, the small sandy cove of **Hope**
was so called because it offered the first shelter along this
troublesome stretch of coast for seamen in distress. For
some, however, such hope proved to be false or premature –
the only Armada galleon wrecked in England came to grief
here in 1588. Tales of the discovery of silver coins dating
from this period buried in the small sandy cove may account
for the enthusiasm of the sandcastle builders, but most
visitors come simply to soak up the sun on the beach or to sit
outside the thatched pub enjoying a drink. There are also
exhilarating cliff walks to Bolt Head or west to Thurlestone
on Bigbury Bay.

Thurlestone, with its long sandy beach and golf course,
gets its name from the arched rock that lies just offshore (the
Saxon *thyrl* means pierced). In 1772 the *Chanteloupe*, on the
way home from the West Indies, was wrecked here. One of
the passengers, a Mrs Burke, dressed herself in her finest
clothes and jewellery in the hope that any rescuers would be
impressed by her wealth and try even harder to save her. She
hadn't, however, reckoned on the avarice of the locals: when
she was washed ashore her fingers were hacked off to get at
her rings, her ear-rings were torn out of her ears, and her
body was buried on the beach. Today's Thurlestone seems
infinitely more civilised, with pretty gardens and thatched
cottages, though the attractive church was once used as a
storage depot by smugglers.

Reached from Thurlestone by a very narrow undulating
road, **Bantham**'s undeveloped beach sits at the mouth of the
Avon estuary. It's a beautiful area, though the views of
Burgh Island and the surrounding hills sometimes covered in
buttercups and grazing cows tend to be ignored by the sun-
seekers stripping off and sizzling between the dunes. The

beach has fine golden sand – but watch out for warning signs about bathing at low tide. The sixteenth-century Sloop Inn, once the haunt of local smugglers, offers local seafood as well as the usual basket meals for those who forget to bring a picnic.

Easy as it looks to swim across from Bantham to Burgh Island or Bigbury-on-Sea when the tide is out, it's not recommended: the currents and distance are deceptive. The only safe way is to take the long way round, backtracking to Aveton Gifford and climbing back up the other side of the valley through Bigbury itself to reach **Bigbury-on-Sea**. When the tide is out it's possible to walk over the sandy beach to Burgh Island, where a signpost pointing towards the mainland reads 'England 282m'. (If the tide is in, a curious contraption known as a sea tractor operates.) Once known as St Michael's Rock, **Burgh Island** is probably best known for its hotel (see p. 157), originally built by millionaire Archibald Nettlefold as a personal hideaway for entertaining his friends. Its art deco glory has now been restored, and it's worth a visit just to peek at the peacock dome ceiling, Lloyd loom chairs and etched glass uplighters. Famous guests have included Agatha Christie, who wrote some of her books here, Noël Coward and the Duke of Windsor and Mrs Simpson.

The only other building on the island is the fourteenth-century Pilchard Inn, notorious meeting-place for thieves and smugglers in years gone by. Most notable of these was the Elizabethan Tom Crocker, who was shot dead by a revenue officer after a life of wrecking, plundering and smuggling. Today it's a popular pub (see p. 159). Pilchards provided a more honest living for local fishermen until the mid-nineteenth century; at the island's highest point are the ruins of the Huer's Hut, from where a hue and cry would be raised when frothing shoals of pilchards were spotted in the surrounding waters.

From Bigbury-on-Sea it's more backtracking on the B3392 to skirt the Erme estuary and arrive at the twin villages of Newton and Noss, as they're known locally. **Newton Ferrers** is a peaceful fishing village sloping down to the bank of the Yealm. Rows of whitewashed cottages decorated with hanging baskets overlook the river, home of another yacht club. A precarious-looking wooden walkway across the river, usable when the tide is out, leads to **Noss Mayo**, with groups of palm trees and a church containing an art nouveau chancel.

Plymouth to Tavistock

Plymouth, almost completely flattened by German bombers during the Second World War, sits strategically at the junction of four estuaries: the Tamar, the Tavy and the Lynher to the west and the river Plym to the east. The Royal Devonport Docks in the Tamar are still the navy's main port, and Plymouth's successful post-war recovery means that it's developed into the south-west's largest conurbation. Imaginative planning makes it a shopper's delight: Armada Way – a large pedestrianised precinct – leads from the station to the Hoe, surrounded by a ring road with plenty of car parks.

Probably the best place to start is on the **Hoe**, the great limestone ridge separating Plymouth's harbour from the city centre. A peculiar cross between a park and a military drill ground, the Hoe has always been used as an open space by Plymothians. Sheep and cattle used to graze here, and up to Elizabethan times two giant figures carved in the turf – Gog and Magog – were regularly kept in trim. Now the grassy expanses are broken up with large war memorials, though Francis Drake also has his place, with a statue of the great Elizabethan and a bowling green. **Plymouth Dome** (open all year, daily, hours are seasonally adjusted. Closed 25 Dec), right on the sea-front, traces Plymouth's maritime and wartime history, with a particularly good audio-visual presentation on Drake's circumnavigation of the world, the voyage of the Pilgrim Fathers and James Cooke's exploratory forays – all started from Plymouth.

Just behind the dome rises the red and white **Smeaton's tower**, the third Eddystone lighthouse, which was moved from the reef to the Hoe in 1882 when its foundations were undermined by the sea. The Eddystone Reef, lying 14 miles out to sea, was a hazard to shipping before the first lighthouse, with a beam of 24 candles, was built in 1698. But only five years later a violent storm swept away both the lighthouse and its builder, Henry Winstanley. A second lighthouse, made of granite and wood, was constructed by John Rudyerd in 1711, but this was destroyed by fire in 1755. The lighthouse-keeper, too, was killed after swallowing some molten lead as it fell from the lighthouse cupola. Leeds engineer John Smeaton pioneered the use of waterproof cement and interlocking masonry in his lighthouse, completed in 1759 with a candlepower of 67. The fourth lighthouse, designed by Sir James Douglass, was built on an adjacent rock and still stands today, with a candlepower of 570,000. On a clear day you can just make out the Douglass lighthouse flashing twice every ten seconds.

Closer at hand, a smaller lighthouse stands at the western end of the **Breakwater**, built to protect Plymouth Sound from the gales that used to ravage the harbour. In the centre sits a derelict island fort, part of Palmerston's plan in the 1860s for a circle of forts surrounding Plymouth; at the eastern end a six-foot hollow globe of gun-metal sits on top of a beacon.

During the Civil War Plymouth, a staunch supporter of the Parliamentarian cause, was much coveted by the Royalists for the safe anchorage it offered. Despite several hard-fought battles, the Royalists never managed to take Plymouth, and

Sir Francis Drake

Drake of Chatham? The pairing sounds unlikely, particularly to natives of Tavistock. But although Francis Drake was born in Devon, just south of Tavistock, in 1541 or 1542, his family moved to Kent when he was seven or eight. Here the young Francis, one of 12 boys, lived on a boat and received his first training in how to pilot a barque.

In his early twenties Drake moved back to Devon, where he used his connections with the famous seafaring Hawkins family to get taken on as a junior officer in their merchant fleet. A couple of skirmishes with the Spanish, combined with Drake's strongly Protestant upbringing, sharpened his hostility towards Spain, and he soon turned to privateering. With the unofficial blessing of Elizabeth I, who received her share of the spoils, Drake's raiding and plundering of Spanish ships made him one of the richest men in the West Country.

In 1577 Drake embarked on another challenge – to sail through the Straits of Magellan to discover the unknown continent believed to lie beyond. Despite a near mutiny, attacks by South American Indians and the loss of one of his ships in a severe storm, Drake's Golden Hind *succeeded in passing through the Straits to reach the Pacific, whereupon he wreaked havoc on the Spanish settlements around the Peruvian coast. Finally, unable to carry any more*

when the monarchy was restored Charles II had the massive granite **Royal Citadel** built east of the Hoe, as a symbol of the lack of royal trust. The guns pointed at the town as well as out to sea, just to remind the townsfolk who was in power. The citadel is now the home of 29 Commando Regiment Royal Artillery.

From its battlements you can look down on **Sutton Harbour**, where the English fleet massed before attacking the Armada. Several stone tablets commemorate, among other events, the colonisation of Virginia in 1584, the homecoming of the Tolpuddle Martyrs in 1838 and the landing of the first transatlantic flight in 1919. But pride of place goes to the Pilgrim Fathers, whose embarkation point is marked with a pillared arch and fluttering British and American flags. **Island House**, a white gabled building on

---

treasure, Drake headed home again, not through the North-West Passage as originally planned but right across the Pacific, through the Spice Islands and round the Cape of Good Hope. Nearly three years after he set out, he rolled triumphantly into Plymouth, the first Englishman to circumnavigate the world. Honours and a knighthood followed, and Drake settled down for a while at Buckland Abbey, former home of the Grenville family. Not that he was idle: as a favourite of Elizabeth, he was expected to attend court regularly, and he also had duties as mayor of Plymouth and MP for Bossiney, in Cornwall.

But probably Drake's most famous achievement was his victory over the Spanish Armada in 1588. Many Devon towns sent ships to join the English fleet, even Tavistock, an inland town. The Spanish ships were cumbersome and slow, and Drake's original plan was to sail out and meet the Armada off Spain, instead of waiting for the Spanish to come to England. But unfavourable winds forced him to return to Plymouth for fear of missing the Armada altogether. Finally, in July 1588, the first Spanish ships were sighted in the Channel, and the message was passed to Drake, who was playing bowls on Plymouth Hoe. Owing to contrary winds and tides, he was unable to sail immediately: the English fleet did not leave Plymouth until that night.

Although a couple of battles ensued, and Drake disabled and captured one of the prize Spanish ships, the Rosario, *the Spanish were in fact defeated not so much by Drake and the English as by the*

---

the corner of the harbour, is where they are supposed to have stayed before their voyage; a board lists the names of the 150 who made the 67-day trip.

Behind the harbour is Plymouth's historic quarter, the **Barbican**. The tiny Saxon fishing village on the north side of the harbour expanded during the Middle Ages as the fishing trade increased, and extended further south as Elizabethan merchants built themselves fine houses along Southside and New Street. Its cobbled medieval streets escaped the bombs of the Second World War, and the mixture of Elizabethan houses, timber-framed shops and pubs, and converted warehouses makes it an interesting area to explore. The Elizabethan house on New Street has a pole staircase made out of a ship's mast, while further along is a small Elizabethan garden, with knot and rose gardens and herb

---

weather. More than a third of the Armada fleet was shipwrecked by storms on the coasts of Scotland and Ireland. The English throne was in any case saved and Drake became a national hero.

As a local resident, one of his most notable achievements was to build a leat (a waterchannel) to bring fresh water from the River Meavy high on Dartmoor down to Plymouth. Little more than a ditch six feet wide, the leat nevertheless ran for 17 miles and was completed in only four months by a workforce of 35. Drake himself dug the first turf in December 1590; the following April he was leading the celebratory opening, with wine, feasting, trumpeters, and guns firing salvoes as the sluice gates were opened. The story goes that Drake was so excited that he leapt on to a white horse and galloped along the leat bed, ahead of the water, all the way to Plymouth. By the time word of this reached the Spanish, who already credited him with supernatural powers, Drake had apparently uttered magic words over a Dartmoor spring, which then followed him and his horse back to Plymouth!

Drake's later seafaring expeditions were not so successful. An operation to take Portugal from the Spanish ended without achieving its goals or a profit. His final voyage, to the Caribbean, was plagued by disease among the crews and hindered by better Spanish defences. Drake's cousin Sir John Hawkins, co-commander of the fleet, died early on from dysentery, and on 28 January 1596 Drake followed him. He was buried at sea in a lead coffin.

borders. An old monastery at the end of Southside Street is now home to the **Black Friars Distillery**, one of the manufacturers attracted by the soft-water springs that emerge in this area. You can visit the premises (open April to end Sept, Mon to Sat, 10.30 to 4) to see how gin is made.

Closer to the modern shopping centre, two other old buildings escaped the bomb blast of the Second World War. The **Merchant's House** (open all year, Tues to Sat, 10 to 5.30, Bank Hol Mon, 10 to 5; Easter to Oct, Sun 2 to 5) is the best example of Tudor architecture in Plymouth: an oak-timbered, gabled building originally constructed in the sixteenth century but altered and embellished by William Parker, a Plymouth privateer who shared Drake's penchant for raiding Spanish treasure fleets. So successful was he that he was later made mayor of Plymouth. The house is now a museum of local history, with exhibits arranged according to the old rhyme 'Tinker, Tailor, Soldier, Sailor', with the Beggarman being replaced by an Apothecary.

Just round the corner is the even older **Prysten House** (open April to end Oct, Mon to Sat, 10.30 to 4) built in 1490 by Plymouth merchant Thomas Yogge. The Bishop's Room contains an old bishop's chair made from the ends of medieval pews, while off the central galleried courtyard is a small room containing the 'Finewell' – a limestone hole that was the inhabitants' water-source before Drake built his leat bringing water from Dartmoor. Neighbouring **St Andrew's Church** is a largely post-war reconstruction, but has six interesting stained glass windows designed by John Piper, one of which was given by the Astor family, who lived locally. Finally, north-east of the centre, **Plymouth City Museum and Art Gallery** (open all year, Tues to Sat, 10 to 5.30, Sun 2 to 5) has examples of Cookworthy's English hard-paste porcelain (see p. 147) and a collection of portraits by Joshua Reynolds donated by William Cotton.

Just south-east of Plymouth with part of the grounds overlooking the River Plym, **Saltram House** (house open Easter to end Sept, Sat to Thurs and Fri, 12.30 to 6; October, Sun to Thurs, 12.30 to 5; gardens open on the same days at 11) is worth a visit. A large pale cream and white house, it was built in the sixteenth century and added to in the eighteenth. John Parker commissioned Robert Adam to design the saloon and dining-room, and they remain two of the best-preserved Adam interiors in the country. An interesting collection of pictures includes several portraits by

Joshua Reynolds, and after you've admired the interior you can walk past the sparkling white orangery and up the magnificent lime avenue.

From Plymouth the A386 heads north up to Yelverton and Dartmoor National Park. It's worth turning off before Yelverton to visit **Buckland Abbey** (open Easter to end Sept, Fri to Wed, 10.30 to 5.30; October, Fri to Wed, 10.30 to 5; Nov to Easter, Sat & Sun, 2 to 5), a Cistercian monastery that became home to Sir Richard Grenville and later, Sir Francis Drake after the dissolution of the monasteries in 1539. The highlight is the great hall, with plasterwork satyrs supporting the ceiling and scenes of retired knights, installed by Grenville. Drake, by contrast, seems to have left little impression on the building, but his drum, banners from the *Golden Hind* and portraits of the great sailor with Queen Elizabeth I are on display in the Drake Gallery. The Great Barn, bigger than the abbey church itself, impresses by its sheer size.

Drake was born less than five miles away from Buckland Abbey, at **Tavistock**. The original statue of the town's most famous son (locals are quick to point out that the better-known statue at Plymouth is only a copy) stands a little way out of town overlooking the canal. Tavistock's importance grew during the thirteenth-century 'tin rush', and it became one of the four stannary towns in Devon, where people came to weigh, stamp and sell tin from the Dartmoor mines. In the seventeenth century the declining tin industry gave way to a prosperous wool trade, which in turn was replaced by copper mining. It was at this time that a canal linking Tavistock to Morwellham, on the Tamar, was dug, mostly by French prisoners of war. **Morwellham Quay** is now a visitor centre, with tableaux of copper mines and costumed actors playing the parts of quay workers. Tavistock life today centres on the pannier market, hidden behind the castellated walls of the Gothic town hall. Both the town hall and the Bedford Hotel were erected in the nineteenth century by the Dukes of Bedford, whose fortunes had been made from the copper mines.

Highlights

** *Dartmouth, Dart Valley Railway, Salcombe, Shaldon, Totnes.*

* *Buckland Abbey, Burgh Island, Cockington, Dawlish, Plymouth.*

Where to stay

For a key to prices, see p. 12

Bantham

Sloop Inn

Bantham, Nr Kingsbridge, Devon TQ7 3AJ. Tel Kingsbridge (0548) 560215/560489
This cosy, cheerful, sixteenth-century inn is only 300 yards from a lovely beach. It has a strong nautical atmosphere created by imaginative use of wood – one of the bars rests on what looks like a ship's hull. Wooden chairs and tables spread across the shiny flagstoned floor of the beamed seating area, with a few more comfortable chairs tucked into a corner. Popular with locals as well as trippers, it serves excellent seafood and there's a choice of à la carte or bar food. Bedrooms, although plain and fairly small, have all the modern facilities. Self-catering accommodation is also available.
£ *Closed mid-Dec to mid-Jan*

Bigbury-on-Sea

Burgh Island

Bigbury-on-Sea, Devon TQ7 4AU. Tel Bigbury-on-Sea (0548) 810514. Fax (0548) 810243
A very special and unusual

hotel which, as the name suggests, is on an island. If you arrive at high tide, a sea tractor takes you through the water from the mainland. Built in the 1930s the house is kept brilliant white with a green roof. Inside is like entering an art deco time-warp. Tony and Bea Porter set about restoring it to its original glory in 1985, finding a perfect setting for their own art deco collection. Decor, furniture and atmosphere are all in keeping; and all bedrooms are suites. Depending on your fellow guests, it can be a very theatrical experience. The price includes dinner.
£££££ *Open all year*

Dartmouth

The Royal Castle

11 The Quay, Dartmouth, Devon TQ6 9PS. Tel Dartmouth (0803) 833033. Fax (0803) 835445
In an excellent position overlooking the harbour, this unusual and pleasant hotel was originally four separate Tudor houses, now linked by a glass roof and staircases. The restaurant on the first floor overlooks the boats and specialises in seafood; you can relax with coffee in the cosy

157

library. Bedrooms are priced according to the view rather than the size – some are very small – and are attractively furnished.

£££ Open all year

Dittisham
Fingals

Old Coombe, Dittisham, Dartmouth, Devon TQ6 0JA. Tel Dittisham (080 422) 398. Fax (080) 422 401

A very peaceful setting in the Dart Valley although only three miles from Dartmouth. Richard Johnston runs his hotel and restaurant in a very relaxed, sociable way. Guests are encouraged to fraternise and usually all eat at one big table. He used to run a restaurant in London and the food is of a high standard. The sixteenth-century house with a Queen Anne façade has been well restored and stylishly furnished and decorated. The library/sitting-room is spacious and comfortable, and the panelled dining-room and snooker room give the place a traditional feel.

££ Closed New Year to Easter

East Portlemouth
Gara Rock

East Portlemouth, Nr Salcombe, Devon TQ8 8PH. Tel Salcombe (054 884) 2342. Fax (054 884) 3033

Originally built in the 1840s as a coastguard station, this hotel has wonderful views along the cliffs and out to sea. It is a happy, informal place very much geared to families, with games rooms, pools and a tennis court; in summer there's organised entertainment for both children and adults and the beach is just a few minutes down the steep cliff path. Decor and furnishings are lived-in rather than stylish, with candlewick covers in the bedrooms. Self-catering accommodation is available at the rear of the hotel.

££ Closed Nov to Easter

Kingsbridge
Buckland-Tout-Saints

Kingsbridge, Devon TQ7 2DS. Tel Kingsbridge (0548) 853055. Fax (0548) 856261

This attractive Queen Anne manor house is in a secluded spot with wonderful views across the hills. There are fine, well-proportioned rooms with ornate plasterwork and marble fireplaces. Staff are young and friendly, and the food is exceptional, though expensive. Bedrooms vary in size but none is cramped and the furnishings are all well co-ordinated. A very civilised place to stay.

££££ Closed Jan

North Huish
Brookdale House

North Huish, South Brent, Devon TQ10 9NR. Tel Gara Bridge (054 882) 402/415

This peaceful country house hotel used to be the rectory. A Grade II-listed Tudor Gothic-style building, it has been sensitively maintained, with moulded ceilings and many other original features, and luxuriously furnished. The atmosphere is very civilised without being formal and you can settle down in the comfortable sitting-room or the small panelled bar and enjoy the quiet. The bedrooms are all different, all comfortable, and

have everything you might want during a stay here.
£££–££££ *Closed 3 weeks Jan*

Salcombe

Tides Reach

South Sands, Salcombe, Devon TQ8 8LJ. Tel Salcombe (054 884) 3466. Fax (054 884) 3954
This is very much a seaside hotel, with many leisure facilities – indoor and outdoor sports, games room, salon etc – and its position is superb, just across the road from a sandy bay on a lovely part of the coast. The colour schemes are predominantly blues and greens, and with the lush jungle-like fabrics the place feels exotic rather than West Countryish. Some of the bedrooms, all done in different colours but favouring jungly greens, blues and apricots, are a bit overwhelming. In the top-floor bedrooms you can escape on to your balcony. Following a more Mediterranean style, the main sitting-area is incorporated with the lobby and has a huge window with views straight out to sea. It is a place for action rather than sedentary pursuits.
£££££ *Closed Nov to Feb*

Where to eat

For a key to prices see p. 12

Burgh Island

Pilchard

Burgh Island. Tel Kingsbridge (0548) 810344
You can see the sea from the snug bar in this twelfth-century inn. Meals and snacks served most of the day. Bookings only for seafood and salad bistro in the evenings.
Open Mon to Sat 11 am–11 pm

Dartington

Cranks

Dartington Cider Press Centre, Dartington. Tel Totnes (0803) 862388
Self service vegetarian food. It can get very busy in summer.
[£] *Open Mon to Sat 10–5, all day Sun in summer*

Dartmouth

Cherub

11 Higher Street, Dartmouth. Tel Dartmouth (0803) 832571
Fourteenth-century pub with very good seafood.
[£] *Open all week 12–2, 7–10; bar 11–3, 5–11*

Kingsteignton

Old Rydon Inn

Rydon Road, Kingsteignton. Tel Newton Abbot (0626) 54626
Lovely old inn with a walled garden. Choice of Chinese and Indonesian dishes as well as more traditional dishes.
Open all week Mon to Sat 12–2, 7–10; bar 11–3, 6–11 Sun 12–3, 7–10.30 Closed Christmas Day

Lifton

Arundell Arms

Lifton. Tel Lifton (056 684) 666

Very charming creeper-clad inn. Light lunches may include mussels or toasted stilton.
[£] *Open all week 12–2.30 Closed 4 to 5 days over Christmas*

Modbury
Modbury Pippin
35 Church Street, Modbury. Tel Modbury (0548) 830765
Well-cooked local produce in a family-run restaurant.
Open Mon to Sat 12–2, 7–9.30 (exc Mon winter) Closed Jan

Paignton
Natural Break
75 Torquay Road, Paignton. Tel Paignton (0803) 524771
Café on the main road serving wholefood such as homity pie and vegan bake.
Open Mon to Thurs 12–3, Fri and Sat 12–3, 7–10

Plymouth
Clouds
102 Tavistock Place, Plymouth. Tel Plymouth (0752) 262567
Simply decorated restaurant with good choice of vegetarian and ordinary dishes.
[£] *Open Mon and Tues 12–2, Wed to Sat 12–2, 7.30–10*

Kurbani
1 Tavistock Place, Sherwell Arcade, Plymouth. Tel Plymouth (0752) 266778
Exotic, cheap food; a choice of vegetarian dishes too.
Open all week 12–2.30, 5.30–11.30

Training Restaurant
Plymouth College of Further Education, Kings Road, Devonport. Tel Plymouth (0752) 385186

Very good value and plenty of choice provided by the catering students.
Mon to Fri 12.15–2.30, Tues to Thurs 7.15 (one sitting) Closed Sat, Sun and college hols

Yang Cheng
30A Western Approach, Plymouth. Tel Plymouth (0752) 660170
Chinese restaurant serving authentic Cantonese dishes.
[£] *Open Tues to Sun 12–2.30 (3 Sun), 6–11 Christmas Day and Boxing Day*

Torcross
Start Bay Inn
Torcross. Tel Kingsbridge (0548) 580553
Popular inn specialising in fresh fish.
[£] *Open all week 11.30–2, 6–10, Sun 12–2.30, 7–10.30*

Torquay
Mulberry Room
1 Scarborough Road, Torquay. Tel Torquay (0803) 213639
Attractive furnishings in a simple little café.
[£] *Open Wed to Sun 12.15–2.30, Sat 7.30–9.30*

Totnes
Willow Wholefood Vegetarian
87 High Street, Totnes. Tel Totnes (0803) 862605
A very 'green' place with organic ingredients and wholemeal flour used whenever possible.
Open Tues to Sat July to Sept, Oct to June Wed, Fri, Sat 10–5, 6.30–10. Closed 2 weeks Christmas

Yelverton

Buckland Abbey

Buckland. Tel Yelverton
(0822) 855024
Generous helpings of
nourishing food served in what
used to be the Old Monk's guest
house. Plenty for vegetarians.
Open all week, Fri to Wed 12–2
Closed Nov to 31 Mar

Dartmoor

Dartmoor, the largest of the granite upland masses forming the backbone of the south-west peninsula, offers the sharpest of contrasts. There is the great moor itself, a plateau sloping south to north with the highest points rising over 2000 feet above sea-level; while to the east is a superb blend of upland and lowland: beneath the wind-blown wastes lies an intricately folded landscape of verdant slopes and clear rivers within deep gorges, sunken lanes and villages sleeping beneath thatched roofs.

Throughout the region, eroded rock outcrops known as tors punctuate the wastes and often provide exciting viewpoints. Formed of hardened magma, the tors have surprising individuality – block-like chunks, pinnacles, pillars and buttresses, much grooved by the effects of Ice Age freeze-thaw weathering. Evidence of prehistoric occupation is scattered everywhere, but today this is the largest unpeopled area in southern England – a bleak expanse, much of it bogland with a distinctive, eerie beauty of its own.

Since 1951 Dartmoor has been a national park, with visitor information centres at Bovey Tracey, New Bridge, Okehampton, Princetown, Postbridge, Steps Bridge and Tavistock. This is principally an area to experience the outdoors, although scenic drives along unfenced roads can be highly rewarding – keep a lookout for traffic-oblivious sheep and Dartmoor's famous ponies. Some 2500 ponies, all cross-bred since 1918 when alien stallions were introduced (true Dartmoor ponies are found only on stud farms), roam wild but all are privately owned, and in autumn some are rounded up for sale.

Organised sightseeing opportunities are very limited: there is Castle Drogo house, castle ruins at Lydford and Okehampton, museums at Ashburton and Okehampton, and *animal attractions near Bovey Tracey, Buckfastleigh and Moretonhampstead. But Dartmoor offers wonderful walks that range from rambling along river banks or up to a nearby tor, to solitary treks over pathless (and often boggy) moors. Or you can explore the moor on horseback; there are plenty of stables offering mounts for all ages and levels of experience for details, contact local information centres, pp. 322–25).*

Bovey Tracey to North Bovey

The national park headquarters and a visitor centre are on the edge of **Bovey Tracey**, a cheerful if uneventful town just outside the south-east corner of Dartmoor's boundary; from here a number of routes make inroads into the national park. To the east, one road rises abruptly to the foot of **Haytor**, the boldest and most visited tor in Dartmoor. If it appears hostile from below, there is nothing unfriendly about the gentle grassy track up to the top, where there is an enthralling view over the south Devon coast around Teignmouth, the South Hams near Totnes, and eastern Dartmoor in the other direction, with Hound and Honeybag tors prominent in the foreground. Other grassy tracks around Haytor were once track-beds for tramway lines built in 1820 to serve the granite quarries which supplied the stone for London Bridge and the British Museum, among other buildings. The quarries were deserted by 1860 and you can now only walk along the seven-mile track.

From Bovey Tracey, the B3344 takes a wayward and sluggish route, passing **Parke Farm**, (open Easter or beginning April to end Oct, daily, 10 to 5), where there is a collection of rare farm breeds. The entrance to **Yarner Wood Nature Reserve** soon appears on the west side of the road: from a car park inside the wood, two nature trails lead around the site (descriptive leaflets are available). It has been managed by the Nature Conservancy Council since 1952, and is worth visiting for its woodland (birches and oaks predominate) and moorland plant, insect and bird life. Pied flycatchers, once a Devon rarity, have been successfully encouraged to nest here. Back on the main road, views dramatically open out almost immediately north of Yarner Wood at **Trendlebere Down**. You can park here to admire the natural wonders of the deep gorge carved out by the River Bovey, densely wooded but edged on its far side by a

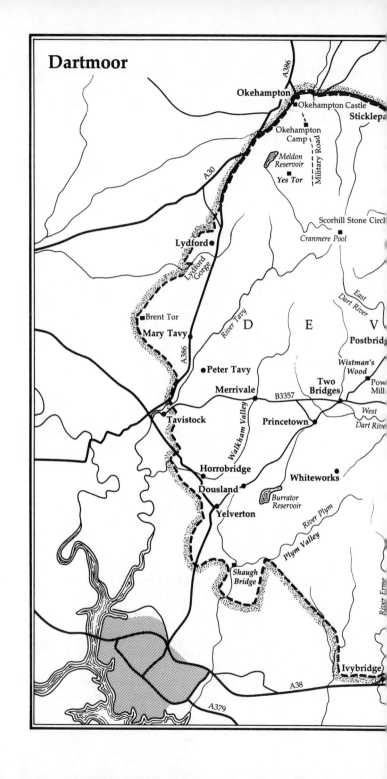

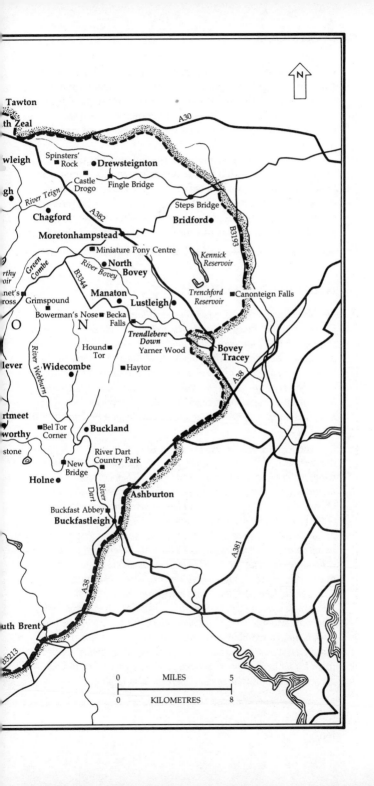

fine moorland ridge capped by the outcrop of Sharpitor. It's a considerably greater spectacle for much of the year than nearby **Becka Falls**, which can dry up to a mere dribble in summer; the falls are approached by following the well-trodden path from Dartmoor's most expensive car park (£1.50).

A mile on from Becka Falls lies the village of **Manaton**, bypassed and secluded beside a long green. Look inside its spacious church for a fine carved screen; Cromwell's men defaced what they could but failed to obliterate the screen's charm completely. The church crouches below Hayne Down, with **Bowerman's Nose** in profile, a natural rock, 20 feet high

Man and the landscape

The influences of man are found even in the emptiest tracts of Dartmoor's 365 square miles. Early prehistoric activity consisted of summer visits by foragers, who came here to hunt and left flint and chert tools as evidence of their visits. Neolithic people were the first to settle permanently, and although their villages have not survived some chamber tombs, built for multi-occupation, can be seen: the best-known examples of these are Spinsters' Rock near Drewsteignton and the remoter site on Corringdon Ball north-west of South Brent.

Settlers in the Bronze Age (1,800 to 800 BC) brought with them metal-making skills and streamed the tin-rich gravels of the moors – using water to extract the surface deposits. They left stone monuments, some clustered in sites such as Shovel Down (west of Chagford) and the upper Plym Valley, others spread across the rest of the moor. Many of them are marked on Ordnance Survey maps, but to find them can be far from easy, since they are often overgrown to the point of invisibility and even those that aren't tend to be camouflaged among the sheep. About 60 instances of stone rows exist – consisting of single, double or triple lines of granite boulders – thought to be processional routes to burial places; the most remarkable is a single row, Europe's longest, stretching two miles from Stall Moor to Green Hill above the Erme Valley. In the Bronze Age the dead were often buried in mounds or cairns; about a hundred cist tombs – burial sites containing stone coffins, each intended for a single occupant and originally covered by mounds – are scattered across Dartmoor. There are also 12 stone circles,

and unmistakable for its likeness to a human caricature; it immortalises a local man who hunted on the Sabbath and was said to have been turned to stone for his sins. If you venture up to this granite portrait, you are likely to be drawn to **Hound Tor** along a lane to the south, whose shattered rock piles make up one of Dartmoor's most memorable features. The view from its summit epitomises the extraordinary blend of scenic elements found on the eastern side of the national park – gentle, green fertility side by side with startlingly severe tors and barren wastes. South-east (towards Greator Rocks, the next group of outcrops), a few hundred yards off, lie the remains of a medieval village,

---

thought to have been erected for a religious or ritualistic purpose; Scorhill Circle near Gidleigh is the only one not to have been restored. Dartmoor's hut circles, dating from the second millennium BC, were originally round structures consisting of a wooden frame supporting a turf and heather roof on a low wall of granite boulders. The number of known sites goes into thousands – Grimspound (north of Widecombe) being the outstanding example – although few are more than dark patches in the vegetation. Boundary banks, or reaves, denoted land allocations within a community or family, and can still be traced in places.

A worsening of the climate around 1,000 BC led to the gradual desertion of the higher lands, moorland vegetation took over again, and the moor was never intensively reoccupied. On the eastern fringes, the Saxons built churches on Celtic sites and renamed villages to reflect a change in administration. In medieval times Dartmoor became a royal hunting forest; some farms were established and 'newtakes' of land enclosed by landowners.

The major activity in the Middle Ages was tin streaming and, from the sixteenth century, mining, with Dartmoor becoming the richest source of tin in Europe. By the late nineteenth century, however, foreign competition was bringing about the decline of the industry, and the last mine closed in 1930. The legacy of this busy mining past is all around, including the remains of about 50 blowing-houses, where tin was smelted, besides numerous gullies, shafts and spoil-heaps. Fine examples of dry-stone granite 'clapper bridges', erected over rivers in medieval times to enable packhorses to carry the tin in all weathers, survive at Postbridge, Dartmeet and Bellever.

Tavistock, Plympton, Ashburton and Chagford prospered as medieval stannary towns, where tin was brought to be officially

---

excavated in 1960 – with an English Heritage explanatory sign making identification easier than at most archaeological sites in the area. A series of tiny stone-walled enclosures comprises 11 buildings, including three longhouses (long dwellings for both humans and animals) and outbuildings, with fireplaces and entrances discernible. They represent the final stage of occupation, *c*.1200–1350, and may have been built on dwellings of Dark Age origin, perhaps dating to the eighth century. Mixed agriculture was carried out here – cereal-growing as well as stock-rearing; why the village was

weighed and stamped. Whiteworks and Eylesbarrow (both near Princetown), Birch Tor (near Warren House Inn) and Holne Moor were some of the main mining areas in the last century. Water channels, or leats, constructed to carry water to the mines, mills and farms (and to the entire town of Devonport), can still be seen on the moor. Cuts made through the bog to enable hunters and farmers to cross the moor, and numerous boundary markers, are among further superimpositions.

Since 1951 the National Park Authority has had the responsibility of balancing the interests of conservation, residents, landowners and visitors. Common land today accounts for 94,000 acres of the area, much of it owned by the Duchy of Cornwall – the major landowner along with the Ministry of Defence, the Forestry Commission and water authorities. Ministry of Defence ranges cover most of the northern moor, and many people feel that it's time the army moved out. Dartmoor is the only national park in Britain where the area of broad-leafed trees exceeds that of conifers, but the sizeable conifer plantations of the Forestry Commission interrupt the emptiness of the moor quite rudely. Several of the plantations have been developed for leisure use, offering sheltered walks and picnic spots – an attraction for some visitors, an alien intrusion for others. Reservoir building has meant that Dartmoor now supplies two-thirds of Devon's water; two man-made lakes have been created since national park designation. The waters have popular appeal – Burrator and Meldon reservoirs are particularly attractive – both for trout fishing and other leisure activities. But conservationists rue the loss of wildlife habitats, archaeologists the disappearance of prehistoric sites, and purists the over-taming of parts of the landscape.

abandoned is not known, although the Black Death (1348–50) may have been responsible.

North Bovey, north of Manaton, is an unspoilt delight; its narrow lanes have kept out the invasions of tourists who flock into its more accessible neighbour Widecombe. A rectangular green shaded by oaks is surrounded by thatched cottages, seventeenth century and earlier; the Ring of Bells tavern, plus the village pump, mounting-block and ancient stone cross, complete the picture. A depiction of three rabbits chasing each other on a roof boss in the chancel of the church is thought to be an emblem of the tin-miners, who financed the rebuilding of many churches in the district; the collection of regilded roof bosses is worth some neck-craning and also includes some royal heads, said to represent Edward I and his wives Eleanor and Margaret.

Lustleigh to the Teign Gorge

Lustleigh lies just west of the A382, with its church on an island site between stone-walled lanes and everything else sloping one way or the other. At the village's heart is a thatched and yellow-washed tea-room called Primrose Cottage (see p. 185), a mecca for connoisseurs of cream teas, and a pretty pub called the Cleave. A path descends to the brook where you may find water-spiders dancing on the surface – or a stray cricket ball from the adjacent ground – and where admiring visitors photograph the pretty back gardens. The church has undergone thorough Victorianisation but has a good screen made in the time of Queen Mary and a fine chancel arch. Here too is one of only four inscribed stones found in Devon churches, the Latin legend commemorating a 'Datuidoc, son of Continoc' and dating from the fifth or sixth century.

North-east from Lustleigh the scenery is secretive and pleasantly rolling, although not of major interest; **Trenchford**, **Tottiford** and **Kennick Reservoirs**, built 1861–1907 to supply Torbay, are sombre places surrounded by conifers. Woodland walks have been laid out starting from the car park by Trenchford Reservoir, while access to the other waters is for trout-angling only. **Canonteign Falls** (open Easter to Nov, daily, 10 to 6; Nov to Easter, Sun, 10 to 4) to the east is much the highest waterfall in the National Park; the estate in which it is located has been developed into a small country park, with a woodland walk and a junior commando course, so to see it means paying a substantial admission fee. Further north is little-visited **Bridford**, a straggly village with an old centre huddled around the church, of interest for its early sixteenth-century painted screen. Unusually, it does not depict saints but everyday folk, one of them dancing and lifting his robe to reveal a leg; although the faces were damaged in Cromwell's time, this is still considered to be the best rood screen in Devon, with its colours particularly well preserved.

The River Teign defines the eastern boundary of the national park but the celebrated **Teign Gorge** is further north – about six and a half twisting miles of delectable scenery from Steps Bridge just south-west of Dunsford to Castle Drogo. The gorge's densely wooded slopes of mixed coppice and the river itself provide a rich habitat for wildlife: dippers, kingfishers and pied wagtails by the riverbanks, buzzards high above; carpets of daffodils in the woods in spring followed by wood anemones and bluebells; and numerous mammals, among them fallow deer, mink and, exceptionally, otters. Roads scarcely give a glimpse of the beauty of the gorge, its precipitous fringes and shady salmon pools, but a level path follows the river all the way, with easy access at **Steps Bridge** and further west at the ever-popular **Fingle Bridge**, where the road ends in front of an inn and a sixteenth-century pack-horse bridge. On the far side of the river a path leads up through the trees past a cross marking the grave of a Royalist officer killed in a Civil War skirmish.

A signposted pedestrian route heading west called the Hunter's Path gives a buzzard's-eye-view over the gorge and is an alternative way from the road to arrive at **Castle Drogo**. (Castle open Easter to end Sept, Sat to Thurs, 11 to 6 (5 Oct) garden open for same periods, daily, 11 to 6 (5 Oct)). The 'castle' was erected between 1910 and 1930 to the design of Sir Edwin Lutyens for Julius Drewe who had made his fortune as a partner in the Home and Colonial Stores chain. Lutyens planned the house to be three times larger than it is, but had to change his plans in mid-flight: the architect showed ingenuity and originality in marrying the styles of country-house opulence with the characteristics of a medieval castle. Its hallmarks are the imaginative use of granite, with much vaulting in the corridors and subtly proportioned steps, and the painstaking attention to detail which extends to the concealment of radiators behind oak screens and carefully shaped chopping-boards in the sky-lit kitchen.

Among the interesting contents are an Edwardian doll's house in the corridor and sixteenth-century Flemish tapestries in the library. Geometric yew hedges, an architectural feature in themselves, forming an outer barbican at the entrance, encircle a croquet lawn and dominate the terraced flower-beds.

Drewsteignton, east of the entrance to Castle Drogo, is a compact village with a charming central square that happily combines thatch and yellow-orange rendered granite. The Drewe Arms forms its centrepiece with the church sealing off the far end.

Moretonhampstead to Sticklepath

Moretonhampstead developed at an important crossroads of the present-day A382 and B3212, and a number of hotels and inns (see p. 186) survive from its days as a stop-over for stage-coaches. It's an agreeable enough small town, well placed for exploring Dartmoor, although with little of intrinsic interest; traffic is noisy in the day-time but dies down appreciably at night. A series of fires in the nineteenth century obliterated much of the town, but a handsome row of seventeenth-century arcaded almshouses in Cross Street, at the edge of town, escaped damage. Three miles west on the B3212, the **Miniature Pony Centre** (open Mar to end Oct, daily, 10 to 5) has various small breeds in addition to rare miniature ponies, including cattle and pigs. Visitors are encouraged to meet and stroke the animals.

North-west of Moretonhampstead and about the same size, **Chagford** has a more villagey, relaxed atmosphere; Evelyn Waugh wrote *Brideshead Revisited* here. The heart of the town is ranged informally around an octagonal turreted market-house in the middle of a somewhat shapeless square chock-full of tea shops and including a thatched Lloyd's Bank, a hardware store with its original shop preserved as a 'museum' within the present premises, and the imposing Three Crowns Inn. New Street leads off the square, giving glimpses of the moors and hills between its cottages.

Out to the west, signposted from Chagford, **Fernworthy Reservoir** lies half-surrounded by hundreds of acres of sitka spruces; it's a place of organised leisure – picnic sites by the water's edge and forest walks for Dartmoor's numerous rainy days. Decidedly less tame is **Shovel Down**, to the north, dotted with prehistoric hut circles and Bronze Age stone rows, and overshadowed by the towering natural form

171

of Kestor Rock, which helps one to find a route across the austere expanses of the moor. A mile further north is **Scorhill Stone Circle**, consisting of 23 upright stones, and the only one of 12 Bronze Age monuments in Dartmoor not to have been restored. It is a bleak and lonely spot, although reached by an unchallenging walk of about ten minutes. Park at Scorhill Farm at the end of a no-through road west of Gidleigh, and follow the left-hand wall; where this veers sharply off to the left, carry straight on across the open moor: away to the left of the circle is Teign e-ver, a small granite bridge over an attractive stretch of the North Teign river. Continuing by car north on winding lanes, you reach **Throwleigh**, which looks forgotten by the twentieth century; cottage porches are draped with rambling roses, tawny-coloured walls are flecked by hydrangea bushes and pots of fuschias, and a thatched lychgate partly screens a sturdy granite church.

Dartmoor's most easily reached Neolithic tomb is **Spinsters' Rock**, signposted off the A382 1½ miles south of the junction with the A30. Standing in a field opposite a farm, the (restored) structure (*c*.3500–2500 BC) consists of three uprights supporting a capstone, denuded of the earthy mound which would originally have covered it. The name derives from a legend that a trio of spinsters erected the tomb before breakfast one morning.

If you could look at **South Zeal**, just north of the A30, from above you would see the extent to which it has retained its medieval pattern: narrow plots of land extend three or four hundred yards behind houses on either side of the sloping main street. A tiny chapel built in 1713 beside a medieval market cross lies in the middle of the street, which has a handsome inn, the Oxenham Arms, with mullioned windows: originally a Norman monastery, it was later the manor house of the Burgoyne family. A seventeenth-century memorial to the Burgoynes – Robert and his wife in kneeling position above a slate panel depicting their children – can be seen in the imposing parish church just north along the lane at **South Tawton**. The church has a fine fifteenth-century west tower, a roof of the same date – displaying human and mythical faces among its bosses – and an exceptional eighteenth-century pulpit inlaid with panels representing the evangelists. To the west at **Sticklepath**, a village cut in two by the A30, Finch's Foundry operated from 1814 to 1960, making agricultural and mining hand-tools until competition from mass-production techniques led to its final demise. The premises, since rescued from dereliction, now form part of a small museum (open Mar to Dec, Mon to Sat, 10 to 5; also June to end Sept, Sun, 10 to 5) about the foundry and its products, with the main foundry area and machinery much as they were.

The northern moor

Four miles south-west from Moretonhampstead on the B3212, you can park at **Green Combe** and view the lush, green expanses of the north-east side of the national park, with central Devon and distant Exmoor beyond. Half a mile on, the Widecombe turn-off gives access to **Grimspound**, the most famous of Dartmoor's Bronze Age village sites, on a saddle of Hamel Down: follow the lane for a mile, stopping at an unsigned parking space by an obvious bend in the road, where a short flight of rough steps indicates the beginning of the quarter-mile long path to the site. Dating back three thousand years, Grimspound comprises a walled enclosure, encircling some four acres, within which you can see the outlines of 24 buildings or hut circles; these would have originally supported a wood and turf roof. It isn't a very hospitable spot, but its inhabitants probably settled here because of the proximity of tin, rich in the stream-beds at that time; the grown-over workings from Birch Tor and Vitifer mines, in evidence across the valley, tell of a flourishing nineteenth-century tin industry.

Back on the main road towards Postbridge and half a mile north-east of the solitary Warren House Inn, **Bennet's Cross** lies on an ancient route from Moretonhampstead to Tavistock (closely followed by the modern highway, which was constructed as a turnpike road in 1792). The cross is medieval, intended, like many others in Dartmoor, as a way-marker for travellers. The hamlet of **Postbridge** has the finest example in Dartmoor of a medieval clapper bridge (see p. 167). The straight main road no longer uses the bridge, bypassing it by a few yards. There is another good example off the B3212 a short distance south at **Bellever**. The Lich Way starts here, an ancient cross-country route used in medieval times by farmers and coffin-bearers on their way to the distant church at Lydford (see p. 175), which has one of the largest parishes in the country. Forest walks from Bellever take you through a sheltered conifer plantation: one track leads up to open ground at the foot of Bellever Tor, an impressive viewing-platform over central Dartmoor.

Continuing south-west on the B3212 from Postbridge, you will see the old chimneys of a disused gunpowder mill, now functioning as **Powder Mills Pottery** (open Easter to Christmas, daily, 8 am to 7 pm), with a pottery workshop, and gallery as well as a small exhibition on the mills. Further on at a bend in the road by prominent trees, **Crockham Tor** is physically unremarkable but historically important as a meeting-place in medieval times for stannary parliament – the administrative body which regulated tin mining.

From the crossroads of the B3212 and B3357 at **Two Bridges**, which is little more than its name suggests, a 20-minute walk north from the car park opposite the hotel leads to **Wistman's Wood**, the best known of the three copses on the otherwise bare moor (the other two being Black Tor Copse on the West Ockment river and Piles Copse near Harford). The oaks are stunted by severe exposure to the elements, and they have only grown at all because of the granite clitter – the shattered remains of surface rock – which has sheltered the seedlings.

The main road soon dips to reach **Merrivale**, dominated by the spoil and ugly sheds of its granite quarry, opened in 1876 and the only one still functioning in Dartmoor. From the first small car park a quarter of a mile back towards Two Bridges, a 300-yard walk across the moor in a beeline towards distant King's Tor will bring you to a double stone row, one of Dartmoor's more accessible Bronze Age monuments (probably used for a ceremonial purpose): you can see two lines of low granite pillars stretching 200 yards on either side of a modern drainage channel. South from Merrivale, the woods and green farmland of the **Walkham Valley**, once dotted with blowing houses (for tin smelting), provide a mellow contrast to the central moor; abandoned quarries lie on the eastern side with Vixen Tor half a mile distant, the tallest rock pile in Dartmoor – 90 feet from top to base.

North of Tavistock the A386 soon passes through an old mining area developed in the last century and including the charmingly named Peter Tavy and Mary Tavy (referring to the local River Tavy). Where the road crosses the open moor the abandoned but preserved engine-house of **Wheal Betsy** is visible just below the road on its east side, above a former lead mine. Extraordinary **Brent Tor**, west of Mary Tavy, comprises a solitary church perched high on a tor-capped hillock of volcanic rock, in direct communion with the elements; the fascinating view extends from the western buttresses of Dartmoor close by in one direction to Bodmin Moor, the highest land in Cornwall, in the other. The church, dedicated to St Michael, dates from the twelfth century (but has little of interest inside); its site must long have been important since vestiges of an earlier earthwork exist below the rock.

A few miles east are the two entrances to **Lydford Gorge** (open all year, Easter to Oct, daily, 10.30 to 6, Nov to Easter, daily, 10.30 to 4), where 450,000 years ago the River Lyd, which had been flowing southwards, diverted its course along an existing stream to rush across the area where the present gorge is situated. The National Trust run the site today and charge admission: a one-way path circuit that has been hacked out of the rock in places takes you on a walk of at least 1½ hours through woods and past whirlpools in the honeycombed shiny rock, edged by dripping moss. By using the car parks at either end of the gorge you can take in the two main highlights without doing the whole walk: the White Lady Waterfall, a slender column of water tumbling down to unite a tributary with the main river, and the Devil's Cauldron, a dark, strange place where water swirls into a gloomy chasm.

There is a free view of part of the gorge where the road crosses it on the way up to **Lydford**. The village was important in the Dark Ages, when King Alfred made it a stronghold against the Celts and Danes, and in Norman times when a castle was built; the keep, built a century later, was erected as a stannary court, with a dungeon for those who fell foul of the stannary laws. It became notorious for its grim conditions ('Oft have I heard of Lydford law, How in the morn they hang and draw, And sit in judgement after. . . .'), where those found guilty of adulterating tin would have molten metal spooned down their throats. The village declined in significance and in 1800 the stannary court was moved to Princetown. Lydford today is a quiet spot – the ruined keep still standing close by the thatched Castle Inn (see pgs. 184, 186) and the church of St Petrock. The latter once served the largest parish in England, including much of central Dartmoor, corpses being carried great distances over the moor from Postbridge and environs for burial. Its churchyard has numerous beautifully lettered slate tombstones of the eighteenth and early nineteenth centuries, the most famous of which has the punning epitaph to 'the outsize case of George Routledge, Watchmaker . . . Integrity was the mainspring, and prudence the regulator, of all the actions of his life'. It ends:

He departed this life
Nov. 14 1802
Aged 57
Wound up
In hopes of being taken in hand
By his Maker
And of being thoroughly cleaned, repaired
And set-going
In the world to come.

To the north the A386 defines the national park boundary, with no opportunities to explore the sharply rising moors immediately to the east except for a lane leading up to **Meldon Reservoir**. Imposingly set beneath towering slopes, the reservoir was completed in 1972 and was the last addition of its kind to the Dartmoor landscape. Nearby Meldon Quarry still produces limestone, which is used for agricultural fertiliser.

The main attraction of **Okehampton**, on the edge of Dartmoor National Park, is the small museum of Dartmoor life (open Mar to Dec, Mon to Sat, 10 to 5; also June to end Sept, Sun, 10 to 5). Tucked away behind a small cobbled courtyard, it has exhibitions on the history of tin mining, granite quarrying, and the Haytor granite tramway. There's also a mention of another less successful industry – the Dartmoor ice-works. For a few years during the 1870s, the western slopes of Dartmoor were the site for ice production and storage. Spring water was piped into specially dug, long shallow pits, where it formed blocks of ice, which were stored in deep trenches and covered in earth and turves. Unfortunately, much of the ice melted during its long wagon journey to Plymouth and other large towns, and the industry never really took off. Okehampton's Church of All Saints, reached along the cobbled Choir Boys Path leading uphill in the western part of town, has some interesting windows by Pre-Raphaelite artists Holman Hunt and William Morris.

Okehampton Castle (open Easter to end Sept, daily, 10 to 6; Oct to Easter, Tues to Sun, 10 to 4. Closed 1 Jan, 24 to 26 Dec), signposted on the south side of town, stands on a grassy spur above a deep wooded valley, with Okehampton just in view. It was erected by the Normans when they created the town, to guard the route from Cornwall. The ruins of a double keep dating from the twelfth century dominate the north bailey below, which was added in the fourteenth century by Hugh Coutenay, Earl of Devon, and consists of the remains of the chapel, kitchens, great hall and lodgings. If you miss the opening times, the spiky ruins can be seen virtually in their entirety from outside.

Also on the south side of Okehampton, and signposted from the town centre, are the army ranges of **Okehampton Camp**, offering a drive into some of the loneliest and wildest scenery in England. There is public access at weekends, in August and other (variable) times to the three ranges which occupy much of the northern part of Dartmoor: full details are available from national park information centres and by recorded telephone information – Okehampton (0837) 52939. From the high-security fences of Okehampton Camp, the **Military road** loops around the empty moor; military activity is evident from the pot-holes in the tarmac and signs pointing the way to ranges or underlining the dangers of unexploded ammunition. Added to the frequently inhospitable weather conditions on this elevated ground, the area can be menacing and even scary, yet it's a favourite for tough walkers intent on testing their map-reading techniques and survival skills against the great outdoors.

In Victorian times Cranmere Pool, right out in the middle and still hard to locate (commonly approached from Chagford) was a popular challenge for adventurous tourists. The first of Dartmoor's 'letterboxes' was placed here in the 1850s: a self-addressed postcard would be left by one walker and be picked up by the next walker to take and post from his or her town or village. A second box was installed at Plym Head south of Princetown in 1938, and in the last 50 years well over 400 more boxes have appeared all over Dartmoor, each with a rubber stamp and inkpad to provide proof of visit.

For those prepared for a long trek there are magnificent outcrops on Fur Tor and Hare Tor, some miles to the south of the road. Much closer is the ridge to the west with High Willhays (2038 feet) and Yes Tor (2029 feet) – the highest ground in England south of the Pennines.

The southern moor

Buckfastleigh grew up as a modest market town, but always played second fiddle to nearby Ashburton. Today it is known for places on its periphery – the terminus of the **South Devon Steam Railway** (see p. 144) and the **Buckfast Butterfly Farm and Dartmoor Otter Sanctuary** (open Easter to end Oct, daily, 10 to 5.30 or dusk; tickets include both sites) – the latter run by the same trust as the sanctuary at North Petherwin. A little further out in the Ashburton direction is **Buckfast Abbey**, the site in medieval times of a Cistercian monastery and rebuilt in the 30 years prior to 1937 by a Benedictine foundation. Its re-creation is an impressive feat, showing great dedication to purpose, though some may find the architecture a bit austere. The monastic range is not open to the public, but you can wander into the huge abbey church, its style a blend of Norman and Early English. The abbey's own tonic wine and honey are on sale at a shop at the entrance.

Holne, north of Buckfastleigh, is interesting mainly for the fact that the vicarage (since rebuilt) was the birthplace in 1819 of Charles Kingsley, author of *Westward Ho!* and the *Water Babies*; but the village stands in glorious countryside on the southern side of the Dart Valley. In particular, the drive north-west to Hexworthy should not be missed; its best view is just after Venford Reservoir at **Combestone Tor**, reached in seconds from the car park. East, at the T-junction with the B3357, **Dartmeet** is an attractive picnic and beauty spot where, as the name suggests, the West and East Dart rivers merge at a clapper bridge; it is very popular in summer but you can leave the crowds by following the river to the north along a peaceful dale. For travellers heading west, Dartmeet signals a transition from the complicated wooded valleys and blend of rugged and tamed landscape of eastern Dartmoor to the lonely tracts of the central moor.

Princetown, on the B3212 south-east of Two Bridges and close by the 668-foot BBC transmitter on North Hessary Tor, is in the midst of wildest Dartmoor, and the highest town in England (if you reckon it a town rather than a village), at 1400 feet above sea-level. The prison is its claim to fame – a vast grey bulk originally intended for prisoners from the Napoleonic Wars, and built by Sir Thomas Tyrwhitt who had earlier developed the village to house labourers for his flax-growing and granite-quarrying enterprises. The prison lay in disuse from 1814 until Prince Albert recommended it should house long-term convicts. A gift shop selling coffee mugs stamped 'Dartmoor Prison', a national park information centre and a few tea-shops cater to the curious public, but the prison-officers' mess and the overwhelming greyness of the place state that this is not somewhere to enjoy. But it's easy to escape, for non-convicts anyway.

A drive south from Princetown penetrates the wilds, coming to the end of the road at **Whiteworks**, where an isolated row of houses stands incongruously in a place of almost sensational bleakness; close by are the ruined buildings of one of the major Dartmoor tin mines, abandoned in the last century. Out on the moor to the south the seven-foot-high Nun's Cross, the highest medieval cross in Dartmoor, marks the Abbots' Way, an ancient route connecting the abbeys at Buckfast and Buckland. It is around here that Conan Doyle envisaged his fictitious Hound of the Baskervilles to have met its end.

Yelverton, Horrobridge and Dousland are large, suburban villages within close range of Plymouth, but **Meavy** just south of Dousland has a real village centre. Its green is notable for the ancient oak tree (reputedly 800 years old) – hollow and precariously kept together by metal rods. In the churchyard, facing the east window of the church, is the celebrated, easily missed epitaph of 1826 to a village blacksmith:

My sledge and hammer both declined
My bellows too have lost their wind
My fire's extinct, my forge decayed
And in the dust, my vice is laid.
My coal is spent, my iron's gone
My nails are drove – my work is done.

Burrator Reservoir to the south of the B3212 has a particularly pretty setting beneath conifer plantations and the splendid summits of Sharpitor (easily reached from the B3212) and Sheeps Tor; it's immensely popular, especially on fine Sunday afternoons, the more so because of its proximity to Plymouth. High above to the east the **Devonport Leat** snakes elaborately for 15 miles from the moors north of Two Bridges: it is the largest water channel in the region, built in 1796 to supply Devonport when it was still a separate town from Plymouth.

The River Meavy flows west and south, entering fine

woods and meeting the Plym at **Shaugh Bridge**, a beauty spot laced with paths along the river and up to the Dewerstone Rock, which looks down on Plymouth. The River Plym's upper reaches lead through a valley studded with ancient sites in the neighbourhood of Ditsworthy Warren, including a well-hidden set of cist tombs beneath Legis Tor. China-clay workings dominate the area to the south-east around **Lee Moor**: great terraces of white spoil and dusty roads.

Ivybridge has an industrial character and owed much of its expansion to the Victorian paper mill at the top of the town, but just to the north the River Erme is green and pleasant. Moorland near the river source is crossed by Europe's longest Bronze Age stone row, linking a stone circle on Stall Moor with a cairn on Green Hill two miles distant; it's a long way from the road, and easier walks can be found on the east side of the valley along the track-bed of an old tramway built in 1910 to serve the Redlake china-clay works. **South Brent**, one of many Dartmoor places that hover somewhere between village and town in character, has a few quiet shops and some docile charm in its colour-washed houses. A board of charges, dated 1889, lists the fees for parking animals during the market fair. Cottages with tubs of geraniums make an attractive corner by the church, which has some Norman work, including a fine tower and a sandstone font.

Ashburton to Widecombe in the Moor

Ashburton, with a population of 3500, is the largest town in the national park. Tin and wool brought it wealth from medieval times, when it was a stannary town as well as a centre where cloth was brought to the fulling-mills. It's still a conspicuously well-cared-for place, with two echoey and densely built main streets arranged in a T. These are lined with old inns, antique shops and prosperous-looking, slate-hung Georgian houses. You might not guess Ashburton has Dartmoor on its back doorstep, so few are the signs of either the hills or of tourist culture. A free museum shows pictures of the town in the last century: it doesn't seem to have changed much, but a model of a splendid market house, which graced the centre for 500 years until demolition, hints at a sad loss.

To the west by Holne Bridge is **River Dart Country Park** (open Easter to end Sept, daily, 10 to 5), a 90-acre site offering woodland and riverside walks within the landscaped grounds of a Victorian mansion, plus adventure playgrounds, pony rides and a bathing lake: 'country fun for everyone', the brochure promises. A mile further west the road crosses the Dart again at **New Bridge**, a fourteenth-century arched granite structure; the spot is busy in summer with picnickers and walkers using the pretty riverside path sheltered by broad-leaf trees. A tiny lane leads north-east to the point where the Webburn encounters the Dart: a gate gives access to a nature reserve path by the former river. Most traffic zigzags uphill from New Bridge, passing the hamlet of Poundsgate and then **Bel Tor Corner**, where the road emerges on to the open moor and you can look over the deep Dart Valley. Dr Blackall of Spitchwick Manor near Poundsgate liked the view so much that he had a special carriage ride constructed in the 1870s; following the track, still called Dr Blackall's Drive, is an easy and enjoyable walk from Bel Tor Corner for about a mile in the New Bridge direction.

East of the River Webburn, the church at **Buckland in the Moor** has an appealingly humble interior and a charming screen painted with saints, but is particularly renowned for the gilt letters in place of numerals on its church clock that spell out 'my dear mother'. The local lord of the manor had them painted on as a memorial in 1928, and was also responsible for erecting the inscribed **Ten Commandments Stone**, more remotely located on Buckland Beacon high up to the east of the village – worth climbing to for the views.

A couple of miles up the Webburn Valley brings you to **Widecombe in the Moor**, immortalised by the folk song 'Widecombe Fair' ('Uncle Tom Cobley and all . . .'). It looks a treat from a distance, its shapely church tower gracing the vale, and in mid-winter should live up to its promise, when you can get the pocket-handkerchief of a village centre and some fine medieval buildings to yourself. In the summer months the tiny village can get intensely overcrowded and its two car parks, tea-room and National Trust shop (within the picturesque Church House – once the village school) become jam-packed; the busiest day of all is when Widecombe Fair takes place, on the second Tuesday of September. But the late fourteenth-century church is large enough to accommodate plenty of visitors, and deserves them: its roof shows off an exceptional collection of bosses – among them a scapegoat, a green man, an angel, a pelican and three interlocking rabbits representing a sign of the tin-miners as at North Bovey (see p. 169). During divine service here on Sunday, 21 October 1638, a thunderbolt struck through the roof, killing four and injuring many more; the churchwardens recorded the incident in verse, displayed on boards in the tower.

Highlights

** *Brent Tor, Castle Drogo, Dart Valley, Haytor, Hound Tor, Lydford Gorge and village, Teign Gorge.*

* *Bridford Church, Burrator Reservoir, Chagford, Drewsteignton, Lustleigh, North Bovey, Okehampton Camp Military Road, Scorhill Stone Circle, Spinsters' Rock, Widecombe in the Moor.*

Where to stay

For a key to prices, see p. 12

Ashburton

Ashburton Hotel

79 East Street, Ashburton, Devon TQ13 7AL. Tel Ashburton (0364) 52784
This attractive Georgian house in the centre of town has been well renovated by the owners, new here in 1989; it has small, comfortable bedrooms decorated in soft, plain colours, a lovely Victorian conservatory, and specialises in organic food.
£ *Open all year, exc Jan*

Holne Chase

Ashburton, nr Newton Abbot, Devon TQ13 7NS. Tel Poundsgate (0364) 3471. Fax (036 43) 453
In a beautiful position beside the River Dart, the hotel has been run by the same family for over 20 years. The grounds allow for croquet and cricket but only a few minutes walk brings you into woodland – it's a secluded spot. The updated decor and additional rooms blend well with the overall, hunting-lodge style, which is comfortable and welcoming. Dinner is a set price with five courses.
£££ *Open all year*

Bovey Tracey

The Edgemoor

Haytor Road, Bovey Tracey, Devon TQ13 9LE. Tel Bovey Tracey (0626) 832466. Fax (0626) 834760
This creeper-clad Victorian house right on the edge of Dartmoor used to be a grammar

school. There is only a hint of the schoolmaster in Mr Stephens, who has recently bought the hotel with his wife. They have redone the decor, and the old Assembly Hall, complete with minstrels' gallery at one end, is now a bright comfortable sitting-room. Bedrooms are cottagey and cheerful, all with their own bathrooms. In the evenings you can choose between an à la carte or reasonably priced table d'hôte menu served in the fairly formal dining-room.
£££ *Open all year*

Chagford

Gidleigh Park

Chagford, Devon TQ13 8HH. Tel Chagford (0647) 432367. Fax (0647) 432574

At the end of a bumpy lane, this 1920s Tudor-style house is set in 40 acres of formal gardens, with croquet lawns and landscaped water gardens. Large comfortable public rooms overlook the gardens: chintz and fresh flowers are the order here. Friendly efficient staff serve delicious food. The bedrooms vary in size and price but all are luxurious and supremely comfortable with lots of pampering extras. A great treat for which you pay handsomely.
£££££ *Open all year*

Mill End

Sandy Park, Chagford, Devon TQ13 8JN. Tel Chagford (0647) 432282. Fax (0647) 433106

The house was converted about 70 years ago from a flour mill and the old wheel still turns in the courtyard. There are plenty of rooms to relax in – you can

choose between a couple of sitting-rooms and bar or the tv/reading room. There's a definite fishing bent and the hotel offers special summer weekends for novice anglers. Bedrooms vary in style and decor, the most modern being on the ground floor with patios. A daily changing menu gives a good choice at lunch and dinner.
£££ *Closed 12 to 22 Dec and 10 to 20 Jan*

Thornworthy House

Chagford, Devon TQ13 8EY. Tel Chagford (0647) 433297

A winding single track leads to this Victorian house which is very much a family home, with lots of personal touches from portraits of the Jevons' children to a collection of china dachshunds. It has a good atmosphere and is a comfortable, peaceful place to stay: you can see the open moor from the large garden. The bedrooms are light and pretty with floral fabrics; three are in the main house and the others, in the converted outbuildings, can be used either as ordinary hotel rooms or on a self-catering basis. Dinner, served promptly at 8, offers a choice of dishes at each course.
££ *Open all year*

Doddiscombsleigh

Nobody Inn

Doddiscombsleigh, Nr Exeter, Devon EX6 7PS. Tel Christow (0647) 52394

It's off the beaten track, tucked away among high-hedged lanes close to Dartmoor National Park, but many people seem to find their way here. It is a very friendly, hospitable place that

serves delicious food: snacks in the oak-beamed bar or a full dinner in the candlelit restaurant. The bedrooms are pretty and simple, some above the pub, others in Town Barton, the eighteenth-century manor house under the same ownership: it's only a couple of minutes down the road but tends to be a bit quieter. There's an attractive garden with tables for eating out in good weather.
£–££ Open all year

Haytor
The Bel Alp House

Haytor, Nr Bovey Tracey, Devon TQ13 9XX. Tel Haytor (0364) 661217. Fax (0364) 661292
Surrounded by eight acres of gardens and woodland this white Edwardian house has lovely views south towards Torbay across the rolling hills. It is a very peaceful setting and the whole atmosphere of the place is quiet and civilised. The owners want people to feel at home and guests are introduced to each other (but sit at separate tables); the public rooms are spacious enough for a full house of guests to be comfortable. The bedrooms vary in size and price, and some of the grander rooms have huge Victorian baths on marble stands. Sports on offer include croquet and billiards.
£££££ Closed Dec, Jan; restricted opening Nov, Feb

Haytor Vale
The Rock Inn

Haytor Vale, nr Bovey Tracey, Devon TQ13 9XP. Tel Haytor (0364) 661305. Fax (0364) 661242
A fairly traditional pub high up on Dartmoor, cosy and cheerful with a half-panelled bar, high-backed settles, beams, polished old wood tables and Windsor chairs. It has a good reputation for food and atmosphere, and can be very crowded at weekends. You can eat either in the two bar rooms or in the snug restaurant. Bedrooms are quite simple and old-fashioned in style but adequately comfortable for the price.
££–£££ Open all year exc 25 Dec

Lydford
The Castle Inn

Lydford, Okehampton, Devon EX20 4BH. Tel Lydford (082 282) 242
The name is rather misleading for the small pink roadside inn complete with trailing roses. The ruined medieval tower close by marks the remains of the castle. There is a twin-roomed bar with low ceilings, stone-flagged floors, high-backed settles and old wooden chairs; the walls in one area are decorated with china plates and you can sit by the huge open fire and relish hot home-made soup. In summer the pretty gardens behind the inn make a lovely setting for an alfresco lunch or evening meal. Bedrooms are unremarkable but neat, and not all have bathrooms.
££ Open all year, exc 25 Dec

Sourton
Collaven Manor Hotel

Sourton, Nr Okehampton, Devon EX20 4HH. Tel Bridestowe (083 786) 522. Fax (083 786) 570
If you want to be close to Dartmoor National Park this creeper-clad manor house

provides a comfortable base, if slightly lacking in atmosphere. It's part fifteenth-century, part Victorian, and has a pretty, well-kept garden. The interior is varied: white walls and beams in some rooms and a mixture of antique and reproduction furniture on patterned carpets with chintzy curtains. The restaurants – the Inglenook and the Hamilton – are both beamed with high-backed wicker chairs (simpler and cheaper fare in the Inglenook). Bedrooms are light and pretty with traditional furnishings.

££££ *Closed 2 weeks Jan*

Where to eat

For a key to prices, see p. 12

Doddiscombleigh
Nobody Inn

Doddiscombleigh. Tel Christow (0647) 52394
Plenty of places to sit in this cosy partly fifteenth-century inn.
[£] *Open all week 12–2, Tues to Sat 7.30–9.15*

Bovey Tracey
Granary Café

Devon Guild of Craftsmen, Riverside Mill, Bovey Tracey. Tel Bovey Tracey (0626) 832223
Clean, simple café in the craft centre.
Open Mon to Sun 10–5

Chagford
Gidleigh Park

Chagford. Tel Chagford (0647) 432367
Excellent cooking at this grand country house (see p. 183).
Open all week 12.30–2, 7–9

Lustleigh
Primrose Cottage

Lustleigh. Tel Lustleigh (064 77) 365
Very pretty thatched tea-room,
serving teas and delicious lunches.
[£] *Open all week 10–5.30 Closed 6 weeks from end of 2nd week in Dec*

Lydford
The Castle Inn

Lydford, Okehampton. Tel Lydford (082 282) 242
Pretty pink pub with rooms (see p. 184), it serves good bar food with a cold buffet their speciality in summer.
[£] *Open all year, exc 25 Dec*

Mary Tavy
The Stannary

Mary Tavy, near Tavistock. Tel Mary Tavy (0822) 810897
Quite adventurous dishes, they hope to have something to suit everyone. A cross between a tea-room/restaurant and guesthouse.
Open most days 7–9.30 Closed some lunchtimes in winter

Moretonhampstead
White Hart Hotel

The Square, Moretonhampstead. Tel Moretonhampstead (0647) 40406

Pub/hotel with a good atmosphere serving reasonably priced food.
[£] *Open all week 11.30–2.30, 6–8.30*

Peter Tavy

Peter Tavy Inn

near Tavistock. Tel Mary Tavy (0822) 810 348
A jolly local inn with good homemade dishes; emphasis on wholefood.
[£] *Open all week Mon to Sat 11.30–2.30, 6.30–9.45; Sun 12–2.15, 7–9.45.*

South-east Cornwall

Cornwall's grandest harbours are in this region – contained within drowned river valleys or rias formed by rises in sea-level. Carrick Roads, the name given to the Fal estuary, is a yachting haven as well as a deep harbour for freighters and tankers, and is flanked by Pendennis and St Mawes castles; it's a superb sight, best seen from a boat. Fowey Harbour is more enclosed in character and its port towns more picturesque. The coast is partly low-lying and partly characterised by fine cliffs, although seldom with the rugged appearance of west and north Cornwall. You will find working fishing villages, with fishing-trips and scenic boat-excursions on offer. Polperro and Mevagissey are the most famous examples, and consequently very touristy in season; Looe is more of a seaside resort; Portloe and the joined-together villages of Kingsand and Cawsand are unspoilt and less visited. Around Falmouth and Truro the mild climate and fertile soil produce the right conditions for charming landscaped gardens, some full of exotic plants, many open to the public. Views inland often feature the Hensbarrow Downs china-clay moonscapes near St Austell, but elsewhere the hinterland has a soft, fertile appearance; Lanhydrock House, close to the remains of Restormel Castle, is well worth the trip some way inland for a taste of Victorian opulence. Further east, the River Tamar defines the county boundary with Devon and provides broad estuarine landscapes near Plymouth; while its close environs contain a number of country houses, including two of Cornwall's finest – Antony and Cotehele.

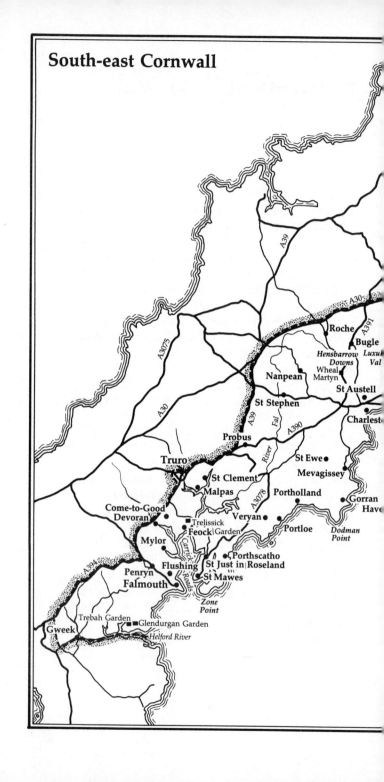

South-east Cornwall

Roche

A39

A30

A391

Bugle

Hensbarrow
Downs

Luxul
Val

Wheal
Martyn

Nanpean

St Austell

A3075

St Stephen

Charlest

A30

Fal

A39

A390

Probus

Truro

St Ewe

Mevagissey

River

St Clement

Malpas

A3078

Portholland

Gorran
Have

Come-to-Good

Devoran

Veryan

Trelissick
Feock Garden

Portloe

Dodman
Point

Mylor

Carrick

Flushing

Porthscatho
St Just in Roseland
St Mawes

A394

Penryn
Falmouth

Roads

Zone
Point

Trebah Garden

Glendurgan Garden

Gweek

Helford River

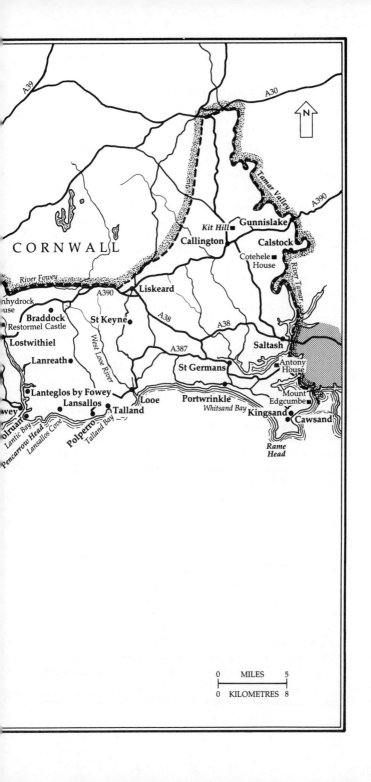

Whitsand Bay and Mount Edgcumbe

Joined on to the rest of Cornwall by a one-and-a-half-mile-wide neck of land, the peninsula sheltering the west side of Plymouth's great natural harbour fills up with Sunday trippers from Plymouth but it is still possible to find pockets of seclusion. **Mount Edgcumbe Country Park** (open all year, daily, 8 to dusk; free) is one of these. Reached by frequent passenger-ferry services from Plymouth to Cremyll (every day, half hourly; hourly during the week in winter), it lies at the easternmost tip of Cornwall and the views back towards Plymouth – the city, harbour, creeks and boating, from the smallest-scale sailing dinghies to huge naval vessels – are well worth the trip. An estate of fine trees, formal gardens and follies, and a grand avenue leading up to the rebuilt family mansion are the legacy of the Edgcumbes who established themselves here in the sixteenth century, preferring a new home to updating their old one at Cotehele (see p. 194). The gardens were laid out in the early nineteenth century in French, English and Italian styles, with hedged enclaves and pavilions; the nearby orangery now functions as a café, with cane furniture interspersed with potted palms in a high-ceilinged room. By the water's edge a blockhouse fort, one of the two earliest parts of the Tamar defences erected by Henry viii, with other fortifications being added over the next three centuries, looks out to Drake's Island and naval Plymouth. In the Civil War the Edgcumbes supported the Royalist cause and guns were fired from here at the ships making their way into Parliamentarian Plymouth; otherwise the blockhouse has spent much of its life as a garden ornament – the Edgcumbes later attached a pavilion and used the guns to salute arriving guests.

Further up the road and still in the estate, isolated **Maker** church has the best roadside views over the harbour; the church car park is an alternative approach up the slope to **Mount Edgcumbe House** (open Easter to end Oct, Wed to Sun and Bank Hol Mon, 11 to 5.30). The original house was built in 1539 to an unusual design based on a central hall lit at the top instead of the quasi-fortified courtyard plan of the Elizabethan manor house. Extensive remodelling was carried out in the seventeenth and eighteenth centuries, when Doric columns were placed in the hall and the west wing was rebuilt with an oval dining-room. But the whole was reduced

to little more than rubble in 1941 when a stray incendiary
bomb fell here instead of on the Devonport docks. What is
seen today is a faithful reconstruction of the sixteenth-
century plan with its later classical touches and crisply lit
polygonal rooms, the whole built with a steel frame and
concrete floors – in a sense, a rare post-war stately home.
Plymouth City Council have now taken it over (the
Edgcumbes having moved away) and have filled some of the
rooms with furniture and paintings from the Edgcumbes'
other houses at Cotehele, Stonehouse and London.

Local knowledge is necessary to work out the dividing line
between **Kingsand** and **Cawsand**, although if you look hard
you can still find a marker opposite the Halfway Hotel
denoting the pre-1844 county boundary when Kingsand was
in Devon and Cawsand in Cornwall. They're really one large
village, at the recess of Cawsand Bay and crammed into the
corner where the cliffs make a sharp turn. Plymouth
suddenly feels miles away as you wander round the winding
lanes and swooping alleys of the little fishing port with its
charming shuttered cottages; a cottage called Penlee
Narrows, at the Kingsand end, huddles in a terrace opposite
the Rising Sun, looking comically thin. Behind the beach,
where four ferries a day land from Plymouth and return, a
quiet square is fronted by the unsurprisingly named
Smugglers Inn. Commercialism here means one chip shop
and a bakery-cum-tea-shop selling fresh crab sandwiches.

Rame Head, a peninsula within a peninsula, is east
Cornwall's answer to the Lizard, a satisfying knob of land
that extends sufficiently far south to give views along 50
miles of Cornish coast, and eastwards to the Great Mew
Stone and Wembury Bay; even the Lizard reveals itself on a
clear day. From the car park by a coastguard lookout post, a
well-trodden path to the point takes a few minutes to walk.
At the top is the shell of a primitive fourteenth-century
chapel, dedicated like so many other hilltop places of
worship to St Michael, and reputedly built on the site of a
Celtic hermitage.

In contrast to the complicated indentations and
promontories of the north side of the peninsula, **Whitsand
Bay** presents a clean four-mile sweep of sand from Rame
Head to Portwrinkle, with the beach uncovered at low tide
for its entire length. Access involves tricky paths, and the
waters are dangerous for swimming, although life-guards
patrol in season; there are attractive views from the road,

despite one of the most random-looking of Cornish shack developments on the clifftops halfway along the bay.

The northern side of the peninsula is a busy traffic route from Torpoint, really a suburb of Plymouth with naval barracks on its fringes, where a vehicle ferry links Cornwall to Devonport. In complete contrast, **Antony House** (open April to end Oct, Tues to Thurs & Bank Hol Mon, also June to Aug, Sun, 2 to 6; garden mid-Mar to mid-June and Aug to end Oct, Mon to Sat, 11 to 5.30, Sun 2.30 to 5.30) hides north of the A374 in parkland laid out by Humphrey Repton and extending to St Germans River. The most distinguished classical mansion in Cornwall, built of brick faced with stone, it was designed by an unknown architect (possibly James Gibbs, architect of the Radcliffe Camera in Oxford and of London's St Martin in the Fields) and completed in 1721 for Sir William Carew. The Carew-Poles still live here, and because the National Trust owns only the house itself and not its contents, admission is by guided tour only. The tour begins in the halls, where the portraits include one of Richard Carew who wrote the seminal *Survey of Cornwall* (1602) and one of Charles I during his trial, at which John Carew was a judge (the king's beard is grey, having lost its colour during the trial); the smaller inner hall has a fine oak staircase and retains its original Queen Anne globe-lights. Portraits by Reynolds and Van Dyck hang in the dining-room; a painting of two Carew boys dated 1793 is of special interest for its early depiction of cricket bats and kit. A number of fine clocks stand in the inner hall, on the landing and in the tapestry room. Upstairs, the bedrooms are roped off but can be glanced into; among these is a room where Daphne du Maurier stayed and was fascinated by a portrait of Rachel Carew, inspiring her book *My Cousin Rachel* (though the two Rachels had very different lives, Rachel Carew dying as a young woman). Outside, a swathe of grass leads between clipped hedges, giving access to the Summer Garden.

To the north-west, the village of **St Germans**, just off the peninsula itself, was once the seat of the bishops of Cornwall, the bishopric set up by Athelstan in about 936. A century later this merged with Crediton and a new diocese was created, with its see at Exeter; St Germans continued to be a place of religious importance from the mid-twelfth century when a priory of Augustinian canons was founded. The remaining priory church, much restored, has hints of cathedral proportions, notably in its great Norman doorway, surrounded by seven receding arches, on the otherwise strikingly austere double-towered west front. The original east end and the north aisle no longer exist, but the interior still impresses with its lofty scale and Norman plan. A north transept was built in 1803, and the stained glass in the east window was designed by Burne Jones for the William Morris Company. Port Eliot, the house of the earls of St Germans and originally the priory, stands nearby; it was mostly rebuilt in 1802–6 to the designs of John Soane, architect of the Bank of England. It is not open to the public but you can see it from the church. At the west end of the village's main street, lined with rust-coloured cottages, is a row of almshouses, dated 1583, with a communal first-floor balcony and slate-hung gables.

The Tamar Valley

From its source in north Cornwall, the River Tamar defines the county boundary with Devon for most of its length, the best of the Tamar Valley lying south of Launceston. The valley has long been celebrated fruit-growing country – apples, pears, plums, strawberries and above all Tamar cherries – though it has dwindled in importance this century. The meandering waterway that was a major trading route for many centuries is, however, elusive: you can glimpse it occasionally from the road and at bridges, enjoy it briefly from the train on the line from the Tamar Bridge to Gunnislake, and follow it intermittently on broken stretches of footpath. The only way to enjoy all of it is by a boat-trip from Pheonix Wharf in Plymouth's Barbican to Calstock; tickets are available for taking the boat one way and the train the other (for information telephone Plymouth (0752) 221300).

The ideal introduction is to start at **Saltash**, a suburb of Plymouth on the Cornish side of the river, with little intrinsic interest until you get to its oldest street above the quay, thrillingly sandwiched between the two Tamar bridges – the concrete road bridge carrying the A38 and Brunel's far from graceful Royal Albert railway bridge (1859). The latter, a suspension and arched structure combined, was a considerable feat of engineering in its day: Brunel had to solve the problem of allowing at least 100-foot clearance for shipping. Its sausage-shaped tubular arches were floated into position, jacked up, and the piers built underneath; the central pier, constructed inside a great cylinder, plunged 80 feet below high water. Equilibrium is achieved by the outward push of the arches against an inward pressure of chains below. A huge crowd watched Brunel direct the operation to raise the first truss in 1857, but by the time the second was due to go up he was too ill to take charge.

Neal Point to the north, overlooking mud-flats that form part of a nature reserve, with the Tamar bridges in the distance, draws the occasional birdwatcher for close-up views of the estuary's large bird population – curlews, oyster-catchers, redshanks and shelducks among them. To reach it, park at Landulph church, follow the road around to the left and at the entrance to Landulph House take a stile on your right; a path along the left edge of the field reaches the water at the nature reserve sign.

Further upriver is **Cotehele House** (house open Easter to end Sept, Sat to Thurs, 11 to 6 (5 Oct); garden, mill and museum open all year: April to Sept, daily, 11 to 6 (5 Oct); Nov to Mar, daily, daylight hours) a fascinating time capsule, virtually unaltered in the last 400 years. It was Edgcumbe property until given over to the National Trust in 1947, and instead of modernising it to keep up with modish architectural style and decor, the Edgcumbes re-established themselves in the seventeenth century at Mount Edgcumbe (see p. 190) and kept this house as a retreat for elderly relatives. Built at a time of lawlessness in the area, it is defended from the outside world, with small windows and a courtyard plan. Inside rooms are dark, and contain a magnificent array of antique furnishings and tapestries. In the chapel, the pre-pendulum clock is the oldest to be found in England still in its original state and position. The gardens, astride a valley with the estuary as a backdrop, slope down past a medieval dovecot shading a lily pond.

Cotehele is of special interest for the extent to which the estate buildings have been preserved, and the water-mill complex can be visited separately from the rest. Clustered together here are the smithy, with tools ready for use and the forge smoking away, the wheelwright's, carpenter's and saddler's shops, the cider press and mill – all left as if their craftsmen have just walked out of the door. This area can be reached by a level walk beside the brook running from the carefully preserved **Cotehele Quay**, through which granite, coal and Tamar fruit used to pass when the Tamar was a trading route; since the Second World War the river has carried no commercial traffic. The quay has a small museum, an outpost of the Royal Naval Museum, explaining the functioning of the port and its craft. The last surviving ketch-rigged barge, once a common sight on the river, is moored by one pier: *The Shamrock* was in use until 1970, rescued from dereliction in recent years by the National Trust.

The railway viaduct aptly dominates the whole of riverside **Calstock**, a tin and copper-ore port that had the life sucked from it when the railway opened. It is far from busy, but attractive enough, on a hillside climbed by a few narrow streets and terraces.

Of the numerous holy wells in the West Country, **Dupath** is outstanding for its state of preservation. Signposted off the main roads near Callington, it lies below a farm in a small field from which water seeps into a channel that feeds a basin in the simple chapel. The waters are supposedly a cure for whooping cough – perhaps the active pond-life floating in it provides vital medicinal sources.

A mile or so north **Kit Hill** is an extraordinary place – a pudding-shaped hill with the abandoned chimneys and workings of the South Kit Hill Mine (tin, copper, tungsten and arsenic) and traces of granite-quarrying dotted around the heathy granite upland. A road leads all the way to the top, or you can earn the view by following the two-mile circular Kit Hill Trail starting at the car park halfway up. One of the most impressive panoramas in inland Cornwall takes in the heights of Bodmin Moor and the Hensbarrow Downs china-clay country to the west and Dartmoor (with the mast on North Hessary Tor prominent) to the east.

Liskeard to Lanreath

In medieval times **Liskeard** was an important stannary town, but there is not much to show for it today. It has a few streets busy with shoppers, and a square centred on an odd lamp-fountain structure; just off it a one-room **museum** (open Mon to Fri, 10 to 12, 2 to 4, Sat, 10 to 12; free) displays snippets of Liskeard's past. Two well-preserved old shops have proudly ignored modernisation – Ham & Huddy (jewellers) in Fore Street, and just round the corner, Ough's grocery/delicatessen, which is almost like a Cornish heritage museum with its mahogany shop-fittings and behatted assistants serving items loose from jars and glass-fronted cabinets. On the way out of town on the road to Looe, glass-making demonstrations take place at Merlin Glass in Station Road; the factory shop is open seven days a week.

Just to the west of Liskeard, **Dobwall's Theme Park** (open Easter to end Oct, daily, 10 to 6; Nov to Easter telephone Liskeard (0579) 20578 for details of opening times) is worth a visit. The main activities are outside but it can also be a place for a rainy day. Don't miss 'Mr Thorburn's Edwardian Countryside', a recreation of Edwardian England; it includes an exhibition of Archibald Thorburn's work. Mr Southern, owner of Dobwall's, has been collecting his pictures since he was a boy and has the most extensive collection in Britain of this great wildlife artist's paintings. They are brilliantly displayed in reconstructions of their landscapes with accompanying sound effects.

The **Paul Corrin Musical Collection** (open Easter to end Oct, daily, 11 to 5) is obscurely located by a disused watermill south of Liskeard and east of St Keyne, in the soft landscape of the East Looe Valley. It gives a fascinating display of mechanical music-making in some of its most visual guises: allow at least an hour to listen to the machines. You can hear a Belgian fairground organ rattling off polkas and marches with clashing cymbals; piano-rolls giving renditions of jazz and Grieg playing his own compositions; a player-piano lighting up to reveal a built-in xylophone and proceeding to tinkle with the demure sounds of Edwardian parlour music; and a very rare 'Orchestrion' – looking a little like an antique dresser – whizzing through the highlights from *Carmen*. The owner finishes off the show with his own demonstration of popular numbers on a Wurlitzer cinema organ whose huge workings are concealed behind the wall.

In common with much of inland Cornwall, this area's attractions are sparsely scattered and reached by twisting, narrow roads. **Braddock** (Bradoc) **church** has a 'back of beyond' feel to it, half forgotten behind a lane edged with high grass and cow parsley, and in a lovely churchyard of beech trees and hydrangeas. Its wood-carvings are the most interesting feature and include, on the front of the pews, Father Time bearing a corpse's head under his arm.

At **Lanreath**, the **Folk Museum** (open Easter to June and Oct, Sun to Fri, 11 to 1, 2 to 5; June to Sept, Sun to Fri, 10 to 1, 2 to 6) uses a taped commentary to pick out highlights, while a full catalogue details every exhibit if you want to know more. All kinds of local objects – wagons, apparatus from a telephone station, a Bronze Age coffin, antique domestic appliances – are housed in an old tithe barn; craft demonstrations take place upstairs between two and four in the afternoon. The village has a dual attraction, for **Lanreath church** is a beauty: beneath its ancient oak roof is a crude Norman font with zigzag decoration, a rare wooden monument of 1623 masquerading as a costlier item of marble and plaster, a pulpit carved with a two-headed eagle, and a fine rood-screen with ten bays spanning the width of the church.

Looe to Lantic Bay

East of Looe near the coast is **Murrayton Monkey Sanctuary** (open two weeks at Easter, May to Sept, Sun to Fri, 10.30 to 5.30), the world's first protected breeding colony for Amazon Woolly Monkeys; talks are given, and the social manners necessary to gain acceptance with the animals are explained to you.

The chief attraction of **Looe** is its site, in a steep-sided valley on the coast, just below where the wooded West and East Looe rivers join. At the town's fore is a sandy beach and fishing harbour – herring-gulls perch on period street lamps and anglers line up on the pier wall beside boards offering shark-fishing trips. There's a bright and breezy resort atmosphere, with crazy golf, amusement arcades, canoes for hire, stripy deckchairs and shops selling trinkets made of shells. East Looe has the town-centre elements, with most of the shops in Higher Market Street; the old guildhall houses a museum (open Sun to Fri, 10 to 7) featuring Victorian Punch and Judy puppets and an old pilchard press. This central area has a number of restaurants that stay open late at night, most of them concentrated in a grid-iron network of lanes too narrow for cars to pass along.

East Looe is predominantly residential and stretches around the corner to the west, looking out to St George's (or Looe) Island; this was a hermitage in the twelfth century and bombed in the Second World War when the enemy mistook it for a battleship. Further west, **Talland Bay** has an easily accessible beach, though with rather more rock than sand; Talland church nearby has a detached belfry, a beautifully sited churchyard and an exceptional slate monument to John Bevill gracing an oak and granite interior.

Most traffic doesn't attempt to enter the old part of

Polperro, a mile west of Talland Bay, thanks to dire warning notices about the difficulties of parking in the centre. This is as well, since the sheer number of pedestrians at peak times virtually fills the village's narrow lanes and alleys to capacity. Minibuses and a horse-drawn wagon shuttle visitors from a giant car park half a mile inland; other people walk along the road and a few choose to avoid the tackier side of Polperro by walking along the coast path from Talland Bay (20 minutes each way, all on the level beneath the cliff).

Fortunately what everyone comes to see still enchants: the wooded valley in which Polperro is tightly set is too narrow to allow expansion in any other direction than inland along its floor, and the harbour has been carefully preserved. Commercialisation has been genteel and discreet – of the hand-painted sign and bottled-glass window variety – and there's nothing in the way of 'amusements' beyond a model village and a wishing-well tucked away in a back yard (calling itself the Land of Legend and Model Village). Well-fed cats doze with half an eye open on the fishing boats; cameras click at gulls squatting on slate roofs; flower boxes adorn uneven walls; and boards advertise 30-minute boat-trips along the coast. The whimsical Shell House is covered with an inlay of shells, scallops around the windows, and shell depictions of boats and the Eddystone Lighthouse. The ancient House on Props, now a restaurant, stands precariously beside a swan-populated stream draining into the harbour itself. In the past, smuggling supplemented the income of the village; a cellar once allegedly used for the purpose now houses a **museum** (open Easter to end Oct, daily, 10 to dusk) devoted to the history and practice of this lucrative activity, showing tricks of concealment – a hollowed-out book, a turtle-shell and a doll among them – and how and where smugglers carried out their business. The display ends didactically with a stern anti-drugs message.

Lansallos, signposted to the west from Polperro, is little more than a hamlet, though with a good church – finely roofed and containing an unusual bench end showing a negroid head with its nose being pecked by a fabulous bird. From here a path leads half a mile down to secluded Lansallos Cove, a beach of small stones and a patch of sand, with rock-pools left by the tide. There's a more ruggedly set beach at **Lantic Bay**, a majestic crescent of sand reached from a stile on the Polperro–Polruan road at a National Trust sign for Pencarrow Head, then via a zigzagging path from the clifftop; under-currents can be strong however and it's not a place for inexperienced swimmers.

Fowey to Bodmin

In medieval times **Fowey Harbour** was Cornwall's major port and it is still one of the great sights of Cornwall. A mass of boats fills the estuary – pleasure yachts and tug-drawn ships transporting china clay from the docks just upriver; the towns of Fowey and Polruan cling to the slopes on either side, each with its blockhouse fort which together once held a chain across the harbour entrance to slice masts off any incoming enemy ships. On the west side, **Fowey** (pronounced Foy) rises steeply, stacked up terrace by terrace from the Fowey river; zigzag paths provide short cuts from the main car park at the top of the town, past balconied villas and cottages with postage-stamp gardens, all competing for the best view. Halfway down, Place Hall (not open to the public), with its nineteenth-century romantic castellations, is the family seat of the Treffry family whose ancestor Joseph Thomas Treffry brought much prosperity to Cornwall and to himself (see p. 204).

At the bottom, the town centre is a cheerful jumble with the bulk of the shops, pubs, eating-places and galleries concentrated around Fore Street, which runs close to the water's edge (seldom giving sight of it); it continues past the overhanging double-gabled house, now an art shop, known as Noah's Ark, to an eighteenth-century house that is Fowey's main post office, where the road rises and becomes Customs House Hill. An aquarium and museum of local history are housed in a granite building near the quay and lifeboat headquarters, looking out across the harbour. Fowey's famous regatta takes place in August – when there are boat races, bands and fireworks, with the bunting staying up well into September.

You can take the foot-passenger ferry across the heart of the harbour to the village of **Polruan**, from where stepped paths between crooked terraces lead up to more grandstand views of Fowey and the boating scene. A footpath signposted to the hills north-east from Polruan's quay runs along the top edge of the Pont Pill river valley, dropping after a mile to the river at **Pont** where the National Trust have restored an old quay; the shipping dues payable in 1894 are posted on the farmhouse. Just south from here, **Lanteglos by Fowey** church stands beside a farm on the rise. The Perpendicular building is one of the finest of its period in Cornwall, and was sensitively restored in 1900–6, retaining the endearingly drunken angles in its arches.

Beside the B3269 near the roundabout with the A3082, look for the **Tristan Stone**, standing seven feet high and with an identifying plaque. The sixth-century monolith is thought to commemorate Tristan, son of King Mark (of the Tristan and Iseult/Isolde legends), and was originally placed close to Castle Dore, an Iron Age fort lying beside the B3269 just north of the Golant turning. **Golant** itself gives rare access to the riverside. Just before the lane dips to the water-front village, you can see Golant church at the top of the slope. Its interior matches the beauty of its location: the building is all fifteenth century, with original roofs and three surviving box pews; pulpit and stalls are made from old bench ends, showing a fool's head, a jug and a head upon a chesspiece-like castle.

Lostwithiel, further north on the Fowey, was an important medieval port and stannary town (where tin was brought for stamping) but it's no longer a centre of great regional importance. The A390 bisects the town rather fiercely, but the old town has been kept intact and has a few villagey streets of Georgian granite and colour-washed houses, prettified by pots of geraniums and hanging baskets. Everything of interest is here, within the compact medieval grid-pattern of streets. A small town museum in Fore Street has the old town gaol as its main exhibit; and you will find a curious corner-stone in a cottage wall at the junction of Malthouse Lane and North Street granting a 3000-year lease (due to expire in 4652) to a Walter Kendall. The parish church, with its decidedly un-Cornish lantern tower, has a battered old font that still displays interesting carvings, pagan and sacred, on its eight sides – including depictions of the Crucifixion, a bishop, a hunting scene and a head entwined with snakes. In contempt of Church and Crown, Cromwell's men, who used the building as a prison, christened a horse Charles here.

Signposted from Lostwithiel, **Restormel Castle** (English Heritage, open Easter to end Sept, daily, 10 to 6; Oct to Easter, Tues to Sun, 10 to 4; closed 1 Jan, 24 to 26 Dec) crowns a conical hillock sited upon a long spur of land above the Fowey river. Norman keeps have frequently been reduced to grassy humps among stinging-nettles, but Restormel has escaped stone-pilfering and its walls stand to their original height. A galleried walkway gives a view of the site from on high, looking down into what were the kitchen, great hall and other rooms inserted into the twelfth-century structure in the following century. The keep was probably erected to command the crossing of the Fowey river, where there was a hermitage chapel; from about 1270 it belonged to the earls of Cornwall, who occupied it until its ruination in the sixteenth century. A hundred years later, it became a Parliamentarian stronghold under Lord Essex until Sir Richard Grenville's forces drove them out in 1644.

North-west of Restormel is **Lanhydrock House** (National Trust, house open Easter to end Sept, Tues to Sun & Bank Hol Mon, 11 to 6 (5 Oct); garden open all year, Apr to Sept, daily, 11 to 6 (5 Oct) Nov to Mar, daylight hours), a vast mansion with formal gardens within a sizeable estate. It is approached along an avenue of beeches and sycamores that sweeps across sheep-grazed parkland; a vintage car ferries visitors from the car park to the house, for those who wish to save their feet. The house looks Carolean, but most of it was devastated in a fire in 1881, and only the north wing, the gate-house and the entrance hall survive from the seventeenth-century structure, which was built for the Robartes, a family who had made their fortune as Truro bankers and merchants. After the fire, the rebuilding kept to the old layout but introduced the latest in gadgets and creature comforts, including central heating, electric light, an opulent bathroom and a lift for taking trunks up to the luggage room for storage. The house vividly evokes nineteenth-century high living, with the whole interior, from the servants quarters upwards, laid out much as it would have been then – kitchen equipment, cakes on the tea-table, snooker table at the ready and tobacco-pipes in a rack. The gallery running 116 feet along the length of the north wing, survived the fire, and its impressive plaster ceiling incorporates 24 panels displaying incidents from the Old Testament – the whole lit by large mullioned windows that look out over the 38 clipped yew hedges in the garden. It's an absorbing visit, taking at least an hour, longer if you walk around the gardens; the church at the back of the house is uninteresting but has a Saxon cross outside.

Hensbarrow Downs

This area has one of Britain's strangest industrial landscapes:
the brilliant-white lunar scenery created by the china-clay
workings on a 1,000-foot-high granite plateau with its apex at
Hensbarrow Downs, visible for miles around. China clay is
the result of the partial decomposition of felspar, a mineral
found in granite, which changes into a white powder; it is
found along with mica and quartz, and the purification
process which involves separating out these other minerals
creates seven parts of waste to one of usable product. The
results are all around: spoil heaped up into toy mountains,
and – increasingly since the Aberfan disaster of 1966 when a
spoil heap engulfed a Welsh primary school – layered in
'finger-tipped' terraces. In between are the pits, some
working, others abandoned and forming deep, brilliant-
turquoise pools, occasionally overshadowed by the
abandoned towers of engine-houses. Villages are cement-
coloured and dusty, spangled with overhead wires.

China clay, or kaolin (from the Chinese for high ridge),
was originally used to make porcelain; a closely guarded
secret of the Chinese for well over a thousand years. The
search for this material in Europe began in 1718, and in 1746
William Cookworthy was the first to discover it, on
Tregonning Hill near Helston, enabling his manufacture of
the first English 'hard paste' porcelain, at Plymouth. Pits on
the Hensbarrow Downs were later leased by Staffordshire
firms, such as Wedgwood, Spode and Minton.

Extraction methods have been updated over the years, and
the final product is now mostly used as a filler for paper-
making, but the general process is still fundamentally the
same. It involves removing the soil overburden, breaking up
the clay face with water – done today by the use of spray
nozzles – then separating the mica and quartz from the china
clay; this is done by passing water over the clay and allowing
the waste material to settle in a solution prior to thickening
the liquid. All this is well-illustrated at the open-air museum
at **Wheal Martyn** (open daily, Easter to Oct, 10 to 5) at
Carthew on the A391 north of St Austell. After an audio-
visual introduction, you follow a marked trail past
waterwheels (used for pumping the clay to the surface),
settling-pits and a pan-kiln where the clay was dried.
Exhibits also include the methods over the ages of
transporting the final product – horse-wagon, railway and

lorry (a rare Peerless lorry of 1916 has been rescued from a state of advanced decay). Tacked on to the main visit, a nature trail leads past reclaimed spoil heaps to a spectacular view over two working pits.

If the area's unearthly appearance intrigues you it is easily explored further – from the car – by driving north to Bugle, then north-west to **Roche**. The latter takes its name from the French for rock, referring to an igneous outcrop on the Bugle road on the east side of the village. A hermitage chapel was built on its summit, and was dedicated in 1409 to St Michael; the last male heir of Tregarrick was reputed to have come here as a leper, tended by his daughter Gundred whose devotion led to the village church being dedicated to her. The chapel ruin survives, approachable by a steep iron ladder; it broods over green farmland in one direction and over spoil heaps, pylons and housing estates in the other. Whichever road you chose, the drive south-west past Nanpean in the general direction of **St Stephen** has more views of this strange, despoiled scenery. Just to the west of St Stephen, on the A3058, **Automobilia** (open June to Sept, 10 to 6, Apr, May and Oct, 10 to 4) displays motoring nostalgia – an accumulation rather than a museum – featuring restored cars, old RAC badges, tops of 1930s petrol pumps and more.

St Austell is the headquarters of English China Clays and has expanded with the growth of the industry into a busy town. Its church, in an area of sloping streets, has a handsome fifteenth-century tower, but the rest of the town is quite plain.

Almost joined on to St Austell on the latter's south-eastern side, **Charlestown** is a rare example of an industrial port small enough in scale and sufficiently unchanged to have strong visual appeal. China clay is loaded here through shutes dusted with that tell-tale chalky whiteness; the neatly ordered rectangular harbour was developed by Charles Rashleigh in the 1790s for shipments of ore, pilchards and clay. The **Shipwreck and Heritage Museum** (open Mar to Oct, every day, 10 to 4, later in high season) on one side of the harbour, has a few life-size tableaux of village craftsmen and a cottage parlour, but the main interest is the shipwreck display: stories of wrecks all around the British coast and substantial quantities of salvage – coins, rusty penknives, torpedo components, and the entire rescued material from an eighteenth-century warship.

To the east lies **Par**, full of lorries and clay dust, developed as a mineral port by entrepreneur Joseph Treffry in the early nineteenth century. Since 1964 the harbour has been owned by English China Clays, and together with Charlestown and Fowey exports two million tons of clay each year. Treffry built a canal to transport granite from Ponts Mill, situated to the north, to Par. You can see remains of his grandiose scheme in the woods of the **Luxulyan Valley**, now a place of quiet beauty. South of Luxulyan and spanning the valley with the British Rail line at the bottom, the redundant **Treffry Viaduct** – 95 feet high and 650 feet long – is unusual in carrying a leat, or water-channel, beneath what was a horse-drawn tramway for pulling trucks of pink and black-speckled granite known as Luxulyanite. Treffry solved the problem of linking the high-level tramway with the canal at Ponts Mill by engineering the leat to feed a waterwheel which hauled the trucks up Carmears Incline, rising 325 feet over a distance of 2781 feet. Today, footpaths lead from the bottom of the valley floor and the leat, incline, waterwheel and viaduct can be explored on foot.

Helman Tor, north-east of Luxulyan, provides one of the best viewing platforms over central Cornwall; it is in surprisingly remote country, but signposted from a maze of tiny lanes, with a footpath taking you the last few yards from the car park. Granite boulders strewn over the summit overlook Hensbarrow Downs, Lanhydrock Woods and the Gilbert Monument near Bodmin. Around the base of the hill is Red Moor Nature Reserve, a former wasteland of tin-streaming, now interesting as a site of mixed heath and bog with its own nature trail.

Mevagissey to Veryan

The coastal village of **Mevagissey** can get monstrously overcrowded but the vast car park keeps most cars out of the centre: 'park and ride' signs greet you on the approach from the B3273 south from St Austell, in case the car park is full. What people come for is a slice of picturesque Cornwall in the area around the harbour. Commercialisation has arrived in force: the first thing you see on leaving the car park is a hut selling a vast population of garden gnomes, then you pass the postcard racks, chippies, picture galleries and tea-shops. But Mevagissey is still an important fishing village in its own right, with brightly painted working craft crammed into the inner harbour and terraces of crooked cottages on its northern side. From vantage-points along the harbour walls you can take in the whole scene. Three indoor attractions open in the tourist season: a museum of local artefacts of all kinds in a former workshop on one side of the quay; an aquarium in the lifeboat house on the other; and an elaborate model railway layout inside a building behind Fore Street. Fishing- and pleasure-trips are advertised in the harbour, and angling shops give details of deep-sea fishing trips.

To the north, **St Ewe** has a happy-looking centre, with flower-tubs adorning the walls of the Crown Inn and a pleasant array of cottages around the stepped platform of an old market cross. All Saints' church is older than most Cornish churches, with a fourteenth-century tower and a medieval roof over its south aisle. Particularly eye-catching is the woodwork of the carved screen, showing a naked man with dragons and birds entwined in foliage. There are a number of monuments, including one to William Mohun (1737), with a bust and fruit decoration.

South from Mevagissey along the coast, **Gorran Haven** has unremarkable modern outskirts but possesses a pocket of unordered quaintness around Church Street, less than six feet wide in places and steep in typical Cornish fashion: a mêlée of potted hyacinths on doorsteps, carriage-lamps by the doors, cottages with names such as Cabin and Upper Deck, and a diminutive church.

The splendid coast path south from here to **Dodman Point** passes above Vault Beach – accessible to the energetic and often deserted – before reaching the landmark cross on the point itself. This is the site of one of Cornwall's largest Iron Age cliff castles, and the 2,000-foot-long ditch enclosing its landward side is still obvious; there's quicker access from a car park at Penare farm a mile north of the point.

The coast west from here is remote in character and the closest road to it takes a crazily roundabout route. You can reach sea-level at two lovely beaches, **Hemmick Beach** and, a little further on, **Porthluney Cove**, which is backed by trees and the mock-medieval Caerhays Castle (not open to the public) which John Nash designed in 1808 for the Trevanion family. The road covers three times the distance of the coast path to arrive at **Portholland**, an unspoilt hamlet over a cove, with doves on a dovecot and a chapel hiding behind the hill.

A few miles west **Portloe** gives a rare insight into what much of Cornwall must once have been like. The village snuggles at the mouth of a deep and wild-looking valley, above an inlet where smocked fishermen draw their boats on to the quay; the coast path south-west to Jacka Point gives an impressive view over it all. There's virtually no room for new building, and certainly no manoeuvring space for coaches; with the slow and tortuous lanes around here Portloe must be one of Cornwall's best-kept secrets. **Veryan** inland to the west, has five 'round houses' – cottages of circular plan – scattered throughout the village, erected in the early nineteenth century by the Rev Jeremiah Trist, the local squire and vicar. Probably the most photographed are the pair of thatched rustic conceits topped by crosses flanking either side of the road on the south side of the village.

The fishing industry in Cornwall

Cornwall's fishing activity accounts for much of the county's picturesque character beloved of artists, visitors and the heritage industry. Its most colourful types – bewhiskered, weather-beaten fishermen and scarlet-cloaked, black-hatted Newlyn fishwives among them – have disappeared, but fishermen's cottages survive, huddled beside the quays. The trawlers provide local colour and display registration numbers prefixed by letters denoting the port authority – FH for Falmouth, FY Fowey, PW Padstow, PZ Penzance, PH Plymouth and SS St Ives.

From medieval times, the humble pilchard (an adult sardine) was the keystone of the Cornish fishing economy – collected over many centuries by the process of seining and later by drifting. In the seine system, three boats operated two nets: the 40-foot-long 'seine boat' and the 'follower' each took a net and seven or eight men, and were guided by the master seiner in the 'lurker' or 'cock boat'. The seine was rowed out in the early morning and directed by the 'huer' on land: on spotting a shoal of pilchards, appearing as a purple patch on the water, he would shout through a loudspeaker trumpet 'hevva, hevva!' (from the Cornish 'hesva', meaning shoal), and signal using white hoops, known as bushes. Each seine company (larger fishing centres had several companies) patrolled an allocated area of water.

The shoals could be enormous – perhaps half a mile across and containing 10,000 pilchards; a record catch at St Ives in 1868 numbered 5600 hogsheads, or 16,500,000 fish. The seine-net had

Truro to St Mawes

Truro feels as if it ought to be Cornwall's capital and its largest town, though in fact it's neither – Bodmin is the county town, and Falmouth and Camborne-Redruth (sometimes counted as one place) are bigger. But Truro has a confident character, a smart shopping centre, some Georgian buildings and streets, and the first cathedral to be built in England since Wren's new St Paul's.

The **cathedral**, built 1880–1910 after Truro had appointed its first bishop in 1876, was the masterpiece of John Pearson, who showed considerable ingenuity in dealing with a

---

floats on one side and weights on the other, allowing it to be suspended in the water in a semicircle, with the area enclosed by a stop-net. Great care was needed to bring the valuable catch back towards the shore, where attendant boats helped lower a tuck-net into the captive shoal, which little by little was decanted into baskets and taken to the fish cellars. Here, in this pre-refrigeration era, the fish were 'bulked': cleaned, pressed, salted and stacked neatly layer upon layer, a job usually carried out by women.

Many people were employed in jobs ancillary to fishing, including fish merchants, rope- and net-makers, smiths, coopers, shipwrights and boat-builders. But the industry was a volatile one. Demand in England for pilchards was never high, and most were sold in Mediterranean countries; in times of war prices plummeted. The dangers of the sea – natural and piratical – and the fickle appearances of the shoals caused massive fluctuations in the wealth of a community. Village life was close-knit but frequently hard: the pilchard season extended from July or August to October or November, six days a week, with little opportunity for the fishermen to rest except on the strictly observed Sabbath. Mackerel and herring fishing were sometimes carried out in other seasons.

Seiners came into competition with drifters, who hung strung-together nets in the water, forming great walls up to a mile long, to trap the pilchards. This practice sometimes broke up the shoals and was the cause of considerable dispute between seiners and drifters, but by the mid-nineteenth century drifting predominated. Fish cellars became redundant as tanks were built to cure pilchards, a system thought to have been first introduced at Mevagissey. Further

---

cramped site on which the old parish church of St Mary stood. He integrated the church's south aisle into the outer aisle of the new building, and created a sense of height and rhythm, invoking the Early English style without achieving mere pastiche. There was no space for a grand cathedral close, so his design was around three spired towers, the tallest soaring 250 feet and dominating the city centre. Money was not plentiful – there was more wealth in Methodism than in the established church in the county – and Pearson's chapter house adjoining the cathedral was never completed: the arches were removed and installed in a school by the river, and a concrete structure was built in its stead in 1967.

Tin and copper mining made fortunes for some in the eighteenth and nineteenth centuries, and Truro became one of the fashionable social centres of the day. Only bits and pieces have survived from this heyday, but Lemon Street, leading up from Boscawen Street, is especially handsome Georgian, strikingly unified by the use of Bath stone; a memorial to Richard Lander (1804–34), a pioneer explorer in West Africa, is at the top of the street. Tiny Walsingham Place curves elegantly beneath the cathedral spires from Victoria Square.

Also worth a look when in Truro the **County Museum and Art Gallery** (open all year Mon to Sat, 9 to 5; closed Bank

---

change occurred with the opening of the Tamar Bridge and the arrival of the railway in Cornwall in 1859, London now providing a market for spring mackerel, which had to be landed in time for the early afternoon train to Paddington. Faster boats were built, and Newlyn became, and still is, the main Cornish fish depot.

Around the turn of the century the pilchard shoals disappeared from the Cornish coast; the last big catch was made in 1907. Drifting or trawling was probably the cause since the nets extracted indiscriminately, taking infant fish and their food sources with them. Seiners and drifters were united in their opposition to the trawlers, whose activities often broke the drift nets, probably deliberately at times, and brawls were not uncommon. With the decline of stocks of fish near the shore, fishing boats had to travel out further from the coast, and today deep-sea trawling for a variety of fish is the rule.

Holidays) in River Street has a collection of paintings by Cornish artists, mineral exhibits and archaeological finds; with a coffee-shop attached.

Two miles south-east of Truro, **Malpas** and **St Clement** are on separate no-through roads, both enjoying quiet waterside views; from the latter an attractive path leads alongside the Tresillian river.

Cornwall's tallest church tower dominates the centre of **Probus**, on the A390 between Truro and St Austell. At the east end of the village, the **County Demonstration Garden** (open May to Sept, daily, 10 to 5; Oct to Apr, Mon to Fri, 10 to 4.30), run by the Cornwall Education Committee, is an excellent place for stocking up on gardening ideas whatever your horticultural constraints and aspirations. The $7\frac{1}{2}$-acre area is laid out as a series of plots showing plant varieties, techniques and how to tackle particular problems – creating a rock garden, supporting plants on fences and walls, choosing what to grow in exposed sites. An adviser is on duty on Thursdays, from 2 to 5.

Virtually next door to the east, **Trewithen** (garden open Mar to Sept, 10 to 4.30; house open Apr to July, Mon and Tues, 2 to 4.30) has grounds extending over 30 acres. The park was created soon after the building of the fine Georgian house in 1723, but little else happened until George Johnstone inherited the estate in 1904 and set about transforming the walled garden – by then taken over by the washing-line – into a formal feature; he created a glade in front of the house and introduced many rare shrubs and trees, including exotic species; look out for one of only two mature specimens found in this country of Rehderodendron Macrocarrum, a tree brought to Britain in 1934. In late spring and early summer, there are blazes of rhododendrons, azaleas and magnolias; plants on sale in the nursery are mainly propagated here. If you catch the house open, it's worth taking the guided tour.

The Roseland peninsula extending south along the east side of the great natural harbour of Carrick Roads is green and fertile, but its name has nothing to do with roses; it derives from the Cornish 'ros' meaning headland. The King Harry Ferry links the two halves of the B3289 across the River Fal, saving miles if you are coming from Truro or Falmouth. Further south, **St Just in Roseland** is known solely for its churchyard: sloping steeply down to a creek, it is luxuriant with Chinese fan-palms, tree-ferns, magnolias, Chilean myrtles and fuchsias. In the early part of this century the Rev Humfrey Davis placed granite stones along the main path, each inscribed with verses and texts ('God is Love'; 'O sweet St Just in Roseland, thy name forever dear. . . .'); some he devised himself, others taken from scriptures or hymns. It all verges on sentimentality, but the atmosphere is exquisitely restful unless you visit during the tourist season.

The A3078 leads south from here down into **St Mawes**, the harbour full of yachts and the main street, ribboned along the harbourside, busy with yachtsmen and visitors who may have arrived by the little ferry from Falmouth. One road, Church Hill, clambers up a one in three slope past candy-coloured houses to a minute church, and steps lead from the Victory Inn to a corner of slate-hung and ivy-clad cottages. For all its charm, there is little old-world about St Mawes, though it has retained its Tudor **castle** (English Heritage, open all year, Easter to Oct, daily, 10 to 6 (5 Oct to Easter), Closed 1 Jan, 24 to 26 Dec), as pristine as its twin Pendennis (see p. 213) across the harbour. The compact fortress has a round tower and lobed bastions on three sides in clover-leaf formation, enclosed by a curtain wall abutting the coast; it was designed to enable cannons to control as large an arc as possible, firing at four levels, but the castle and its guns were never used.

The Perthcuel river divides the southern part of Roseland into two, making its eastern side all the more remote. **Towan Beach**, south of the tranquil but considerably expanded coastal resort village of Porthscatho is sandy. The beach is concealed from the road but easily reached by a short path from a National Trust car park. At the end of the road, the promontory of **Zone Point**, fortified in Napoleonic times, juts out as Roseland's southernmost tip, giving a glorious view over the Carrick Roads, Falmouth Harbour and Pendennis Castle. Immediately below, but hidden from the top, St Anthony lighthouse is open to the public.

Truro to Falmouth

Before the river system flowing south from Truro broadens out into Carrick Roads, two places deserve seeking out for their intrinsic interest. **Come-to-Good**, on an unclassified road east of Carnon Downs on the A39, derives its name from the Cornish cwm-ty-quite (the house of the valley of the woods). The hamlet is known for its primitive but fetchingly pretty Quaker Meeting House of 1710 – thatched, with diamond-leaded windows and green shutters. Inside all is barn-like simplicity: free-standing benches on a wooden floor, with the thatch showing above. Off the B3289 east of Come-to-Good, close by the King Harry Ferry, is **Trelissick Garden** (open April to end Sept, Mon to Sat, 11 to 6 (5 Mar & Oct) Sun, 1 to 6 (5 Mar & Oct), the grounds of a classical mansion (not open to the public) built in 1825 around the core of an earlier house. The rebuilding was carried out for Thomas Daniell, son of Ralph Allen Daniell – who made a huge fortune in Cornish mines – but in 1832 Trelissick was sold and Thomas Daniell left the country. The house was inherited in 1937 by Ida Copeland, and she and her husband enlarged the shrubbery, adding a splendid range of rhododendrons, azaleas, and various other shrubs and trees. These are seen from winding paths and spacious lawns; there is abundant colour here all year round. The park spreads down to the water's edge, looking far out to Pendennis Castle; industrial ships anchored nearby in the deep harbourage offered by the Fal look huge beyond the foreground of beeches and oaks.

The Fal estuary, otherwise known as **Carrick Roads**, is one of Britain's prime yachting centres and a superb sight in itself, dotted with craft of all sizes from dinghies to ocean-going freighters. One of the largest natural harbours in the world, Carrick Roads proper extends a mile across, but the numerous creeks that feed it are much more intimate and sheltered. Green farmland sweeps almost to the water's edge, and waterside villages and walks are mostly low-level. Pleasure cruises from Falmouth to Truro are an excellent way to take it all in.

Villages on the estuary such as **Feock**, **Point** and **Devoran** are invariably pleasant, dominated by yacht-masts and large well-kept houses; there is little to distinguish one place from the next. The quay at **Mylor Churchtown**, halfway down on the west side, was constructed by the admiralty early in the nineteenth century as a place to train young naval cadets. In the churchyard here is the tallest (when measured from its base) Saxon cross in Cornwall, though some of it lies below present ground-level. **Flushing**, just north of Falmouth, was renamed after the Netherlands town by Dutch engineers who lived here in the seventeenth century while working on the construction of Falmouth harbour and the sea walls. The

211

Dutch influence goes beyond the name: the simple, uniform rows of rendered cottages don't look quite English. Passenger ferries ply regularly across from here to Falmouth.

Penryn, north of Falmouth, is bypassed by the A39, from which it appears to be quite nondescript, and as a result is, quite unfairly, little visited. The creation of Falmouth gradually eclipsed this town, which had prospered as a port dealing particularly in the shipping of granite from quarries nearby at Mabe. But Penryn did not lose its handsome centre – ranged along and around a cambered main street built on the spine of a ridge. It is a town of tawny-coloured granite houses, of slopes and unexpected peace in secretive alleys, dominated by the town hall which splits the main street in two, with an Italianate Methodist chapel and the Teetotal Hall close at hand. Mutton Row, much prettier than it sounds, is stepped and decked out with hanging baskets of flowers; Bank Cottages and Easom's Yard – both near the town hall – are quaintly flagged and cobbled. The main street broadens out at the site of the old fish market by the King's Arms, and attractive Thomas Street descends past Queen Anne Cottage (1700), next to a Georgian house of alien red brick, to a pub called the Famous Barrel. To the right, a field with the fragments of an arch in it, is the site of Glasney College, renowned in medieval times as a seat of learning but demolished soon after the dissolution of the monasteries.

Falmouth, at the west mouth of the estuary and the largest town in Cornwall, sprawls inelegantly but has a wonderful site, and is best viewed from the water itself. The town divides into a deep-water port on the town-centre side and a beach resort of lush gardens, bay-windowed B&Bs and rows of semis on the other; the promontory, capped by the fortification of Pendennis Castle, abuts in between. A somewhat undistinguished square is the obvious centre, flanked on one side by a public library with a newly opened **gallery** of paintings in the town's collection – works by Alfred Munnings, Laura Knight and J.W. Waterhouse in particular. At the corner of High Street and Church Street the Morning Price Gallery offers Far-Eastern tribal masks and carvings for sale. From here, the long main street runs parallel with the water, though you only catch glimpses of the estuary and its boats down stepped alleys. From the pier boat-trips will show you the best of the estuary and passenger-ferries cross to St Mawes and Flushing. Further on is the harbour, full of trawlers, nets and local colour, with the porticoed Customs House backed by a red-brick chimney known as the King's Pipe, where seized contraband used to be incinerated. The steam tug *St Denys*, built in 1929, is berthed here, forming part of the **Maritime Museum** (open all year, daily, 10 to 4), and can be visited by anyone agile enough to manage its narrow ladders; the main museum is on land, signposted opposite Marks and Spencer, and concentrates on the seafaring history of the area, including stories of shipwrecks and the Carrick Roads fortifications, model ships and quays, and nautical equipment. Close by, the parish church is unusual for its dedication to Charles I and for its interior, mostly of 1896, blending Gothic and classical styles.

Further along towards the mouth of the estuary you'll find a pyramidal monument to the Killigrew family, opposite a fragment of their former home, Arwenack House, where they lived from the fourteenth century. The Killigrews were Royalists in the Civil War and after the Restoration of the Monarchy, Charles II rewarded them by granting a charter to create a port below Penryn and Truro. The new port of Falmouth prospered with the advent of the mail-packets in 1688, shipping mail to and from international destinations, and doubtless enabling lucrative smuggling opportunities for crew members. By 1827, 39 ships from all over the world brought mail here, but a quarter of a century later the trade was taken over by Southampton and Liverpool. Falmouth lives on as a major deep-water port, with a busy area of docks, shipyards and warehouses, marked by a forest of cranes dominating the skyline near the estuary mouth; close by the port, new marina developments are appearing on the scene.

Just beyond is the promontory crowned by the fortifications of **Pendennis Castle** (English Heritage, open Easter to end Sept, daily, 10 to 6; Oct to Easter, Tues to Sun, 10 to 4. Closed 1 Jan, 24 to 26 Dec), erected under Henry VIII as part of the national defences against a possible French invasion, but only used in the Civil War as a successful Royalist stronghold. The castle, entered across a drawbridge and encircled by a curtain wall, is immaculately preserved, an outstanding example of military architecture, designed to maximise the angles of fire: one of the octagonal gun rooms has been set up as it would have looked with the guns manned. Another reason to visit is for the tremendous panoramic view over Carrick Roads.

Falmouth to Gweek

West of Falmouth on the road to Constantine you will see the entrance to **Lamanva Military Vehicles Museum** (open Easter to end Sept, daily, 10 to 5, Oct to Easter, Mon to Fri, 10 to 5. Closed 2 weeks Christmas and New Year). The Second World War theme predominates, and period pop music throbs in the background, although many of the jeeps, armoured vehicles and army trucks are replicas made for feature films.

To the south, two superb gardens lie side by side on the road from Mawnan Smith to Helford Passage, in this lush and mild country. Both occupy sinuous valley sites that slope down to the Helford river. **Glendurgan Gardens** (National Trust, open Mar to end Oct, Tues to Sat & Bank Hol Mon, 10.30 to 5.30, closed Good Friday), the grounds of a nineteenth-century house (not open), were the creation of Alfred Fox in the 1820s and 1830s. He planted a laurel maze, built a walled garden and landscaped the whole with fine trees, including *Liriodendron tulipifera* (tulip trees) on the east side of the glen; in this century Cuthbert Fox, a descendant of the earlier owner, was responsible for planting many of the shrubs. Glendurgan has a dreamy quality, softly coloured (according to the time of year) with yellow king-cups or pink and purple rhododendrons, graced with a shady lily pond and sheltered from the wind by its natural site. Glimpses of the river entice you down to the bottom, where there is the tiniest of hamlets on a pebbly cove, with lobster-pots piled up outside a house called Postbox Cottage. **Trebah Garden** (open all year, daily, 10.30 to 5) next door was also Fox property and is just as romantic. It is particularly memorable for its exotic plants and trees: towering palms and 60-foot-high rhododendrons, with a zigzag path through a collection of Mediterranean plants and a tunnel perforating thick growths of gigantic Brazilian rhubarb. Trebah has more organised activity for children than Glendurgan, with a play area and a garden trail; plants are for sale in a nursery shop at the entrance.

At the large village of **Gweek** the B3291 crosses the Helford river where dinghy masts bob in a pretty creek. Signposted from the village centre the **Cornish Seal Sanctuary** (open Easter to Nov, daily, 9.30 to 6; Nov to Easter, daily, 9.30 to 2; limited facilities during winter) carries out rescue work on sick and injured seals and sea-lions found on shores anywhere round the country; exhibitions explain the project. While the sickest animals recuperate in the 'hospital', others flip around in pools, bark at each other or snore blissfully on rubber tyres.

Highlights

** *Antony House, Carrick Roads (Fal Estuary), Cotehele House and Quay, Fowey Harbour, Lanhydrock House, Polperro.*

* *Charlestown, Come-to-Good Meeting House, Glendurgan and Trebah Gardens, Hensbarrow Downs (China Clay Country), Kingsand and Cawsand, Kit Hill, Lanreath, Mevagissey Portloe, Probus, Restormel Castle, St Just-in-Roseland, Trelissick Garden, Truro.*

Where to stay

For a key to prices, see p. 12

Calstock
Danescombe Valley Hotel
Calstock, Cornwall PL18 9RY. Tel Tavistock (0822) 832414
A stunning position on the bend of the Tamar river and only a woodland walk away from the lovely Cotehele estate. The Georgian house has a wide verandah with first-floor bedrooms opening on to it. Style is evident throughout: pretty and comfortable without being overdone, lots of books and games in the cosy bar, and lovely watercolours by a local artist hanging all round the house. Price includes a four-course dinner.
££££ *Nov to Mar; Wed, Thurs*

Fowey
Marina Hotel
The Esplanade, Fowey, Cornwall PL23 1HY. Tel Fowey (0726) 833315
Guests can unload luggage at the hotel and then leave their cars further up in the car park of this extremely pretty seaside town, built into the hillside. It is a compact, very well-run hotel whose hill position makes for a rather odd arrangement of rooms. The sitting- and dining-rooms are one floor down from the entrance hall, with an adjacent terrace and small garden where you can sit and watch the comings and goings in the estuary below. The bar, separated from the dining-room by a white trellis intertwined with trailing plants, has a quite genteel atmosphere; a small

chintzy sitting-room has cosier comfy seating. Bedrooms are equally neat and light, with pine furnishings and pretty floral fabrics; not all overlook the estuary so book early to ensure a lovely view.

££ Closed Nov to end Feb

Mawnan Smith

Budock Vean

Mawnan Smith, nr Falmouth, Cornwall TR11 5LG. Tel Falmouth (0326) 250288

A sporting hotel complex with a comfortingly old-fashioned atmosphere in spite of the informality. A golf course surrounds it and outbuildings house a swimming pool, further accommodation, games rooms etc. It is in a lovely spot with grounds stretching down to the sea; guests can sit out in the loggia and admire the view. A number of large, high-ceilinged beamed sitting-rooms, with huge open fireplaces and stags' heads on the walls, are comfortable and informal. A long and varied menu offers bar snacks, more substantial dishes and a formal dinner in the unusual open-plan dining room.

££££ Closed early Jan to late Feb

Meudon Hotel

Mawnan Smith, nr Falmouth, Cornwall TR11 5HT. Tel Falmouth (0326) 250541. Telex 45478 Meudon G. Fax (0326) 250543

The subtropical gardens of this hotel stretch down to the sea and are one of its most remarkable features. The sitting-rooms overlook them, the dining-room opens on to them and nearly every small seating area can take advantage of them. It is very much a family-run hotel with two generations of the Pilgrim family organising their guests – many of them regulars, even with the fairly high prices. It has an old-fashioned feel, with traditional furnishings in some of the public rooms. The bedroom block, separate from the main building, is modern and characterless but all rooms face the garden and are light and peaceful; they have recently been refurbished in a variety of colour schemes.

£££££ Closed Jan, Feb

Nansidwell Country House

Mawnan Smith, nr Falmouth, Cornwall TR11 5HU. Tel (0326) 250340. Fax (0326) 250440

An exceptionally pretty house built of Cornish stone, creeper-clad and with mullion windows. You can sit on the terrace and look out across five acres of subtropical gardens leading towards the sea. The atmosphere is one of easy informality although the service is entirely efficient. Decor and furnishings throughout are stylish and understated, and guests undoubtedly have a relaxed comfortable stay. The bedrooms are individually decorated: stripped old pine and antique cotton in some, patchwork quilts and antiques in others.

££££–£££££ Closed 27 Dec to 1 Feb

St Austell

Boscundle Manor

Tregrehan, St Austell, Cornwall PL25 3RL. Tel Par (072 681) 3557

A couple of miles east of St Austell, this mainly eighteenth-century house has acres of grounds and gardens although is itself quite close to the road. The Flints are busy planting and landscaping when they can spare time from being extremely friendly hosts: they give a high standard of service and cooking while retaining a relaxed informality. Public rooms and bedrooms echo this with a mixture of antiques and modern furnishings.

££££ Closed mid-Oct to Easter

St Keyne
The Well House

St Keyne, Liskeard, Cornwall PL14 4RN. Tel Liskeard (0579) 42001

It's quite a surprise to come upon this hotel, tucked discreetly off a tiny lane. Nick Wainford has decorated and furnished the house (built in 1894) in pale sophisticated colours, modern-style, to create a smart very well-equipped hotel. The sitting-room and restaurant overlook the terrace and swimming pool across to the hills. The bedrooms are neatly co-ordinated and have lots of luxurious extras. The five-course menu does not come cheap but won't disappoint.

££££ Open all year

St Mawes
Hotel Tresanton

St Mawes, Cornwall TR2 5DR. Tel St Mawes (0326) 270544. Fax (0326) 270002

Built across a number of terraces at different levels, this hotel gives wonderful views out to sea: the modern dining-room has a whole wall of glass. Guests have to pass through the

cosy bar to reach the dining-room or terraces but there's a more private, if slightly gloomy, sitting-room at the side. Bedrooms are slightly old-fashioned, some with candlewick covers or chintz, and vary in size and outlook but they are generally comfortable.

£££ Closed Nov to Mar, exc Christmas to New Year

Talland
Talland Bay

Nr Looe, Cornwall PL13 2JB. Tel Polperro (0503) 72667. Fax (0503) 72940

The subtropical gardens surrounding this black-and-white house have some unusual plants and shrubs. The hotel is well placed for holidays, only a few minutes from the rocky beach and the cliffs. The decor is old-fashioned but the atmosphere peaceful and friendly, and the bedrooms comfortable.

££££-£££££ Closed Jan

Tregony
Tregony House

Tregony, Truro, Cornwall TR2 5RN. Tel Tregony (087 253) 671

The house, right in the centre of this quiet village, is part-seventeenth, part-eighteenth century. The front has high-ceilinged spacious rooms – the residents' lounge among them – while at the back the dining-room shows its earlier origins with a low ceiling and black beams. The lounge isn't particularly cosy but is comfortable enough, with TV and plenty of books and games. By contrast the dining-room, with a small bar at one end, is cosy and welcoming. Bedrooms are simple and pretty, not all with en suite bathrooms. The atmosphere is more that of a guesthouse than a hotel and the friendly owners do everything themselves.

£ *Open Mar to Oct*

Truro

Alverton Manor

Tregolls Road, Truro, Cornwall TR1 1XQ. Tel Truro (0872) 76633. Fax (0872) 222989
This well-restored Victorian manor house used to belong to the bishop of Truro; very close to the centre, it is set back from the dual carriageway up on a hill and is surprisingly quiet. Everything is smart, newly refurbished and beautifully co-ordinated, and the service is immaculate, but there is not much atmosphere. The bedrooms, though extremely comfortable and with all the luxuries, feel rather self-conscious. It will all probably take a little time to soften up. The food is delicious and beautifully presented.

£££ *Open all year*

Veryan

The Nare Hotel

Carne Beach, Veryan, Nr Truro, Cornwall TR2 5PF. Tel Truro (0872) 501279. Fax (0872) 501856
Another hotel in a wonderful position – overlooking one of the secluded beaches in the Roseland peninsula. The hotel itself is no beauty; everything has been sacrificed for the view. Bedrooms facing the sea have sliding windows, floor to ceiling, so you can lie in bed looking straight out to sea. Rooms on the ground floor open on to the garden and in the summer you can wander on to the terrace with a cup of tea or evening drink. Public rooms are quite smart, with some interesting pieces and modern pictures, but the atmosphere is informal and children are welcome (check the safety of bedroom windows if not on ground floor). The beach is only a few minutes' walk and there's plenty to do in the hotel with tennis, sauna and swimming.

££–£££ *Open all year*

Where to eat

For a key to prices see p. 12

Blackwater

Long's Restaurant

Blackwater. Tel Truro (0872) 561111
A smart conversion of the former headquarters of a tin-mining company. Lots of choice, well-presented and finely cooked.

Open Wed to Sat, 7.30–10, 12.30–1.45, Closed 4 weeks during winter

Calstock

Danescombe Valley Hotel

Lower Kelly, Calstock. Tel Tavistock (0822) 832414
Attractive house in a lovely

position. Need to book if a non-resident. Delicious food.
Open Fri to Tues 7.30 for 8.
Closed Nov to Easter

Fowey
Food for Thought

Town Quay, Fowey. Tel Fowey
(072 683) 2221
On the quayside, only open for
dinners. Simple and elaborate
dishes expertly cooked.
Open Mon to Sat 7–9.30 Closed
Jan/early Feb

Falmouth
De Wynne's Coffee House

55 Church Street, Falmouth. Tel
Falmouth (0326) 319259
Bow-windowed coffee/tea shop
right on the waterfront.
[£] *Open all week Mon to Sat
10–5, Sun 11–4*

Feock
Trelissick Garden Restaurant

Truro. Tel Truro (0872) 863486
A simple, good café serving
visitors to the garden. Lots of
salads and hot dishes.
Open all week Mon to Sat 11–6,
12–4 Sun. Closed Jan and Feb

Grampound
Eastern Promise

1 Moor View, Grampound. Tel
St Austell (0726) 883033
Popular Chinese restaurant
with well-cooked if not unusual
dishes.
Open Thurs to Tues 6–11

Gweek
Mellanoweth

Gweek. Tel Mawgan
(0326) 22271
In the summer you can get good

cheap lunches here, mainly
filled crêpes, soups and salads.
[£] *Open all year 7.15–9, summer
all week 12–2*

Mevagissey
Mr Bistro

East Quay, The Harbour,
Mevagissey. Tel Mevagissey
(0726) 842432
Fish and chips and more
sophisticated dishes served in
this converted pilchard store.
[£] *at lunch. Open all week 12–3,
7–10 Closed Nov to Feb*

Mylor Bridge
Pandora Inn

Restronguet Creek, nr Mylor
Bridge. Tel Falmouth
(0326) 72678
Overlooking the tidal creek and
specialising in seafood, this is a
very popular pub in summer.
[£] *Open Mon to Sat 11–11,
Sun 12–3, 7–10.30*

Philleigh
Roseland Inn

Phillleigh. Tel Portscatho
(087 258) 254
Very pretty pub serving simple
but tasty bar food.
[£] *Open all week 12–1.45,
summer 12–1.45 7–9 Closed
Christmas Day*

Polperro
Kitchen

The Coombes, Polperro. Tel
Polperro (0503) 72780
Small cottagey restaurant offers
a selection of set menus
including a vegetarian option.
Open Wed to Mon 6.30–9.30,
Fri and Sat only in winter

Sun Lounge

Little Green, Polperro. Tel
Polperro (0503) 72459
A good place for a late breakfast
as well as lunch and dinner.
Quite a simple place but the
food is well cooked.
[£] *Open Mon (Wed in winter) to
Sat 10–2.30, 6.30–10, Mon and
Tues in winter, and 2nd week Jan to
Easter*

St Dominick

Cotehele Barn

Cotehele Estate, St Dominick.
Tel Liskeard (0579) 50652
Beautiful National Trust manor
house with the restaurant in the
barn. Good wholesome food.
Sunday lunch particularly good
value.
[£] *Open Sat to Thurs; 12–5.30,
open spasmodically 31 Oct to Good
Fri or Apr 1*

St Keyne

Well House

St Keyne. Tel Liskeard
(0579) 42001
Very good food in this smart
restaurant. Also has rooms
(see p. 217).
*Open Tues to Sun 7.30–9; lunch by
arrangement only*

Tideford

Heskyn Mill

Tideford. Tel Landrake
(0752) 851481
The dining-room is upstairs in
this pretty mill. Some elaborate,
some plain dishes.
Open Tues to Sat 12–1.45, 7–10

Truro

Alverton Manor

Tregolls Road, Truro. Tel Truro
(0872) 76633
Come here for a special lunch or
dinner. Beautifully presented
food in a formal setting (see
p. 218).
*Open all week 12.15–1.45,
7.15–9.45*

Piero's

Kenwyn Street, Truro. Tel
Truro (0872) 222279
Bistro atmosphere in this
brasserie run separately from
the Mounts Bay Trading
Company. Wide selection of
dishes including pastas, pizzas
and quiches.
*Open Tues to Sat 9.30–5.30, 6.30–
10, Mon 9.30–5.30 Closed 25 and
26 Dec*

Bustopher Jones

62 Lemon Street, Truro. Tel
Truro (0872) 79029
Popular bistro with a good
atmosphere.
[£] *Open Mon to Sat 12–2, 6–10,
Sun 6–10*

Pottles

Pannier Market, Back Quay,
Truro. Tel Truro (0872) 71384
Simple and efficient café
serving casseroles as their
speciality. Also do takeaways.
Open Mon to Sat 11.30–5

North Cornwall

*A wild and highly impressive coastline from Morwenstow to
the Camel Estuary, with occasional easy access to the beaches
such as at Bude. From the Camel to St Agnes, the seaboard
includes a sequence of excellent bathing and surfing beaches,
although the scenery is much spoilt by holiday development;
Newquay and its hinterland have a monopoly of family
activities. A lack of sheltered harbours on this wind-buffeted
coast has meant only a handful of ports have developed, the
most attractive today being Port Isaac, Boscastle and
Padstow, with Crackington Haven and tiny Porthquin worth
a look for their locations. Tintagel has suffered for its fame,
but the castle's romance survives. Inland, the chief scenic
attraction is Bodmin Moor, not as featureless as it first
appears, with tors and prehistoric and industrial remains
providing the main interest. North Cornwall is graced with
some superb country churches, the most rewarding including
those at Launcells, Altarnun, Morwenstow and St Neot's;
Launceston and Bodmin have grander but more restored
churches.*

Morwenstow to Crackington Haven

The north Cornish coast begins in style, with majestic cliffs
around **Morwenstow**, reached via narrow lanes from the
A39. To sample some of the best of this bizarrely sculpted
coast of contorted grey rock, pinnacles and inlets, park by
the church and follow a well-trodden field path to the sea.
Higher Sharpnose Point to the left soars between two narrow
combes, creating an exciting sense of plunging depth,
looking south towards the alien mushroom-like structures of
the Composite Signals and Organisation Station, with
Tintagel and Trevose Heads far beyond. The coast has
claimed many wrecks; onshore winds often doomed boats

North Cornwall

Port Gaver
Port Isaac
Porthquin
Pentire Point
Camel Estuary
Polzeath
S
Endel
Trevose Head
St Minver
Padstow
Rock
Wadebri
Bedruthan Steps
C O R N W A L L
St Mawgan
Newquay
A3059
Castle
Downs
A30
Kelsey Head
St Columb
Major
A3075
A3058
A39
Goonhavern
St Agnes Head
St Agnes Beacon
Trerice
St Agnes

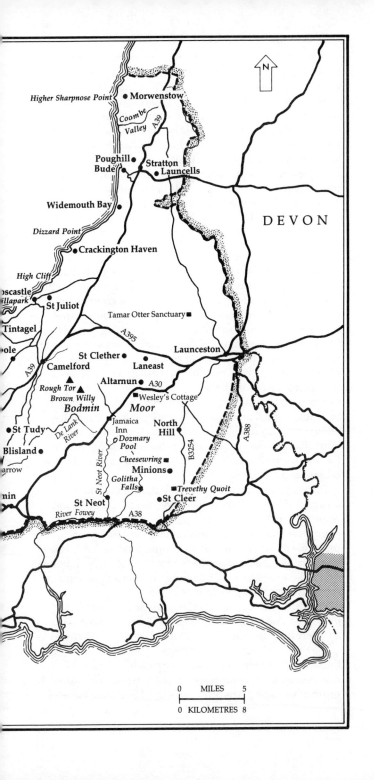

straying south of Hartland Point. The Reverend Robert Stephen Hawker, vicar of Morwenstow from 1834 until his death in 1875, made great efforts to salvage corpses from the wrecks and give them a proper churchyard burial. Perched by the cliff, and signposted just below the Coast Path before Higher Sharpnose Point is reached, Hawker's Hut is a wooden driftwood shack he built as somewhere to go to contemplate and in which to smoke opium. It may well have been where he penned the words of the ballad which has more or less become a Cornish national anthem:

And have they fixed the where and when?
And shall Trelawney die?
Here's twenty thousand Cornish men
Will know the reason why!

Hawker, who is also remembered as the originator of church harvest festivals, rebuilt the vicarage in curious style, with five of its chimney-stacks representing churches at places where he had earlier lived; the sixth chimney was styled on his mother's tomb. Above the vicarage stands Morwenstow church, which has some exceptional Norman work, including the admirable zigzag work above the porch and the carved heads, human and bestial, within three remarkable arches in the north arcade. Also outstanding is the set of sixteenth-century bench ends, with the original benches, and a fine wagon roof. Conspicuous among the several churchyard graves of shipwrecked sailors, for whose burial Hawker was responsible, is the figurehead from the *Caledonia*, wrecked in 1843, positioned as a memorial to the captain and crew.

Tautologically named **Coombe Valley** to the south is an area of dense woods owned by the Forestry Commission and National Trust but partly managed as a local nature reserve. Some deciduous species grow among the conifers, including the rare wild service tree, and in springtime daffodils blaze on the banks of a river populated by kingfishers and dippers. Access is via a nature trail, leading off from a tight bend in the road from Duckpool to Stibb.

Poughill (pronounced 'Poffle'), on the outskirts of Bude, manages to retain a separate village character and possesses an interesting church. The best of its bench ends were carved at the time of Henry VII, depicting symbols of the Passion; the later, Elizabethan ones show markedly inferior craftsmanship. The north aisle arcades are of Caen stone, the south of Cornish granite, all beneath a handsome barrel-vaulted roof. Medieval wall-paintings of St Christopher were lost beneath plaster for over four centuries, but uncovered in 1894 and repainted.

Once a port and now unmistakably a resort, **Bude** has a disjointed and rather bleak appearance, its rows of Edwardian guest-houses broken up by golf-links and sports pitches, but it's blessed with a deep sandy beach large enough to absorb a hefty swelling of the town's population in summer – sandcastle-builders, deckchair-loungers and kite-fliers spread out impressionistically. But surfing is Bude's present-day claim to fame, as the cargo of every other car roof-rack and the concentration of surfing shops testify. Crooklets Beach, half a mile north, is the venue for surfing and life-saving championships.

Most of Bude is Victorian or later, the sparse remnants of the pre-resort era lying alongside the Bude Canal. This waterway was 33 miles long when built for transporting the lime-rich sand (used for fertiliser) to the quay for shipping; two miles of navigable length remains. A **museum** (open in summer, daily, 10 to 4) on the quay is full of local history, with photographs of Bude as it was, and material on the canal and shipwrecks. A popular walk over carpet-like turf leads southwards past a lookout tower on Compass Point to the summit pillar on Efford Beacon, where a view-indicator identifies coastal features stretching down past Tintagel Head and the Rumps to Trevose Head. Beneath the low cliff, a series of horizontal rock sills, undercut by wave action, project across a beach containing a small natural arch.

Bude's outskirts almost overlap those of **Stratton**, whose centre could hardly be more different: the sleepy Georgian main street winds up to the church, inside whose porch the door of the old town jail is exhibited, the word 'clink' embedded into it with nails. The church interior has a brass of 1561 in memory of Sir John Arundell of Trerice (see p. 250) and his two wives, while casualties of the Battle of Stratton (1643), in which the Royalists defeated the Parliamentarians, were buried more humbly in unmarked graves in the churchyard.

Launcells church, signposted off the A3072 between Stratton and the Devon border, has a calm air of seclusion as it stands among trees screening it from a small group of cottages and a Georgian manor. It lies off an obscure lane a mile east of Stratton, but should be seen by anyone with a liking for untampered medieval country churches. What is most immediately striking about the interior is the quality of the light, a product of clear-glass windows, which illuminates Cornish craftsmanship in a range of local materials – oak, slate, granite and stone from the nearby Polyphant quarries. Superb bench ends depict symbols of the Passion (a towel for the Washing of the Feet, a table with loaves for the Last Supper, an open coffin for the Resurrection, and so on), and the sanctuary floor is patterned with fifteenth-century Barnstaple tiles featuring pelican and lion motifs. Some restoration was carried out in the eighteenth century, but basically Launcells is strongly fifteenth century in character, even its oak roof and flagged floor having escaped modernisation.

The low-lying coastline continues southwards to **Widemouth Bay**, with its mile of sands and scattering of beach shops, before rounded cliffs rise abruptly and majestically. Crumbly shale cliffs are topped by stunted oak woods, blasted by the prevailing wind around **Dizzard Point**. Aptly named **High Cliff**, at 731 feet, is the highest point on the Cornish seaboard, lying just to the south of Crackington Haven, and readily accessible from a National Trust sign on the road. The more energetic can walk to it from **Crackington Haven** itself, once a limestone and coal port. The tiny hamlet's own beach has level access from the road, and a tremendous location beneath the cliffs, though its limited size means it fills up rather easily.

Boscastle to Porth Quin

This is a magnificent and largely undeveloped stretch of coast, with the bonus of two of north Cornwall's most absorbing coastal villages – Boscastle and Port Isaac – and the much-visited site of Tintagel Castle. While you won't easily find family beaches with safe bathing and lots of facilities, the cliff scenery offers grand views and secretive coves.

Boscastle, at the junction of the B3263 and B3266, is squeezed into the only available land between the plunging slopes of a deep wooded combe, part of the village – including its newer outskirts – up on the hill, and the old fishing area lining the bottom. The village's charm lies in its site, notably the harbour and the tortuous inlet that links it to the open sea, rather than in its buildings, although there are some intriguingly misshapen slate roofs to be seen in the low and high parts of the village. It looks at its best from the lookout tower on Willapark, the headland to the west, reached easily in 15-minutes walk; it makes a good escape from the crowds who come in along the road: take the steep road by the Wellington Hotel (with a 'no entry' sign), until the first sharp right turn; cross the main road and find the lane opposite and to the right of Melbourne House. A path immediately on the right here leads past the church to Willapark. There's nothing parklike about this rugged headland; with such stupendous views it comes as no surprise to learn that this was the site of an Iron Age cliff castle; far below, guillemots' cries echo noisily from among slatey inlets. Boscastle's rocky-sided and distinctly perilous-looking twisting creek then appears, the occasional pleasure-boat threading its way along it.

The village's busy days as a port are long over, eclipsed, like the other ports along this coast, by the arrival of the railways to north Cornwall in the 1890s. Apart from the present-day lack of activity, the scene can't have changed all that much in a hundred years. Further inland lies Boscastle's inoffensively commercialised area: the pixie shop has a wishing-well and garden gnomes, and is topped with a sagging grey roof resembling an inexpertly erected tent – a sort of Cornish equivalent to the gingerbread cottage. Somehow it looks inspired by the nearby **Museum of Witchcraft** (open Easter to end Oct, daily, 10 to 8.30), a strange display of 'genuine' bits and pieces associated with (mostly local) witches, giving ghoulish pleasure to some – spells, curses, charms, a dried frog and a stuffed cat.

St Juliot's church, a mile inland, can be reached by a footpath along the wooded Valency Valley, which is partly owned by the National Trust. The medieval church was on the point of 'irredeemable dilapidation' in 1868, and Thomas Hardy, then a young architect working for a firm in Weymouth, was appointed to deal with the rebuilding. When he arrived in 1870 he could have scarcely predicted the watershed in his life that came about. For here he met his future wife Emma, the vicar's sister-in-law, whom he used to court on Strangles Beach between High Cliff and Cambeak. After the completion of the new church in 1872, Hardy returned to read the lessons. While on this visit he received a letter offering architectural work in London. Emma encouraged him to turn it down, urging him to pursue his career as a poet and novelist. Emma became the model for the heroine of his third novel, *A Pair of Blue Eyes* (1873), in which Boscastle appears as Castle Boterel, and Cornish cliffs and woodlands provide many of the settings. Thomas and Emma married in 1874 at Paddington after the completion of his next novel, *Far from the Madding Crowd*. Emma's memorial of 1913 was erected at the church by Hardy during a poignant visit which culminated in his great *Poems 1912–13*, tinged by sentiments of love and regret, of which 'At Castle Boterel' recalls his courtship days.

Hardy's architectural drawings of the old church are hung inside the present building; he was said to have regretted the destruction of the medieval building, and his drawing of the bench ends gives a hint of what was lost.

Further south-west along the coast, **Tintagel** attracts the crowds for its historically doubtful links with King Arthur, whose court of Camelot might have been here. Tintagel Castle, as it is known, is fragmentary but real enough, the twelfth-century structure built by Earl Richard of Cornwall, younger brother of Henry III, probably sited here as a sop to Cornish patriotism because even then the place had Arthurian associations. It certainly was no site for a strategic base. While Welsh chronicles record a British leader who led his forces against the Anglo-Saxons and was killed at Camlaun (possibly near Winchester), the renowned legends of Arthur were largely invented by Geoffrey of Monmouth in the twelfth century, by Sir Thomas Mallory some 300 years later, and further added to in the nineteenth century by the hugely popular works of Tennyson, Matthew Arnold and Swinburne. So the flood of tourists began in Victorian times and hasn't ebbed since, drawn part by legend and part by the undeniable romanticism of the castle site, on a towering headland, with a cave piercing the neck of rock that connects the castle to its mainland section. A long staircase, on which visitors pause for breath, climbs to the top of the 'island'; up here are the scant ruins of a twelfth- and thirteenth-century building and a few remains of an earlier building, requiring a lot of imagination to bring the place back to life. Not much is known about the site's early history; pottery finds point to third- or fourth-century activity, but little evidence has been found to back up theories of an early Christian monastery. Any sense of disappointment you may get from the castle itself should be offset by its sensational natural site, commanding views south towards Rumps Point and north towards Devon.

Tintagel village is a fairly extreme and well-established

example of the pilgrimage industry; some countries have religious kitsch, but here in north Cornwall it's Arthurian – an accumulation of ice-cream stands and gift shops (a plaster statue of King Arthur stands on a canopy above a Cornish piskie store). Looking completely out of place among all this is the **Old Post Office** (open late Mar to late Sept, daily, 11 to 6; Oct, daily, 11 to 5). Despite the name it collected in the nineteenth century, this is probably Cornwall's finest example of a simple medieval manor house of cottage character, modest in size but highly evocative and worth going well out of your way to see. Its spectacular roof, wildly sagging and precarious-looking, is a sight in itself, and its interior too is almost miraculously well preserved, thanks to the foresight of a Miss Catherine Johns. She purchased the building at an auction in 1895 while the rest of Tintagel was being ripped apart by the advent of the Arthur industry, and arranged for its repair and conservation, selling it to the National Trust in part-exchange for a lifetime lease. The Trust took over a shell and have filled it with oak furniture once typically found in most Cornish farmhouses, and have hung the whitewashed walls with old samplers, while the post room has been furnished as a Victorian post office. Try to go first thing in the day to avoid the crowds, as it feels cramped even with a dozen people in it.

Tintagel's other attractions include a small mineral museum – featuring a collection of stones from all over the world – and King Arthur's Hall of Chivalry. The latter is a curiously masonic-seeming building with hints of a set design from a film epic in what looks like a suburban house, with a 'Round Table', Throne Chamber, a vast hall and stained glass commemorating Arthur's circle.

Tintagel's church occupies a lone and blustery spot near the cliff, but is easily reached by a short walk from the castle. The building has undergone heavy restoration but has some unusual features – a Saxon doorway and tiny windows in its north wall, a Roman milestone inscribed MPCQ VA LIC IIV (or LICIN), referring to Emperor Licinius, a Norman font adorned with carvings of faces and serpents, and a little brass *c*.1430 to a lady, one Johanna Kelly.

A few miles inland, **Delabole** by contrast is a grey village of industrial terraces and Nonconformist chapels, famous for four centuries as the home of Delabole slate, the roofing material of so many Cornish homes, from humble terraces to stately homes such as Pencarrow (see p. 236). The vast hole excavated for this prized rock extends half a mile across, with yellow JCB's and trucks at work several hundred feet below the public viewing-platform – a minor tourist sight in itself. To reach the public viewing area, turn off opposite the Bettle and Chisel pub (named after quarrymen's tools) in the village centre. Through the showroom is a yard where stacks of slate house numbers and names are on sale, and lettered plaques can be made to order.

From the tiny cove hamlet at Port William, where there is road access to Trebarwith Strand – the most popular beach for bathing and surfing around Tintagel – begins a remote length of coast accessible only to walkers on the coast path, with the road over a mile inland for most of the way. The first settlement reached to the south is **Port Gaverne**, with a handful of houses and a hotel (see p. 253). Just over the hill in the next cove lies the far more frequented **Port Isaac**, busy with sightseers enjoying the epitome of the Cornish fishing village. The streets are barely a car's width, and it is best to leave your car at the top of the village, outside the restricted parking zone, and walk down Rose Hill (which begins half way down the slope), a crooked lane of whitewashed cottages with rambling roses, steepening as it nears the sea and dwindling to a path before depositing you in the hub of the village. Booths around the harbour announce fresh lobster on sale, together with hake, megrim, Dover sole and sea-trout; lobster-pots are clustered next to the lifeboat house; a caravan by cars parked on the tidal stony shore advertises fishing-trips for pollack and mackerel. The fishy smells and haphazard arrangement of lanes and alleys, with stone stairways leading to unseen first-floor doors, and white or candy-coloured cottages between minute gardens, all contribute to a memorable sense of place. You have a good view of the village from the Old School House (see p. 254). Delabole slate, evident on every roof, used to be shipped from here, before rail and then road took over.

A short distance inland from Port Isaac, on the road to St Endellion, **Long Cross Victorian Garden** (open during daylight hours), occupying a small site by the hotel to which it belongs, has recently been restored from a tangle of undergrowth into ornamental shrubberies, with a pond and a recreated folly and dovecote for period effect. **St Endellion** church has a beautiful timber roof with modern bosses in the form of bishops, and bench ends carved with heraldic motifs. In the south aisle the intricately carved slate tomb-chest is reputed to be that of St Endelienta, a hermit who lived on cow's milk; a coat of arms comprises heifers' heads, a ruminant cow, a hill and a crown. Performances of choral, chamber and orchestral music are given here during music festivals at Easter and in early August.

Further south-west, **St Minver** is little more than a tiny half-forgotten street of stone cottages dipping to the wall of the grounds of the former manor house-turned-campsite. The church, reached by an alley on the right, has more carved bench ends, Adam and Eve together with various secular themes, and a brass dedicated to Roger Opy (1517); a carved bird, neck cowed, adorns a pew top in the central aisle.

Barely a hamlet, **Porthquin** comprises a few National Trust-owned cottages, the road rising one in five in both directions, the steep cliffs giving some shelter to the harbour. The Coast Path on the right-hand side of the bay heads up on to **Kellan Head**, which looks over the pinnacle beneath the Rumps; closer by stands a small folly 'castle', built in 1827 by a former governor of Wandsworth Prison as a retirement home. Just beyond it, shafts mark the site of old antimony mines, which together with the pilchard industry used to provide Porthquin with its livelihood.

Launceston

In contrast with the uneventfulness of several of Cornwall's inland towns, Launceston has considerable distinction in its compact centre. Its hilltop site, crowned by the Norman keep of its **castle**, which dominates the view as you enter town, has something of a Continental flavour at first glimpse. Climb the spiral steps up the castle keep (open Easter to end Sept, daily, 10 to 6, Oct to Easter, Tues to Sun, 10 to 4) for the best panorama over the town, grey slate roofs making an abrupt transition into rural sheep-grazed hills on one side of town, with Bodmin Moor and Dartmoor in the distance. The castle site was selected by William the Conqueror's half-brother, Robert de Mortain, as a base from where he could rule over Cornwall, and subsequently used by the earls of Cornwall as their seat. Thus, Launceston became the Cornish capital and the centre of law and order, with executions carried out in the castle grounds until 1821 and (although the castle was abandoned after 1376) the North Gate functioning as a jail. George Fox, founder of the Quaker movement, was imprisoned in a cell here for distributing leaflets connected with his activities and for his over-long hair. Launceston lost its county-town role to Bodmin when roadbuilding in the early nineteenth century made the latter more accessible and central.

For all its narrow, winding, medieval and Georgianised streets, Launceston lives on as an unprecious market town, inviting enough to wander around at will, with minor delights tucked away in back streets. Plaques identify major buildings described in a free town trail leaflet available at the tourist information centre.

The money for the building in the fifteenth century of **St Mary Magdalene church** came from bereaved Sir Henry Trecarrel, a wealthy landowner. Much expense was put into this grand building, which possesses a unique exterior, virtually covered with granite carvings of little motifs – ferns, roses, pomegranates and thistles, while St Mary herself adorns the porch. Inside, the roof timbers are said to run to half a mile of carved oak, including 162 angels and 400 bosses.

Southgate Arch, the only survival of four gates in what was the only town wall ever built in Cornwall, spans Southgate Street. Castle Street, a favourite of John Betjeman's and the best in Launceston, is reached from the castle grounds (which are always open, even when the keep is closed), and consists of a series of fine Georgian residences. Among them is **Lawrence House**, now the town museum (open Apr to mid-Oct, Mon to Fri, 10.30 to 12.30, 2.30 to 4.30), built for an attorney and mayor, Humphrey Lawrence. The museum contains costumes, coins, typewriters and tools, as well as a room about Launceston, Tasmania (which also has a River Tamar).

At the bottom of town is the old Launceston station. From here, the **Launceston Steam Railway** operates: historic engines pull open-sided carriages on reinstated track of the old Launceston to Padstow line, which closed in 1962. The route runs for two miles through the fields, at times within sight of the river. At the Launceston end there's a layout of a model railway, a shop selling reproduction railway maps and an engine shed with a collection of vintage cars and motor bikes.

Out of town at North Petherwin, signposted off the B3254 to Bude, is the **Tamar Otter Sanctuary** (open end March to end Oct, daily, 10.30 to 6). The conservation project to boost

Britain's fast-dwindling otter population was begun at Eartham in Norfolk, and its success encouraged the setting up of a branch here in 1986. Some of the otter breeds you see will be released into the wild. You can also see various species of waterfowl and owls.

Bodmin Moor: the south-east

To reach **North Hill**, turn off the B3254 south-west of Launceston on to a quiet lane. This compact, sturdy-looking and quietly enjoyable village possesses a surprisingly large church with three spacious aisles. Among several memorials worth seeking out are those to the Spoures and a haunting slate one to Thomas Vincent, his wife and 15 children, showing a dragon and skeleton representing Christ overcoming sin and death.

At Upton Cross to the south, **Sterts Open-Air Theatre**, opened in 1990, occupies a small grassy amphitheatre and in summer puts on a varied programme, including family shows, drama, concerts and occasional performances by Opera South-West.

Close by to the west but belonging much more to the moor, **Minions** is 995 feet above sea-level and Cornwall's highest village. It lies amid derelict engine-houses and disused quarries in an area once busy with copper, tin and granite production, but now dominated by the television transmitter masts on Caradon Hill: a mournful scene to some, while others will find the eerie, wind-blown character of its vicinity irresistible. A track at the west end of the hamlet heads north past **The Hurlers**, three Bronze Age (*c.*1500 BC) stone circles up to 140 feet across, enigmatically spread in the heather; local folklore explains them as men turned into stone as a punishment for playing the game of hurling on Sunday. The track continues an undemanding course to the strange weathered outcrops called the **Cheesewring**, so named because they resemble a stack of drying cheese, perched above rock-climbers tackling a vertical quarried rockface. Views on Bodmin Moor don't come better than this – over the brooding stillness of the central moor to Brown Willy and Rough Tor, and eastwards across lush patchwork farmland to the foreboding barrier of western Dartmoor, with the suburbs of Plymouth further to the south. Walk back southwards on the well-defined bed of the old railway track that once served the quarries, later branching off left, if you want to extend the walk towards Kilmar Tor.

Two well-signposted antiquities are found to the south close to Darite. One is **Trethevy Quoit**, reached along back lanes, an impressive burial chamber standing on a small rise in a field and consisting of seven stone uprights, one of which has fallen, under a tilted capstone some 12 feet across. Inside, an upright divides the tomb into two chambers, the larger once housing the dead and the smaller probably for the dead's possessions, long since looted by treasure-seekers. **King Doniat's Stones**, of lesser interest, are upright granite slabs standing beside the road west of Darite; an inscription on one of them is supposed to translate as 'Doniert ordered this cross for the good of his soul', but as it's now entirely illegible this has to be taken on trust. Doniert was a ninth-century Cornish king who allegedly drowned in the River Fowey near Draynes Bridge while out on a wild boar hunt; bones excavated at the base of the stones may have been those of Doniert's horse. Nearby, the church at **St Cleer** is known for its fine tower, buttressed and

Bodmin Moor

Cornwall's highest ground resembles Dartmoor in miniature, with great moorland expanses frequented by wild ponies and topped by the occasional granite tor, a jagged outcrop above a smoothly rolling landscape. Most of the moor is over 800 feet high, with Brown Willy, at 1,311 feet, its highest point. And like Dartmoor, Bodmin Moor attracted prehistoric settlers; Ordnance Survey maps mark tumuli, hut circles, standing stones and stone circles, only a few of which are actually obvious on the ground. Bronze Age man carried out tin-streaming on a large scale in the valley gravels.

The moor's high rainfall and infertility deter development and – on the more elevated ground at least – agricultural improvement. But the area's primeval character has been nibbled in places by conifer plantations and reservoirs, some of the latter used for leisure – canoeing, yachting and fishing in particular. Few roads penetrate this bleak wilderness; the A30 traffic gets a fleeting idea of it, but there is much to see around the edges, and if the idea of a walk across the largely pathless moor doesn't appeal, there are a few excellent viewpoints from which you can look over the area.

pinnacled and rising in three stages; north of the churchyard is a fifteenth-century holy well within a small building.

Further west, **Golitha Falls**, signposted on the road to Draynes, are a series of modest rapids, but set amid sufficiently attractive woodland to merit a short walkabout. A way-marked trail follows the swift-flowing River Fowey through part of the 18-hectare site of oaks, ashes and beeches, the largest surviving remnant of the tree-cover that once spread across the moor before clearance by early man, and now designated a National Nature Reserve. Lichens and mosses grow here in abundance and variety; two botanical rarities are Tunbridge Filmy fern and *Fissidens polyphyllus* moss.

South of Colliford Lake, the moor's largest reservoir, **St Neot** feels well out of the way but receives visitors seeking out its church, renowned for the quality of its fifteenth- and sixteenth-century stained glass, which is by far the best in Cornwall. St Neot himself, reputedly only 15 inches high, appears in the most famous of the windows, which shows Neot ploughing with a team of stags after his oxen had been stolen, and the story of the three fishes (an angel ensured an everlasting supply of fish provided Neot took only one a day from the fish-well; when Neot fell ill, a monk brought two fish, but ordering them to be placed back, together with prayers for forgiveness, resulted in the reinstatement of the miraculous fish-well). The Creation and Noah's story are charmingly illustrated in other windows, well explained in the church guide.

The road from here to the A38 takes in an attractive wooded stretch by the St Neot river, with little hint of the austere moor close by. On the way to the main road is the entrance to **Carnglaze Slate Caverns** (open Easter to Sept, daily, 10.30 to 5), which were worked from medieval times in an open-cast quarry; later operations moved under ground before excavations ceased in around 1903. The guide switches on dim lighting to show what conditions were like in the days when 60 men worked in the caves (today 60 bats live here) with a further 20 dressing and splitting the slate prior to shipping from Polperro. The miners' lives were made harder by the fact that wages were paid only as tokens redeemable at the mine company's shop at St Neot. Altogether the tour takes in four chambers, some with mock-ups of miners at work, and culminating at a subterranean pool, followed by an invitation to take as much souvenir slate

as you can carry. Wear something warm – the dank chill can
be quite a shock on a summer's day.

Bodmin Moor: Bodmin and the west

Most of the places of interest at **Bodmin** are scattered around
the town's fringes. Its county-town status and shopping
streets bring in local people, but the centre does not really
entice one to linger. Cornwall's largest parish church is here,
suffering a traffic-ridden position with some dignity, its
much restored fifteenth-century interior of interest for a slate
monument to Prior Vyvyan and an exceptional Norman font.
And there is a free museum – well laid out but small in extent
– by the classical Shire Hall.

On Bodmin's east side, on the B3268 to Lostwithiel, the
Duke of Cornwall's Light Infantry Regimental Museum
(open all year exc. Bank Hols, Mon to Fri, 8 to 4.45) is housed
in the Quartermaster's Stores of the regiment, whose
proudest achievement was the defence of Lucknow during
the 140-day siege of 1857, in which many lives were lost.
Relics of this occasion are on display with memorabilia,
letters and medals, and weapons through the years from the
attack on the Spanish in Vigo Bay in 1702 up to the Second
World War. Across the town is the terminus of the **Bodmin
Steam Railway**, on track which links up to the main British
Rail line at Bodmin Parkway, taking 20 minutes each way for
the 3½-mile trip. The preservation society which reopened the
line in 1990 after it had laid inactive for six years is hoping to
extend the operation in the other direction to Boscarne along
what in 1834 was Cornwall's first railway, and one of the
earliest anywhere; the later stages of track are now a
pathway called the Camel Footpath (see p. 244). Carriages
are old British Rail stock with compartments, although one
luggage van has been quaintly fitted out with pews.

On the way to Bodmin Parkway you catch glimpses of the
144-foot **Gilbert Monument**, erected in 1844 to the memory
of Walter Raleigh Gilbert, a general who lived most of his life
in India but who was not as well known as the prominence of
the structure suggests.

The Molesworth family built and their descendants still
own **Pencarrow** (open all year, daily exc Fri and Sat, 11 (1.30
in winter) to 5, located off the main road between Bodmin
and Camelford and approached by a mile-long drive that
runs between rhododendrons and banks of hydrangeas. The

fourth Sir John Molesworth commissioned the architect
Robert Allanson to build this formal Palladian mansion,
three-storeyed beneath a roof of grey Delabole slates, and
standing in grounds that extend to a lily pond flanked by
cypresses, a formal Italian garden and an American garden.
One of the Molesworth's visitors in the last century, a Mr
Charles Austin, was shown an *araucaria* tree brought here
from Australia and observed 'That tree would puzzle a
monkey', and thus the popular name 'monkey-puzzle' was
born.

Pencarrow's interior was remodelled in Victorian times by
Plymouth architect George Wightwick. He added the alcove
in the music room, which destroyed the acoustics; the piano
now stands in the drawing-room, approached by a hidden
doorway made to look like part of the bookcase. While
staying here as a house guest in 1882, Arthur Sullivan
composed the first-act finale of the music of the comic opera
Iolanthe using this very piano. The hour-long guided tour is
of special interest for the antiques, furniture and paintings,
which include Sèvres plates, a group of family portraits by
Joshua Reynolds in the dining-room, and a Ch'ien Lung
famille rose bowl with a Chinese artist's depiction of the house
which he had never seen (though he made a pretty good job
of it).

Further north, **St Tudy** has informal verges merging into
floral borders, the village noticeboard integrated into the bus
shelter below a spreading chestnut tree, across the street
from the smithy, village pump and ancient horse-trough.
When the owners are around, the well-tended garden of
Tremeer House is often open; it is on the edge of the village
(follow the signs to Camelford until the gate-posts appear on
the left). A grass terrace provides the centrepiece to
ornamental rockeries and a noted collection of camellias and
rhododendrons. Leave a donation in the tin to the National
Gardens Scheme, and try not to startle Mildred the pheasant.
A few miles north-west, **Lamellan Garden** is open some days
in April and May, and has a noted collection of
rhododendrons in its sheltered position in a valley.

Closer to Bodmin Moor both geographically and in
essence, and seeming a shade less refined and more
weatherbeaten than St Tudy, **Blisland** is the surprising
possessor of a village green – quite a rarity for a Cornish
village – furnished with metal benches installed for Queen
Victoria's Jubilee year. Below the grey-stone cottages stands

the church, which has an intricate and very colourful screen installed by F. C. Eden in 1894, said to give a good idea of how medieval screens looked when new. John Betjeman pronounced the building his West Country favourite and remarked 'as a restoration – even improvement – of a medieval church, this can hardly be bettered'.

North of here, the no-through road from Blisland to Pendrift gives access to the **Jubilee Rock** (keep straight on at a crossroads, park at the end of the road, walk up the track to the right, then further on through a gate), whose carvings of Britannia and various coats of arms were the handiwork of Lieutenant John Rogers to commemorate 50 years of the reign of George III in 1810.

The drive north-east from Blisland to St Breward takes in a sample of open moor, the unfenced lane crossing the De Lank River at a granite clapper bridge of ageless appearance.

Bodmin Moor: central and northern

The busy A30 provides the longest uninterrupted drive across the moor, and most visitors' only view of it. About the only place to stop at is **Jamaica Inn**, and this fact, coupled with Daphne du Maurier's famous novel which is set here, has made the place very busy, with a large and hectic car park and a gift shop tacked on to the ancient slate-hung inn itself. Integrated into all this is **Potter's Museum of Curiosities** (open Mar to late Oct, daily 10.30 to dusk; Nov to Easter, weekends only), recently moved here from Arundel in Sussex, a highly eccentric and somewhat creepy storehouse of objects ethnic, zoological, archaeological and plain odd. The most famous of them are the series of tableaux created by a Victorian taxidermist, including the Duelling Squirrels, the Rabbits' Village School and the multi-bestial Who Killed Cock Robin?, in questionable taste but done with an extraordinary eye for detail. An extract from the catalogue gives an idea of the strange juxtapositions of the hundreds of items in this collection:

37. *Clock alarm gun which fires bullets when set, nineteenth century.*
38. *Young pig with three legs (it can be seen in the 1901 newspaper No. 3)*
39. *Little dog – lived about 28 hours.*
40. *Paper model of Brighton railway station prior to 1883.*
41. *Great spotted woodpecker.*
42. *A specimen of Star Quad telephone cable containing 2020 wires, as at present in use between London and Worthing.*

43 *(a). Californian quail (male), western states of America. (b). White
  pheasant. (c) Chinese silver pheasant.*
44. *The House that Jack Built.*
45. *The Guinea Pigs' Cricket Match.*
46. *Lamb with two heads born at Wattle Corner Farm near Rye in 1887.*

Two minor roads head south from here: the one along the
River Fowey offers nothing scenically, but another passes
close to **Dozmary Pool**, a desolately sited pond which is one
of several sites in the country into which King Arthur's
sword Excalibur was allegedly hurled; the latter road is
intermittently open-sided as it proceeds to St Neot (see
p. 235).

Slow down at Trewint if you wish to see **Wesley's Cottage**,
marked by a tiny signpost beside a narrow lane on the south
side of the A30. This was where in 1744 John Wesley visited
the cottage's inhabitant, Digory Isbell, a stonemason whose
wife Elizabeth had a year earlier entertained two of Wesley's
agents. The sincerity of the Wesleyans inspired Isbell to
found what is now the smallest Methodist preaching place in
the world in a one-up, one-down cottage. The rooms are
simply furnished, with stick-back chairs against
whitewashed walls, a preacher's desk, Wesley's letters and
prayer-cards, and a fireplace with a range, all lit by tiny
windows and feeling like a step back in time.

Despite this, the Isbells remained church people, and their
tomb can be seen in the churchyard at **Altarnun**. The huge
church tower dominates this village of grey stone spangled
with colourful hanging flower-baskets, the houses ending in
front of a pack-horse bridge over the swiftly running
Penpont Water – all in mellow and soft contrast to the
bleakness of the moors on each side of the A30. A former
chapel wall is adorned by the effigy of John Wesley, carved
by Nevil Northey Burnard, who was born in the village and
later enjoyed national repute for his craftsmanship, but fell
on hard times and died a pauper. The 70-odd bench ends
(*c*.1510–30) in the church are as good and interesting as any,
and feature a fiddler, a jester, a bagpiper and a bearded
demon-like figure; and for once the artist, Robert Daye, has
recorded his name. At first glance the church's proportions
seem incongruously grand for such a small village, but its
parish boundaries extend for miles around. Spanning the
width of the church is a notable fifteenth-century screen,
from which period most of the church dates, although the
font, crafted with bearded faces and a double-headed snake,

is Norman. A Celtic cross in the churchyard is the sole survival from the time of St Nonna, mother of St David, from whom the church takes its dedication and the village its name.

Laneast church, reached by tortuous lanes to the north, has more good bench ends, not quite in the Altarnun class but in a little-restored and touchingly simple building. High-hedged lanes lead to **St Clether**, where a well-marked path

---

John Wesley and Methodism

In the middle of the eighteenth century the Church of England clergymen were often younger sons of the landed gentry who joined the clergy less for religious reasons than for social position, taking the income from their church livings but doing little to alleviate the grim, poverty-stricken circumstances of many of their parishioners. Absentee clergymen and those with more than one parish were quite common. So the arrival of John Wesley and his brother Charles in Cornwall in 1743 was something of a shock to the establishment. They both belonged to the Church of England but believed that the church should return to the basic teachings of the Bible, leaving out any ceremony or frills; the priest, they thought, should live and work among his parishioners.

They had set up a club at Oxford and as well as religious devotions, visited prisoners and the sick, and helped the needy. The term methodist described the way they ran their lives: very methodically with strict discipline. The brothers travelled all over the West Country preaching and trying to demonstrate a new kind of lifestyle based on the Bible. They preached in towns and village squares, on open ground and beaches – wherever anyone would listen to them; they slept where they could find a bed. Their initial reception was to be expected: they were considered cranks and madmen, stones and mud were thrown at them and their sermons met with jeers. But gradually when it was seen that they practised what they preached, people started to listen. Their success was not only a measure of their personal conviction but of the spiritual need of eighteenth-century England. The church was set against them: they were preaching dangerously egalitarian ideas; some local magistrates tried to prevent them speaking and some early supporters were punished by employers and landlords.

John Wesley visited Cornwall about 40 times. He organised

from the back of the churchyard advances along the side of the remote Inney Valley, fringed with bracken and the occasional rock outcrop. After a quarter of a mile you reach a holy well, adjacent to a fifteenth-century chapel that stands on the site of a Celtic hermitage. The chapel has been restored but is still dark and primitive, with a rough floor, a granite altar and a plea to put 3d in the box.

Camelford, between Bodmin Moor and the sea at Tintagel,

---

groups of Methodists in the towns and cities he and his brother had visited and appointed leaders who carried on the work in their absence. Wesley considered himself to be part of the Church of England and had no wish to form a separate organisation. But in 1743 he issued a strict book of rules for Methodists and in 1744 he set up what was to become an annual conference of leading preachers. In the same year he ordained some of his preachers to serve in America and in the following years ordained others to serve in Scotland and England. This was a breach of Anglican episcopal order. Every divisive step was taken reluctantly by Wesley yet inevitably (as he felt) in order that he could more effectively spread the word of God. His sermons were calm logical expositions of scripture with particular emphasis upon the doctrine of justification by faith.

He preached anywhere, but one of his favourite places in Cornwall was Gwennap Pit near Redruth: a large, deep hollow formed by the collapse of underground mine workings, it made a natural amphitheatre. He discovered it by chance when trying to preach on a windy day nearby; he was forced to move into the pit where he could be more easily heard. Later, ledges were cut into the bank providing seating for thousands. He was still preaching there when he was over 80 years old, and on one of his last appearances preached to a congregation of over 30,000. This was his own estimate and is likely to be a slight exaggeration, but the entry from his journal confirms that it was a memorable occasion: 'I think this my ne plus ultra (no further can I go). I shall scarce see a larger congregation till we meet in the air.'

Methodism became a new way of life for thousands. But there were obviously many who disagreed with his preachings and an opponent in the nineteenth century was reported to have remarked: 'The man Wesley corrupted and depraved instead of improving the west of England . . . He found the Miners and Fishermen an upstanding, rollicking, courageous people. He left them a

---

is a not over-busy small town, with a town hall adorned with a camel (a red herring, so to speak: the river and town probably take their name from the Cornish *cam pol*, meaning 'crooked river'), and fourteenth-century Darlington Inn obviously predating the predominant Georgian-cum-Victorian flavour of the place. On its edge is a **museum** (open April to late Sept, Mon to Sat, 10.30 to 5) of folky objects collected from the area – carriages, agricultural implements, cobblers' lasts, the town stocks, Truro pottery and bygone tools from the slate quarry at Delabole (see p. 229). **Rough Tor** (pronounced Row Tor, to rhyme with 'cow') is signposted off the A39 east of Camelford, although you have

---

downlooking, lying, selfish-hearted throng.' But there is no doubt that he did some good. He went especially to areas where social problems, particularly poverty, were acute. The industrial revolution had caused population shifts that left communities badly depleted and Wesley brought them new hope and a sense of purpose; he encouraged preaching by anyone who felt they had something to contribute.

Over 50 years Wesley travelled about 250,000 miles, usually on horseback, and preached over 50,000 sermons. Most of the roads were no more than rutted and pot-holed tracks and he often travelled 30 miles a day, preaching four or five times.

He was a short man and tried to find a high spot from where to deliver his sermons. At Heamoor, just outside Penzance, a rock from which he preached has become the base of a pulpit in the Methodist chapel built in 1842 and called the Wesley Rock Chapel. Denied a place in their existing parish churches, the Methodists began building their own chapels; usually very simple, built of stone or cob, then whitewashed inside and out. No statues, no ornaments or religious pictures, not even a candle, just simple chairs gathered round the pulpit: this was all they needed. The modern chapels are grander – the Wesleyan church in Bodmin is a fine example – but generally in Cornwall, Methodism was very strong in the poorest and most hard-working communities – fishing and mining villages – as you can see by the size of the chapels in Camborne and St Just.

John Wesley died in 1791 having founded a way of worship which has spread all over the world and is still a powerful force in Cornwall.

---

to walk the remaining three-quarters of a mile from the car park at the end of the road: allow an hour up and down, with time to enjoy the view. To the right at the bottom of the ascent over the springy turf is a memorial to Charlotte Dymond, found murdered here in 1844. Charlotte, a maid at Penhale, went for a walk on the moor with her lover, Matthew Weekes; only he returned, saying she had gone on to visit a Tom Prout. Days later, a search began and Weekes disappeared; the corpse was found, and Weekes located in Plymouth. His subsequent conviction and hanging appears to have depended on circumstantial evidence, leaving the true course of events something of a mystery.

Further up the slope the granite blocks begin, broken off by freeze-thaw weathering, making progress a little trickier in the final stages. They give Rough Tor a rugged character befitting the panorama over the central moor, quite impressive in a drab kind of way; the seaward aspect is dominated in its foreground by conifer plantations and a china clay pit. You can continue across the moor past the memorial to the Wessex Regiment, which gave the hillside to the National Trust, to Brown Willy.

The Camel Estuary and Bedruthan

Nothing prepares you for the sudden change from the jagged coastline of indented cliffs to the north and south and the smooth outlines and pastel shades of the **Camel Estuary**. The Camel broadens above **Wadebridge**, once an important link in the shipping of granite from the De Lank Quarries on Bodmin Moor – stone for the building of Blackfriars Bridge passed this way. In June the town becomes the centre of attention when it hosts the Royal Cornwall Show, the major event of its kind in the county, extending over several days. For the rest of summer, though, the town is mainly remembered as an unfortunate bottleneck on the A39, crying out for a bypass, with one of the slowest traffic lights in Cornwall and traffic grinding over its noble 17-arched, fifteenth-century bridge (said to have been built on foundations of wool-packs). North-west of the town, well hidden in the lanes but worth a visit, is the **Cornish Shire Horse Centre** at Trelow Farm, Treddinick (open Easter to Oct, daily, 10 to 5).

Much better things happen further downriver. **Rock**, on the east bank and joined on to wonderfully named Splatt and

Pityme, is a resort village with lots of yachts both on trailers and in the water. A passenger-ferry crosses from here to Padstow, on the opposite bank. Sand-dune hillocks conceal a golf course and an oddly sited Norman church, **St Enodoc's**, on a site once vulnerable to the drifting sands. By the early nineteenth century the church had actually become engulfed, and the vicar made a hole in the roof so he could get in and hold services, which was necessary for the church to collect tithe dues from fishermen and farmers. The church was dug out of the sand completely in 1863 and is now famed as the burial place of Sir John Betjeman, Poet Laureate from 1972 to 1984, who knew the area from his childhood and whose gravestone can be seen in the churchyard. His poem 'Sunday Afternoon Service in St Enodoc Church, Cornwall' recalls:

> *The modest windows palely glazed with green,*
> *The smooth slate floor, the rounded wooden roof,*
> *The Norman arch, the cable-moulded font –*
> *All have a humble and West Country look,*
> *Oh 'drastic restoration' of the guide!*
> *Oh three-light window by a Plymouth firm!*
> *Absurd, truncated screen! oh sticky pews!*
> *Embroidered altar-cloth! untended lamps!*
> *So soaked in worship you are loved too well. . . .*

Just to the north, **Daymer Bay** was where St Petroc landed from Ireland in the sixth century before going on to found a monastery in Padstow. The bay now marks the tip of a large holiday-resort development spreading to **Polzeath**, which has happened largely because of a huge sandy beach, the windsurfers often outnumbering the bathers. Its northern end, **New Polzeath**, is the starting-point for a delightful walk around Pentire Point and the Rumps.

The west side of the estuary is undeveloped between Wadebridge and Padstow, and the track of the old railway line from Bodmin now provides a four-mile foot and cycle route, the **Camel Footpath**, along the water's edge. Bridges span the creeks, and the footpath is ideal for viewing the estuary's large wader population, Canada geese, terns, teal and swans. An obelisk on Dennis Hill commemorating Queen Victoria's Jubilee presides over the scene.

Padstow looks unremarkable from the other side of the Camel, and nineteenth-century guidebooks, such as *Ward's Thorough Guide to North Devon and North Cornwall*, were unenthusiastic ('a mean-looking place, of woe-begone aspect'). But the town does have vitality and charm, with a bustling harbour looking across a sand spit to a procession of yachts. Boutiques and fudge shops proliferate in the amiable little streets, but plastic shop-signs haven't, and Padstow seems well healed and restrained. It's strong on places for eating and drinking at (you can buy delicious homemade Cornish pasties at some of the shops): and for a special treat try the Seafood Restaurant (see p. 254) on the quay. Also on the quay are blackboards offering mackerel and sharking expeditions and pleasure-boat trips up and down the estuary and out to sea. In the days when Cornwall's minerals and other products were transported by ship, the town offered the most sheltered harbour on the Cornish north coast, with the Doom Bar sandspit at the harbour mouth. Historic quayside buildings can be seen in places, but have changed function – on South Quay stands Raleigh's Court, where Sir Walter Raleigh presided as Warden of Cornwall, and fifteenth-century Abbey House was probably an assembly house for merchants.

In its leafy churchyard below the main car park, the church is dedicated to St Petroc, who founded a monastery here in the sixth century and was the source of the town's original name, Petrocstow. Two features to look for inside are a satirical bench end depicting a bishop preaching to a gaggle of geese and a fifteenth-century font of local slate displaying carvings of the 12 Apostles and once thought to bestow immunity from the gallows upon anyone baptised in it – until the hanging of a local man in the eighteenth century confounded the theory.

A **museum** (open late Mar to late Sept, Mon to Fri, 10 to 1, 2 to 5), above the library, has old photographs, local and nautical history and a 1920s 'Obby Oss', the last a strange pantomime-horse-like costume donned on May Day for what may be Europe's oldest dance festival. The 'horse', accompanied by musicians, dancers and singers, and taunted by a club-bearing Teazer, wends its way through the crowd, taking women and girls under the cape of the costume in accordance with what is very likely a pagan fertility rite. The crowd joins in the last line of each verse of the 'Morning Song', of which at least 17 verses are known, and the chorus:

Unite and unite, and let us all unite,
For summer is a-come unto day;
And whither we are going we will all unite,
In the merry morning of May.

Further into the back streets, the **Tropical Bird Park** (open all year, daily: summer 10.30 to 7, winter 10.30 to 4; closed Christmas Day) has scarlet ibis and golden harp pigeons among its 40 species of brilliantly coloured exotic birds housed in an ornamental garden. **Prideaux Place** (open for two weeks from Easter, spring Bank Hol to end Sept, daily, 1.30 to 4.45) is on the edge of town but only a few minutes' walk from the centre. Its handsome Elizabethan exterior, with pointed gables and castellated bays, beside a deer park, can be enjoyed from outside if you do not have time to take in the hour-long tour. Still the home of the Prideaux (now Prideaux-Brune) family for whom it was built, the manor has sumptuous Strawberry Hill Gothick alterations, more evident from within. A row of miniature cannons by the entrance, traditionally fired to mark the start of Obby Oss day (until one exploded and the practice was abandoned), stands by the entrance, from where you are taken into a dining-room of dark panelling cobbled together from three smaller rooms and rich in Spanish marquetry with plant and animal decorations. By the door, an *art nouveau* lightswitch is a reminder that this was the first house in Cornwall to have electricity. Beyond, the hallway and staircase introduce the Gothick theme. The highlight of the first floor is the Great Hall, with a splendid plaster ceiling showing the story of Susanna and the Elders; this was made by a firm of Devon plasterers who also worked at Lanhydrock (see p. 201). Virtually every room has fine porcelain, and there are numerous portraits, most notably by Lely, Zoffany and the leading Cornish portrait-painter, John Opie.

Urban Padstow is beachless, but good sandy beaches are all around; the nearest is reached by a tarmac path from the north side of the harbour out to a war memorial and then down to the shore. An easy and enjoyable hour's walk continues northwards to **Stepper Point**, its prominent column acting as a navigational aid for shipping.

Acres of caravans and hillsides of white bungalows dominate much of the Padstow to Newquay section of coast. The abundant sandy beaches which attracted the developers in the first place are excellent for bathing. Bays such as Trevone, Harlyn, Constantine, Mawgan Porth and Watergate have easy level access and are good for families. Treyarnon Beach attracts surfers. All of these can get very crowded. Less accessible beaches, such as Beacon Cove, reached by track from Trevarrian, may give a bit more seclusion.

Trevose Head protrudes well out into the Atlantic, and on a clear day commands a wide view along the north Cornish coast and into Devon; a toll road from near Harlyn leads out to the lighthouse, from where it is a short walk before views open out north. But by far the most striking scenic feature of this coast is a series of highly dramatic pinnacles and headlands of slate and shale, standing above a chain of rocks taking on the appearance of gigantic stepping-stones, collectively known as the **Bedruthan Steps**. Follow the sign for Bedruthan midway between Padstow and Newquay, and then walk from the large National Trust car park. Stairs to beach-level get wonderful views, but landslips mean that access to the bottom is often barred.

Newquay

Cornwall's largest and liveliest seaside resort has none of the ordered quaintness of St Ives or Padstow, and its scale and list of organised attractions by far outstrip those at Bude. The centre becomes frantically busy in season, most of the daytime visitors dressed for the beach and wandering along hectic shopping streets lined with fast-food outlets and surfboard stores, with racks of T-shirts and fluorescent plastic buckets and spades; notices proclaim the heart of Newquay an 'alcohol-free zone'. The central street is no less active at night. Hotels and guest-houses are everywhere, but in August the town fills to capacity, with scarcely a 'Vacancies' sign to be seen, and the population swells to several times its permanent figure. A replica 1910 London General bus winds a circular route nine times daily in season from the Great Western Hotel on Cliff Road through the crowds, giving a carefree opportunity to see the town; breaks of journey with the same ticket are allowed, and the half-hour trip can be picked up alternatively from the zoo or the Atlantic Hotel.

While the bulk of the main central streets and the town's far-spreading suburbs have little of distinction, the beaches are excellent – clean and sandy, contained in a series of bays, well below the level of the town itself. The B3276 on the north side of town dips to give access to **Porth Beach**, towered over by Trevelgue Head, and edged by caves. **Tolcarne Beach** lies more centrally, below Victorian hotels: three tiers of beach huts and a beach café look on to the sands. At the heart of seaside Newquay and the resort's most famous scene, **Towan Beach** has a detached rock topped by a strangely ordinary bungalow (it deserves a folly tower at least), linked to the mainland by a suspension bridge; huddled by the cliff, the Cosy Nook Theatre puts on seaside variety shows. Above, white picket fencing encloses a putting-green and neat municipal flower-beds.

The 'new quay' was constructed in the fifteenth century and modified in the 1840s, when Thomas Treffry built a tramway through a tunnel leading inland; the tramway was intended to facilitate the shipping of Cornish minerals to smelters in South Wales by providing an improved link from the mines to the port. The most evident hangover from Newquay's days as a small port, before the arrival of passenger rail traffic in 1876 transformed its potential into a holiday town, can be seen around the **harbour**, where yellow-aproned fishermen clean nets in front of onlookers. Beyond are a weatherboarded fishermen's mission chapel and the mouth of Treffry's tunnel, which now houses an aquarium of local fish and shellfish. A path leads up to the Huer's House, a vaguely castellated, whitewashed shelter. From here, men watched for shoals of pilchards, which looked like purple patches on the water, and, on sighting them, would cry 'Hubba, hubba!' ('hevva, hevva!' elsewhere in Cornwall) down a trumpet-style loudspeaker to alert the fishermen below to put to sea. From the house it's only a ten-minute walk across the grass, past the lifeboat station, to **Towan Head** for a view into **Fistral Bay**, backed by golf links and easily the longest of Newquay's beaches, a favourite with surfers.

Trenance Gardens, on the southern fringes of town, is an attractive swathe of mature trees, lush lawns, hydrangeas and palms set against an imposing railway viaduct. Incorporated into them, the **Trenance Cottage Museum** (open end Mar to end May, mid Sept to end Oct, Sun to Fri, 10 to 4; June to mid Sept, daily, 10 to dusk) contains an array of oddities from all over the world – tribal masks, nineteenth-century musical boxes, ships in bottles, butterfly collections, oriental curios and stuffed animals.

A little closer to the town centre, municipally run **Newquay Zoo** (open daily, 10 to dusk) is probably the West Country's major animal attraction, well set out like a park, with plenty for children (farmyard animals and a children's zoo, adventure trail and maze) as well as a substantial collection of exotic species, including lions, penguins, monkeys and an aviary. Combined tickets are available for the adjacent **Waterworld**, which has a 25-metre and a 'fun' pool. Next door, a miniature railway, toboggan run and pitch-and-putt course are side by side.

St Columb Major to St Agnes

St Columb Major has a main street of two-storey houses and cottages gently dipping from its cattle market to the faintly ludicrous Barclays Bank, all turrets and stepped overhangs in alien red brick. Few cars make their way through this small town now that it is bypassed by the A39, and only a coaching-inn remains as a reminder of the town's staging-post days. The Liberal and Conservative Clubs, three-storey rarities, face each other across a small square. Seventeenth-century Glebe House, crooked and slate-hung, stands at the entrance to the churchyard of a spacious church, venue of an August music festival.

If the town has something of the air of having retired from the world, on Shrove Tuesday and the Saturday following, the town wakes up to a raucous game of hurling. The goals are stone troughs a mile apart at each end of town, the teams are Town and Country (from the parish), and the pitch is the town's main streets, necessitating much boarding-up of windows the night before. Play commences with the silver-coated applewood ball being hurled high above the crowd, and the rest is pretty much an amicable free-for-all as the ball is caught, taken, passed, hurled and dropped. The winning team keeps the ball as a trophy; it is cleaned and dunked in a celebratory barrel of beer – or cocoa, if the scorer of the winning goal is a teetotaller. Traditionally, hurling, a likely ancestor of football, was played in many places in Cornwall and elsewhere in Britain, but the event at St Columb is a rare survival, and probably has pagan origins as a spring fertility rite. A stone plaque, dated 1926, on the Red Lion Hotel commemorates another product of the town's athleticism: James Polkinghorne, former landlord of the pub, was an accomplished wrestler and a Cornish hero.

Return to the A39 at the roundabout at the south end of town and go east along an unclassified road. Three miles on, a track on the left leads part of the way up **Castle Downs**, with a path across gorsy ground for the last few hundred yards. The view from the Iron Age ramparts crowning the mildly protruding hill is quite impressive southwards over the strange whitewashed toy mountains of the china clay country.

More conventionally rural charm is found at **St Mawgan**, where there are slate tables (and barbecues held in the evenings in summer) in the garden of its Falcon Inn; a bonsai nursery and a craft shop are elsewhere in the minute village. St Mawgan's church has a carved pulpit and painted screen but is chiefly memorable for its collection of brasses, many of them sixteenth century and commemorating the Arundell family. Outside in the churchyard are an ancient and elaborately carved cross and a boat-shaped wooden memorial to a crew who in 1846 drifted ashore at Tregurrian Beach, just north of Newquay, and were found frozen to death.

South of the A3059 between St Columb Major and Minor, **Porth** is the location for Cornwall's largest coarse fishery, run by South-West Water (day permits available).

Cornwall has steadily been filling up with organised farm attractions. **Dairy Land**, on the A3058, is one of the biggest, and offers a milking plant with a viewing gallery (milking takes place from 3 to 4.30), a well-displayed collection of country bygones, and a farm trail taking you past a herd of munching Friesian cattle and sundry farmyard animals to a site created as a wetland habitat for wildlife. Dairy produce is on sale at the entrance.

Turn off the A3058 at Kestle Mill for **Trerice** (open late Mar to late Sept, Wed to Mon, 11 to 6; Oct, Wed to Mon, 11 to 5), a manor built in 1572 for the Arundell family, but owned throughout the last century by the Aclands and since acquired by the National Trust. Sheltered within a walled garden, the house is a typically Elizabethan E-shape and has five scrolled gables, transomed and mullioned windows, and tall chimneys, the whole handsomely crafted from silver-yellow limestone; parts of an earlier house survive in the south wing. The ornate plaster ceilings, overmantels and Great Hall, with its musicians' gallery, are original, and many of the contents are eighteenth century, some earlier still. John Opie (1761–1807), who was at the time Cornwall's only nationally known artist, appears in a self-portrait in the drawing-room. An outbuilding contains what must be the only National Trust-owned collection of vintage lawnmowers (1875 to 1969), while an excellent tea-room operates in a converted barn.

Much of the low-lying coast between Newquay and St

Agnes comprises big sandy beaches backed by holiday camps, the sand-hills of **Kelsey Head**, the site of an ancient cliff castle, giving relative remoteness. Sands have completely covered the ruins of St Piran's church, north of Perranporth, but **St Piran's Round** nearby survives as a curiosity. To reach it, take the B3285 from Goonhavern towards St Agnes; park after three-quarters of a mile by a bus shelter on the right and walk back a hundred yards or so to a point opposite a guest-house, then turn left. This sizeable amphitheatre, enclosed by ten-foot banks of turf, is in the field immediately to the left of a storage tank. Of uncertain origin, perhaps an Iron Age fortification, the amphitheatre was in use in 1602 for the performance of Cornish miracle plays.

On Goonhavern's eastern side is **World in Miniature** (open daily, 9.30 to one hour before dusk), where you can see scaled-down versions of the world's most famous sights, set in immaculately tended miniature gardens, each enclosed by clipped hedges, some with theme music emanating mysteriously from the lawn: 'The Stars and Stripes Forever' for the Statue of Liberty and twangy oriental music for the Taj Mahal. Entry tickets include a visit to a full-scale mock-up of a Wild West 'street' with moving models, shops and a bar.

Another theme park is **St Agnes Leisure Park** (open Mar to Oct, daily, 9.30 to 6 (closes 10, May to Sept)), the first thing you see as you turn off the A30 roundabout on to the B3277. It offers Cornwall in Miniature, full-size model dinosaurs, a fairyland and gardens.

St Agnes, once one of the richest tin- and copper-producing areas in Cornwall, feels more of an ex-mining town than a resort. The St Agnes Miners' and Mechanics' Institute of 1893 still stands on the crooked main street and further down there's a terrace of ex-miners' cottages along a tiny lane called Stippy Stappy (which probably simply means 'steep'). Untidy outskirts somewhat mar the approach to the sea, but the old chimneys, from long-closed mines with names like Wheal Friendly and Wheal Kitty, on the hills and clifftops enhance the place's Cornishness. One of the most famous of all the county's scenic industrial remains, **Wheal Coates Mine** (now National Trust and with unrestricted access) stands on the cliffs two miles west of the village, approached by a short track from the road or by the coast path rounding St Agnes Head, home for hundreds of kittiwakes. Above, the heathery hill of **St Agnes Beacon**, 630 feet above sea-level, commands a good view over the head and of inland Cornwall, with St Michael's Mount and shipping near Falmouth visible on a really clear day. The whole hilltop is owned by the National Trust and is laced with footpaths.

Highlights

** *Bedruthan Steps, Boscastle, Padstow, Pencarrow, Port Isaac, Tintagel, Trerice.*

* *Altarnun, Blisland, Crackington Haven, The Hurlers, and the Cheesewring, Launcells Church, Launceston, Morwenstow, St Agnes Beacon and Wheal Coates, St Neot.*

Where to stay

For a key to prices, see p. 12

Little Petherick

Molesworth Manor

Little Petherick, Wadebridge, North Cornwall PL27 7QT. Tel Rumford (0841) 540292

About two miles out of Padstow, the manor is tucked up beside the road and it's easy to miss the entrance. The house dates from the eighteenth century and the present owners have been carefully restoring it. So far they have completed ten bedrooms, all spacious and comfortable, with modern facilities. Furnishings throughout are unfussy and suit the character of the house, a former rectory. The library, TV room and drawing-room give guests plenty of places to relax. Dinner is available with a little bit of notice. A good-value base for the area.

£ *Open all year*

Padstow

The Seafood Restaurant

Riverside, Padstow, Cornwall PL28 8BY. Tel Padstow (0841) 532485

The views across the estuary from some of the bedrooms above the restaurant are stunning, and sitting out on the large terrace gives a 180 degree view. Bedrooms vary in size and are priced accordingly; all are stylishly decorated in pale colours with a few well chosen objects and pictures, and the marble bathrooms are fully equipped. Decent sitting areas with comfortable chairs and sofas compensate for the lack of a public sitting-room. The restaurant and conservatory bar are simple and stylish with strongly scented trailing jasmine, whirring fans and framed exhibition posters on the walls. As its name suggests the speciality is fish and seafood and it is extremely well cooked and presented.

£££ Closed mid-Dec to mid-Feb; restaurant closed Sun

St Petroc's House Hotel

4 New Street, Padstow, Cornwall PL28 8EA. Tel Padstow (0841) 532700
The fifth oldest building in Padstow, this freshly painted white seventeenth-century town house is only a few minutes' walk up from the harbour. The decor throughout is simple and neat with wooden tables on a polished wooden floor in the dining-room and bar, softened by the occasional rug. Bedrooms, painted white with old-fashioned beds and en suite showers are adequately comfortable – all very neat and unfussy. Dinner can be eaten here most nights.

££ Closed Jan to Mar

Portgaverne

Port Gaverne

Portgaverne, Nr Port Isaac, Cornwall PL29 3SQ. Tel Bodmin (0208) 880244 Fax (0208) 880151
Just round the headland from very busy Port Isaac, the hotel in this tiny hamlet is also the local inn. Dating back to 1608 it has, rather surprisingly, been owned and run by an American and his wife for the last 20 years. It strikes the right balance between a hotel and a pub with rooms. The bars are beamed and decorated with sea and fishing pieces. A cosy, jolly atmosphere prevails in the evenings and you can have bar food or order from the fuller menu and eat in the large low-ceilinged dining-room. Bedrooms are both in the main house and in a separate building slightly up the hill and are quite simple and pretty. The sitting-rooms above the bar tend to be cramped and rather gloomy but it's more fun sitting in the bar anyway.

£££ Closed early Jan to mid-Feb

Poughill

Reeds

Bude, Cornwall EX23 9EL. Tel Bude (0288) 352841
Over the last ten years the owners have completely renovated this Edwardian country house and rescued the gardens from a wilderness. They run it on the lines of a house party, with only three bedrooms, all as spacious and immaculate as the rest of the house. Pre-dinner drinks are taken around the fire in the hall in winter and everyone sits down to dinner together at 8 pm. Two sitting-rooms give guests plenty of space to relax.

££ Open Fri to Tues; closed 25 Dec

Where to eat

For a key to prices see p. 12

Bodmin

*Pots Coffee Shop and
Restaurant*

55 Fore Street. Tel Bodmin
(0208) 74601
Huge hot-pots, baked potatoes,
sandwiches and puddings in an
informal atmosphere.
[£] *Open Mon to Sat 9–5.30*

Waffles

Market House Arcade, Fore
Street. Tel Bodmin (0208) 75500
A good selection of lunchtime
dishes; also does takeaway
food.
[£] *Open Mon to Sat 8.30–5*

Chapel Amble

Maltsters Arms

Chapel Amble, nr Wadebridge.
Tel Wadebridge (0208) 812473
Fresh fish and other dishes
ordered from blackboard menu.
Good puddings too.
[£] *Open all week 11–3, 6–11*

Launceston

Greenhouse

Madford Lane, Launceston. Tel
Launceston (0566) 3670
A cross between a bistro and a
coffee bar. Light and airy with a
wide choice of vegetarian
bakes, pizzas and salads.
*Open Mon to Sat 10–4 Closed 1
week after Christmas*

Marhamchurch

Bullers Arms

Marhamchurch, nr Bude. Tel
Bude (0288) 361277
Fax (0288) 361877
Cosy, friendly village pub

serving traditional English food
and seafood.
[£] *Open all week 12–2, 6.30–9.30
(9 in winter)*

Padstow

Seafood Restaurant

Riverside, Padstow. Tel
Padstow (0841) 532485
Excellent fish restaurant. It's
only open in the evening and
you need to book; also has
bedrooms (see p. 252).
Open Mon to Sat 7–10

Port Isaac

The Old School Hotel

Port Isaac. Tel Bodmin
(0208) 880721
Great place to sit out when the
weather's warm and watch the
activities on the beach below.
Food served all day.
Open all week 8.30 am–9.30 pm

St Breward

Old Inn

St Breward, Bodmin, Tel
Bodmin (0208) 850711
Bar snacks in the daytime are
unexciting but reliable. You can
choose between the snug and
the dining-room in the evening.
[£] *Open Mon to Sat 12–2.30
(11.30 in summer) 6–11 and Sun
12–3, 7–11 Closed Christmas
evening*

Trebarwith

House on the Strand

Trebarwith Strand, Trebarwith
nr Tintagel. Tel Camelford
(0840) 770326
Right on the beach this slate

house, with tables outside, is open all day and is a good place for families.

[£] *Open all week 6–10, also daytime during summer and weekends.*

Wadebridge

Janner's Bistro

34 Molesworth Street, Wadebridge. Tel Wadebridge (0208) 812833
A good value, stylish wine bar with mediterranean influences. *Open all week 12–2, 6–9.30 Closed New Year's Day*

West Cornwall

The two geographical extremities of West Cornwall provide much that is rewarding. The Penwith peninsula, little commercialised except at the English mainland's westernmost point – Land's End – has a superbly dramatic coast splattered with relics of a busy industrial past, and a rich archaeological heritage from Bronze Age stone circles to Iron Age villages, much of it to be found inland. St Ives on the north coast, within a crescent-shaped bay abutting Penwith, has lots of self-conscious charm and excellent family beaches. The Lizard peninsula, mainland Britain's most southern point, is remarkable for its rugged cliff scenery: strange formations of serpentine rock and small sandy coves; to the north-east is the contrasting delight of the mild, wooded creeks of the Helford estuary. Between the two peninsulas, Mounts Bay spreads out, its sweeping sandy beaches dominated by the romantic outline of St Michael's Mount, an isle topped by a castle.

Porthtowan to Hayle

The north Cornwall coast from St Agnes south-west to Hayle is a mixture of its copper- and tin-mining heritage and modern holiday developments, with occasional solitary and unspoilt cliffs. **Porthtowan** and **Portreath** are both ex-mining villages which have expanded in recent years to become beach resorts. Inland from Portreath on the B3300 towards Redruth, a huge shop called the National Gold Centre, displaying a massive sign, sells all things gold and looks incongruously swish next to the ramshackle arrangement of sheds, stamping-machinery and shaking-tables (for crushing and sifting ore) that constitute the **Tolgus Tin Streaming Works**. Tin streaming – using water to separate the ore from the spoil discarded by the tin mines – was once common in this valley, and these works were the last of their kind in use in Cornwall.

The B3301 from Portreath to Hayle runs closely beside the clifftop, and there are plenty of (unsigned) car parks from which you can survey a wave-battered coast, two of its inlets starkly named Deadman's Cove and Hell's Mouth. **Godevry Point**, reached by a National Trust toll road, is considerably gentler, a low-lying expanse of grass looking out to a lighthouse (see p. 270) on a tiny island. From here to Hayle, the B3301 is well screened from the sea by miles of sand-dunes, themselves concealing acres of caravans. Beyond them lies a three-mile-long beach, popular in the summer and a good spot for surfers and kite-fliers.

Hayle, a port since the Bronze Age, is now an industrial-looking town dominated by an electricity generator and the shell of Harvey's Foundry, where huge boilers and steam engines were manufactured for the Cornish mines. Coal used to be shipped in from South Wales for this purpose and for feeding the copper- and tin-smelters located here. The Hayle river leading seawards from the harbour is now a peaceful place, where you can see wading birds and waterfowl in great numbers on and around the mud-flats. For more exotic birds, go to **Paradise Park** (open May to Sept, 10–6; Oct to May 10–4; for information about flying display times telephone Hayle (0736) 753365)), on the edge of Hayle, where endangered species from all over the world are bred. The park is also undertaking a project to breed and introduce otters into Cornwall in an effort to boost the mammal's dwindling populations; another project aims to re-establish the chough, a red-beaked, crow-like bird which was once a common sight on Cornish clifftops.

West from Hayle, **Trencrom Hill** is one of those Cornish protuberances that rise to no great height but when you've climbed up, it feels like the top of the world: the view spreads over St Ives Bay to the north, Penwith to the east, and Mounts Bay (with St Michael's Mount) and the Lizard to the south. The hill was presented to the National Trust as a memorial to the people of Cornwall who died in the two World Wars.

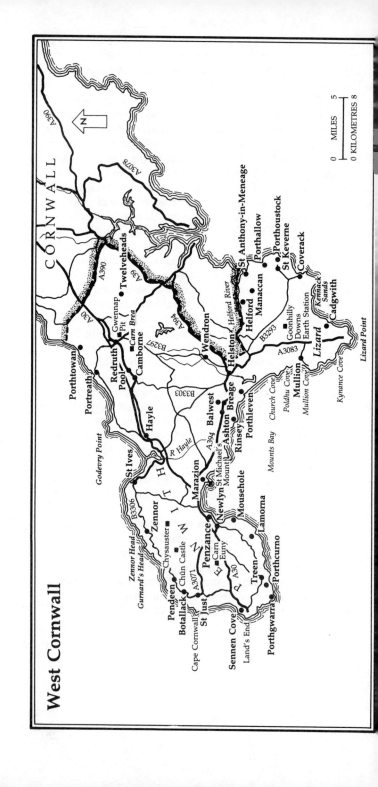

West Cornwall

St Ives

If you want to avoid traffic jams and parking problems in St Ives, you can walk from Carbis Bay to the south: go past Carbis Bay church to the hotels above the beach, cross over the railway and follow a leafy path until the whole of **St Ives** appears below. The picturesque fishing port, with its firm sandy beaches and near-Mediterranean light, has attracted artists and holiday-makers for many years. Turner, Sickert and Whistler worked here, and in the 1930s an internationally noted artists colony grew up, as Ben Nicholson, Naum Gabo and the potter Bernard Leach settled here. After the Second World War a middle generation which had strong links with the New York Abstract Expressionists continued the tradition, and the sculptor Barbara Hepworth made the town her home. Today, with the huge influx of summer visitors, studios on street corners invite passers-by to look and purchase artists' works. The two largest galleries are the St Ives Society of Artists and the Penwith Galleries, both of which make a small admission charge; the Bernard Leach pottery still flourishes. Plans are under way to establish the Tate Gallery's collection of St Ives paintings and sculpture in an old gasworks above Porthmeor Beach.

At the harbour, blackboards offer fishing-trips and parascending (a cross between water-skiing and hang-gliding with a parachute); there's a mild degree of tourist razzmatazz here: fast-food places, shell shops, and an amusement arcade. By contrast, immediately behind are huddled streets and winding alleys with names like Love Lane and lots of floral tubs, stone steps and B&B signs. This area was once a slum known as Downlong where the fishermen lived when St Ives was an important centre for pilchard seining (see p. 206). Fore Street gets packed with pedestrians; cars don't even attempt to enter. Shops are touristy and sometimes twee; but it's fun. Close by you will find the Sloop Craft Market, where leather-craft, stained glass and wood sculpture are on sale.

Signposts lead you to the **Barbara Hepworth Museum** (open all year, April to end June, Mon to Sat, 10 to 5.30 (6 in July and Aug, Sun, 2 to 6; Oct to April, Mon to Sat, 10 to 4.30), in Trewyn Studio where the sculptress lived and worked for 26 years, dying here in a fire in 1975 at the age of

72. Coats and overalls are hung in her studio beside unfinished sculptures, and on display in an upstairs room, the conservatory and secluded back garden is much of her characteristic work – standing or pierced figures, and double forms. Another Hepworth sculpture, *Madonna and Child*, can be found in the lady chapel of the parish church of St Ia, dedicated to a fifth-century Irish missionary who gave the town its name.

At the west end of the harbour, the town **museum** (open mid-May to 30 Sept, Mon to Sat, 10 to 5, Sun 11 to 4) tells of fishing and shipwrecks which were both a source of wealth and disaster for the townsfolk over many centuries; the building itself was once used for curing and packing pilchards for export to Italy, and later became the premises of the British Sailors Society Mission, providing accommodation for shipwrecked mariners awaiting repatriation. Out on the promontory – known as the Island – friars used to bless fishermen at **St Leonard's Chapel** before departing on often perilous voyages; a plaque lists some of those who never made it back. On the far side of the Island stretch the mile-long sands of **Porthmeor Beach**.

South of the harbour, the town becomes a sedate resort, with gabled Victorian guest-houses and hotels above the putting-green, and games of beach cricket in progress below close to the deckchairs and beach-huts.

Camborne to St Day

The conurbation that sprawls nearly four miles from the western fringes of Camborne to Redruth is the most industrial urban landscape in the county. It isn't for seekers of the picturesque, but the towns have a distinctive flavour, with straight nineteenth-century terraces and views of South Crofty tin mine, the only tin-producer left in Cornwall. Outside the library in **Camborne** is a statue of inventor Richard Trevithick, who was born here in 1771; he is depicted holding a model of the Cornish mining-engine he developed.

Abandoned engine-houses which served the mines are an unmistakable feature of the area. You can survey the whole scene from **Carn Brea** (pronounced bray), 738 feet above sea-level, a moorland hill encircled by Iron Age ramparts and the site of an early Neolithic settlement. The granite tor topping the hill towers over Redruth and Camborne, giving views to both coasts – the nearby cliffs around Portreath and St Agnes Head, and Mounts Bay to the south. Old engine-houses can be seen scattered around the towns' outskirts, and decaying beside transmitter masts and hedge-fringed fields. Two prominent features on Carn Brea itself are misleading from a distance: the apparent chimney turns out to be an obelisk erected in 1836 in memory of Francis Basset of Camborne, a landowner whose benevolence improved miners' welfare; the bleak-looking castle is in fact a Victorian fantasy based on a medieval structure, and today houses a tea-room and restaurant. To reach the summit, either drive up from Carnkie on the southern side, or walk up from the Pool side (turn off the main road by the Railway Inn and park at the base of the hill).

The National Trust has acquired two engine-houses (open Easter to end Sept, daily, 11 to 6 (5 Oct)) adjacent to Pool's sizeable industrial estate, on the main road (the old A30) between Camborne and Redruth. **East Pool Whim**, designed to haul men and copper ore to the surface, was built in 1887 by a Camborne firm and powered by steam; electricity is now used for working demonstrations, so you have to imagine the heat and smell of the hot oil and coals used in the high-pressure steam system patented by Trevithick in 1802. Across the road is the much larger beam-engine which pumped water on a different shaft of the same mine, a product of the great Harvey's foundry at Hayle, it was originally installed at Carn Brea mine and was moved here in 1924, making it the last Cornish engine to be erected. After this mine closed, it continued to work for neighbouring South Crofty until electricity made it redundant in 1954. Close by is the apt setting for the Camborne **School of Mines**, exporting mine technology to the world, and containing an excellent geological museum (open all year, Mon to Fri, 9 to 5, closed Bank Hols).

Rurally sited to the east of Redruth and signposted off the B3298 near St Day, **Gwennap Pit** is one of the cradles of Cornish Methodism, famous as the place where John Wesley preached in 1762; the abandoned sunken pit in which a large crowd of miners gathered to hear him was later made into an amphitheatre (see p. 241). An annual sermon still takes place here on Whit Monday.

A drive around the St Day and Twelveheads area, to the east of the B3298, will take you into the strange landscape of abandoned mines and urban-looking villages amid dairy pastures and isolated scraps of moorland.

Camborne to Helston

Distant views of the coast can be glimpsed from quiet roads 600 feet or so above sea-level in this unfrequented area of pasture-land and agricultural villages, where there are a few organised attractions but not much else to detain you. At Wendron, off the B3297 north of Helston, **Poldark Mine and Heritage Complex** (open Apr–Oct, daily, 10 to 6, May to Sept, daily, 10 to 6, Thurs, Fri & Sat, 10 to 10), is a mining

Cornwall's tin and copper mines

Only two mines – Geevor near St Just and South Crofty near Camborne – survive from what was the foremost copper- and tin-producing centre in the world. Today the decaying and at times spectacular legacies of this busy industrial past are a major feature of the Cornish landscape – ruined engine-houses, brick-topped chimneys, spoil heaps, fenced-off ventilation shafts and more. Although their function has changed, the mining towns and villages are still very much alive; chapels, miners' institutes and straight rows of cottages live on in many places, such as St Agnes, St Just, St Day, Redruth and Camborne.

The huge increases in need for metal products in the Industrial Revolution caused a significant rise in demand for tin and copper. The peripheries of the granite uplands of Devon and Cornwall, which coincide with a ring of metamorphic oriole – rocks known locally as 'killas' – yielded the metals that made fortunes for some entrepreneurs and gave employment to many in what had been an economic backwater.

Tin and copper are often found together. Tin, which occurs only in small quantities, is more valuable – a little is mixed with copper to make bronze and with lead to make pewter. Both minerals are found in veins within the rock – known in Cornwall as lodes – which were created when fissures occurred in the cooling granite and filled with mineral vapours and solutions which then crystallised; some lodes contain quartz and fluospar, others tin or copper. Also present are zinc, a by-product of tin, copper and lead (produced until recently at Wheal Jane), and arsenic, an impurity in tin; iron and wolfram were also mined in small quantities.

In prehistoric times, Bronze Age man found tin readily available

and Cornish heritage museum, centred on a 25–30-minute walk into the mine (called Wheal Roots in its working days). Donning a hard hat to protect your head from inevitable encounters with the low and uneven rock ceiling, you can take your time on the walk; labels point out features of the mine and the rock veins or 'lodes' which yield the tin and copper, while one or two model miners at work help recreate the experience and former work conditions. The longest walk involves negotiating a narrow mesh staircase that drops steeply into a chamber with mock-skeletons. At surface level,

from eroded lodes and on the surface in the valley gravels on Dartmoor, Bodmin Moor and Penwith; the streaming process, whereby water run over the gravel sorted out the heavier tin, was sufficient for many centuries. When surface deposits ran out, excavations began. By medieval times, tin had become so important to the regional economy that a stannary court and stannary parliament were set up to make laws and maintain gaols at Lydford and Lostwithiel; Dartmoor was by now the foremost tin area in Europe. Ingots of tin were stamped and weighted to establish the duty to be paid to the Duchy of Cornwall at stannary towns, which included Liskeard, Lostwithiel, Helston, Truro and Penzance. 'Coigns' or corners were struck off to test for quality at special 'coinagehalls'. The system went on until 1838, and the stannary courts were not dissolved until 1896.

Industrial expansion in the nineteenth century led to the development of fishing ports such as those at Boscastle, Newquay, Fowey and Penzance. In many places mineral railways took over from pack-horse routes as a means of transporting copper ore from the mines for shipping to the Wye Valley and Bristol en route to the smelters in the South Wales coalfield. Tin and lead, however, were always smelted in Cornwall.

Cornish miners had a tough and often dangerous life, working in damp and dusty conditions. Innovations were essential for progress. Penzance's most famous son, Sir Humphrey Davy, invented the miner's safety lamp, replacing tallow and providing good light without risk of explosion from gas combustion. Sled hammers, wielded by one man to strike a bore held by two, inevitably resulted in numerous accidents and were replaced by the rock-drill, invented in 1867. William Bickford's safety fuses for explosives were manufactured in Camborne from 1831 to 1961. The perennial problem of how to pump water from the mines was first tackled by

an audio-visual display gives a thumbnail sketch of mining in Cornwall, and an extensive exhibition area shows miners' tools and glimpses into their domestic lives, with reconstructed miners' cottages and displays of flat-irons, coronation mugs and antique packets of cocoa. There is a range of playthings for children, and an amusement parlour which you can't avoid going through on your way out.

Just south of Helston, **Flambard's Theme Park** (open Easter to Nov, daily, 10 to 5.30 (8.30 end July to Sept)) is one of the biggest attractions of its kind in the West Country. In addition to fairground rides and activities, there is a reconstructed Victorian street where a barrel organ plays in the dark gaslight, and evocative smells emanate from shop

---

water-, horse- and man-power; early achievements with the steam engine followed, notably in 1777 when a Boulton and Watt engine was installed at Chacewater. Richard Trevithick was a pioneer of early beam-engine designs – the first steam-powered beam engine was installed in 1812, and over 600 engines were in operation in the 1860s; the one at South Crofty was in use until 1955 when electricity took over. The dangers of entering and ascending from mines were mitigated by the invention in 1842 of the man-engine (a series of moving platforms), and later the cage, operated by a 'whim engine'. Steam-engine technology was also used in dressing-sheds, where ore was crushed into the consistency of fine sand.

Underground operations were supervised by mine captains. Workers were either 'tut workers', on contract for so much money per fathom of ground broken, or 'tributers', who got a share of the price gained. Prospective tributers auctioned themselves for work – the lowest bidder was employed for a month, but had to provide his own tools, light and explosives; they had the potential to make fortunes if they had secret knowledge of a rich lode within a mine. Men worked in eight-hour shifts, using sled hammers before the days of gunpowder and high explosives. Women ('bal maidens') and children were employed in the dressing-sheds on the surface.

Highly susceptible to domestic and foreign competition, the Cornish mining economy wobbled in the late eighteenth century when there was a flurry of open-cast mining in Anglesey, and fell into terminal decline a century later under competition from South

and domestic interiors. The chemist's shop at the end of the street comes from the Somerset village of South Petherton and was re-erected here exactly as it was when it served its last customer in 1909, to be locked up and forgotten until 1987. The nostalgia theme continues with the 'Britain in the Blitz' street, complete with smoke, rubble and sandbags, a wireless crackling out the news from a 1940s living-room, and a grocer's shop with meagre, rationed goods on display. The adjacent aeropark houses a collection of Second World War fighter planes, Falklands and RAF memorabilia, as well as a prototype section of the front of Concorde. If you visit after three o'clock the admission charge is reduced, and for a few pence you can get a season ticket entitling cheap readmission.

America, the United States and Australia. The 'cost-book system' used in Cornwall was part of this downfall: the 'mine adventurers' (the business partners) injected more money when times were lean, but any profits that accrued were immediately shared out, with little thought for the long-term economic stability of the mine. As the Cornish industry foundered, many miners and entrepreneurs found a demand for their skills overseas and emigrated. The lead industry died in the 1870s, but tin production continues albeit on a much smaller scale.

The tourist industry has taken over from lead and copper, and has woken up to the potential crowd-pulling qualities of Cornwall's unique heritage. Geevor Tin Mines are open to the public, giving a lengthy tour of the treatment works and of the mines themselves, while Poldark Mine (originally called Wheal Roots) near Helston has dressed itself up more as a family attraction. The National Trust has preserved a number of engine-houses as derelict landmarks, and has restored two with their pumping systems intact – at Pool between Camborne and Redruth. Wheal Jane, which in 1991 was the last mine to close, may become a mining heritage museum, and the tin-streaming works at Tolgus outside Redruth have been retained for the public to view. Many of the gaunt ruins of engine-houses can be seen for free – notably from the summit of Carn Brea above Camborne, from the car in the much despoiled St Day area and on the coast path at such memorable places as Wheal Coates, Bottalack Mine and at Rinsey.

Helston, the northern gateway to the Lizard peninsula, was for 600 years one of the five stannary or coinage towns of Cornwall, tin being stamped at the Coinage Hall in the main street (Coinagehall Street). The hall has vanished but buildings tell of Georgian and earlier prosperity; the broad main street, unusually grand for Cornwall, slopes down past the thatched Blue Anchor tavern – which advertises home-brewed beer – and the Angel Hotel (once the town property of the Godolphins; see p. 274). At the bottom, the street tapers out in front of a memorial arch, screening a bowling green. Helston's **folk museum** (open all year, Mon & Tues, Thurs to Sat, 10.30 to 1, 2 to 4.30, closed Wed) behind the town hall is housed in the old butter and meat market; displays include a reconstructed forge, farm implements, a cider press, Cornish kitchen, Victorian photographs and toys. The town has few pretensions to be a tourist destination apart from on 8 May when the age-old Furry (or Flora) Dance takes place in the streets – a day-long event with dances performed by hundreds of pairs of local people in formal dress. The festival has pagan origins as a spring fertility rite, but over the years it has come to commemorate St Michael, Helston's patron saint, who reputedly saved the town from the Devil.

Lizard, west of A3083

The southernmost tip of mainland Britain has long held a fascination for travellers, not just for its geographical extremity but for the fine cliff scenery, which is characterised by small coves and the rare 'serpentine' rock, so-called because of its snakeskin appearance: mottled and veined green, red and yellow. Inland, much of the Lizard is pancake-flat, and of great botanical value for its flora, which includes the rare Cornish heather (*Erica vagans*). **Porthleven**, south-west of Helston, is the largest tourist-oriented place on the Lizard; it is devoted mainly to angling and boating, centred on a quay built in the last century for the shipping of copper ore, china clay, china-stone from Tregonning Hill and soap-rock used in porcelain manufacture. South-east along the coast, **Loe Pool** is hemmed inland by Loe Bar, a great spit of shingle that was built up by the sea and dammed a river, creating a lagoon speckled with water-lilies, a habitat for waterfowl and trout. It can be explored on foot from the Porthleven side.

At **Church Cove** near Gunwalloe, a solitary church snuggles behind a small headland, its detached tower built tightly against the rock; nautical rope borders the churchyard path. You can drive there or walk to it over the cliff from **Poldhu Cove**, which has a sandy beach overlooked by a large Victorian hotel. To the north, a memorial marks the spot of the first transatlantic wireless transmission in 1901 when three faint 'dots', Morse code for the letter S, were heard by Guglielmo Marconi far away in St John's, Newfoundland. Marconi's experimental station on the Lizard was later taken over by the Post Office, and in 1909 it received its first ship distress signal; daily news to shipping was sent from here until 1922.

Mullion village, inland and south-east, has a pleasant, unexceptional centre; the church has good carved bench ends, some featuring sea-horses and Jonah and the whale. On the village's outskirts, the **Mullion Model Museum** (open daily, 11 to 5) has vintage penny-in-the-slot machines (which take only old pennies) in addition to a model coal mine, railway and city. **Mullion Cove**, separate from Mullion, a hamlet consisting of little more than an old hut surrounded by tyres, an upturned boat, lobster-pots and nets, is squeezed between tilted and overhanging wedges of rock; it looks out to Mullion Island – T-shaped and looking like a gigantic rusting anchor sprawled in the bay. Superb cliff walks south from here to Lizard Point offer the most rugged scenery on the peninsula and some of the best in Cornwall, though there is no feasible inland return route that avoids using roads. A haul up on to the top and along Mullion Cliff to Predennack Head gives you an excellent taster as the view opens out beyond Vellan Head.

A drive through flat moorland brings you to **Kynance Cove** where a National Trust car park much larger than the beach itself gives access to the stepped path leading a quarter of a mile down to the beach. The cove's famous beauty draws the crowds: the sands are sheltered by strange cliff and serpentine rock formations, and you can explore the caves, clamber up the offshore rock of Asparagus Island (where the delicacy once grew wild) at low tide, or picnic on grassy clifftops. The beach disappears at high tide.

At **Lizard Point**, just beyond the commercialised village of Lizard itself, a row of shacks, one selling serpentine rock handicrafts, compete for the most southerly site on the British mainland; hardy visitors scramble on to the rocky shore to get to the very end. The lighthouse above, on Cornwall's oldest lighthouse site, controls all of the rock lighthouses in the south-west (see p. 270); its beam shines out over 20 miles of perilous sea. A few hundred yards to the east, the roof of a cave collapsed one night in 1847 leaving in its stead a great vertical funnel known as the Lion's Den.

Lizard, east of A3083

The serpentine stone is too flawed for widespread use as a building material, but it can be seen in the rose-hung walls of thatched cottages at the picture-postcard village of **Cadgwith**, north-east of Lizard Point and nestling in a deep valley ending at a cove. A board on a café door in the centre lists the service record of the lifeboat station from 1873 to 1955, its proudest year being 1907 when 227 men from the Liverpool ship *Suevic* were saved. Five minutes' walk south along the coast path brings you to another reminder of this coast's dangers: at the **Devil's Frying Pan**, the waves swirl menacingly through an arch and into a gigantic cauldron-like hole – a cavern until the roof fell in. Car-parking problems and traffic-jams in the steep and narrow lanes of Cadgwith can be avoided by arriving on foot by the coast path from **Kennack Sands** a mile or so to the north-east. This is the largest beach on the Lizard and offers good opportunities for collecting colourful serpentine pebbles; easy access makes it a popular family destination.

Further along the coast the village of **Coverack** lies in a sweeping bay, attractively sited beneath a promontory, Dolor Point; anglers try their luck from the stone pier, and steps lead down the long harbour wall to a small beach, covered at high tide. Inland, a mile or so to the north, the large village of **St Keverne** has a central square with an urban feel to it, and a churchyard full of graves of shipwreck victims. A granite cross marks the communal resting-place of 106 sailors from the *Mohegan* which foundered in 1898 on the notorious Manacles reef a short distance offshore. Porthoustock, close by, is dominated by an ugly quay serving road-stone quarries.

Further north along the coast, the small yachting resort of **Porthallow** marks the geological end of the Lizard; the serpentine rock gives way to gabbro – dark igneous rock – and the infertile plateau gives way to green and lush country known both as the Meneage ('land of monks', where monasteries were established in pre-Norman times) and the Garden of Cornwall. This north-east side of the peninsula shelters a delightful complex of wooded creeks leading from the Helford river; mild and shady, they are far removed from the rugged grandeur of the rest of the Lizard coast. Villages are small-scale, with front gardens sporting the occasional palm tree. **Helford** itself is the pick of them: houses line both sides of a creek full of yachts beached on the tidal mud; swans float on the water, and customers at the Shipwrights' Arms enjoy the scene from the pub garden. In spring, the adjacent woodlands are full of primroses. **Frenchman's Creek**, just to the west, inspired Daphne du Maurier's novel of the same name. Inland a short way south, **Manaccan** church, at the heart of a quietly attractive village, may be unique in having a fig tree growing out of its wall. A couple of miles to the east, **St Anthony-in-Meneage** consists of little more than its church, beautifully sited beside Gillan Creek. A car park here provides a starting-point for gentle walks along the much-wooded coast path to Helford, with a good viewpoint at Dennis Head on the way.

At the inland heart of the Lizard is **Goonhilly Downs Earth Station** (open Easter to end Oct, daily, 10 to 6), looking like something out of science fiction – huge white satellite dishes gleam on the flat, windswept moor, dominating the view for miles around. Following the pioneering achievements of Marconi at Poldhu (see p. 267), it was the first satellite tracking station in Britain, set up in 1962 with the launch of the telecommunications satellite *Telstar*; since then, the tracking station at Madley in Herefordshire has opened. International telephone calls are sent and received from here via a network of microwave towers across the country linking up with the British Telecom Tower in London. Goonhilly also receives television pictures by satellite, making history in 1962 when it received the first live television transmission from the United States beamed across the Atlantic. Forty-minute guided tours take you into an old control tower for a view of the space-age architecture of the site and past the operation's nerve centre – nicknamed Starship Enterprise. The guide proudly explains that the tracking station stands in a nature reserve which is important as the habitat for Cornish heather and rare clovers, buttercups and orchids. The futuristic visitor centre contains gadgets for you to try out in its displays of telecommunications, from old Morse code and telephone exchange equipment to fax machines and dishes capturing sound waves.

To the north, signposted off the B3293 at Garras, the **Trelowarren** estate has craft and garden shops, a campsite and a gallery of nineteenth- and twentieth-century paintings on sale, besides the Elizabethan/Strawberry-Hill Gothick house of Trelowarren itself, which is run as an Anglican retreat but also hosts classical music concerts in summer.

Lighthouses on the Cornish coast (listed anti-clockwise)

	light flash	range in miles	date of present structure	date of original structure
Trevose	every 5 secs	25	1847	
Godevry	every 10 secs	17	1859	
Pendeen	4 every 15 secs	27	1900	
Longships	every 10 secs	19	1873	1795
Wolf Rock	every 15 secs	23	1869	
Round Island	every 10 secs	24	1887	
Penninis	every 20 secs	20	1911[1]	
Bishop Rock	2 every 15 secs	28	1850[2]	
Tater Du	3 every 15 secs	23	1965	
Lizard	every 3 secs	29	1751	1619[3]
St Anthony	every 15 secs	22	1835	
Eddystone	every 10 secs	24	1882	1698[4]

[1] *Replaced St Agnes Lighthouse (1680; the first to be erected by Trinity House), which is now a private house but the tower is painted white as a day-mark.*

[2] *Collapsed when it was about to receive the lighting apparatus; rebuilding completed 1858; heightened 1881.*

[3] *Originally a private light; two towers were built in 1752.*

[4] *Also rebuilt 1699, 1709 and 1759.*

There are tours (Wed and Bank Hol Mons, 2.30 to 5) around the building, but few interesting original features have survived. A designated woodland walk (open Easter to end Sept; leaflet available at house) gives access to Halliggye fogou, an Iron Age underground chamber of unknown purpose, and considered to be one of the best examples in Cornwall.

Cornish Lighthouses

Cornwall has always lived in uneasy alliance with the Atlantic and English Channel. The sea provided bounty for fishermen but dangers for sailors. From early times the wind, fog and unpredictable tidal currents have claimed wrecks; one of the most treacherous black-spots, the waters around Land's End and the Isles of Scilly, confounded navigation – until the first navigational charts were made in the late eighteenth century – because of a 'circular' tide that changes direction every few hours. Headlands deflect tidal streams and many vessels foundered (and still do) in bays between two such features.

A royal charter granted by Henry VIII in 1514 gave Trinity House general powers to regulate pilotage, and Elizabeth I, in 1566, passed an Act of Parliament giving the Corporation powers to erect sea-marks. Trinity House subsequently became the Lighthouse Authority for England, Wales and the Channel Islands.

Local interests in plundering wrecks did not go hand in hand with the development of the lighthouse network: 50 years of local opposition delayed the building of the first Lizard lighthouse, finally erected in 1619. In 1698 the first Eddystone lighthouse, in the Channel, south of Plymouth, was erected, but was washed away by waves before it could be occupied; its third rebuilding, by John Smeaton in 1759, was the first use of interlocking masonry blocks in place of timber.

The main spate of lighthouse building took place in the nineteenth century. Innovations boosted progress: oil-lighting took over from coal and wood fires (which were hard to keep alight and blackened the glass), prismatic lenses and reflectors concentrated a weak oil-lamp into something akin to a modern car headlight, and a rotational action enabled the light to be brought to a point. A major improvement in the 1780s was the circular wick blown by a current

Breage to St Michael's Mount

The people of **Breage**, just off the A394 west of Helston, were
once known, along with the residents of Germoe further
along the coast, for looting shipwrecks – inspiring the sailors'
rhyme, 'God save us from rocks and shelving sands/And
save us from Breage and Germoe men's hands'. The former
mining village now seems a docile place, better known for
the wall-paintings in its handsomely arcaded church, the
third on the site, and dating from the fifteenth century. The
nine paintings that have been uncovered since the 1890s after
disappearing in Elizabethan times include depictions of St
Christopher, Christ of the trades, St Giles and St Thomas of
Canterbury; they display great vitality and are of
considerable rarity value in a county with few such church
decorations. The church also includes monuments to the
Godolphins (see p. 274) and a Roman milestone inscribed

---

*of air, to produce a brighter and cleaner flame. In 1822 a
Frenchman, Augustin Fresnel, was the first to mount the apparatus
in front of rather than behind the light source, with a revolving lens
and flashing mechanism.*

*Two of the most notorious Cornish wrecking-grounds where
navigational lights play an important role are Stones Reef near
Godevry Lighthouse in St Ives Bay, and Seven Stones reef between
Land's End and the Scillies, where a light-vessel warns of the two-
square-mile danger zone and is moored by a four-ton anchor
attached to a 300-fathom chain.*

*One light used to look much like another, but today navigation is
made easier by deliberate differentiation of light colours and flash
frequencies. Flashing lights comprise a flash or flashes, alternated
with a longer period without light; occulting lights make a long light
with a short period of dark; isophase lights are of equal periods of
light and dark; sector lights give a different colour from the main
light, its arc showing a particular danger area; fixed lights (not
flashing) are also used. In addition, there are day-marks,
unilluminated beacons – examples are on Stepper Point just north of
Padstow, Gribben Head near Fowey, and eastern Chapel Down on
St Martin's, Isles of Scilly. At times of poor visibility fog signals
have been given in the past by firing cannon, ringing bells and*

---

with the name of Emperor Marcus Cassianus Posthumus.

West from Breage along the A394, a turning to the north at the main-road village of Ashton for Balwest, where a lane leads steeply up to the right, gives access to the top of **Tregonning Hill**. Here in 1746 the chemist and Quaker preacher William Cookworthy made the first discovery of china clay in England, enabling him to manufacture the first true English porcelain. The view from the top of the hill extends in all directions, with St Michael's Mount conspicuous in Mounts Bay.

Also from Ashton, a side-turn on the south side of the A394 for **Rinsey** takes you down a narrow lane, dwindling to a bumpy track before ending in a small car park by the cliffs; there is no wilder place on the coast between the Lizard and Penwith, and the ruined engine-houses of Wheal Prosper and Wheal Trewavas mines are among the finest sited in Cornwall (there is unrestricted access to the sites). Wheal Prosper thrived only modestly and briefly, producing small

---

sounding gongs or horns, but radar has lessened the need for them and fog signals have now been discontinued at some stations.

The lighthouse-keeper is also gradually being phased out by automation – all offshore lighthouses are scheduled to be automated by the mid-1990s and land lighthouses by the end of the century. Trinity House has adopted microwave radio links to monitor unmanned lighthouses, and has established eight base stations around the coasts of England, Wales and the Channel Islands for this purpose; eventually it may be possible to monitor all lighthouses from one central base. In 1982 Eddystone became the first remote-controlled automatic lighthouse, capable of being monitored and controlled from Penlee Point near Plymouth. Each automated lighthouse has an attendant who lives locally and who visits the lighthouse regularly to perform husbandry tasks. Lighthouse-keepers at land stations live on the site with their families; rock lights are manned by a principal keeper and two assistant keepers, working on a four-week rota, or turn, with another crew.

Many land lighthouses are open to the public, and further information may be obtained from the Information Officer at Trinity House, London EC3N 4DH. In addition there is a National Lighthouse Centre at Penzance which is open to the public for a fee (see p. 276).

---

quantities of copper and tin from 1860 to 1866; its engine-house has now been restored by the National Trust. Wheal Trewavas, solely a copper mine, was worked in the 1830s and 1840s.

Further west, **Praa Sands**, a sweep of sand extending a mile from headland to headland, is popular for bathing and surfing, with plenty of rock-pools for the marine-life enthusiast; there is easy access from a car park and a café close by. A resort village and holiday camp has been developed behind the bay. **Prussia Cove**, further west and reached by a no-through road from Rosudgeon on the A394, lies in a rugged complex of slit-shaped coves and miniature headlands; the sea here can be a brilliant turquoise, and the best view is from the coast path rounding Piskies' Cove and Cudden Point. This is old smuggling country: in the late eighteenth century Captain Henry Carter, the 'King of Prussia', who gave the cove its name, carried out a lucrative trade in illicitly obtained liquor.

Godolphin Hall (open May and June, Thurs, 2.30 to 5, July and Sept, Tues and Thurs, 2 to 5, Aug, Tues, 2 to 5 and Thurs, 10 to 1, 2 to 5) is a few miles north of Breage, off the main tourist routes but worth finding. What you first see is the early seventeenth-century façade, neatly symmetrical and mostly raised on columns. Beneath it an Elizabethan gateway leads into a secluded courtyard where on sunny days visitors spill from the adjoining tea-room (serving good-value tea and cakes). The Godolphin family lived here until the mid-eighteenth century, and portraits of them and of a famous stallion called Godolphin Arabian hang on the linen-fold panelling in the fifteenth-century dining-room. Rooms upstairs are roped off but can be looked into; they include a library, an Elizabethan bedroom with a bed made in about 1590, and the King's Room – named after a visit from Charles II. The Godolphins were staunch Royalists, and maintained the house as a stronghold in the Civil War, raising Cornish regiments for the king. A small exhibition tells of the Civil War, and there are occasional 'Living History' re-enactments of military practice in the seventeenth century.

St Michael's Mount (open Easter to end Oct, Mon to Fri, 10.30 to 5.45, Nov to Easter guided tours tide and weather permitting; also open some weekends for charity events) rises like a fairy-tale vision out of Mount's Bay. Very similar, though smaller in scale, to Mont-St-Michel in Normandy, it is an island approached by a causeway, with a village huddled around the base of the soaring mound which is crowned by a medieval building. The similarity to the French isle is not coincidental: St Michael's Mount belonged to the Benedictine foundation of Mont-St-Michel from the eleventh century up to the war with France in the early fifteenth century, and it was the French Benedictines who founded a church on the island's summit during this period. After the dissolution of the monasteries the island became Crown property and was used as a fortress because of its commanding position. In the Civil War it was a Royalist stronghold until the Parliamentarians captured it under the command of Colonel John St Aubyn in 1646. The St Aubyn family, still the owners, bought the Mount in 1659 and what you see today is a residential castle adapted for comfortable living from the earlier monastery and fortress. The monks' refectory is now a hall called Chevy Chase – after a seventeenth-century plaster frieze of the 'Ballad of Chevy Chase'. The rooms are an intriguing mish-mash of styles, shapes, sizes and contents – from the modest panelled library to the opulent eighteenth-century Rococo drawing-rooms hung with portraits by Gainsborough and Reynolds; in the map room you can see the family butler's attempt to model St Michael's Mount from champagne corks. The best views over Mounts Bay and far inland are from the South and North Terraces, the latter presided over by a granite lion, made in Egypt *c*.400 BC. The church, which can be entered from this terrace, is the most obvious survival of the monastic foundation of 1135; it was substantially rebuilt after an earthquake in 1275 and its windows enlarged in the fifteenth century.

The causeway is submerged at high tide, so if you are visiting the island, enquire locally about times before setting off; there is no vehicle access for the general public so you have to cross the causeway on foot. There is no admission charge if you want to visit only the island village and its small harbour. Boat services operate to and from the village of **Marazion** on the mainland. This is the closest point to the island, and gives a peerless view of the Mount across the large sandy expanse at the village's fore. The meandering main street has some pretty cottages and in summer there is an aquarium of local marine life (repatriated into the sea at the end of the season).

Penzance and Newlyn

The town of **Penzance**, finely sited on the west of Mounts
Bay, is no great beauty but it has hidden pleasures. Tin and
smuggling contributed to its early prosperity; in 1769 the
mayor was a renowned smuggler, and in the nineteenth
century Penzance became a stannary town as Cornish tin
production reached its peak. It further developed in the early
nineteenth century as a seaside resort – Regent Terrace on
the sea-front retains something of its early architectural
character – and more trade came with the opening of the
railway in 1859. Today a one-way system and car park have
spoilt the view of the harbour, but quiet Chapel Street in the
centre of town is a pleasant urban backwater; it is well
endowed with carefully preserved Georgian houses,
restaurants, old pubs and antique shops, with a small arts
centre functioning in an old chapel (around the corner in
Parade Street). Among these buildings the **Egyptian House**
(open April to Dec, Mon to Sat, 9 to 5; Jan to March, Mon,
Tues, Thurs & Sat, 10 to 4) with its colourful lotus columns
and stylized cornices stands out for its exuberant
architecture. Built in 1835, it is a virtual copy of the Egyptian
Hall (1812) which stood in London's Piccadilly until 1904: the
inspiration for both designs came from the Temple of
Hat-hor at Dendra, Egypt. The Landmark Trust have
restored the building and let out the upper floors for holiday
lets, renting the ground floor to the National Trust for use as
a shop.

Further along the street towards the quay, at No. 19, the
Maritime Museum (open April to end Oct, Mon to Sat, 10 to
5), looks like an agreeable town-house but the interior has
been entirely remodelled to recreate an early eighteenth-
century man-of-war, on four decks. The realism extends to
neck-craningly low ceilings, creaking floorboards and a smell
of tar; the exhibits are primarily a fun collection – ship
models, shipwreck and flotsam debris, guns and old diving
gear. Opposite the main car park on Wharf Road, the
National Lighthouse Centre (open all year, daily, 11 to 5,
closed Christmas holidays) has a replica of a lighthouse-
keeper's room, and an absorbing exhibition shows the
development of the lighthouse – optic systems and signalling
equipment, foghorns, model light-vessels (see p. 270).

A statue of the town's most celebrated son, Sir Humphrey

Davy, inventor of the miner's safety lamp, stands in prime position in the town centre. By it is the domed and porticoed market house, the dominant building of Penzance; a small market still operates here but a bank now occupies most of the space.

Flowers and vegetables flourish in and around Penzance, owing partly to the mild climate and partly to the rich soil, and the area has become a centre of market gardening. On the west side of town, **Morrab Gardens** displays this fertility with palms and other exotic plants, colourful flower-beds and fine lawns. The small mansion in Penlee Memorial Park, to the north across Morrab Road, is the home of the town **museum** (open Mon to Fri, 10.30 to 4.30, Sat, 10.30 to 12.30); several rooms are devoted to the work of local artists, and there are small displays on mining, archaeology, the police and natural history.

To the south **Newlyn**, now within the borough of Penzance but a separate place in character, attracted a colony of artists in the nineteenth century – including Stanhope Forbes, Lamorna Birch, Laura Knight and Alfred Munnings – whose paintings recorded the fishing village's inhabitants and picturesque character. That old-world charm of winding alleys and basket-bearing fish-wives has virtually gone; Newlyn today is the south-west's prime fishing port, headquarters of a major canning firm and with a daily fish market. Cornish and French trawlers, among others, dock in the harbour and you can hear an assortment of languages spoken in the quayside pubs. **Newlyn Art Gallery** (open all year, Mon to Sat, 10 to 5) exhibits works of the Newlyn School along with those of other British artists.

Mousehole to Land's End

South of Newlyn is **Mousehole** (pronounced Mouzall), which probably takes its quaint name from the Cornish 'mouz hel' meaning maiden's brook. The most western of the fishing ports on Mounts Bay, it still has an important-looking quay at its centre, where weather-beaten cottages and inns huddle around streets congested with cars in the summer season. A plaque on a nearby house records a former inhabitant, Dolly Pentreath, who died in 1777 at the age of 102 and is said to have been the last person to speak no other tongue but Cornish; her resting-place is up the hill in the churchyard in the smaller village of **Paul** – a typically

Cornish arrangement of a 'churchtown' separate from the main village; her monument is in the church wall.

Lamorna to the south is a scattering of cottages with well-tended gardens, artists' studios and a pub called the Wink, alongside a trout stream in a green and rather overgrown valley; the road ends at Lamorna Cove, a popular spot in summer, when parking can be a serious problem. If you have managed to park at Mousehole and are not in a hurry, you may do best to follow the coast path, which leads off at a corner in the road south of the village and runs along the cliffs for two miles before the cove suddenly reveals itself.

Travelling west from here by the B3315, through mildly undulating farmlands, there is a concentration of prehistoric sites that are easier to find than most in Penwith. If you are coming from Newlyn, the **Merry Maidens stone circle** is in a field on the left just after a hotel sign ($\frac{1}{2}$ mile past the turn to Lamorna): the 19 stones in a 75-foot-diameter circle were erected in the Bronze Age, and later tradition held that they were maidens turned to stone as a punishment for dancing on the Sabbath. Across the road, two standing stones or menhirs (probably burial stones) known as the **Pipers**, were supposed to have been the musicians who played for the merry maidens. A short distance along the road to the west, a labelled burial chamber can be seen in the verge. Weather-worn Celtic stone crosses stand alongside the roads particularly in the neighbourhood of **St Buryan**, a compact grey-stone village whose 92-foot church tower can be seen for miles around; there are more crosses in the churchyard itself.

The coast is, however, the chief attraction of this southern side of Penwith from Penberth Cove near Treen to Land's End; for sheer drama it is virtually unparalleled in England, and makes for glorious if sometimes arduous walking. (You may have to rely on public transport to get you back to your starting-point.) At **Penberth Cove**, owned by the National Trust and let to tenants, navy-smocked fishermen haul boats into a tiny harbour, the quayside wall piled with rope and lobster-pots. To the west, **Treryn Dinas** juts into the sea, a fearsome-looking promontory with a jagged top of crags and huge tumbled boulders, where traces remain of the Iron Age ramparts of a cliff castle. On it is the famous Logan Rock, a large stone that could be set rocking; when a naval lieutenant succeeded in pushing it over the edge in 1824, a public outcry forced him to erect a complex system of poles and hoists to reinstate it – it is said to be harder to budge now. The easiest access to it is by a signposted path through fields from the car park by the village shop at **Treen**, which has a cosy inn called the Logan Rock.

Porthcurno straggles along a valley dominated by radio masts and a training centre for Cable and Wireless. A pyramid on the cliffs on the east side of the sandy cove marks the site of the first cable to link Britain with America (via Brest in France), and a diamond-shaped marker on the beach indicates the point of mainland departure of the present transatlantic cable. But the village's real claim to fame is the open-air **Minack Theatre** (exhibition centre open Mar to Sept, 10 to 5.30, Oct, 10 to 4), founded in 1932 by Rowena Cade. She built a granite terrace adjacent to her cliff garden for an outdoor performance of *The Tempest* by local actors, and steeply tiered concrete benches were later installed on this breathtaking site, with the sky, the Atlantic and the Penwith cliffs forming the backdrop. A varied programme runs from late May until late September, featuring Shakespeare, modern drama, opera and musicals.

The cliff path west of here continues to provide astounding views but walking is not too demanding as far as the remains of St Levan's Well, which still supplies water for baptisms, above idyllic **Porth Chapel** beach. This path provides perhaps the best way to get to **St Levan church**, which is at a dead-end where parking space is restricted. The church, snugly sheltered beneath a slope, is one of Penwith's most charming; the interesting array of wood-carving includes a sixteenth-century rood screen decorated with Passion motifs and an entertaining set of bench ends depicting clowns, fish and faces. Outside, a Saxon cross stands close to the communal grave of the crew from the *Khyber*, a grain ship that was wrecked a few miles to the west at Porth Loe in 1905. A tortuous road leads to the coastal hamlet of **Porthgwarra**, where the surroundings are essential viewing. From a tiny beach fringed by small caves, the coast path ascends above deeply fissured cliffs and past two marker beacons to reach **Tol Pedn Penwith**, a great hole in the headland dropping the full height of the cliff.

The wild natural majesty continues into the bays of Porth Loe and Nanjizal, after which you rejoin the crowds at **Land's End**. Following the A30 to its conclusion, which will often entail queuing for the vast car park, brings you to the heavily commercialised Land's End complex (open all year, daily, 10 to 4, 10 to dusk in high season, closed 25 Dec). A signpost indicates mileages to New York, Brazil and John O'Groats: for a fee you can be photographed with the name of your own home town and its distance from Land's End added to these. A revamped Victorian hotel now stands amid the theme-park development, with souvenir shops, a 'shipwreck' play area, and a train and horse bus conveying visitors to various viewpoints. Combined entry tickets are sold for exhibition areas featuring two museums – 'Man Against the Sea' and 'The Spirit of Cornwall' – and the 'Last Labyrinth' sight and sound presentation – smugglers, Arthurian legends, shipwrecks and cackling witches. But the real Land's End is still impressive: piles of dark rock named Dr Syntax's Head form the mainland extremity, a natural look-out to the lighthouse on Longship Rocks, with the Isles of Scilly beyond. It is worth being there in time for the beautiful sunset view; or else you can earn the satisfaction of arriving on foot from Sennen Cove, a mile's walk from the north-east.

Sennen Cove to Zennor

Sennen Cove is a major holiday development; the fishing hamlet is engulfed by bungalows and 1930s villas, and a surviving fisherman's hut by the lifeboat shed functions as a craft shop. The attractions are a fine beach of clean sand – the best bathing-place for miles around – and the walk south on the coast path, starting unpromisingly from the toilet block, to Land's End (allow half an hour each way). You can enjoy aerial views of the Land's End area by taking short pleasure flights from St Just Aerodrome (telephone Penzance (0736) 778771), beside the B3306 just north of the A30.

Cape Cornwall, accessible by car from St Just, marks the southern extent of a once busy tin- and copper-mining area; many of the ruined mine buildings, crouching on cliff edges, have a haunting beauty. The chimney of the old Cape Cornwall Mine stands on a low headland overlooking the shingle beach at Priest's Cove, with Land's End in the distance and Kenidjack mine to the north. The coast path south joins the end of a road from St Just, where beside a trig point you can see **Ballowall Barrow**, an elaborate late Bronze Age (*c.*1400–600 BC) cairn riddled with deep burial chambers.

St Just is a small inland town, characterised by streets of grey-stone miners' cottages and the ubiquitous Methodist chapel, compactly arranged around a triangular centre. The B3306 heading north-east is worth taking at leisure in order to enjoy its views and neighbouring archaeology – ancient and industrial. At Bottalack, a lane by the telephone box takes you north-west towards the coast. After the road ends, a short track leads to the two much-photographed engine-houses of **Bottalack Mine**, perched on the cliff; 11 engines were working here in 1865, but only 30 years later tin mining stopped when prices fell irretrievably. Continuing along the path to the north-east, **Levant Mine**, also extinct, sprawls over a large area; it was the scene of one of Cornwall's worst mine accidents when in 1919 the man-engine (a type of lift) collapsed, killing 31 men.

Just inland on the B3306 at Pendeen are the **Geevor Tin Mines** (open Easter to end Oct, Sun to Fri, 10 to 5 (Sat in school holidays), closed Sat; last underground tour at 3; last surface tour at 4; advance booking advisable for underground tours – telephone Penzance (0736) 788662)). The mines still function, although on only a 'care and maintenance' basis until such time as tin prices rise sufficiently to enable economic extraction to resume. Geevor presents a unique opportunity to see a working tin mine from the inside: you descend by cage into the depths of the mine, which extends under the bed of the sea. The four-hour underground tour is expensive but thorough; you can save money and time, and still have an idea of the process, by restricting yourself to the surface tour of the mining museum and the treatment plant where the tin concentrate is produced. Signposted from the main road at Pendeen and accessible by car, **Pendeen lighthouse** (open to the public in daylight hours) stands on a headland known as Pendeen Watch; it retains its original $2\frac{1}{2}$-ton lens apparatus installed in 1900 (see p. 270).

One of the best spots on this superlative coast is **Gurnard's Head**, which juts into a wild sea edged by indented cliffs and looks like a clenched fist-salute. On this natural buttress Iron Age settlers built a cliff castle, of which you can just see faint traces of the ramparts. To reach it, leave the B3306 at the Gurnard's Head Hotel between Morvah and Zennor, park in this lane and take the signposted footpath at the end; the headland is directly below. To the east lies the broader Zennor Head, flanked by fine coves. **Zennor** itself is a one-street village, with St Zenara's church at the top end. The church has an unusual seat made from a bench end carved with a mermaid; a village legend tells how the squire's son, the best singer in church, was lured away by a mermaid and went to live with her on the sea-bed in Pendour Cove beneath Zennor Head. At the other end of the street, the **Wayside Museum** (open Easter to end Oct, daily, 10 to 6) originated over half a century ago when a retired colonel who had settled here rescued a scrap pile of locally made tools. His collection expanded to include mining, domestic and agricultural artefacts – and new owners have extended the museum into the cottage where some rooms have been set up as a recreation of a Cornish home around the 1800s.

Evidence of early settlers in Cornwall

Penwith can compete with Wiltshire in the concentration and interest of its reminders of early man and archaeological sites are also found on the Isles of Scilly and Bodmin Moor. Ordnance Survey 1:50,000-scale Landranger maps show the locations of many of these sites, although sometimes there is little to see. Only a few of the best-preserved are signposted or labelled: map-reading, patience and luck are needed to find the more obscure places – many of them on private land untraversed by public footpaths – and we have tried to make life easier by locating some of the ones most worth visiting. A description of the various kinds of sites, listed roughly chronologically, is given below.

The Late Stone Age covers the period from 3000 to 1800 BC; the Bronze Age from 1800 to 700 BC; and the Iron Age from 700 BC to the Roman invasion in AD 43. These stages represent an approximate level of cultural development in southern Britain, and are not closely defined.

Henges *These Late Stone Age oval earthworks, like arenas, are the oldest surviving monuments in Cornwall; they are thought to have been used for ceremonial purposes. Only three are known – Stripple Stones at Blisland, Castlewich at Callington and Castilly at Luxulyan.*

Megalithic chamber tombs, *known also as barrows, quoits, giants' graves, dolmens and cromlechs. They were erected in the Late Stone Age and early Bronze Age by peoples from the*

The Penwith uplands

A short distance west of Madron and beyond the northern
outskirts of Penzance, **Trengwainton Gardens** (National
Trust, open Easter to Oct, Wed to Sat & Bank Hol Mons, 11
to 6 (5 Mar & Oct)) are at their best in spring with great blazes
of rhododendrons and primulas; they are also noted for
mature woodlands and rare plant species from the Far East,
the Antipodes and Chile. The grounds, high above Mounts
Bay but endowed with a mild climate, were developed by

*Mediterranean, especially Iberia, who had spread over France and
colonised Britain. The Late Stone Age tombs were mass graves,
often with as many as 20 bodies in each tomb, although the trend
later was for single cremation burials. The tombs were placed on the
surface (the dead were not buried underground) and covered with
earth and stones – though this covering has to be imagined today.
Two main types of chamber tomb are found in the region. **Scilly
entrance graves**, are distinguished by an entrance passage leading
into the vault – of the 50 such sites, examples are Innisidgen on St
Mary's and Ballowall Barrow on the mainland near St Just.*
***Penwith Tombs**, of which 13 survive, typically consist of half a
dozen slabs supporting a capstone; most are found in Penwith – for
example, Lanyon and Chûn Quoits – although the famous Trethevy
Quoit is on the edge of Bodmin Moor.*
***Bronze Age barrows or tumuli** are the graves of a civilisation of
immigrant hunters who brought with them a knowledge of metals
and ore, and were doubtless attracted to Cornwall because of the
wealth of copper and tin found in the valley gravels. The barrows,
appearing today as circular or elongated humps, were the first true
underground burials, with the dead placed in compact stone coffins
called cists (pronounced 'kists'). About a thousand of these sites
survive in the county, although many more have been obliterated by
farming practices over the centuries.*
***Bronze Age standing stones** also called menhirs (from the Cornish
'men'=stone, 'hir'=long) and long stones. Some of these upright
stones, often of a considerable height, stand alone, others are found
near stone circles or beside tombs. Many are thought to have been
tomb markers. Nearly 90 exist, of which the Pipers, near Lamorna,
are among the best known.*
***Bronze Age stone circles** About 20 of these enigmatic monuments,*

Rose Price, the son (sic) of a wealthy West Indian sugar planter. Price bought the estate in 1814, added a granite façade to the house (not open to the public), constructed a drive and planted woodlands; Trengwainton later passed into the ownership of Lt Col. Edward Bolitho whose head gardener created a new garden of exotica; Bolitho handed the garden to the National Trust in 1961.

To reach the remains of **Carn Euny** Iron Age village, under the guardianship of English Heritage but unstaffed, means a lengthy drive west from Sancreed and Penzance along narrow lanes; occasional signposts keep you encouraged. Perseverance is rewarded: park at the end of the lane, and a clearly indicated path through the fields will take you to one of the archaeological wonders of Cornwall. As at Chysauster (see p. 286), the remains of the village, occupied from about 500 BC to AD 400, are substantial, and the flagged floors and stone walls still survive. In the middle is an outstanding

---

thought to be connected with pagan religious ritual, can be found today, mostly on Bodmin Moor and in Penwith; a few are of Late Stone Age origin. The stones are sometimes evenly spaced but many circles have stones missing or fallen and the tallest is seldom more than a couple of feet above ground. The Merry Maidens near Lamorna, the Nine Maidens near Morvah and the Hurlers on Bodmin Moor are impressive examples.

Iron Age hill forts Strategic defensive sites protected by ramparts and ditches were established by well-organised Celtic invaders from the Continent who came equipped with a knowledge of iron – which proved to be a better material than bronze for making tools and weapons. The forts usually crowned summits of sharply defined hills, many of which can be visited today as viewpoints, such as Carn Brea near Redruth and Trencrom Hill near St Ives; Chûn Castle near Morvah has stone ramparts dating from reoccupation in the Dark Ages.

Iron Age cliff castles These defensive sites were similar to the hill forts but occupied commanding points on the coast, particularly on headlands. There is now little to see in the way of remains, but the sites often have a natural splendour – such as Treryn Dinas near Treen, Gurnards Head near Zennor (also with the Cornish name of Treryn Dinas), and the Rumps at the mouth of the Camel estuary near Polzeath.

example of a fogou (see below), deep enough to stand up inside. Its unique feature is a circular chamber leading off it – its purpose, like that of the fogou itself, unknown, but perhaps used for storage or ritual.

A mile and a half south-west by foot, but much further by road, is **Carn Brea**, not to be confused with its namesake near Redruth, but a hill that offers a similarly grand viewing-platform. Turn off the A30 four miles from Land's End at a well-preserved milestone by an ancient cross and a sign for 'Aerodrome 1¾'. From an easily missed car park on the left side of the lane, a track brings you in minutes to the summit – giving the widest panorama of this end of England, with sea on three sides; a view indicator helps identify Penzance, Lamorna Cove, Goonhilly Downs on the Lizard and the Isles of Scilly.

The road from Madron to Morvah has some of the most famous Penwith landmarks in the game of archaeological

Iron Age courtyard house villages *All of the 20 or so British examples are found in Penwith; the 'villages' consisted of a group of houses, each with a series of rooms giving on to a courtyard. Chysauster and Carn Euny, maintained by English Heritage, are the best known, the former subject to opening hours.*

Iron Age fogous *The function of these low, semi-subterranean passages, roofed and lined with slabs, and mostly curved and open-ended, is a mystery; storage or hiding places have been suggested. Carn Euny in Penwith and Halliggye on the Trelowarren estate are excellent examples.*

Inscribed stones *About 25 stones from the Dark Ages, dating from the sixth to tenth centuries AD can be seen, although the lettering is often badly weathered. The inscriptions are in Latin and often commemorate a chieftain; King Doniat's Stones on Bodmin Moor and the Tristan Stone near Fowey both occupy roadside verges and have descriptive plaques.*

Celtic crosses *There are over 300 of these early Christian relics dating from the Dark Ages, found in churchyards, on roadsides, paths and private land. They had a variety of purposes – to commemorate the dead, to mark land boundaries, to guide people on their way to church and to mark sacred sites. The parishes of Lanivet (near Bodmin) Sancreed (in Penwith) and Wendron (near Helston) are particularly rich in such crosses.*

hide-and-seek. **Lanyon Quoit** stands within yards of the road, on the east side, but needs careful locating – it's a quarter of a mile on the Penzance side of Lanyon Farm. Formerly covered by an earth mound 90 feet long, the burial chamber comprises three vertical stones and a flat, 17-foot capstone; the purple moors with the sinister outline of the abandoned engine-house and chimney of Ding Dong Mine high up on the horizon are a memorable setting. The quoit is Neolithic but was re-erected in 1824 after it had collapsed nine years earlier, and the supports were lowered to ease the task of replacing the capstone.

Further north-west is a concentration of prehistoric sites, scenically located and all reached by an easy walk from the main road. **Men-an-Tol** – signposted on the east side of the road close to a telephone box, and a gentle half-mile walk up a stone-walled track – is an enigmatic holed stone set on its edge; known locally as the Crick Stone, it was thought to bring relief from back pains and rickets to anyone who passed through the hole. A little further along the same track (where it stops climbing) **Men Scryfa**, a stone standing alone in the centre of a field on the left, has a Latin inscription of the fifth century commemorating someone called Riolobran, son of Cunoval. Soon after, the track ceases to be walled and forks in front of a ruin: by keeping half right on a path that leads over the highest ground, you reach the Bronze Age **Nine Maidens** stone circle – the tallest 'maiden' standing over six feet above ground. The path continues along the ridge to Ding Dong Mine, with the north and south coasts in sight. Returning to the telephone box, a side-turn alongside takes you to a farm and parking space, from where a way-marked path ascends to **Chûn Castle**, primeval in spirit and occupying an exposed site high above the north coast. The dry-stone ramparts of this Iron Age fort, reoccupied in the Dark Ages, still crown the hilltop, and close by is **Chûn Quoit**, a well-preserved chamber tomb.

Penwith's most rewarding archaeological site, with formal opening hours and ticket booth, is **Chysauster ancient village** (English Heritage open Easter to Oct, daily, 10 to 6; Oct to Easter, Tues to Sun, 10 to 4, closed 1 Jan & 24, 25 Dec), north of Penzance but signposted from the B331. It was built during the Roman period and six of nine 'courtyard' houses have been excavated, with walls standing to a height of three or four feet. Common to all the dwellings are a thick-walled entrance leading into a courtyard, a Round Room containing a stone with a socket likely to have supported a timber upright, and a Long Room. Originally the courtyards were paved, but the stone has been removed over the centuries for use as building material. Towards the south boundary of the site, you can see but not enter a fogou (see p. 285).

Highlights

** *Cape Cornwall to Pendeen Coast, Carn Brea (near Redruth), Carn Euny and Chysauster Ancient Villages, Helford River, Mullion and Kynance Coves, Penberth Cove to Land's End Coast, St Ives, St Michael's Mount.*

* *Cadgwith, Carn Brea (near Land's End), Goonhilly Downs Earth Station, Lanyon Quoit, Men an Tol and Chûn Castle, Mousehole, Penzance, Rinsey, St Levan Church, Trengwainton Gardens.*

Where to stay

For a key to prices, see p. 12

Helford

Riverside

Helford, Nr Helston, Cornwall TR12 6JU. Tel Manaccan (032 623) 443

In a very special position on the side of the Helford river close to the estuary, Riverside is made up of several of the houses built into the bank from the road. More of a restaurant with rooms than a traditional hotel, the buildings are connected by flower-lined paths and the bedrooms can feel very private; they are generally large and extremely comfortable. Extras include fresh milk, home-made biscuits and a selection of teas. The small dining-room and bar are in the central cottage and although not particularly cosy have a good atmosphere – and the food is delicious.

£££ Closed 6 weeks late Dec to Feb.

Mullion

Polurrian Hotel

Mullion, Helston TR12 7EN. Tel Mullion (0326) 240421. Fax (0326) 240083

On the west coast of the Lizard overlooking the sea, this is very much a family hotel: 12 acres of grounds, swimming pools, leisure club and particularly good sports facilities. When the hotel is full or a function is on, the four sitting-rooms, four bars and two restaurants are needed. Bedrooms are comfortable and nicely

decorated but it isn't the place to come for a quiet weekend. The emphasis is on activities, families and friendliness.
££££ Open Mar to Nov

Penzance

The Abbey

Abbey Street, Penzance, Cornwall TR18 4AR. Tel Penzance (0736) 66906
From the top bedrooms you can look out across the harbour and watch the ferry come in from the Scilly Isles. The house was built in 1660 and has some wonderful angles and creaking staircases. The atmosphere is distinctly bohemian. A large high-ceilinged sitting-room on the first floor with a huge fireplace and gloriously comfortable sofas is packed with fascinating pieces collected from India, Africa and other exotic places. Book-shelves are stacked with books and games, and you can choose your own music from the pile beside the gramophone. Dinner is downstairs in a simple wooden-floored dining-room; the French cuisine is served by the French waiter who brings you a drink before dinner and delivers coffee upstairs afterwards. There's no ceremony or formality, and it's an extremely relaxing place to stay.
£££ Open all year

St Ives

Garrack Hotel

Burthallan Lane, St Ives, Cornwall TR26 3AA. Tel Penzance (0736) 796199. Fax (0736) 798955
A friendly, family-run hotel up on the hill at the south end of St Ives with lovely views across the garden to the sea. An indoor pool with a sauna and coffee bar is set apart from the main hotel. It's popular with families and the dining-room is unstuffy, with young staff serving the meals under the supervision of Mr Kilby junior. His father takes his turn in the newly decorated, cosy bar. Furnishings throughout are a mixture of old and new, and the bedrooms, although adequately comfortable, are a little dull.
££ Open all year

Where to eat

For a key to prices see p. 12

Hayle

Lelant Garden Centre Restaurant

Nut Lane, Hayle. Tel Hayle (0736) 753732
Good café serving nourishing hot dishes. Part of the garden centre but you don't have to be buying plants.
Open all week 10–5.30

Helford

Riverside

Helford, nr Helston. Tel (032 623) 443
Small well-run restaurant; delicious choice of dishes including aperitifs and chocolates; bedrooms (see p. 287).

*Open all week 12.30–1.30 season,
7.30–9.30 Sat and Sun only out of
season Book in advance*

Shipwright Arms

Helford. Tel Manaccan
(032 623) 235
Fish dishes and more traditional
pub food at this pretty thatched
inn. Tables outside by the
riverbank.
[£] *Open all week (exc Sun and
Mon evening in winter) 12–2, 7–9*

Manaccan

New Inn

Manaccan. Tel Manaccan
(032 623) 323
Good plain food in this
charming sixteenth-century
pub. Very busy in summer.
[£] *Open all week 12–2, 7–9*

Marazion

Sail Loft

St Michael's Mount, Marazion.
Tel Penzance (0736) 710748
In a converted carpenter's shop
and boat store, this good café/
restaurant is run by the
National Trust.
[£] *Open all week 12.15–5 Closed 1
Nov to Easter*

Newbridge

Enzo's

Newbridge. Tel Penzance
(0736) 63777
Italian cooking in a plant filled
conservatory. It seems
incongruous in an old Cornish
house but the food is very good.
*Open all week 7–9.30
(9 Sun) in summer*

Penzance

The Abbey

Penzance. Tel Penzance
(0736) 66906
Original, comfortable house
(see p. 288). Delicious French
cooking in a very good
atmosphere.
*Open all week 7.30–8.30 Booking
advisable*

Parrot of Penzance

Abbey Slip, Penzance. Tel
Penzance (0736) 50515
Elegant restaurant with good
views of the harbour and
Mounts Bay.
[£] *Open Easter to Sept Mon to Sat
12–3, 7.30–10, Sept to Easter
Thurs to Sat 7.30–10 Closed
Christmas Eve and Sun to Wed
Sept to Easter*

Isles of Scilly

Life in the Scillies is dominated by the sea and by the weather, which are constantly changing. The number of shipwrecks that feature in the history books and the museums reinforces this. The Scillians are proud of their islands and staunchly independent; flowers, tourism and fishing are their main industries. Each island has its own distinguishing characteristics – both in the landscape and the inhabitants – from St Mary's, the most populated, with a thriving town, to St Agnes, the smallest of the inhabited five. They make good hosts with a certain weather-beaten charm. Both visitors and inhabitants respect the supremacy of the boatmen on whom they totally depend. You can island hop or just stay put – life is simple for the visitor: for long peaceful days the only distractions are the sea and the birds.

From the air – or on the map – the isles of Scilly look like scattered jigsaw pieces unlikely to fit, and in no memorable pattern. Twenty-eight miles off Land's End, they are not distant in modern terms, but antique names and references stress their inaccessible mystery: the Islands of the Blest, the Kingdom of Atlantis. If they were ever part of the mainland it was long before human history, but the Cornish legend of Lyonesse, which claims they were once joined to Land's End, is embedded in poetry, both British and Breton. The legend became linked with King Arthur: the surviving knights of the defeated Round Table fled westwards, so the story goes, pursued by Mordred and his rebel force. As they crossed the fertile land of Lyonesse towards Scilly, the wizard Merlin caused an earthquake behind them, engulfing Mordred and drowning for ever 140 villages.

There is real evidence that the major islands were linked, if swampily, until about AD 600, and inhabited since the Bronze Age. An astonishing concentration of barrows and burial mounds suggests a geographic location for the Hesperides, the Greeks' mythological resting-place beyond the Pillars of Hercules where dead heroes found immortality and perpetual summer. The social status of the Scilly graves reveals the burial of chieftains, perhaps brought here by their successors in the belief that spirits of the dead could not return across water to plague them. Living souls in Scilly, according to the evidence of archaeology, were much humbler folk.

The Romans used *Silia Insula* as a place of banishment and a source of tin; the Saxons almost certainly never got here, but the Vikings did, beginning Scilly's tradition of lawlessness and piracy. In 980, according to Scandinavian saga, an island hermit converted to Christianity the mighty Olaf Tryggvason, who thereafter offered his Norwegian subjects the stark choice of baptism or death. By the early twelfth century there was a Benedictine priory on Tresco, then called St Nicholas' Isle, and until the sixteenth-century dissolution of the monasteries reluctant monks shared the islanders' meagre existence, in constant fear of the freebooters and social outcasts who converged on Scilly. The English Crown took little interest in this unprofitable part of the Duchy of Cornwall until after the Spanish Armada, when Elizabeth I ordered the building of a properly deterrent fortress. Star Castle on St Mary's, ugly but effective, was unchallenged until the Civil War, when a Parliamentary force bombarded it into submission from a gun-base on Tresco. Through the seventeenth century the castle served as a lodging for passing VIPs, and a secure remote prison for political offenders.

Scilly was poor in the seventeenth century, poorer in the eighteenth. The people fished and farmed, depending heavily on the potato harvest. One economic mainstay was kelp, an alkaline substance then used in the manufacture of glass and soap, produced by the kiln-burning of great quantities of seaweed. When demand disappeared, a small shipbuilding industry provided some work. Smuggling became a way of life: the advantages of an income from contraband spirits, wine and tobacco far outweighed the risks. There was a running war with the Customs and Excise Office. By the 1790s a protection vessel was stationed full time in Scilly, and its revenue officers received a share of the proceeds from contraband they captured. This stimulated them to such efficiency that smuggling dwindled rapidly, and economic distress in Scilly became severe. In the early nineteenth century £9,000 (then no mean sum) was raised by subscription following a grim report of conditions in the islands, but the pilchard fishery it financed never came to much. Then in 1834 salvation came to Scilly in the person of Augustus Smith.

Though the Isles of Scilly were included in the Duchy of Cornwall, created in the fourteenth century for the Black Prince, their ownership came to be an individual leasehold from the Crown, a holding of some prestige but little profit. For 250 years from the time of Elizabeth I Scilly belonged to the Godolphin family or its agents, a connection maintained until in 1831 the leaseholder elected not to renew the lease and the islands reverted to the Duchy.

In 1834 Augustus Smith bought the lease and became the live-in Lord Proprietor of Scilly. He set about reforms with the autocratic powers of a benevolent despot, beginning with the reallocation of farming land which, because no rule of

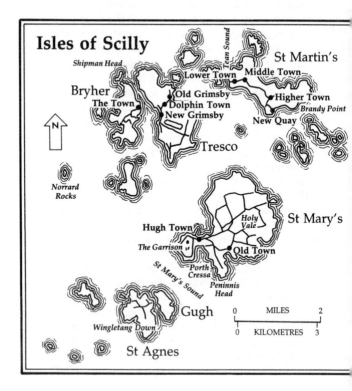

primogeniture had ever applied in Scilly, was worked in scattered subdivided plots. Now the eldest sons would inherit compact farmholdings, while younger children found employment in an extensive building programme: Hugh Town's church and extended quay, island schools and Tresco Abbey, the Lord Proprietor's new home.

Shipbuilding prospered for a while – by the mid-nineteenth century there were five shipyards on St Mary's – and by the time the demand for wooden ships was over Scilly had a promising new source of income: the flower industry was largely developed by the Dorrien Smith heirs of Augustus, who today still hold the island of Tresco, on lease from the Duchy of Cornwall.

The introduction of the island's oldest narcissus, the Scilly White, is variously attributed – to the monks of St Nicholas' Priory and to a Dutch sea-captain, who presented some to Star Castle. According to the story, the governor's wife thought that narcissi were unpalatable onions and threw them out, but they sprouted and spread around the moat. In 1879 a farmer who had replanted St Mary's abundant wild narcissi in his gardens sent a hopeful hat-boxful to Covent Garden. The fashion for cut flowers was just reviving, and the price obtained was gratifying; a couple more farmers joined in. The Dorrien Smith of 1882 studied bulb cultivation in Holland, planted 190 varieties in Tresco Abbey gardens, made bulbs in quantity available to his tenants and built them working sheds. Narcissi are still bestsellers – particularly 'sols', the early Soleil d'Or, with its cluster of sweet-scented yellow flowers on every stem.

The combination of frost-free climate and cunning horticultural technology produces flowers in bud in the little open fields from November or early December; daffodil varieties follow narcissi with peaks in February and March; iris and tulips wind up the season in mid-April. In the fields and the sheds people pick, bunch or pack all winter, geared day and night to local tides and the loading times of the steamer, whose winter sailings make no concession to passengers. Other stages of the flower business – lifting the bulbs, checking and grading them, treating and replanting them – are the work of the full-time farmers. The rest of the islanders man (and woman) the guest-houses, cafés and boats for Scilly's summer industry.

'In the winter we do the flowers, and in the summer we do the visitors,' a small boy is reported to have told Harold

Wilson. (There aren't many stories about Prime Ministerial residence in Scilly, though you may hear about the picture window in the wrong wall of the bungalow.) On 3 June 1989 Prince Charles, Duke of Cornwall, threw a switch activating an underwater cable from the mainland: 28 miles from Land's End, the western outposts of his Duchy received their first electricity from the national grid. It's not revolutionary – just a cheaper power supply than by oil generator – but the invisible link will make life easier for a population of some 2,000 and their annual influx of holiday-makers.

In Scilly it is impossible not to be aware of how many necessities, from building materials to butter, are imported, in the big battered containers that are swung from ship to quay. All year the arrival and departure of the Isles of Scilly Steamship Company's *Scillonian III*, with a preliminary blast of her siren, structures the day – except Sunday, when she doesn't come, and nor does the helicopter, and the newspapers wait until Monday; The absence of day-trippers makes quite a difference, at least to St Mary's, the communications hub.

But this holiday area is not going to become overcrowded. Both the Duchy of Cornwall and the Isles of Scilly Environmental Trust, which manages untenanted land, are unlikely to permit further housing development: available accommodation limits the number of visitors. As it is, in July and August there is the potential problem of demand on the water supply exceeding the St Mary's storage capacities – it already exceeds the daily output of the island's wells – and the appeals for restraint in consumption go up each season outside the town hall, along with the regulations to conserve the stocks of shrimp, and the prohibition of metal-detectors.

For birdwatchers and botanists, sailors and skin-divers, Scilly is so full of interest that holidays may be hectic. For birdwatchers (affectionately called 'twitchers') late October – the migration season – is an intense time. Exhausted, often rare birds stop off here on their way south. Within hours of a sighting the islands can be crammed with twitchers swarming into every corner to search out and record some unusual bird. The crackling of walkie-talkies and the determination to find the bird, regardless of whose land it's on, annually aggravate the locals. For the non-specialist visitor peace is the goal and exploration the activity. Each morning the boatmen announce the day's possibilities according to weather and tide, and the passenger-launches set out from St Mary's to the off-islands, to the western or eastern rocks to watch seals and sea-birds, and far out to the Bishop Rock lighthouse. Steep slippery quay steps, a soaking by rain, spray or the full wet of a stray wave, choppy passages and tricky landings deter nobody in this archipelago – not even the elderly or infirm. The boatmen simply regard everybody alike as incompetent landlubbers and give equally serene assistance to healthy young hikers, octogenarians, crutches and wheelchairs. The special pleasure of disembarking to explore a new island, just big enough to lose a boatload of solitude-seeking walkers, can be yours four separate times from St Mary's. After that, you'll be revisiting a favourite.

The quick way of getting to the Isles of Scilly is the 20-minute helicopter-ride from the airport a mile east of Penzance on the A30. You can leave your car at the airport, and there is a coach-service from Penzance railway station. Baggage is free up to 33 pounds per person; more can be sent by sea and costs extra. There are several flights daily (except Sunday) to St Mary's, fewer and summer only to Tresco. Details and reservations from British International Helicopters; telephone Penzance (0736) 63871 or Scillonia (0720) 22646.

The boat trip on *Scillonian III*, can be both relaxing and bracing and takes about two and a half hours; she normally leaves Penzance harbour at 9.15 am, St Mary's 4.45 pm, daily in summer (except Sundays; in high season there are Sunday excursion-trips at different times). You can leave your car at garages near Penzance harbour if the Steamship Company's limited parking space is full. Your labelled luggage goes into a container, to be decanted on St Mary's and delivered to your accommodation. Details and reservations from the Isles of Scilly Steamship Company Ltd; telephone Penzance (0736) 62009.

It's advisable to take a light waterproof garment to protect you from spray in the inter-island launches even if it doesn't rain. Umbrellas are useless. In Scilly's combination of wind, sea-light and clean air, most people need a high-factor sunscreen cream to prevent rapid burning.

Dogs are usually welcome, except on Tresco, where they must be kept on a lead. Only St Mary's has mains water supply: small guest-houses, B&B and self-catering may not offer a bath, as showers use less water. Camping is permitted only on the authorised sites on St Mary's, St Agnes, St Martin's and Bryher. There are no caravan sites.

For more information, including accommodation lists, contact the Tourist Information Centre, St Mary's, Isles of Scilly TR1 0LW; telephone Scillonia (0720) 22536.

St Mary's

The Scillies' largest island – three miles by two at its widest – is roughly round, with a projecting western knob called the Garrison. It has narrow roads in an undulating inland circle, and paths and tracks everywhere else, between small rectangular bulb-growing fields hedged with tall windbreak shrubs, some of them brown and brittle following a rare catastrophe of snow in Scilly a few winters ago. Every sheltered yard of the island, including cottage gardens, contributes to the flower industry. The coastline is gorse and downland: miles of bays, beaches and headlands that make one magnificent day's walking or can fill several with different rambles.

Hugh Town became Scilly's metropolis when Star Castle (now a hotel) was built on the Garrison as a post-Armada deterrent against the Spanish, and a quay below replaced Old Town's landing bay. Along the isthmus between beaches, the town's main street has terraces of small granite houses, plain but pleasing, built in the late eighteenth century after a fire. Its shops are well stocked with basic and practical needs; you can also buy pottery, paintings, excellent sweaters and some frivolous tourist souvenirs. There are two pubs, several hotel bars and some cafés to idle in. Behind the harbour, a small square copes with regular rush-hours of people from boats and the airport bus, luggage delivery carriers, a few local vans and taxis. At the east end of town near the 'new' church of 1835, the little museum displays an appealing medley of Scilly history and local life: shipwrecks and shells, Roman finds and labelled jars of fresh flower samples, a Victorian kitchen. The Old Town church over the hill is a restored fragment of its twelfth-century self, set in an idyll of a graveyard between a leafy path and the sea.

North of Hugh Town's isthmus, the bay between harbour arm and old lifeboat slipway is full of sea traffic and vessels at anchor, including the modern high-tech lifeboat. Town Beach and its promenade give a grandstand view; south-facing Porth Cressa Beach is more favoured for bathing. A steep slope (Queen Victoria got out of her carriage and walked to save the horses) leads up to the eight-pointed ramparts of Star Castle and the easy path round the Garrison's grassy headland, at its best taken clockwise at sunset for a superb sequence of views.

Improbably, there is a bus-tour around the limited roads of St Mary's (with an entertaining commentary). Bike-hire is popular – it takes you further towards points of coastal interest while allowing you to see over the hedges, listen to the birdsong and smell the fragrant air. But only walking gets you over stiles to the downland paths and the nature trails. The western coast has the out-island views; facing south, the highlight is Peninnis Head, where wind-blown sand and weather have eroded the great granite rocks into smooth, bizarre shapes. Dotted all around St Mary's there are ancient burial chambers, excellently preserved, and in the island's sheltered heart, near the unexpected wooded cleft of Holy Vale, several paths converge on the **Longstone Heritage Centre**, which offers vivid tableaux – a life-size Sir Cloudesley Shovel giving his version of the famous shipwreck (see p. 298) – and an audio-visual show among its displays of history, and an enlightening account of modern bulb-management.

Tresco

Half the size of St Mary's, Tresco has a wild northern end but sub-tropical potential in its sheltered south, and seems to have long been a favoured island. The earliest Christian hermits had retreats here, and in the twelfth century the Benedictines chose the island as the site for a priory. Augustus Smith exercised his Lord Proprietorship from his own Tresco Abbey, the house he built in the 1830s, and his Dorrien Smith descendants still live and 'rule' here, leasing Tresco from the Duchy of Cornwall. The gardens begun by Smith, behind the sheltering pines he planted, are world-renowned among specialists and are Scilly's main tourist attraction. The white-sand, shell-strewn beaches in the south are among Scilly's finest, and gentle inland lanes wind past paddocks and a lake full of wildfowl. This is the only place in Scilly where you can hear the wind sough through the trees. Apart from a few much-treasured trees on St Mary's, Tresco is the only island with mature woods.

There are no cars on Tresco (tractors serve) but a helicopter-service lands deafeningly at the gardens' gate.

Landing by boat from St Mary's (there's a landing charge on Tresco) is generally at **New Grimsby** quay on the west side, though in some conditions it has to be at rocky Carn Near in the far south; at lowest tide it is possible to walk across from Bryher. The few cottage gardens at New Grimsby sport fat palm trees, and above the quay there's an unashamedly touristy souvenir and ice-cream shop. Crossing the waist of the island, you pass the New Inn (see p. 307) and the 'reading room' building, venue for whist drives and other island gatherings.

Dolphin Town in the middle is a cottage or two, a painter's studio and St Nicholas' parish church, full of Dorrien Smith memorials. **Old Grimsby** has the school and two curves of lovely beach of which one – Ravens Porth

Sir Cloudesley Shovel

Cloudesley Shovel was born in north Norfolk in 1650 and first went to sea at the age of 14 under the command of his kinsman Sir Christopher Myngs and later Sir John Narborough. He rose quickly through the ranks and was knighted in 1677 for successful command of the Edgar *in the battle of Bantry Bay. He was promoted to Admiral of the Blue in 1696, commanding a fleet in the Channel and Bay of Biscay, and in 1707 was appointed commander-in-chief for operations off Portugal and Spain. When returning from the Mediterranean in that year, he assisted the allies in the siege of Toulon.*

Shortly after this battle Sir Cloudesley Shovel, leaving behind a squadron of ships for winter service, set sail for home with the rest of the fleet. This consisted of 15 battle ships, four fireships, a sloop and a yacht. The fleet left Gibraltar on about 10 October, and as they proceeded north the weather deteriorated and became very hazy and stormy. On the 21st Sir Cloudesley was able to 'make an observation' – probably the first for many days. The next day he called for soundings which told them the depth was 90 fathoms. He called for a consultation with all the sailing masters of the various ships on board his flagship, the Association, *to try to ascertain the fleet's position. All except the master of the* Lenox *thought they were in the latitude of Ushant and near the coast of France. Sir William Jumper, master of the* Lenox, *judged they were nearer Scilly and that they would be within sight of Scilly lights in three*

beyond the jetty – is private to the Island Hotel (see p. 306) set in gardens above it.

Tresco has three historic monuments: the **Old Blockhouse** at the southern end of Old Grimsby harbour which doesn't quite date back to the Civil War, and on the north-west coast opposite Bryher the remains of a pair of castles which do. King Charles' Castle, set too high, proved useless, but Cromwell's, built nearly a hundred years later, successfully guarded the channel. An austere round tower, 60 feet high, it can be explored. A walk around the northern end of the island, bleak and bare, offers you full Atlantic exposure to compare with a visit to the gardens and also a cave called Piper's Hole, bigger and safer than it looks from the entrance tunnel, with a tiny lake deep inside.

---

hours. Sir Cloudesley, unfortunately but unsurprisingly, adopted the opinion of the majority.

On 23 October he sent three ships, the Lenox, La Valeur *and* Phoenix, *on to Falmouth to escort a merchant fleet. These ships soon found themselves among the numerous rocks and islets which lie to the south-west of the Scillies. The* Phoenix *sustained so much damage, it had to find refuge between St Martins's and Tresco; the other two miraculously escaped through to Broad Sound to the west, anchoring until the next day, then sailing on to Falmouth.*

Meanwhile the admiral had given the signal for sailing to the rest of the fleet at about 6 pm. The three light frigates which had been sent to Falmouth would usually have led the fleet, so it was now the Association *that headed the line. It was a very dark night with a thick haze, gales and rain. The only accounts of what happened to the front three ships are from the reports of those that followed. About an hour and a half after setting sail the fleet found themselves floundering among the rocks of the Scillies; warning guns had been fired by the three lead ships before they sunk, and more by luck than skill the others somehow managed to survive the raging seas.*

The death toll was huge. The Association *with its 96 guns had a crew of 900, the* Eagle, *with 70 guns, and the* Romney *with 50 guns had an almost equal number. It is thought that the total of dead could not have been less than 2,000. The speculation has always been why they were so wrong about their position. But it was before the development of navigational aids, and days of bad weather and poor visibility had disorientated them.*

Sir Cloudesley Shovel's body was one of the first to be washed

The **Abbey Gardens'** achievement is the proliferation of species which grow nowhere else in Britain, through the fertility of the Tresco soil and the absence of frost – but always threatened by wind. The gardens were started in 1834 by Augustus Smith, who cleared and terraced a whole hillside. His first plants came from Kew; presently specimens were arriving from all over the world via Scilly sea-captains. Many of the plants flourish in dense undergrowth, so the gardens seem an ungroomed tangle of colour. There are some splendid effects for the non-botanical – the steep perspective of the Neptune Steps, for instance, climbing to a dominant statue from a 'gateway' of square-cut foliage, each side a whole tree. Vestigial ancient walls and an archway, remnants of the twelfth-century Benedictine Abbey, support crevice and climbing plants. Near the main entrance the **Valhalla**, an open-sided building, houses a collection of figureheads from ships wrecked on Scilly – they stand vivid

ashore and was found in a sandy cove, Porthellick Bay, on St Mary's. The bodies of Lady Shovel's two sons by her first marriage were the next to be washed up; both had been sailing with their stepfather on the Association; her nephew was drowned too in this devastating tragedy.

The story continues with a macabre twist. The admiral's body was found stripped of his shirt and with marks on his fingers where two rings had been removed. One was an emerald ring set with diamonds – a reward was offered but all efforts to recover it proved unsuccessful. The corpse was temporarily buried under the instruction of a local worthy but after enquiries by one of Sir Cloudesley's pursers he was disinterred, conveyed to Plymouth, embalmed, and then transported to London. The Queen honoured him with a state funeral and he was buried at Westminster Abbey.

The mystery of the missing ring was only solved many years later. A woman from St Mary's, racked with guilt and on her death-bed, called for a priest to take her confession. She revealed that on the day after the shipwreck she had found Sir Cloudesley on the beach: exhausted and faint but still alive. She had murdered him and stolen his valuables. The emerald and diamond ring was produced; she had never been able to sell it in case her guilt was discovered. The ring was eventually returned to Sir Cloudesley's close friend, Lord Dursley, who had given it to him many years earlier.

and brave, restored to their original colours and well
repaired by the National Maritime Museum, Greenwich.
Between the shop and the entrance to the garden is a café;
you can sit either between the trees or sheltered under a half-
roof and share cake with fearless, persistent birds.

Bryher

Less than a mile across, less than two from north to south, its
population about 60, Bryher is a tough little island. In its only
sheltered quarter – east, facing Tresco – the town has a
school, a general store, a church with a graveyard full of
Jenkinses, a hospitable café or two and some accommodation
for summer visitors. There are a few gallantly productive
flower fields, and in the low-lying middle cows graze and
swans occupy a couple of peaceful pools. Off the broken
westward coastline, the Norrad Rocks do little to break the
full force of the ocean and nothing at all at savage Hell Bay
where spray obscures its jagged lines. The length of Bryher is
a switchback of steep hills, gorse-covered in the south, bare
of all but sea-birds and megalithic barrows in the north
where Shipman Down is separated from Shipman Head by a
dizzy chasm. In this terrain the wind is either cut off abruptly
or, emerging from a sheltered area, you are blown off your
feet – walking Bryher is exhilarating but worrying!

Low tide leaves the Quay high and dry, so until recently,
arriving and departing passengers at such times have had, as
the official guidebook puts it, 'an interesting walk along a
gang-plank from the beach'. Sometimes even that was
impracticable and passengers waded ashore at pretty little
Rushy Bay in the south. Now a loading jetty, built under the
direction of Anneke Rice, makes landing easier. The sea
retreats southwards so far that you can cross the sands to
Tresco, while the north of the channel under the craggy rock
called Hangman Island is safe anchorage for boats. Watch
Hill, above the Town, is a most satisfying summit from
which to scan this part of Scilly.

St Martin's

Invisible from Hugh Town and considered a bit untypical of
Scilly, St Martin's is an irregular banana shape, two miles
long and rarely more than half a mile wide. It has slopes but
not steeps, rising highest at each end, and seems flatter

because of an absence of trees; on eastern Chapel Down the big red-and-white-striped stub of the day-mark is jarringly prominent. It is hard to believe that this intensely modern-looking cone was built in 1683; dominating some of the highest ground in Scilly it was erected by an island steward as a guide to shipping. In even a gleam of sunlight, St Martin's glows with intensified colour. Acres of waist-high gorse on the uplands are a dense dazzling yellow in spring; hedge flowers are big and bright, even the grass particularly green; a walk around the island in autumn will reveal an overwhelming crop of blackberries, too many for the islanders' consumption. The island's celebrated beaches are long sweeps of pale gold, the sea pellucid shades of turquoise scattered with a multitude of rocks and islets, a challenging paradise for snorkelling, scuba-diving and the sailing school.

Gig-racing

Scilly's six-oared racing gigs are the 30-foot-long pilot gigs (or facsimiles) that used to compete to reach a ship, when the first man aboard got the pilot's job. For anyone interested, the pilot gig Klondyke, *built in 1873, can be seen in the museum in Hugh Town, St Mary's. They also ferried stores and lighthouse-keepers and had an honourable record of lifesaving and salvage. Now they make up a sport unique to the West Country; teams from the islands compete against each other but only Newquay, from the mainland, can offer the men of Scilly real competition – every September, in the atmosphere of a Cup Final. Brittany is developing a French version of promise so things may change. For speed at sea, the gigs are strong but flexible; seats don't slide, and wooden thole-pins replace iron rowlocks – they break, which is better with a mis-stroke than smashing the gunwale.*

The races, every Friday evening in summer, are beyond question the high spot of the week. The finishing line is Hugh Town quay; the start may be St Agnes, the rock Annet, Tresco, St Martin's or a straight sprint from Nut Rock off the uninhabited isle, Samson. To watch from the quay is tame: all who can pack themselves into St Mary's launches and proceed to the start, gigs in tow. A period of jockeying about gets them lined up in the sunset – the launches jockey too, for the best spectator position is next in the line to the

A population of 100 or so is spread between **Higher**, **Middle** and **Lower Towns**, linked by a small road on which you may encounter a vehicle. New Quay below Higher Town is the usual landing place, but as on Bryher low-tide arrangements may be more adventurous – a punt (flat rowing-boat carried on board) to the rocks east at Brandy Point, or a gang-plank to Lower Town's beach. The south-facing slopes above Higher Town are intricately divided into high-hedged flower fields, while further west the meadows of cows and goats and cottage gardens spilling over the walls are gently pastoral.

On top of the hill in Higher Town, where most of the inhabitants live, there is a complement of church, chapel, post office, cafés and pub, the Seven Stones; and two other establishments mark the extremes both of the linear community and the island style of idyll. Out west the

---

outside gigs – and the air is full of speculation, encouragement and ribald comments. Pitching about in the chop the rowers look casual; stripped to the waist and well padded below is the style, with the coxes huddled in oilskins. The whole flotilla takes up considerable sea room, and boats in the area join in.

When they're off you forget cold, cramp and incipient mal-de-mer. *The instant, total, brutal, unremitting energy of the race immediately generates roars of support for* Shah, Eagle *and* Czar, *all built in the 1870s;* Bonnet, *the veteran from 1830;* Serica *and* Dolphin, *built in the 1960s,* Nornour *of 1971 and* Men-a-Vaur *of 1982. They're evenly matched, and the line stays remarkably straight. Sometimes a gig is entirely hidden by swell. The rowers are soaked and gasping, the hefty launch you're in is fighting the waves, and the pace if anything increases. Time telescopes, but it is unbelievable that such power can be sustained. Nearing the finish, one intently swaying cox galvanises his crew to another spurt and produces a winner, to hoarse acclaim from the launches and fresh roars from the quay – and the scarlet, sweating, cursing, laughing crews collapse.*

The race from Nut Rock is just over a mile, the others between two and three miles. Women race too, equally fiercely over shortened courses. Gigs have been rowed to Penzance. The Nornour *has been rowed to Brittany. They are amazing boats: don't miss a chance to watch.*

---

recently completed St Martin's Hotel (see opposite), of discreetly cottagey aspect, is tucked above the beach by Tean Sound: it offers all modern comforts from its wine list to its audio-visual conference equipment. Out east, Little Arthur Farm makes a go of ecological self-sufficiency, explaining itself on little information boards in the course of a trail past goats, sheep, bees and a donkey; it offers home-made leather shoes, produce and tea.

St Agnes

The smallest inhabited Isle of Scilly lies west of the biggest in the deep waters across St Mary's Sound, sometimes inaccessible in bad weather. Its lighthouse, behind the dangerous western reefs, was superseded in the 1850s by one built far out beyond them on Bishop's Rock; but it still sends out friendly flashes and serves as a high white day-mark. Agnes, as it's locally known, inspires great affection. It is Lilliputian, irregular and harmonious. Its tiny community sits snug in a hollow in the middle, its intricate wriggling coastline is full of interest, and its extension island of **Gugh** across the sandbar is sprinkled with megaliths and burial sites – the nine-foot standing stone called the Old Man is unmistakable, and Obadiah's Barrow is the one that yielded urns of human remains and a seated skeleton.

Above the quay facing Gugh there is an excellent pub called the Turk's Head (some old-hand visitors go no further) and the most expensively constructed public lavatories in Scilly – Agnes has no piped water, and still sprouts electricity-generating windmills. A home-made concrete strip of road leads past cream-tea-dispensing cottages towards the lighthouse (now a private dwelling not open to the public) and the church, which has as many Hicks memorials as Bryher has Jenkinses. Beyond the farming middle of flower and potato fields, and the ornithologists' goal of Big Pool where you can almost always find birds and twitchers, a white-flashed path leads across the coastal downs and along the coast to the Troy Town maze: a pattern of small white stones laid out, maze-like, on the grass, kept in trim since a bored lighthouse-keeper made it in 1729 – at least, that's the most probable account of its inception, in spite of rumours of antiquity. (A modest imitation has recently appeared on Bryher, near Hell Bay.) The rock called the Nag's Head, from where you can see St Warna's Bay, weirdly deserves its name, and there are more, as effectively sculpted as those on St Mary's Peninnis Head. And across Wingletang Down at **Beady Pool**, the tradition that there are still seventeenth-century Dutch beads to be found washed up from a merchant ship is confirmed just occasionally – enough to inspire a hunt.

Highlights

✱✱ *You will probably have time to visit all the islands during your stay. But make sure you don't miss the Abbey Gardens on Tresco.*

Where to stay

For a key to prices, see p. 12

Bryher

Hell Bay Hotel

Bryher, Isles of Scilly, Cornwall TR23 0PR. Tel. Scillonia (0720) 22947 Fax (0720) 23004 As with most of the Scilly Isles Bryher has only one hotel and it doubles up as the local hostelry. A converted farmhouse, it is an extremely friendly place where islanders come in the evening to eat and drink. The position is wonderful, only minutes from sandy beaches and 20 minutes' boat-ride to St Mary's. The décor throughout is unpretentious and bedrooms are in separate buildings set around the courtyard; they can be rented on a hotel or self-catering basis and are adequately comfortable and spacious.
£££-££££ HB *Open mid-March to early Oct*

St Martin's

St Martin's Hotel

St Martin's, Isles of Scilly, Cornwall TR25 0QW. Tel. Scillonia (0720) 22092 Fax (0720) 22298 This hotel, opened in 1989, is in a superb position, on the west side of the island with a landing jetty just below it; you can sit and stare out across the sea to other islands. It is extremely comfortable, built and decorated with reasonable sensitivity to the environment; the rooms maximise the wonderful light, and soft, restful colours help create a great sense of peace and relaxation. The dining-room on the first floor is slightly lacking in atmosphere but if you have a table by the window the view more than makes up for it. Service is polite and friendly and the food delicious. Very expensive for singles.
£££££ HB *Open all year*

St Mary's

Tregarthen's Hotel

St Mary's, Isles of Scilly,
Cornwall TR21 0PT.
Tel. Scillonia (0720) 22540 Fax
(0720) 22089

In one of the best positions on
St Mary's, only two minutes
from the centre of town, five
minutes from the quay and one
minute from the bus pick-up-
point for the heliport. Set
slightly up on the hill it has
the advantage of being away from
the noise while benefiting from
the views. The bold-carpeted
sitting-room is comfortable and
very light, with new chairs and
slightly dated pine panelling;
the dining-room – very pink
and white – has a wall of
windows so diners can fully
appreciate the scenery. Locals
use the restaurant and bar
which gives the place a friendly,
informal atmosphere and
families are made very
welcome. Bedrooms aren't as
comfortable as you might
expect for the price and tend
towards candlewick covers and
fitted modern furnishings; all
have en suite bathrooms.
££££–£££££ HB *Open 3rd week of
March to end Oct*

Tresco

The Island Hotel

Tresco, Isles of Scilly, Cornwall
TR24 0PU. Tel. Scillonia
(0720) 22883
Fax (0720) 23008

The hotel is in a quiet, secluded
spot at the north end of the
island. Many of the visitors to
Tresco are day-trippers who
come to see the gardens and
then return to St Mary's, so the
hotel manages to keep its
restful, peaceful atmosphere.
The garden slopes down to the
sea and in this superb setting
you can sit in the lounge gazing
out across the sea towards St
Martin's. The public rooms
were undergoing complete
refurbishment in the winter of
1990 and some more new
bedrooms added. This can only
enhance what was already a
comfortable, friendly hotel. The
bedrooms completed last year
are neat and attractive – co-
ordinated colours, quilted
bedcovers and modern wooden
furniture with good en suite
bathrooms. Service is old-
fashioned: polite and respectful
without being too formal.
£££££ HB *Closed Nov to Mar*

The New Inn

Tresco, Isles of Scilly, Cornwall
TR24 0QQ. Tel. Scillonia
(0720) 22844

A much simpler, cheaper
option to the Island Hotel, the
inn is run by Chris and Lesley
Hopkins. The only one on the
island, it is extremely popular
both with locals and trippers,
and serves good food at lunch
and dinner. It has a jolly,
informal atmosphere, with a
small residents' bar and lounge
for those wanting to have a
quieter time. Bedrooms are
clean and simple, some with sea
views. During the migration
seasons the island can suddenly
become swamped with
twitchers so book well in
advance.
£-£££ HB *Open all year*

Where to eat

For a key to prices see p. 12

Bryher
Hell Bay Hotel
Bryher. Tel. Scillonia
(0720) 22947
Popular and friendly place
serving a good choice of food
and drinks.
*Open mid-Mar to early Oct all
week, 12–2, 2.30–5, 7.15–8.15*

St Agnes
Turk's Head
St Agnes. Tel. Scillonia
(0720) 22434
Very good atmosphere and
friendly service at this cosy pub
with a pine-panelled bar. Enjoy
a home-made pasty looking at
the wonderful view from the
terrace.
*Open all week, 11–4.30, 7–11,
11am–11pm in season*

St Martin's
St Martin's Hotel
St Martin's. Tel. Scillonia
(0720) 22092
You can have lunch, tea or
dinner here if you're not a
resident but you'll need to make
sure of a boat back to your
island (see p. 305)
*Open Mar to Oct, all week 12–
1.45, dinner must be booked in
advance*

Seven Stones
St Martin's. Tel. Scillonia
(0720) 22861

The only pub on the island is a
much cheaper option to the St
Martin's hotel if you fancy a
snack or lunch.
*Open Mon to Sat, 11–5, 7.30–11;
Sun 12–2, 7.30–11*

Tresco
The Island Hotel
Tresco. Tel Scillonia
(0720) 22883
Hotel at north end of the island,
good spot for tea if you're on a
day trip
*Open all week, 3rd week of Mar to
end Oct, 10.30–5.30, 7.30–9.*

The New Inn
Tresco. Tel. Scillonia
(0720) 22844
The only pub on the island.
Very friendly and serving
delicious pub lunches. Can get
very busy in season.
*Open all week 11–4.30, 7–11,
11am–11pm in season*

St Mary's
Longstone Heritage Centre
St Mary's. Tel. Scillonia
(0720) 22924
If you find yourself out of reach
of Hugh Town and in need of
refreshment there's a good
choice of food here served
throughout the day. Special
offers for 'twitchers'.
Open every day 9.30–5.

Walking in the
West Country

The West Country has something to offer every kind of walker apart from the mountaineer. There is some of the finest coastal walking in Europe along the South-West Peninsula Coast Path, splendid rambling in the windswept expanses of Dartmoor, Exmoor and Bodmin Moor, gentle strolling through woods and past waterfalls in eastern Dartmoor, and a few outstanding routes over the Quantocks and Mendips.

For longer walks along the coast, good boots are advisable, although you can easily manage in shoes for most of the shorter sections unless the ground is very muddy. The Coast Path is almost entirely signposted and can be followed without a detailed map, but, to help you pace your day and get the most from it, carry an OS map. The 1:50,000-scale (about 1¼ inches to the mile) *Landranger* series maps (with purple covers) are generally adequate. If you plan to head inland, the 1:25,000 series maps are advisable as they show greater detail, including field boundaries. The green-covered 1:25,000-scale (about 2½ inches to the mile) *Pathfinder* series maps each cover a fairly small area, but for Dartmoor, south Devon and the Isles of Scilly larger coverage is instead given on the yellow-covered *Outdoor Leisure* sheets (regrettably, there is at present no *Outdoor Leisure* sheet for Exmoor).

There's no shortage of walk guidebooks, but the quality of text and selected walks varies. Bartholomew publish inexpensive spiral-bound volumes: *Walk the Cornish Coastal Path* has very clear hand-drawn maps and concise résumés of what you see on the way; *Walk Exmoor and the Quantocks* and *Walk Dartmoor* both have three-colour maps and a well-thought-out format, although many of the routes (especially in the Dartmoor volume) are on the short side.

The *Ordnance Survey National Trail Guides* cover the Coast Path in three books: the maps are excellent – 1:25,000

Pathfinder maps in full colour, with the route picked out in yellow, and there are informative colour photographs. The directions are perhaps a bit over-detailed for what, after all, is mostly a common-sense route; the guides include some round walks based on the Coast Path. The Ordnance Survey also put out three *Pathfinder* guides: *Dartmoor Walks, Exmoor and the Quantocks Walks* and *Cornwall Walks*, with about 25 routes in each: again, *Pathfinder* maps are included with the route highlighted in yellow, and each walk has a short summary of what you see on the way. The degree of difficulty ranges from easy strolls to moderate upland rambles.

Tourist information centres and National Park visitor centres stock leaflets on local walks. Among these are some booklets for Exmoor and Dartmoor published by the park authorities, describing paths and features of interest in great detail but hindering the reader by referring to key maps at the back of the book which take some decoding.

The *Penguin Footpath Guides* include titles for the Coast Path, with text by H. D. Westacott and clear hand-drawn maps by Mark Richards.

Consumers' Association and Hodder & Stoughton also publish two books of walks covering the whole of Britain – *Holiday Which? Good Walks Guide* and *Holiday Which? Town and Country Walks Guide*. Both of these describe the most rewarding walks in the West Country; these are listed below.

Long-distance paths

As well as providing ready-made routes for long-distance walkers, these are often a good basis for day-long walks.

The **Two Moors Way**, a south–north route across Devon, starts at Ivybridge and passes through Dartmoor, the quiet farmland of central Devon and into Exmoor to finish at the sea at Lynmouth. It often takes in the best of the scenery in a locality, and even if you don't want to tackle all of its 103 miles, many parts of the Way can be sampled to give an excellent introduction to some little-frequented and easily missed tracts of country. OS maps show the route. The Devon Ramblers' Association produces a booklet on the Way, with clear OS-based sketch-maps giving enough detail to enable you to find the route across the less obvious sections.

The **South-West Peninsula Coast Path** takes in the entire

coast of the peninsula, including Dorset. The 560 miles of the Coast Path, from Minehead in Somerset to Poole in Dorset, make it the giant of the official long-distance paths in Britain. Few people attempt the path in its entirety, and the path's real value for most visitors is that there is always a coastal walk to hand. Outside towns and villages, where there is no car access to the coast, access to the path is only via public footpaths: these are usually signposted from the road, but the route may involve walking through fields (and the way may not be obvious).

The path is often treated by guidebooks as a set of paths: the Somerset and North Devon Path, the Cornwall Coast Path, the South Devon Coast Path and (beyond the scope of this book) the Dorset Coast Path. Waymarking and signposting throughout is thorough and the way nearly always can be found without a detailed map.

Typically, the Path follows clifftops – with the drop often unfenced – but it often dips, sometimes to sea-level, and rises very steeply in places: walking boots or good stout shoes will make the going much more pleasant. Some shore sections take you over expanses of sands, and on the south coast in particular there are some major rivers to be crossed – either at low tide, by ferry or sometimes by an extensive inland detour. Road walking is necessary for some parts of the route, especially through coastal towns. It pays to beware of underestimating distances: often the path snakes so intricately around coves and headlands that the point you are making for never seems to get any closer.

It isn't always easy to find round walks based on the Coast Path: because the coast itself has a monopoly of the best scenery (with some notable exceptions where there is splendid walking immediately inland, such as in parts of Exmoor) there may not be much point in diverting from the Coast Path. Sometimes the less used paths inland may be blocked or overgrown, making progress difficult for the walker, and map-reading the way can be testing. But the numerous coastal headlands often can be used for rewarding circuits, giving changes of views and requiring only a short walk inland to complete the circle.

East and Central Somerset

Two uplands are the main attraction here: the rolling, heathery Quantocks and the often spectacular Mendips. Both ranges tower above lowland plains and give views out of scale with the small amount of effort needed in getting up them.

Along the broad spine of the **Quantocks** runs a level but exhilarating track for about six miles from above West Bagborough north-west to the abrupt culmination of the plateau above West Quantoxhead, from where there are impressive views over the Bristol Channel. Minor roads give access to the top of the ridge, giving the easiest of walks from strategically sited carparks. For those who may find these too tame, begin from the base of the Quantocks: Holford is a good starting place from where routes lead through Hodder's Combe and into some attractive broad-leafed woodlands before the ascent to the top. There is a multitude of woodland walks in a maze of paths on this east side of the Quantocks, including the waymarked Quantock Forest Trail. At the south-east end, more vast panoramas can be enjoyed effortlessly by a walk from a high-level carpark at Lydeard Hill.

Road walks are not usually worth singling out, but two in the **Mendips** should be tried. Cheddar Gorge and Burrington Combe are the great natural wonders of the area, both followed along their floors by B-roads (quite busy in the tourist season): both give a mile-long walk where you can appreciate the limestone cliffs and formations from below. More ambitious walks on paths above these gorges are worthwhile too. In Cheddar Gorge, head for the wonderful path above the south side, reached at the north-east end of the gorge opposite a nature reserve. The views are astonishing, both into the canyon and across the Somerset Levels to the Quantocks. The Burrington Combe area is blessed with rolling moorland and some sheltered woodlands: here, the most distinguished scenery apart from the gorges is to be found around the western fringes of the upland. Dolebury Warren and Beacon Batch, both moorland hills close to Burrington Combe, have big views northwards over the Severn and towards Bristol.

Elsewhere in the region, the most appealing walking is on detached hills which tower above the sea and the pancake-flat Somerset Levels: Brent Knoll south of Weston-super-Mare has paths encircling it and climbing to its 450-foot summit; north-east lies Wavering Down at the westernmost end of the Mendip range, with a pleasant two-mile stroll along its broad ridge. Several nature trails exist in the Mendips, including some at Cheddar Gorge, Ebbor Gorge and Wells. The West Mendip Way is a long-distance path from Brean Down to Wells via Wavering Down and Ebbor Gorge. Much of the rest of the Mendips is flat plateau, intensively farmed and not that rewarding.

On the coast, Brean Down, on the south side of Weston-super-Mare and projecting one mile out to sea, gives a ridge walk of the highest quality (though of modest altitude) with views all around.

See also *Holiday Which? Good Walks Guide* Walks 1 (Burrington Combe and Dolebury Warren) and 33 (The Northern Quantocks); *Holiday Which? Town and Country Walks Guide* Walk 102 (around Cheddar Gorge).

Exmoor

Exmoor's famous variety is very much at a scale for walkers, particularly in the north. Within a half-day walk you can encompass clifftops, farmland, woods, river valleys and moorland: very few places in Britain can claim this kind of concentration of scenery. The signposting of most paths is thorough. Combe Martin Bay to Minehead, one of the finest sections of the South-West Peninsula Coast Path, has bold, muscular slopes dropping seawards and secretive combes leading inland. From Combe Martin the path climbs the cliff, passing Great Hangman and Holdstone Down (both offering 360-degree viewpoints over 1,000 feet high). Hunter's Inn, north of Parracombe, makes a good starting point for an exploration of the wooded Heddon Valley, leading out to the sea at Heddon's Mouth and into the big sweep of Woody Bay. Lynton, sandwiched between the sea, the Valley of Rocks and Lyn Cleave, lays claim to be the epicentre of Exmoor's walking activity. Westwards, the level cliff path heads to the Valley of Rocks and Wringcliff Bay (don't miss the views from Castle Rock and Hollerday Hill); eastwards, the riverside path from Lynmouth to Watersmeet allures casual walkers, but the less obvious high-level path along the south side of the valley, via Midsummer Hill and the Cleaves, has sensational views before dropping to

Watersmeet. From Countisbury on the main road, the Coast
Path takes a north course to the lighthouse on Foreland Point
for a rugged section along England's highest cliffs to Porlock.

At Porlock Bay the Coast Path drops to sea-level before
rising from Bossington eastwards to Selworthy Beacon (there
is a path beyond Hurlstone Point, closer to the sea, which is a
bit more trying than the official route, but the views are
better). Huge views open out at the top over the Bristol
Channel and eastern Exmoor. You can cheat and drive up to
within a few yards of the Beacon, but if you have time you
may find it more satisfying to plan a round walk taking in
nearby Selworthy village below the slopes to the south: the
hill is laced with paths and tracks.

Inland Exmoor offers some good walking in remote-feeling
river valleys and over occasional patches of moorland and
unspoilt farmland. The best river valleys for the walker are
the Barle from Dulverton to Simonsbath (especially around
Tarr Steps and Cow Castle), Badgworthy Water (south of
County Gate) and the River Exe from Exford to Winsford.
Wimbleball Lake (really a reservoir) and Clatworthy
Reservoir (both east of Dulverton) have nature trails and
attractive waterside paths.

The Brendon Hills offer deep and complicated country,
much wooded. Head for the area around Luxborough, or
Lype Hill a couple of miles south-west. Woodland walks also
proliferate in the hills of eastern Exmoor, with splendid
broad-leafed woodlands around Horner Water south of
Porlock. From Dunster it is worth taking in a very fine ridge
path, above tree-top level, along Grabbist Hill, from where
there are three-way views. The deer park and woodlands
close to Dunster Castle can be taken in from the same walk,
or visited by following the signs from Dunster to Gallox
Bridge. There is a waymarked woodland trail starting from
the carpark at Webber's Post.

Dunkery Beacon (which caps Dunkery Hill), the highest
point in Exmoor, is the nearest thing to a summit in the
National Park, with one of the most extensive views in
southern England: it doesn't require much effort to walk up
to the cairn from the road a mile to the east. Excellent day-
long circular walks to the Beacon start from Horner or
Luccombe. Plan the route so that you walk the ridge of
Dunkery Hill from west to east: as the land slopes gently
down you will be walking into the view (east to west you will
be staring at a large unchanging area of moorland for a long

time). Further west, the attractive but extremely popular walk along Badgworthy Water can be started from Malmsmead; to escape summer crowds, you may like to extend the walk westwards over Malmsmead Hill, which gives a flavour of the central moorlands. On the far side of Lynton is the delightful, but easily missed, Ladies' Mile, a path half-way up the slope which follows the contour of the valley west of Hunter's Inn, offering a fine scenic walk.

The path network inland is well maintained and signposted (although its not that dense, so you may have to resort to road-walking). Carry a 1:25,000-scale OS map if you intend to cross farmland, as field paths may be undefined. The moors aren't particularly hazardous in good weather, but it is sensible to take a compass in case of mist. On the whole there are rather more tracks on the ground than appear on the maps, but these moorland routes in places suddenly disappear in the middle of nowhere.

National Park information centres have details of guided walks organised by the National Park Authority.

See also *Holiday Which? Good Walks Guide* Walks 20 (Watersmeet, Lynton and the Valley of Rocks), 21 (Heddon's Mouth and Woody Bay), 22 (Brendon, Countisbury and the Foreland), 30 (Cow Castle and the Barle Valley), 31 (Hurlstone Point and Selworthy Beacon) and 32 (Horner Woods and Dunkery Beacon; *Holiday Which? Town and Country Walks Guide* Walks 31 (Holdstone Hill and the Ladies' Mile), 32 (Doone Country), 100 (Tarr Steps and the Barle Valley) and 101 (Dunster Park and Grabbist Hill).

North Devon

Virtually all the best walking here is close to the coast. From the Cornish border to Clovelly the Coast Path takes in some of the most dramatic cliff scenery in Devon; beware that windy conditions (which occur most of the time) can make progress tiring. Immediately inland lie some sheltered small-scale valleys, but, as there are few paths, lane walking (most of it very quiet) is unavoidable if you plan to do a round walk. Good objectives include Welcombe Mouth (with Welcombe church and the wooded coombe of Marsland Water inland), the cliffs around Hartland Quay, Speke's Mill Mouth waterfall and Hartland Point lighthouse, with Hartland Abbey and Stoke church just inland, and the Coast Path on the north-west side of Clovelly leading into the village itself.

North of Bideford Bay the coast rounds some big headlands. The best of these for the walker is Morte Point, which can be taken in on a walk from Woolacombe to the lighthouse on Bull Point, with an optional extension to Lee Bay; a minor road from the lighthouse provides a quick return route.

Lundy Island, reached by ferry from Ilfracombe in summer, has a coastal walk most of the way around its seven or so miles, which is fun to do in its entirety; in clear weather there are views of the South Wales and Devon coasts.

See also *Holiday Which? Town and Country Walks Guide* Walk 30 (Hartland Point and Quay).

South Devon

Deep creeks and lushly wooded river valleys meet the sea, creating some highly appealing estuary and coastal landscapes: river ferries can be used at some (but not all) points to join the Coast Path together. Despite the considerable amount of development on this south coast, much remains unspoilt. The Plymouth to Brixham stretch, all 69 miles of it, has the bulk of the best. Views from the Coast Path neatly condense Plymouth's sprawling form into a water-front city of some drama, looking to the Hoe and Drake's Island. Diversions may be in operation at Wembury Point, where there is a Ministry of Defence firing range. Summer ferries take you across the Yealm Estuary to Noss Mayo, and across the Avon near Bigbury-on-Sea; between these two rivers, the River Erme has to be forded at low tide to avoid a lengthy diversion inland.

Tremendous cliff scenery ensues from Bolt Tail to Bolt Head – well worth the not inconsiderable effort it demands – then, after the ferry from Salcombe, the scenic quality continues past Prawle Point to Start Point. From here to Dartmouth the Coast Path includes some dull road walking, but the exciting final mile or so past Compass Cove and Dartmouth Castle should be experienced. The ferry across the Dart to Kingswear is followed by some fairly invigorating cliff walking to Brixham (from where you can catch a bus back to Kingswear).

Budleigh Salterton to the Dorset border, a stretch of about 14 miles, begins mildly from the crossing of the River Otter, whose waterside path can be taken to make a round walk incorporating Otterton and the coast up to a caravan site at

Ladram Bay. The real drama begins east of Sidmouth, with tough gradients as the path drops into deep combes and rises again. Beyond Branscombe, the famous Hooken undercliff presents a chaotically tumbled scene, best enjoyed from the low-level path rather than the clifftop alternative.

Inland, there's rather a dearth of footpaths, despite some attractive and deeply rural country, in particular north of Honiton and south of Totnes; the latter area, known as the South Hams, has a pleasant waterside walk from Tuckenhay along Bow Creek.

See also *Holiday Which? Good Walks Guide* Walks 11 (Bolt Head and Starehole Bay), 12 (Woodcombe Point and Prawle Point), 13 (Dartmouth Castle and Compass Cove) and 14 (Sidmouth and Weston Mouth); *Holiday Which? Town and Country Walks Guide* Walks 29 (Hooken Cliff and Branscombe) and 36 (Tuckenhay and Bow Creek).

Dartmoor

This is the prime inland attraction for walkers in the West Country, with rugged walking in the west side of the National Park over moorland, and something for everybody in the lusher east.

Southern England's largest expanse of wilderness needs to be treated with respect. Boots are almost essential in the bleaker expanses of Dartmoor if you are attempting a long walk, and a compass is recommended, as mists can descend suddenly. A walk in the heart of the moor is not to be missed by anyone with a love of wide spaces and remoteness: the bizarrely outlined tors and windswept archaeological remains provide the main focal points. Additionally, you can try hunting out some of the 450-odd 'letter-boxes' on the moor (see p. 177), at which walkers can record their visit.

Here, probably more than in most parts of the country, it pays to have a walk guidebook if you are unfamiliar with the area. Many clearly defined paths are not marked on Ordnance Survey maps, and some of the paths that are marked are quite invisible. Although there is free access to much of the moor, the army training area to the north of the Tavistock–Moretonhamstead road (the B3212) is open to the public only on public holidays, at most weekends, and during certain spring and summer periods (including all of August).

Although the centre of the moor can be perilous for

inexperienced walkers – losing your way trying to follow ill-defined routes is all too easy, and the terrain can be boggy – there are plenty of easy and middling-difficulty rambles which give a good flavour of Dartmoor. One of the gentlest ways to see the moor close up is to follow old railway tracks or leats (water channels), such as the old track across Ugborough Moor north of Ivybridge (used in part by the Two Moors Way; see p. 309) and the track west of Princetown, past King's Tor and overlooking the lush Walkham Valley. The meandering Devonport Leat (see p. 179) loops around the western moor and has some good distant views for much of the way. Don't miss the wonderful Dr Blackall's Drive, a track specially created as a panoramic coach ride looking over the Dart Valley; join it at Bel Tor Corner north-west of New Bridge carpark.

Outstanding among riverside walks is the wooded Teign Gorge, leading about nine miles westwards from Steps Bridge to north of Chagford; from Fingle Bridge two signposted paths create a loop, the Fisherman's Path along the river and the Hunter's Path high up above, passing the back entrance to Castle Drogo. Also rewarding, the East Dart River between Dartmeet and Postbridge has a fairly rough path which passes ancient clapper bridges; stepping-stones should be attempted only by the extremely agile. Particularly fine, too, is the area west and south of Lustleigh in the region of Sharpitor, the Bovey Valley and the Becka Falls; there is also a nature trail in Yarner Wood, a National Nature Reserve (see p. 163).

Of Dartmoor's 200 or so tors, Hay Tor and Hound Tor (with its neighbouring abandoned medieval village) are among the most visited, being easily accessible. But most visitors who wish to leave their cars will make their own discoveries and find their own favourites, with Vixen Tor, Great Mis Tor, Hare Tor and Honeybag Tor among the prime candidates.

Details of guided and self-guided walks, and of public access times to the firing ranges, are published in the *Dartmoor Visitor* (available free of charge from National Park information centres and from many hotels and shops).

See also *Holiday Which? Good Walks Guide* Walks 15 (Sampford Spiney and Pew Tor), 16 (The Erme Valley and Hangershell Rock), 17 (Dartmoor clapper bridges, Bellever Tor and the East Dart River), 18 (Lustleigh Cleave and Hunter's Tor) and 19 (the Teign Gorge and Castle Drogo);

Holiday Which? Town and Country Walks Guide Walks 33 (Leather Tor and Dartmoor Railway), 34 (Hound Tor and Honeybag Tor) and 35 (Webburn Valley and Dr Blackall's Drive).

South East Cornwall

Cornwall's easiest coastal walking is largely confined to this area, which also offers plenty for the more energetic walker. Spectacular views across Carrick Roads to Falmouth from Zone Point make the Roseland Peninsula memorable, despite the ease of the path, which snakes around estuaries and coastal headlands. The going gets less easy further east, beyond Nare Head, but is then quite gentle as it passes Portloe and Dodman Point, with lovely views across Veryan Bay. St Austell Bay is too developed to be worth going out of your way for, but the pretty townships of Fowey and Polruan have much to offer; in particular, you can use the two ferry services across the harbour to provide links for a charming circuit via Polruan, Pont Pill and Bodinnick, or extend the walk to Lantic Bay, which has a sandy beach. Picturesque Polperro becomes a permanent traffic-jam on summer days, and some may find it more satisfying to walk into it along the low-level path westwards from Talland Bay or Looe. The tranquil West Looe River has a path, lane or track along most of its length.

Just to the west of Plymouth, the Cornish Coast Path finishes with a flourish as it skirts a complex peninsula, rounding Rame Head, and entering Cawsand Bay: here is an opportunity for a half-day walk of remarkable contrasts, with the combined fishing villages of Cawsand and Kingsand, the landscaped woodlands and parklands of the Mount Edgcumbe Estate and some huge views of Plymouth and its harbour, with Dartmoor in the background.

Around St Austell, bizarre landscapes created by china clay workings tempt only the most curious walker – there are very few paths – but the Luxulyan Valley is something of a minor inland oasis, with dense woodlands and some intriguing industrial archaeology.

See also *Holiday Which? Good Walks Guide* Walks 8 (the Luxulyan Valley and the Treffry Viaduct) and 9 (the West Looe River, Talland Bay and Polperro); *Holiday Which? Town and Country Walks Guide* Walks 13 (St Anthony in Roseland), 15 (Pont Pill and Lantic Bay) and 16 (Mount Edgcumbe and Kingsand).

North Cornwall

Cornwall's highest cliffs, between Crackington Haven and Boscastle, present a rounded and muscular appearance, offering a breezy (though not especially demanding) walk; just inland, a wooded valley just south of Crackington Haven provides a sheltered return route. There's a very exciting length of coast between Boscastle and Tintagel, the headlands around the former village stealing the show; if visiting Tintagel, you may like to park a couple of miles north-east on the B3263 and walk down Rocky Valley to the sea before picking up the cliff path. In the extreme north, the short path from Morwenstow church gives easy access to strangely shaped cliffs of considerable grandeur.

Allow plenty of time to walk the (pretty exacting) sections from here to the Camel Estuary: views and scenery are for the most part constantly absorbing, although holiday development is seen in a few places. West of Port Isaac is The Rumps, a headland best approached from New Polzeath, making an easily managed round walk of three miles. The broad Camel Estuary comes as a contrast, with opportunities for strolls along the dunes on its east side or along the old railway track east of Padstow.

The Coast Path continues to be undemanding as it goes along low cliffs past Trevose Head then catches sight of resort villages and caravans, later skirting above long Watergate Beach. Beyond Newquay, a summer ferry or low-tide wade brings you to Crantock Beach and an extended shore-level stretch. Around St Agnes the cliffs are high again, and now peppered with industrial relics, including the memorably sited Wheal Coates Mine. Two short inland ascents are worth seeking out for the views: St Agnes Beacon, close to St Agnes itself, and Carn Brea, south-west of Redruth.

Inland, Bodmin Moor has some devotees, not least for its sense of remoteness and the wealth of antiquities it harbours, but for the most part this is pretty rough country, involving crossing often trackless and boggy ground. If you intend to do anything more than stroll up to a nearby tor, you will probably need a compass in case mist descends. One of the most popular short walks is to Rough Tor, signposted from the A39 just north-east of Camelford. From the car park the route leads gently up over springy turf and clambers over boulders fallen around the base of the impressive tor, from where the view gives a good idea of the emptiness of the moor; a pathless route can be taken south to Brown Willy, the next rise, the highest point in Cornwall. A short round walk not to be missed follows an old quarry railway track from Minions, passing the Hurlers stone circles and veering right past the Cheesewring, a fine tor staring · across Dartmoor and west Devon.

See also *Holiday Which? Good Walks Guide* Walks 7 (Pentire Point and St Enedoc's church) and 10 (High Cliff and Cambeak); *Holiday Which? Town and Country Walks Guide* Walk 12 (Wheal Coates and St Agnes Beacon).

West Cornwall

Westwards from St Ives Bay lies a magnificent coastline, rounding Land's End and continuing east past Penzance and around the Lizard peninsula. Paths leading inland are numerous but are occasionally found to be obstructed. But for those prepared to navigate across farmland and moors some absorbing routes taking in archaeological sites (both ancient and industrial) can be devised.

Apart from some of the developed coast around Penzance, virtually any stretch of the Coast Path is rewarding, but there are a number of special features worth going out of your way for. The cliffs east of Pendeen Watch can be combined with a visit to Chûn Castle, which enjoys fine views, and Men-an-Tol standing stones. Just west of Pendeen, the spectacular remains of the Levant tin mine clutter the cliff. From Cape Cornwall southwards is a relatively easy section; the valleys north and south of it can be used to make an interesting round walk starting from St Just, heading north-west to Boscean and the coast, then continuing south and finally east. A few miles inland, a little too far to be included in a coast walk, Carn Brea is easily climbed from the road and gets views over Cornwall's western tip. If visiting Land's End, you might like to avoid the crowds (which are concentrated only a couple of hundred yards on each side of the carpark) and follow the cliff path a short way; the best entrance to this headland is from Sennen Cove, a mile northeast. South and east of Land's End is what is generally reckoned to be the finest part of the Cornish Coast Path, passing Nanjizal Bay, Hella Point, Minack Theatre and culminating at Treryn Dinas, the grandest of all Cornish headlands, with its famous Logan Rock. Inland scenery is unexciting, but further east at Lamorna you can make a circuit by passing the Merry Maidens stone circle.

The Lizard Peninsula looks for the most part ruggedly remote once you are away from the main carparks: its finest section is from Mullion Cove to the Lizard itself. On its east side, the path dips down past some attractive fishing villages. With such a pancake-flat hinterland on the west side of the peninsula, there is little point in leaving the Coast Path. Closer to the Helford River, however, the countryside's soft, small-scale charm provides one or two beautiful round walks around Manaccan and Helford, incorporating mostly level paths through woods and above river estuaries and tidal creeks.

See also *Holiday Which? Good Walks Guide* Walks 2 (Land's End and Nanjizal), 3 (Lamorna Cove and the Merry Maidens), 4 (Carnyorth Common and the Levant tin mine), 5 (Morvah Cliff and Chûn Castle) and 6 (St Ives and the coffin route); *Holiday Which? Town and Country Walks Guide* Walks 11 (St Levan and the Logan Rock) and 14 (Gillan Creek and the Helford River).

Isles of Scilly

The coast of the largest island, St Mary's, can be followed on foot all the way round by a consistently absorbing coast path – an energetic full day's walking. For shorter routes, just about any stroll will be worthwhile for lovely views over the rest of the archipelago. There is an easy round walk from the west side of Hugh Town past Star Castle and Woolpack Point, and the northern part of the island has some interesting chambered cairns on sites looking out over St Martin's and Tresco.

Information

Tourist information centres

* Operates a seasonal service (April/May to September/October)

* **Axminster,** Devon
The Old Courthouse, Church Street, Axminster EX13 5AQ. Tel Axminster (0297) 34386

Barnstaple, Devon
North Devon Library, Tuly Street, Barnstaple EX31 1TY. Tel Barnstaple (0271) 47177

* **Bideford,** Devon
The Quay, Bideford. Tel Bideford (0237) 477676

* **Bodmin,** Cornwall
Shire House, Mount Folly Square, Bodmin PL31 2DQ. Tel Bodmin (0208) 76616

* **Bovey Tracey,** Devon
Lower Car Park, Station Road, Bovey Tracey TQ13 9AW. Tel Bovey Tracey (0626) 832047

* **Braunton,** Devon
Caen Street Car Park, Braunton EX33 1AA. Tel Barnstaple (0271) 47177

* **Bridgwater,** Somerset
Town Hall, High Street, Bridgwater TA6 3ES. Tel Bridgwater (0278) 427652

Brixham, Devon
The Old Market House, The Quay, Brixham TQ5 8TB. Tel Brixham (08045) 2861

Bude, Cornwall
The Crescent Car Park, Bude EX23 8LE. Tel Bude (0288) 354240

* **Budleigh Salterton,** Devon
Fore Street, Budleigh Salterton EX9 6NG. Tel Budleigh Salterton (0395) 445275

Burnham-on-Sea, Somerset
South Esplanade, Burnham-on-Sea TA8 1BB. Tel Burnham-on-Sea (0278) 787852

* **Camelford,** Cornwall
North Cornwall Museum, The Clease, Camelford PL32 9PL. Tel Camelford (0840) 212954

* **Chard,** Somerset
The Guildhall, Fore Street, Chard TA20 1PP. Tel Chard (0460) 67463

* **Cheddar,** Somerset
The Gorge, Cheddar BS27 3QE. Tel Cheddar (0934) 744071

* **Combe Martin,** Devon
Sea Cottage, Cross Street, Combe Martin EX34 0DH. Tel Combe Martin (0271) 883319

Dartmouth, Devon
11 Duke Street, Dartmouth TQ6 9PY. Tel Dartmouth (0803) 834224

Dawlish, Devon
The Lawn, Dawlish EX7 9AP.
Tel Dawlish (0626) 863589

Exeter, Devon
Civic Centre, Paris Street,
Exeter EX1 1JJ. Tel Exeter
(0392) 265297

Exeter Services, Devon
Exeter Services Area,
Sandygate (M5), nr Exeter
EX2 7NJ. Tel Exeter
(0392) 79088/437581

* **Exmouth**, Devon
Alexandra Terrace, Exmouth
EX8 1NZ. Tel Exmouth
(0395) 263744

Falmouth, Cornwall
28 Killigrew Street, Falmouth
TR11 3PN. Tel Falmouth
(0326) 312300

Fowey, Cornwall
The Post Office, 4 Custom
House Hill, Fowey PL23 1AA.
Tel Fowey (0726) 833616

* **Frome**, Somerset
Cattle Market Car Park, Frome.
Tel Frome (0373) 67271

* **Glastonbury**, Somerset
1 Marchant's Buildings,
Northload Street, Glastonbury
BA6 9JJ. Tel Glastonbury
(0458) 32954

* **Honiton**, Devon
High Street, Honiton. Tel
Honiton (0404) 43716

Ilfracombe, Devon
The Promenade, Ilfracombe
EX34 9BX. Tel Ilfracombe
(0271) 863001

* **Ilminster**, Somerset
Shrubbery Hotel Car Park,
Station Road, Ilminster
TA19 9AR. Tel Ilminster
(0460) 57294

Ivybridge, Devon
South Dartmoor TIC, Leonards
Road, Ivybridge PL21 0SL. Tel
Ivybridge (0752) 897035

Kingsbridge, Devon
The Quay, Kingsbridge
TQ7 1HS. Tel Kingsbridge
(0548) 853195

* **Laity**, Cornwall
Lizard and Helston TIC,
Carnbone, Laity, nr Helston
TR13 0NW. Tel Helston
(0326) 40899

Launceston, Cornwall
Market House Arcade, Market
Street, Launceston PL15 8EP.
Tel Launceston
(0566) 772321/7723333

* **Looe**, Cornwall
The Guildhall, Fore Street, East
Looe PL13 1AA. Tel Looe
(05036) 2072

Lostwithiel, Cornwall
Lostwithiel Community
Centre, Liddicoat Road,
Lostwithiel PL22 0HE. Tel
Lostwithiel (0208) 872207

* **Lynton**, Devon
Town Hall, Lee Road, Lynton
EX35 6BT. Tel Lynton
(0598) 52225

Minehead, Somerset
The Town Hall, The Parade,
Minehead TA24 5NB. Tel
Minehead (0643) 702624

* **Modbury**, Devon
Poundwell Meadow, Car Park,
Modbury PL21 0QL. Tel
Modbury (0458) 830159

Newquay, Cornwall
Municipal offices, Marcus Hill,
Newquay TR7 1AF. Tel
Newquay (0637) 871345

Newton Abbot, Devon
8 Sherborne Road, Newton
Abbot. Tel Newton Abbot
(0626) 67494

Information

* **Okehampton**, Devon
3 West Street, Okehampton
EX20 1HQ. Tel Okehampton
(0837) 53020

* **Ottery St Mary**, Devon
The Old Town Hall, The
Flexton, Ottery St Mary
EX11 1DJ. Tel Ottery St Mary
(0404) 813964

Paignton, Devon
The Esplanade, Paignton
TQ4 6BN. Tel Paignton
(0803) 558383

Penzance, Cornwall
Station Road, Penzance
TR18 2NF. Tel Penzance
(0736) 62207

Plymouth, Devon
Madeira Road, The Hoe,
Plymouth. Tel Plymouth
(0752) 264849/264851/223806

* **Podimore**, Somerset
Somerset Visitor Centre, Trust
House Forte Service Area
(A303), Podimore, nr Yeovil
BA22 8JG. Tel Yeovil
(0935) 841302

St Ives, Cornwall
The Guildhall, Street-an-Pol,
St Ives TR26 2DT. Tel St Ives
(0736) 796297

Saltash, Cornwall
Welcome to Cornwall Centre,
Granada Motorway Services,
Carkeel Roundabout, Saltash
PL12 1XX. Tel Saltash
(0752) 849526

Isles of Scilly
Porthcressa Bank, St Mary's,
Isles of Scilly TR21 0JY. Tel
Scillonia (0720) 22536

Seaton, Devon
The Esplanade, Seaton
EX12 2QQ. Tel Seaton
(0297) 21660/21689

* **Sedgemoor Services**, Somerset
Somerset Visitor Centre,
Sedgemoor Services, M5 South,
nr Axbridge BS26 2UF. Tel
Weston-super-Mare
(0934) 750833

* **Shepton Mallet**, Somerset
2 Petticoat Lane, Shepton
Mallet BA4 5DA. Tel Shepton
Mallet (0749) 345258

* **Sidmouth**, Devon
The Esplanade, Sidmouth
EX10 6NS. Tel Sidmouth
(0395) 516441

* **South Molton**, Devon
1 East Street, South Molton
EX36 3BU. Tel South Molton
(07685) 4122

Taunton, Somerset
The Library, Corporation
Street, Taunton TA1 4AN. Tel
Taunton (0823) 274785/270479

* **Tavistock**, Devon
Town Hall, Bedford Square,
Tavistock PL19 0AE. Tel
Tavistock (0822) 612938

Teignmouth, Devon
The Den, Sea Front,
Teignmouth TQ14 8BE. Tel
Teignmouth (0626) 779769

* **Telegraph Hill**, Devon
Telegraph Hill (A380),
Kennford, nr Exeter EX6 7YW.
Tel Exeter (0392) 833559

Tiverton, Devon
Phoenix Lane, Tiverton
EX16 6LU. Tel Tiverton
(0884) 255827

* **Tiverton Services**, Devon
Tiverton Services Junction 27
(M5), nr Sampford Peverell
EX16 7SB. Tel Sampford
Peverell (0884) 821242

Torquay, Devon
Vaughan Parade, Torquay
TQ2 5JG. Tel Torquay
(0803) 297428

* **Torrington**, Devon
Town Hall, High Street,
Torrington EX38 8HN. Tel
Torrington (0805) 24324

Totnes, Devon
The Plains, Totnes TQ9 5EJ. Tel
Totnes (0803) 863168

Truro, Cornwall
Municipal Buildings, Boscawen
Street, Truro TR1 2NE. Tel
Truro (0872) 74555

* **Victoria**, Cornwall
Mid Cornwall Service Area, A30
Victoria, nr Roche. Tel Roche
(0726) 890481

* **Wadebridge**, Cornwall
Town Hall, Wadebridge
PL27 7AQ. Tel Wadebridge
(0208) 813725

* **Wellington**, Somerset
Wellington Museum, 28 Fore
Street, Wellington TA21 8AQ.
Tel Wellington (0823) 664747

Wells, Somerset
Town Hall, Market Place, Wells
BA5 2RB. Tel Wells (0749) 72552

Wincanton, Somerset
The Library, 7 Carrington Way,
Wincanton BA9 9JS. Tel
Wincanton (0963) 34063/32173

* **Woolacombe**, Devon
Hall 70, Beach Road,
Woolacombe EX34 7BT. Tel
Woolacombe (0271) 870553

Yeovil, Somerset
Petter's House, Petter's Way,
Yeovil BA20 1SH. Tel Yeovil
(0935) 71279

* **Yeovilton**, Somerset
Fleet Air Museum, RNAS
Yeovilton, Ilchester, nr Yeovil
BA22 8HT. Tel Ilchester
(0935) 841083

Entertainment

Theatres and Concert Halls

Barnstaple, Devon
Queens Hall Theatre, Boutport
Street. Tel Barnstaple
(0271) 43239

Bideford, Devon
Bideford College Theatre,
Abbotsham Road. Tel Bideford
(0237) 421951

Brixham, Devon
Brixham Theatre, Bolton Cross.
Tel Brixham (080 45) 2829

Exeter, Devon
Barnfield Theatre, Barnfield
Road. Tel Exeter (0392) 70891

Crediton, Devon
Crediton Drama Centre, East
Street. Tel Crediton
(036 32) 3260

Dartington, Devon
Dartington Arts Society,
Dartington Hall, Shinners
Bridge. Tel Totnes (0803) 863073

Dawlish, Devon
Shaftesbury Theatre, Brunswick
Place. Tel Dawlish (0626) 863061

Dunsford, Devon
Church Army, Sheldon Centre.
Tel Christow (0647) 52203

Exeter, Devon
Northcott Theatre, Stocker Road.
Tel Exeter (0392) 54853
St George's Hall, Market Street.
Tel Exeter (0392) 422137
Exeter Little Theatre Co, 4
Colleton Crescent. Tel Exeter
(0392) 58774

325

Information

Exmouth, Devon
Exmouth Players, Blackmore Theatres, Bicton Street. Tel Exmouth (0395) 276681

Falmouth, Cornwall
Princess Pavilion, Melville Road. Tel (0326) 211222

Frome, Somerset
Merlin Theatre, Bath Road. Tel Frome (0373) 65949/61360

Holsworthy, Devon
Holsworthy Theatre, Bodmin Street. Tel Holsworthy (0409) 253826

Honiton, Devon
Houselight Theatre Restaurant, 14 Argus Close. Tel Honiton (0404) 44083

Ilfracombe, Devon
Pavilion Theatre, Victoria Pavilion, The Promenade. Tel Ilfracombe (0271) 862228

Kingsbridge, Devon
South Hams Theatre & Arts Trust, Town Hall, Fore Street. Tel Kingsbridge (0548) 6636

Newmill, Cornwall
Theatre Rotto, Bosulval Farm House. Tel Penzance (0736) 65158

Newquay, Cornwall
Cosy Nook Theatre, Towan. Tel Newquay (0637) 873365
Lane Theatre, Lane. Tel Newquay (0637) 876945

Paignton, Devon
Festival Theatre, Esplanade. Tel Paignton (0803) 558641
Palace Avenue Theatre, Palace Avenue. Tel Paignton (0803) 558367

Plymouth, Devon
Barbican Theatre, Castle Street, The Barbican. Tel (0752) 267131
Plymouth Athenaeum, Derrys Cross. Tel Plymouth (0752) 266104

Theatre Royal, Royal Parade. Tel Plymouth (0752) 669595

St Buryan, Cornwall
Minack Theatre, Porthcurno. Tel St Buryan (0736) 810471

St Austell, Cornwall
Arts Centre, 87 Truro Road. Tel St Austell (0726) 73949

Sidmouth, Devon
Sidmouth Manor Pavilion, Manor Road. Tel Sidmouth (0395) 514413

Street, Somerset
Strode Theatre, Church Road. Tel Street (0458) 42846

Taunton, Somerset
Brewhouse Theatre, Coal Orchard. Tel Taunton (0823) 283244

Teignmouth, Devon
Carlton Theatre, The Den. Tel Teignmouth (0620) 778991

Torquay, Devon
Babbacombe Theatre, Babbacombe Downs Road. Tel Torquay (0803) 328385
The Little Theatre, St Marks Church, St Marks Road. Tel (0803) 299330
Princes Theatre, Torbay Road. Tel Torquay (0803) 297527

Torrington, Devon
Plough Theatre, 9–11 Fore Street. Tel Torrington (0805) 22552

Yeovil, Somerset
Octagon Theatre, Johnson Hall, Hendford. Tel Yeovil (0935) 22884

Cinemas

Barnstaple, Devon
Astor Cinema, Boutport Street. Tel Barnstaple (0271) 79717/42550

Bridgwater, Somerset
Film Centre, Penel Orlieu. Tel Bridgwater (0278) 422383

Burnham-on-Sea, Somerset
Ritz Cinema, Victoria Street. Tel
Burnham-on-Sea (0278) 782871

Camborne, Cornwall
Palace Cinema, Roskear. Tel
Camborne (0209) 712020

Exeter, Devon
Odeon Cinema, Sidwell Street.
Tel Exeter (0392) 54057

Exmouth, Devon
Savoy Film Centre, Market
Street. Tel Exmouth
(0395) 268220

Frome, Somerset
Westway Cinema, Cork Street.
Tel Frome (0373) 65685

Ilfracombe, Devon
Pendle Stairway Cinema, 134
High Street. Tel Ilfracombe
(0271) 863484

Looe, Cornwall
The Cinema, Market House,
Higher Market Street. Tel Looe
(050 36) 2709

Minehead, Somerset
Regal Enterprises, 10/16 The
Avenue. Tel Minehead
(0643) 702439

Newquay, Cornwall
Camelot Cinema, The Crescent.
Tel (0637) 874222

Newton Abbot, Devon
Alexandra Theatre, Market
Street. Tel Newton Abbot
(0626) 65368

Okehampton, Devon
Carlton Cinema, St James Street.
Tel Okehampton (0837) 52167

Padstow, Cornwall
Capitol Cinema. Tel Padstow
(0841) 532344

Paignton, Devon
Torbay Cinema, Torbay Road. Tel
(0803) 559544

Penzance, Cornwall
Savoy Cinema, Causewayhead.
Tel Penzance (0736) 63330

Plymouth, Devon
Cannon Cinema, Derrys Cross.
Tel Plymouth (0752) 225553
Odeon Cinema, Derrys Cross. Tel
Plymouth (0752) 668825
Plymouth Arts Centre, 38 Looe
Street. Tel (0752) 660060

Redruth, Cornwall
Regal Film Centre, Fore Street.
Tel Redruth (0209) 216278

St Austell, Cornwall
Filmcentre, Chandos Place. Tel
St Austell (0726) 73750

St Ives, Cornwall
Royal Cinema. Tel Penzance
(0736) 796843

Sidmouth, Devon
Radway Cinema, Radway Place.
Tel (0395) 513085

Taunton, Somerset
Cannon Cinema, Station Road.
Tel Taunton (0823) 272291

Teignmouth, Devon
Riviera Cinema, Den Crescent.
Tel Teignmouth (0626) 774624

Tiverton, Devon
Tivoli Cinema, Fore Street, Tel
Tiverton (0884) 252157

Torquay, Devon
Odeon Cinema, Abbey Road. Tel
Torquay (0803) 292324/295805

Truro, Cornwall
Plaza Cinema, Lemon Street. Tel
Truro (0872) 72894

Wadebridge, Cornwall
Regal Cinema. Tel Wadebridge
(0208) 812791

Wellington, Somerset
The Wellesley Cinema, Mantle
Street. Tel Wellington
(0823) 662135

Information

Wells, Somerset
Regal Cinema, Priory Road. Tel
Wells (0749) 73195

Wincanton, Somerset
Plaza Cinema, South Street. Tel
Wincanton (0963) 32223

Yeovil, Somerset
Cannon Cinema, Court Ash. Tel
Yeovil (0935) 23663

Accommodation

At the end of each chapter we list our recommended hotels. B&Bs are available all over the West country and the tourist offices publish a bed and breakfast touring map for the area with a list of over 200 places that have been inspected and graded by tourist board officers. To receive a list contact the West Country Tourist Board, Trinity Court, Southernhay Rast, Exeter EX1 1QS Tel Exeter (0392) 76351

Also available from the tourist office is a list of caravan and camping sites which have been inspected and graded annually by their official inspectors.

Market Days

Axminster, Devon	Thursday
Barnstaple, Devon	Tuesday and Friday (Pannier market)
Bideford, Devon	Tuesday
Bodmin, Cornwall	Saturday
Bridgwater, Somerset	Wednesday and Saturday
Bridport, Dorset	Wednesday and Saturday
Burnham-on-Sea, Somerset	Monday
Camborne, Cornwall	Friday
Chard, Somerset	Saturday
Cheddar, Somerset	Wednesday
Dartmouth, Devon	Tuesday and Friday
Exeter, Devon	Daily; Cattle market Monday and Friday
Frome, Somerset	Wednesday
Glastonbury, Somerset	Tuesday
Hatherleigh, Devon	Monday and Tuesday
Helston, Cornwall	Monday and Saturday
Holsworthy, Devon	Wednesday and Thursday
Honiton, Devon	Tuesday and Saturday
Ilfracombe, Devon	Saturday
Ilminster, Somerset	Wednesday
Kingsbridge, Devon	Wednesday and Friday
Launceston, Cornwall	Tuesday
Liskeard, Cornwall	Monday and Thursday
Newton Abbot, Devon	Wednesday and Saturday

Okehampton, Devon	Saturday
Padstow, Cornwall	Thursday
Penzance, Cornwall	Tuesday, Thursday and Saturday
Redruth, Cornwall	Friday
St Columb, Cornwall	Monday
Seaton, Devon	Monday
Shepton Mallet, Somerset	Friday
Sherborne, Dorset	Thursday and Saturday
South Molton, Devon	Thursday
Tavistock, Devon	Friday
Tintagel, Cornwall	Thursday
Tiverton, Devon	Tuesday, Friday and Saturday
Totnes, Devon	Tuesday and Friday
Truro, Cornwall	Wednesday
Wadebridge, Cornwall	Monday
Wells, Somerset	Wednesday and Saturday
Willand, Devon	Wednesday
Wincanton, Somerset	Tuesday
Yeovil, Somerset	Monday and Friday

Getting around

Maps

See the chapter 'Walking in the West Country' (pgs 308–321) for our recommended maps for walkers.

If you want more detail than the average road maps give you, the Bartholomew Leisure map series at 1:100,000, covers this area and includes sights, nature reserves, gardens and most places of interest. But for finer detail of paths and terrain and less tourist information the Ordnance Survey 1:50,000 series is the most reliable.

By car

Reaching the West Country by car is not a problem. The M5, about 30 miles south west of Bristol, links with the motorway network, both the M6 to the north and M4 to the east. An agricultural show can lead to interminable traffic blocks so it's worth checking dates and locations with local tourist offices when planning a tour around the area.

By train

There are links with the Intercity trains from local stations to London, Birmingham, Sheffield, Newcastle, Glasgow and Edinburgh, all with connections to other major towns and cities. Sleeper services operate between Devon and Cornwall and London as well as between Plymouth and Glasgow and Edinburgh. A wider range of direct destinations are available on Saturdays in summer. Seven-day unlimited travel tickets are available at mainline stations.

Information

Passenger enquiries

CORNWALL
Bodmin, Camborne, Falmouth,
Hayle, Lostwithiel, Newquay,
Par, Penzance, Redruth, St Austell,
St Erth, St Ives, Truro
(08.00–21.00 weekdays,
09.00–21.00 Sundays)   Tel Truro (0872) 76244

DEVON
Liskeard, Looe, Plymouth, Saltash   Tel Plymouth (0752) 221300
(08.00–21.00)
Barnstaple (08.00–18.00)   Tel Barnstaple (0271) 22200
Exeter (07.30–21.00)   Tel Exeter (0392) 433551
Torquay (08.00–19.30)   Tel Torquay (0803) 295911

SOMERSET
Taunton – Travel Centre   Tel Taunton (0823) 283444
Taunton, Bridgwater, Highbridge   Tel Taunton (0823) 283444
(08.00–20.00)
Crewkerne and Yeovil area   Tel Yeovil (0935) 32377
(08.00–20.00)

By coach

National Express operates from London (071-730 0202), the Midlands
(021 622 4373) and the North (0772 51177). Where a direct service isn't
available regular connections leave from London, Birmingham,
Bristol and Plymouth. A network of Rapide routes give access from
many areas of the country operating both by day and overnight. The
service from London Victoria and Heathrow Airport runs six times a
day (travel time to Truro is about seven hours). Tourist Information
offices (see pp 322 to 325) have details of the extensive network of
local bus and coach services.

By air

Regular scheduled services make use of the airports at Bournemouth,
Bristol, Exeter, Newquay, Plymouth and the Isles of Scilly; a regular
helicopter service (Tel 0736 63871) from Penzance and a skybus
service from Land's End (0736 787017) also operate to Scilly.

By sea

Channel ferries dock daily at Plymouth and those arriving at
Fishguard from Ireland have quick access to the West Country via the
M4. The *Scillonian III* offers a regular service between Penzance and
the Isles of Scilly.

General information

Lighthouses

The lighthouses listed below are open to the public, free of charge from 1pm until one hour before sunset, every day except Sunday or during fog, without prior permission from Trinity House. However, work may be in progress at the lighthouses so it is advisable to telephone the Principal Keeper to check before setting out on a visit.

Bull Point	The Principal Keeper, Bull Point Lighthouse, Mortehoe, Woolacombe, North Devon	Tel Woolacombe (0271) 870535
Lizard	The Principal Keeper, The Lizard Lighthouse, Helston, Cornwall	Tel Lizard (0326) 290431
Lundy South	The Principal Keeper, Lundy South Lighthouse, c/o Officer-in-Charge, Trinity House Depot, Swansea	Tel Clovelly (023 73) 455
Lynmouth Foreland	The Principal Keeper, Lynmouth Foreland Lighthouse, Countisbury, Lynton, Devon	Tel Brendon (059 87) 226
Pendeen	The Principal Keeper, Pendeen Lighthouse, Cornwall	Tel Penzance (0736) 788418

Golf Courses

Public golf courses in the West Country (No. in brackets is number of holes on the course).

SOMERSET
Taunton	Vivary Park Golf Club, Taunton, Somerset (18)

DEVON
Chumleigh	Chumleigh Golf Club, Chumleigh, Devon (18)
Ivybridge	Dinnaton Golf Club, Dinnaton, Ivybridge, Devon (9)
Tedbury St Mary	Fingle Glen Golf & Leisure Complex, Tedbury St Mary, Devon (9)
High Bickington	Libbaton Golf Club, High Bickington, Devon (18)
Torrington	Torrington Golf Club, Firze Beam Hall, Torrington, Devon (9)

CORNWALL

Redruth	Radnor Golf Centre, Scorrier, Redruth, Cornwall (9)
Truro	Killiow Golf and Country Club, Kea, Truro (18)

Index

Index

Index

335

Index